ⱵⱵ 1 7 2009

A GLANCE BACK IN TIME:

Life in Colonial New Jersey (1704-1770) as depicted in News Accounts of the Day

Richard B. Marrin

D1228014

Kenosha Public Library
Kenosha, WI

HERITAGE BOOKS, INC.

SW

3 0645 8025716

Copyright 1994 by

Richard B. Marrin

Published 1994 by

HERITAGE BOOKS, INC.
1540-E Pointer Ridge Place,
Bowie, Maryland 20716
(301) 390-7709

ISBN 0-7884-0089-4

A Complete Catalog Listing Hundreds of Titles
on Genealogy, History, and Americana
Available Free on Request

*Dedicated to the Memory of my Father,
Wilfrid E. Marrin, Jr.*

A Glance Back in Time:
Life in Colonial New Jersey (1704-1770)
as Depicted in News Accounts of the Day

TABLE OF CONTENTS

Newspapers, once read daily by virtually everyone, have lost out to television and radio as the principal method by which the American, heading for the 21th Century, learns what is happening about him, locally and internationally. No longer do the citizens of major cities have a choice in both the morning and the evening among several, if not more, publications that will report on the latest events.

But while journals cede dominance on late breaking news to television, fed by satellite, the newspaper remains the only place to obtain a full account of most events, together with much more, from cash off coupons to the sports pages. In earlier years, when news travelled slower and the urgency of the gripping "Special Bulletin/Special Bulletin" did not yet exist, these periodicals performed an even greater role, that of communicator and exchanger of information, the hub of a wheel that kept neighboring farmers as well as neighboring regions in tune with each other on a surprisingly large number of levels. The early newpapers were relevant, useful, and entertaining, and did not require intense study.

Printing presses arrived early to the Americas, in 1638, but not newspapers. While occasionally producing almanacs and oaths of allegiance, the primitive presses were utilized primarily for the printing of Bibles and religious tracts, many in the Indian languages.

In 1690, the first "newspaper" was printed in the Western Hemisphere. A small quarto printed on three sides of a folded sheet, it was named <u>Public Occurrences</u> but published only a single issue, before being shut down by the Royal Government. Considered a "phamlet [containing] reflections of a very High Nature", <u>Public Occurrences</u> was declared illegal as the statutes strictly forbade "anything in print without license, first obtained from those appointed by the Government to Grant the same."

The true ancestor to the news publications of today was a two sided single sheet, with three columns of print on each side, published weekly. Named <u>The Boston News-Letter</u>, it continued, under several owners, for seventy-two years, until the American Revolution[1]. Its first issue, dated April 17, 1704, proposed the purpose of this pioneer publication:

---

[1] The Boston News-Letter never proved a very profitable venture, a condition of newspapers that, unfortunately, has not much changed. Indeed, it often had to make pleas to its patrons and advertisers to better support it or that it could not continue. To increase profitability, it also published part of the Paper as *The Massachusetts Gazette* which became the official organ of the Massachusetts Bay Colony, publishing all the Proclamations of the Courts, Acts and Proceedings of the Government, Legal Notices and similar profitable insertions. But, this acceptance of Government business marked the Paper's doom. Branded a Tory publication by the distressed citizens of Massachusetts, it folded in March, 1776. When the British troops evacuated Boston, the paper's owners followed.

"This News-Letter is to be continued Weekly; and all Persons who have any Houses, Lands, Tenements, Farms, Ships, Vessels, Goods, Wares or Merchandise &c. to be Sold or Let; or Servants Run-away, or Goods Stole or Lost; may have the same inserted at a reasonable Rate, from Twelve Pence, to Five shillings and not to exceed."

Newspapers flourished right from the start. In 1730, there were seven of them throughout the colonies. By the end of the century, there were 180 papers, the combined annual circulation of which was twelve million readers! The newspapers now also had an enhanced image of themselves from those very first days when they had pandered for advertisements:

'Tis Truth (with deference to the College)
News-Papers are the spring of knowledge,
The general source throughout the nation,
Of every modern Conversation.
What would this mighty People do,
If there, alas ! were nothing new?
A news-paper is like a feast,
Some dish there is for every guest;
Some large, some small, some strong, some tender
For every stomach, stout or slender.
The New York Gazette or Weekly Post Boy, April 16, 1770.

These first newspapers together were the precursor, at least in concept, to today's press. There is much that is familiar in them.

Over a century ago, a noble effort was made by a group of public spirited New Jersey citizens to preserve for posterity that state's pre-Revolutionary War history. The result was a multi volume work, entitled <u>Documents Relating to the Colonial History of the State of New Jersey</u> which sought to collect every contemporaneous document regarding the Provinces of East New Jersey and West New Jersey that still survived in archives around America. They included private letters from the first Governors and others, court documents, extracts of wills and much more, including entries *from the news publications throughout the colonies that related to New Jersey or were about New Jersey people. Sadly, this collection is long out of print and available in fragile form only in a few research libraries in the state.*

In the following pages, some of those news articles, notices, advertisements and depictions of life in colonial New Jersey that had been so painstakingly gathered over a century ago are re-published. They have lost nothing over time and are as amusing, informative, dramatic as they were when first circulated among a people beginning to reach for their destiny. Much will be familiar to us as, is often said, nothing really changes. But then, as if to prove that thesis a lie, articles will appear that suggest how different a place America now is, almost three centuries later. One thing is certainly observable, the emergence of a unique spirit of independence and the liberty of the individual, which ultimately led our forebears to begin a new world order, democracy based on the rights of the individual, a revolution that at this very moment continues to sweep the planet.

Special effort has been made, when possible, to keep the spelling, capitalization, grammar and punctuation the same as in the original accounts, even though they vary greatly, sometimes within the same piece. Editor's notes hopefully translate phrases and concepts no longer familiar to those of our century.[2]

One final suggestion. Read slowly and carefully as one walks across a rocky beach. Style has changed. Colonial newspapers were not the direct, well edited journals of today. Often, the "subscriber" (who is not, as we use the word today, the customer, but the advertiser, literally "he who put his name under the notice") was himself the author of the item and he picked the words and phraseology he wanted. This is a blessing, as it provides us the dialects, the grammar, and the vocabulary of the countryside, which is ancestor to how we speak today two hundred and fifty years later. Indeed, the evolution of words, phrases and surnames, and just language itself, can be viewed to a startling degree in these publications. Like daily life back then, the language, spoken and written, is very recognizable to us centuries later, while, at the same time, unmistakably different, sometimes even alien. So again the caveat: <u>don't speed read</u>. It is not only the gist of what is being said that is interesting, but how it is expressed as well.

---

[2] Some of the editor's notes will treat backgrounds or provide explanations that the average reader might think too basic to have required inclusion. However, as it is hoped that this collection may be used on occasion by students, as a supplement to their study of American History, the notes will attempt to be as complete as necessary to assist them.

A Short History of the Colony of New Jersey

Since the events depicted in the following news accounts occurred between two and three hundred years ago, the reader might appreciate a short refresher history of that era so as to better put things into perspective.

From the time of Columbus, it had taken England almost a century to commence its colonization of North America. Spain ruled the seas those days and it was not until Britain's defeat of the Spanish Armada in 1588 that this stranglehold was broken.

During the early 1600s, England quickly became a maritime power of its own, the beginning of a dominance that would extend into the twentieth century. An empire, however, especially a tiny island like Britain, needed colonies to supply it with raw resources. England looked to North America, among other faraway places, to satisfy these needs. Thus, Jamestown was founded in 1607, Plymouth Bay Colony in 1620 and a host of others along the Atlantic Coast and its tributaries.

The process of colonization was slow but steady, considering the enormity of the task. England was hampered by two forces at home. One was a lessening of the absolute rule of the King and the cession of some of his authority to the people themselves, theoretically, via a Parliament. This had not happened before in the world and it did not occur here without its own revolution in 1640, when British Royalty was extinguished for a period of twenty years. Secondly, with the Protestant reformation a century old in England, the Church of England (that had replaced the Church of Rome) was itself feeling the pressure for change. It was in the form of followers of John Calvin and other European religious thinkers that came to be known as dissenters.

Moreover, as it struggled to become the world power, England had to "fight every kid on the block", especially those that still retained their allegiance to the Church of Rome. The wars with Spain and France were frequent during this period and, along with the internal political and religious struggles, sapped some of the money and attention that otherwise would have been directed by the Crown to its overseas colonies.

In several ways, England's distractions were to our advantage. First, it gave these colonies many of their first settlers, those religious dissenters who were causing trouble at home. The first wave proved to be the backbone of the New England and some of the mid-Atlantic Provinces. Another wave, this time of Presbyterian Scotch-Irish beginning in the 1720s were our pioneers westward of the next two hundred years, taming Appalachia, Tennessee, Texas, and Oklahoma, among other frontiers.

The benign neglect of the Crown also had permitted an already independent people to become even more so. The colonists had survived many hardships in a new land and were, although they did not know it at the time, beyond the reach of the old system that believed the King derived his power from God and that all must be subject him. Instead, the colonists were ready to hear the Voice of the Enlightenment that was sweeping Europe--i.e,. God gives the power to the people, who, in turn, for the common good, cede some of it back to a government of their own making and under their own ultimate control, retaining all unceded authority to themselves. They grasped the Enlightenment in the Revolution and expressed it in the Constitution. Ever since, beginning with the French revolution, and as recently as the changes in Russia, that revolution of the rights of man continues to sweep the world and will some day be the common thread of a multi-cultured orb.

New Jersey had been home for ten thousand years to the Leni Lenape Indians and forebears, who divided the area in half, a peaceful clan called the Unamis below the Raritan River and a more belligerent Munsee, who acted as the first line of defense against the warlike Iroquois who lived in New York and the north.

There were some early settlements at New Sweden, Burlington Island and elsewhere along the Delaware River and along the western shore of the Hudson. However, most of the colonization of New Jersey did not begin until 1660 when the Dutch were ousted from New York. Then, the English filled the vacuum and established, not one, but two provinces there, which were known as the Eastern and Western Divisions of the Colony of Nova Caeseria. Perth Amboy was the capital of the Eastern Division, Burlington the capital of the Western Division.

The news accounts set forth in the following chapters are from the period 1704 through 1770, the time during which New Jersey and the other eastern colonies developed their own personalities and priorities. They begin with a province still very much attached to Britain. They end with a Revolution on the horizon.

Not unlike tabloid headlines today, colonial newspapers understood the value of getting the reader's attention by focusing on the sensational or dramatic news event. Good front page material is timeless.

For example, imagine the response of readers two hundred years ago and compare it with your own reaction to the following news accounts, which recreate the dangers and differences of early America:

New-York, February 20. By a Man from Shrewsbury, we are informed that last Week, a Man of that Place, was killed and torn to Pieces by a Panther; that about an Hour after, two Men, knowing nothing of the Matter, went with their Guns into the same Wood, when the Beast leaped from the Branch of a tree where he sat unseen, upon the Back of one of the Men, where the other Man immediately shot and killed him.

They afterwards found the mangled Body of the dead Man, near the Place. *Supplement to the New York Journal or General Advertiser*, February 20, 1768

We hear from East Jersey of the following horrible Tragedy; not long since, about Eight or Ten Men (Irish all) by Night went to the House of a particular Gentleman in that Country, who was noted for a Man of Substance, and having call'd at the Door, diverse of the Family went out to see what the Matter was, whom the Men without immediately fell upon and murder'd. The Gentleman of the House perceiving some Disturbance, went out himself and was murder'd also. Upon which the Gentleman's Wife in the utmost Distress ran up to the Garret, leaving her young child behind her, and hid herself in a Hogshead of Feathers and so escap'd their bloody Hands. The Rogues having entered the House, in a most barbarous Manner murder'd the child, after they had tortur'd it in order to find the Mother saying "Make the Calf Blair and the Cow will come." After they had rifled the House and pick'd up all the Money and Plate they could meet with, they made off, whilst one of them in a Hurry, left his little Dog behind him, shut up in the House. The poor distressed Gentlewoman perceiving they were gone, ventur'd down Stairs and then presented with the most awful Spectacle that ever her Eyes beheld: her Husband, child, and Servants all weltering in their Blood. The Authority being informed of this amazing and almost unparallel'd Piece of Villany, order'd officers with proper Attendants, to pursue and make Search after the Murderers, who turning out the little Dog before mentioned were led to a House where they found seven Men, who appearing suspicious, were immediately apprehended and order'd to Prison. *The Boston Weekly News-Letter*, March 28, 1740

New York, February 4. By a written Account from Richmond County on Staten-Island, and by a Gentleman who brought it, and was himself a sharer in the Calamity, we are acquainted with the following Scene of Distress, viz.

On Thursday Night, the 28th of January, between 7 and 8 o'Clock, the Weather extremely cold, and the Ground cover'd with Snow, the following persons went from the Blazing Star[3], in New-Jersey, to cross the Ferry to Staten Island, (the Wind being moderate and fair, and the Passage judged to be very safe) viz. Mr. William Cornelius George, supposed to be from Rhode-Island and Col. Kolb, a German Gentleman, both lately arrived at Philadelphia from London; Mr. Robert French, lately arrived at Philadelphia from St. Kitts; Mr. John Kidd, of Philadelphia, Merchant; John Tomson, (who has a wooden leg) Stage Driver; William Bury, and a Lad, belonging to the Ferry (the Lad was lately Cabin Boy to a Ship from London to New-York where he left the ship, alleging that the Captain had misused him); a Negro Man, belonging to Mr. Newry of the Jersies, and a Negro Man, belonging to Mr. Provoost of this City, in all 9 Persons and 4 Horses. As they were crossing the Ferry in a scow, a violent wind suddenly arose at N.W. whereby they were driven a considerable Way down the River, and ashore on a Mud Bank, where the Scow was half filled with water; but as it was impractical to land at that Place, they were obliged to put off again, and in their Efforts to gain the Land broke two of their Oars, and were soon driven ashore upon a small Marsh Island, in the Mouth of the Fish-Kill Creek, about half a mile distant from the Ferry-House, where the Scow

---

[3] The Blazing Star is mentioned frequently in the colonial news record. Probably located along the shore of New York Harbor, in what today is Jersey City, it was an important tavern, inn and stage coach stop between New York City, just across the Hudson River, and two day distant Philadelphia.

immediately fill'd, and the People and Horses were obliged to get out. The mud was so soft that the men sunk into it near the upper Part of the Thigh, and were not able to pull out their Feet, without lying down on the Water and the Mud, and assisting with their Hands; but they with great Difficulty at last all got to the highest Part of the Marsh. The poor lame man was rendered even more helpless, by breaking his Wooden Leg. Three Horses not being able to disengage themselves from the Mud, stuck there and perished. The People on their small Portion of Marsh, deep cover'd with Snow, had not the least shelter from the freezing Blasts of the Wind, nor could they make themselves heard by the People on Shore, the Wind being against them. They had no other Resources but to huddle as close together and to give themselves as much Motion as possible. It was then about 9 o'Clock, the Boy soon gave out and sunk down, but the Men took him up, shook him, and did all they could to exercise him and heat him up; but at about Eleven he expired. At one o'Clock, Mr. George, who had till then seemed to bear up as well as any of them, began to falter, and notwithstanding the best Assistance his Fellow-Sufferers could give him, he expired at about three o'Clock; the rest lived out the dreadful Night, and at last, almost quite spent and hopeless, at about nine o'Clock in the Morning, were discover'd and with proper Help, for they had all nearly lost the Use of their Limbs, they were carried to Mr. Mersereau's and all possible Care taken of them. Col. Kolb, after taking off his Boots immediately put his Feet in cold Water, where he held them for half an Hour, during which time he took some Refreshment, and then went to Bed and slept soundly to the Afternoon. And he was the only Person who escaped without Hurt. The Rest sat up, round the Fire, and are terribly frost bitten; it is feared that they all will lose their Toes and that the Feet and Legs of some are in Danger; an Ear of one of the Negroes seems entirely perish'd. Mr. French, Mr. Kidd, John Thomson, Wm. Bury, and the two Negroes, when this Account came away, were at Mr. Mersereau's Ferry-House, opposite the Blazing Star, unable to travel. The two Dead Bodies were carried to the same Place for interment, the Coroner's Inquest having first sat on them. Mr. George, said to be a Man of good Family and Fortune, was buried on Sunday last, with proper Solemnity. His Effects are in the Hands of the Coroner, till claimed by his Friends. Col. Kolb, proceeded on his Journey and arrived here on Monday last. The Horses belonged to Mr. Mersereau. *The New York Journal or General Advertiser*, February 4, 1768

Burlington, October 12. Saturday last at Mt. Holly, about 8 Miles from this Place, near 300 People were gathered together to see an Experiment or two tried on some Persons accused of Witchcraft. It seems that the Accused had been charged with Making their Neighbours' Sheep dance in an uncommon Manner and with causing Hogs to speak and sing Psalms &c. to the great Terror and Amazement of the King's good and peaceable Subjects in this Province; and the Accusers being very positive that, if the Accused were weighted in Scales against a Bible, the Bible would prove too heavy for them ; or that, if they were bound and put into the River, they would swim. The said Accused desirous to make their Innocence appear voluntarily offered to undergo the said Trials, if 2 of the most violent of their Accusers would be tried with them. Accordingly, the Time and Place was agreed upon and advertised about the Country. The Accusers were 1 Man and 1 Woman and the Accuseds the same . . . Then came out of the House, a grave tall Man carrying the Holy Writ before the supposed Wizard &c. (as solemnly as the Sword-bearer of London before the Lord Mayor) the Wizard was first put on the Scale and over him was read a Chapter out of the Book of Moses and then the Bible was put in the other Scale, (which being kept down before) was immediately let go; but to the great Surprize of the Spectators, Flesh and Bones came down plump and outweighed that great good Book by abundance. After the same Manner, the others were served, and their lumps of Mortality severally were too heavy for Moses and all the Prophets and Apostles. This being over, the accusers and the rest of the Mob, not satisfied with this Experiment, would have the Trial by Water; accordingly, a most solemn procession was made to the Mill-pond, where both Accuseds and Accusers being stripp'd (saving only to the Women their Shifts) were bound Hand and Foot and severally placed in the Water, lengthways, from the Side of a Barge or Flat, having for Security only a Rope about the Middle of Each, which was held by some in the Flat. The Accuser Man being thin and spare, with some difficulty began to sink at last, but the rest, everyone of them, swam very light upon the Water. A Sailor in the Flat jump'd out upon the Back of the Man accused, thinking to drive him down to the Bottom, but the Person bound, without any Help, came up some time before the other. The Women Accuser being told that she did not sink, would be ducked a second time, when she swam again as light as before. Upon which she declared that she believed the Accused had bewitched her to make her so light and that she would be duck'd again a Hundred Times, but she would duck the Devil out of her. The accused Man, being surprized at his own Swimming, was not so confident of his Innocence as before, but said, "If I am a Witch, it is more than I know." The more thinking Part of the Spectators were of opinion that any Person so bound and plac'd in the Water (unless they were mere skin and bones) would swim till their breath was gone and their Lungs filled with Water. But it being the general belief of the Populace that the womens Shifts, and the garters with which they were bound, help'd to support them; it is said they are to be tried again, the next warm Weather, naked.[4] *The Pennsylvania Gazette*, October 15, 1730

We have Advice from New York of the 21st of January last that in Summerset County in East New Jersey, on Raritan River, there has lately been a conspiracy among the Negroes there to Murder the English and to assemble together in a Body and make their Escape to settle themselves in some new Country. About 30 of the Conspirators have been apprehended, one of them hanged, some had their Ears cut off and others were whipped. Several of them had Poison found about them. *The Weekly Rehearsal*, February 11, 1734

Perth-Amboy, July 8. On the 30th of last Month, Wequalia (the Indian King) was Executed according to Sentence passed against him for the Murder of Capt. John Leonard. And as said Wequalia had led a base inhuman Life and had Murdered his own Brother and other Indians formerly, so he died a hardened and unpenitent Wretch, not shewing the least Remorse for any of the Actions of his Vile Life; nor would he own the Murder of said Capt. John Leonard, of which he was notoriously Convicted for and deservedly suffer'd Death. He saved us the Labour of Writing his Confession, having made none; he only bid *adieu* to the few Indians that attended him to the Gallows, which were only his near Relations, all the other Indians refused to shew the least Regard. When the Sheriff ask'd if any of the Ministers should Pray with him before he died, he indifferently answered "They might, if they would" and, being asked which of them, he named Mr. Morgan, a Presbyterian Minister and that because he was his Neighbour, which he implied was all the reason for his choice. There was a great Concourse of People at the Execution, together with two Companies of the Militia in Arms, in Order to Protect the Sheriff and Officers from any Insult of the Mob or Indians. *The American Weekly Mercury*, July 6, 1727

---

[4] This piece was undoubtedly written by Benjamin Franklin, who was the sole owner of the Gazette at this time.

Perth Amboy, New Jersey, June 6. The Sloop William, William Fraser Master is arrived here from Jamaica; they sailed from Blewfields the last day of April . . . entering the Gulf, the Pyrates waiting there for them took them and plundered them; they cut and whipped some and others they burnt with Matches between their Fingers to the Bone to make them confess to where their money was. They took to the value of a thousand Pistoles[5] from Passengers and others; they then let them go, but coming on the Coast off the Capes of Virginia, they were again chased by the same Pyrates who first took them; they did not trouble them again but wished them well Home; . . . they are Commanded by one Edward Low. The Pyrates gave us an account of his taking the Bay of Hondoras from the Spaniards, which had surprized the English and taking them and putting all the Spaniards to the Sword excepting two Boys, as also burning the King George and a Snow belonging to New York and cut off one of the Masters ears and slit his Nose, all this they confessed themselves; they are now supposed to be cruising off of Sandy Hook or thereabouts. *The American Weekly Mercury*, June 6, 1723

---

[5] A Spanish coin worth about $4.00.

Murder is still considered to be the worst of crimes, the snuffing out of another's life without justification. We are still appalled by the senseless murder, the thrill killings, the murder of an old lady for a handful of coins. The following series of news accounts report on exactly that type of murder, the slaying of one Joseph Young for the money in his pocket by jailed hardened toughs that society had tried but could not change. The similarities between today and then are apparent as are, quite definitely, the differences, especially with respect to the punishment meted out and the Court's philosophy in ordering it.

Philadelphia. From Glouster there is Advice that three Men are in Goal there, for the Murder of Joseph Young of that County and robbing his House of Money, to the Value of about 40 Shillings[6]. They are old Offenders, have all been in the Goal of this City and have suffered corporal punishment. *The New York Gazette Revived in the Weekly Post Boy*, March 19, 1750

At a Court of Oyer and Terminer[7], held at Glouster, in New-Jersey, on Thursday last, Sentence of Death was passed on John Johnson, John Carrol and Edward Steward for the Murder of Joseph Young and we hear they are to be executed Monday next. *The Pennsylvania Journal*, April 12, 1750

On Thursday the 5th of April, 1750 John Johnson, John Stewart and Edward Carryle, received Sentence of death, at the Court of Oyer and terminer and General Gaol Delivery, holden for the County of Glouster, in New-Jersey, for the Murder of Joseph Young, a Farmer in the said County. Before Judge Nevill pronounced the sentence, he made a Speech to the

---

[6] It is difficult to express the currency of the colonies with its cash equivalent today. A shilling was worth 12 pence or 1/20th of a pound. It is estimated that in Colonial America, each shilling varied in worth from between 12 cents and 16 cents. A rough guess, therefore, was that Mr. Young was slain for about $5 to $7.

[7] A glimpse of the roots of common law can be seen in the courts of "oyer and terminer". Part Norman French in origin, it referred in the colonies to the higher criminal courts which had the authority "to hear and determine" the facts surrounding the defendant's alleged guilt. It is often used together with the phrase "General Gaol Delivery". Indicted persons, awaiting trial, were held temporarily in General Gaol as opposed to convicted felons who were punished and released.

Prisoners and then delivered a Copy of the same to the Sheriff, ordering him to deliver the said Copy to those unfortunate Wretches for their Comfort and Assurance in their unhappy Circumstances; and being desired to publish the same by some of the Hearers, we have a Copy, which should have been published before, had it come to hand sooner, but hope it will not be disagreeable tho' at this Distance of Time, which is as follows:

John Johnson, John Stewart and Edward Carryle, you have all three been indicted for wilful Murder. Upon your indictment, you have been arraigned, upon your arraignment you have pleaded Not Guilty, and for your Tryal you have put yourselves upon God and your Country, Which Country has found you guilty. And now nothing further remains for me to do than to pass that sentence upon you which the Law has awarded for Crimes of this Nature. And that is a dreadful Sentence, indeed! A Sentence which cuts you off from the Communication of Mankind and from the Face of the Earth. Wickedness like yours creates such Disorders of the Body of the common Wealth, that it becomes necessary to dissect the infected and mortify'd Members, in order to preserve the rest of the Constitution. You have all had the Indulgence which the Law allows, a fair Tryal, free Liberty of making your Defence; you have been fully heard without Restraint, and a Jury of twelve Men, upon their sacred Oaths have pronounced you Guilty. The Crime you are convicted of is the most Foul and Shocking upon the List, Murder; the very Name makes a good Man start and tremble; you have defaced the Image of your Maker, deprived the King of a Subject, and left a poor disconsolate Widow and her Children helpless and defenceless; and by one fatal Stroke robb'd them of all the Comforts of their Life, and by taking away the Means of their Subsistence, exposed them to Poverty and Want; you have sent a poor unhappy Man to his Account, loaded with his Imperfections, before that Time which indulgent Nature allows for Repentence. But, it is not so with you for you have Time given you to State your Accounts and make up your Reckonings; and I hope you will make good Use of it, by seriously considering your lost Condition and the deplorable State into which you have plunged yourselves, by the Instigation of the Devil, who hath seduc'd, flatter'd, and deceiv'd you and by subtilly Decoying and Tempting you from Sin to Sin, under the false and deluding Notions of Pleasure, hath at last abandoned you to shame, and disgrace and an ignominious Death; and is still gaping and in hopes of his Reward by making a Prey of your poor Souls . . . . Poor Wretches! You are heavey Laden, indeed! The Guilt of innocent Blood upon your Consciences! Which is a Thousand witnesses. "Everyone one that findeth me shall Slay me" was the Voice of Nature, which the conscience of Cain extorted from him, when he had slain his Brother Abel, Conscious to himself that he deserved Death for the Crime which he had committed. You are justly condemned by the Law of God, the Law of Man and the Law of Nature. By the Law of God, Exodus XXI, 14 "If any Man come presumptuously upon his Neighbour to Slay him with Guile; thou shall take him from my Altar that he may Die." And again, "Ye shall take no Satisfaction for the Life of a Murderer which is guilty of Death, but he shall surely be put to Death;" So that by the Law of God, you are doom'd to Die. The Law of Man, in obedience to the Divine Law, confirms the same, and Nature not bearing to see her beautiful Production thus destroyed, calls aloud for exemplary Satisfaction. . . . *The Pennsylvania Journal*, April 26, 1750

Some of the murders were committed, as they say in the law "with malice aforethought", well plotted and carried out in cold blood:

We also hear from the County of Somerset in New-Jersey, that one - - - - Lawrance, a Glasier, having a small matter of Money in the House, a Person that was a Lodger there, took an Ax and Wounded his Wife so that she dyed; her Husband coming in, he fell upon him, cut and wounded him so, that he was disabled from defending himself. Then the Fellow took the Money and some other Goods and fled, but soon after was pursued, taken and is committed. *The New York Gazette*, March 22, 1736

We hear from New-Jersey, that on the 25th of March last, a barbarous Murder was committed there on the Road between Woodbridge and Piscataway, upon a Man who was travelling on Foot from New York to Philadelphia, and by a Paper found in his Pocket, appeared to have been one of the back Settlers whose Habitation and Effects were destroyed by the Indians, on which Account he had been recommended to the Charitable Assistance of the Public. It appeared that he had changed or shewn 4 or 5 seven Pound Bills upon the Road and that 2 Men dressed like Sailors, who were likewise traveling on foot the same Way, sometimes before and sometimes behind him, had often joined his Company, and from Woodbridge, at their Request travelled with him. That they called at several Taverns and went from the Last in the Night. He seemed to inclined to stay there all Night but was persuaded by the Sailors to go to Brunswick. It is supposed that they murdered him. A considerable Quantity of Blood was found in the Road and a bloody Stick near it. The same Night these two Sailors called up the Ferryman at Brunswick and crossed the Ferry, and, as they went over, were quarreling together about the Division of some Money. The Body of the murdered Man was dragged out of the Road, over a Fence, and covered with Leaves &c., where it lay a Week, and was discovered by a Man who accidentally crossing the Fence at the same Place, jumped upon the Body. The Murderers are not yet taken up. *The New York Gazette or Weekly Post Boy*, April 10, 1766

New York, January 13. From Roxbury in Morris County, East New Jersey, we learn that a Servant Man belonging to one Matthias Auble, died suddenly there; and a Jury being called and his Body opened by the Physicians, it was judg'd his death was occasioned by the Cruelty of his Master a few Days before in chastising him for some Misdemeanour; and Auble was immediately taken up and secure in the County Goal in order to be brought to trial for the same. *The New York Gazette or the Weekly Post Boy*, January 13, 1755

We have advice from the County of Glouster in this Province that a few weeks ago, one Andrew Lashley, a flat-man, who plied between Mantua Creek in the said county and Philadelphia, was found in the flat in said creek in miserable condition, having a large bruise on his head, several marks of violence upon other parts of his body, the rim of his belly very much scorched and his back bone about the kidneys burnt to a cinder, notwithstanding which he lived some days and, at intervals, often spoke and said he would tell who did the mischief but his sense never continued so long at one time as to name the persons, the manner how or the place where it was done. Several persons have been taken up on suspicion, tho' no discovery hath as yet been made who committed this horrid villainy, but the strictest enquiry is still making to find them out, that they may be brought to justice. *The New American Magazine*, February, 1758

New York, December 25. We have an account from the North Branch of Rariton, in New-Jersey, of a barbarous and cruel Murder committed there on Wednesday the 13th instant, on the Body of Mr. Jacob Vaneste, by his own Negro, in conjunction with another of his Neighbours. It seems that all the Provocation was Mr. Vaneste's taking a little of the Fellow's Tobacco, and that evening, having been on a visit to Dr. Van Wagenen's, his Neighbour, the Two Negroes Way-laid him and knocked him off his Horse. They then, with Axes, split his Skull and drag'd him a little out of the Road. The Horse, coming home soon without his Master, gave some Alarm and the next Day proper Search being made, he was found. His Negro was thereupon taken up and brought before the Coroner's Inquest, and being made to touch his Master's Body, the Blood suddenly gushed out of the dead Man's Nose and Ears[8], as it likewise did from the Negro's, who thereupon being sung with guilt, confessed the Crime and was, together with his Accomplice, directly sent to Jail in order to receive their just Demerits. *The New York Gazette Revived in the Weekly Post Boy*, December 25, 1752

---

[8] In the early days, folk lore often mixed with the common law, a prime example of which was the belief that the corpse of the victim would reveal its killer by bleeding from the nose and mouth when the suspect touched the dead body.

New York, January 1. We hear from New-Jersey that the Negro Fellow who committed the Murder upon the Body of Mr. Jacob Van Este, his Master, as lately mentioned, was burnt at Millstone, on Wednesday Last. He stood the Fire with the greatest Intrepidity and said that, they had taken the Root, but left the Branches. *Upham's Collection of English Newspaper Cuttings*

Others were intentional, but the circumstances mysterious:

Philadelphia, August 14. We have the following Melancholly from West New-Jersey near Manc[ ] Creek, that there was found on the Shore a Girl of about 8 or 9 Years of Age; she was Naked, only a Cap on her Head and it is supposed she was Shot, having seven Shot holes in her Breast and two in her Arm. There was also a Man taken up on the shore, sow'd up in a Blanket. *New England Weekly Journal*, August 25, 1729

Philadelphia, July 26. We hear from Cape May that last week the Bodies of three Men drove ashore there; one of them had good Cloaths on, Gold Buttons in his Shirt sleeves, two Gold Rings on his Finger, a Watch and some Pieces of Gold in his Pocket and Silver Buckles in his Shoes, but was shot thro' the Head and the other two had their Heads cut off. About the same time a small Sloop drove on shore about 15 Miles to the northward of the Cape, but it is not known who she or the Men are. We also hear that a Brigantine sailed up our Bays as far as Bombay Hook, then tacked about and stood to Sea. Some think it was the Brigantine bound from Bristol with a number of Convicts[9] and that they have mutinied and Murdered the Master and Men. We expect a more particular Account of this barbarous Murder in a few days. *The New York Gazette* July 30, 1733.

Philadelphia, August 5. Yesterday a Man was found floating near Point no Point, having both his Hands cut off and it is supposed he was murdered. By letters found in his pockets, it appears that he was going up to Trenton. *The Pennsylvania Journal*, August 6, 1752

New York, September 6. About a Fortnight since, was found in the Woods between Long Pond and Charlottesburgh, in New Jersey, a man lying on his back with his Head cut off and laid on one of his Arms. He had no other clothes on than a Shirt and Trowsers, was about 5 Feet 7 or 8 Inches

---

[9] Convicted felons in England were often sentenced to serve their sentences as laborers in America.

high, and to appearances must have been murdered some months before. *The New York Journal or General Advertiser*, September 6, 1770

Still other homicides were the results of emotional flareups. Occasionally, the passions were understood and, while regrettable, treated with some leniency by the Court:

Perth Amboy, August 3. On Thursday last at a Special Court of Oyer and Terminer, held at this Place, one David Simes, Carpenter of the Brigantine *Rachel and Betty* of Whitehaven was Tryed for the Murder of one John Grimes, a Sailor on Board said Vessel, on the 15th of July last. But it appearing to have been done on a sudden Quarrel between them and the Vessel's Crew giving the Prisoner a good Character as being a Peaceable Inoffensive Man, the Jury found him guilty of Manslaughter only, and he was the same day burnt on the Hand[10]. *The New England Weekly Journal*, August 19, 1728.

Other losses of temper were not so easily forgivable.

New York, January 22. We are inform'd from New Brunswick in New Jersey that two men near that Place, having had some Words together, one of them told the other that he would be revenged upon him by setting his House on Fire and, accordingly, he took the opportunity and he set the four corners of the House on Fire, at which Time Two young children were in the House alone, upon whom he barred the Doors on the out-side so that they could not get out. The Man seeing his House on Fire and his Children in it, got into it and took his Children up in his Arms, and, as he was carrying them out, a Beam, that was burnt thro', fell down and struck the poor Children out of their Father's Arms, and the Flames being very furious, he was obliged to leave his Children to save his own Life, and, as the poor infants lay perishing in the Flames, they were heard to cry out "O Daddy! O Daddy!" We have not yet learnt the Mens Names. *The Boston Evening Post*, February 19, 1739

New York, April 23. We hear from Elizabeth-Town, that on Monday last, Alderman Stites of that place, a gentleman generally esteemed, being about to straighten a road, of which he was overseer, by the removal of a fence belonging to one Sears, which was an encroachment upon it.

---

[10] A common punishment of the times.

Sears, having before heard of his design, declared, if he attempted it, he would shoot him and, accordingly, loaded his gun with powder and shot. When Mr. Stites, with his labourers on the high-way approached the fence, he saw Sears with his gun, ask'd him where he was going with it. He relied, "I'tell you, damn ye" and immediately fired on him, lodging the shot in his side and in his belly. Sears was after some resistance secured and sent to gaol[11]. It is thought that Mr. Stites cannot recover, though it is not certain as to whether the shot penetrated his bowels, several have been extracted, but he had a high fever and was in exquisite pain, though still alive on Wednesday morning last. *The New York Mercury*, April 23, 1764

New York, April 30. We hear from Elizabeth-Town that Alderman Stites was still alive Wednesday Morning last, many shot had been extracted and there was some Hopes for his Recovery. *The New York Mercury*, April 30, 1764

Highway robbery was more than just a phrase back then, unfortunately a situation unchanged today:

We hear from Shrewsberry in New Jersey that in that Township, last week, a Pedler[12] was met with a Foot-Pad upon the high Road, who ask'd him if he had a chew of Tobacco to give him? The Pedler answered "Yes", and while he was taking it out of his pocket, the Rogue took hold of his horses's Bridle and then asked him if he had any money, for he must have it? The Pedler answered "no" for he was newly set out with his Pack, &c. The Rogue pulled out a sharp pointed knife and cut his Leg, stab'd him in the Brest and other places, cut open his pack, wherein was ten Pounds in Paper Money, which he took and made off, leaving the Man in his blood, seemingly a dying, but in a little time he got to a house, which was near. They sent for a Surgeon who drest him and it is hop'd he will recover. Diligent search has been made for the Rogue but he is not yet taken. *The New York Gazette*, October 24, 1737

New-York, July 5. Last Saturday three Weeks, John Woodsides, a Pedlar, was robbed by two Men on Horseback, near Andover Iron Works, County of Sussex and Province of New-Jersey, of Cash and Goods to an amount of 160 pounds currency. As soon as the Villains approached

---

[11] To learn what became of the assailant Sears, see page 44 *infra*.

[12] A "pedler" was a travelling salesman of sorts, carrying his stock of goods with him as he visited outlining farms.

Woodsides, one of them discharged a Pistol at him not more than 7 Yards distant, but it happily missed him; he then drew his pistol (having a good one ready loaded by him) and fired it at the Highwayman, but, without Effect also; this Conduct of Woodsides so enraged the Rogues that one of them ran at him with a Cut and Thrust Hanger[13] and intended to have him killed on the Spot, but after he had received a terrible Wound in his right Side and a large Cut in his Shoulder, he took to his Heels and escaped by concealing himself in the Woods. *The New York Mercury*, July 5th, 1762

Twenty Pounds Reward

On the 12th of June last one John Woodside, of the City of Philadelphia, Pedlar, travelling from the House of Peter Drugoe, in Sussex County, East Jersey, on the Road to Anderson Furnace, was attacked by two Men, and after some Resistance made his Escape, having received two Wounds, one on his Left Side the other on the Back of his Neck and was at the same time robbed of Sixty Pounds in Cash and about Eighty Pounds of Goods, such as Calicoes, Cottons, Chintzes, printed linen, long, clear and flowered Lawns, sundry Sorts of Silk and Linin Handkerchiefs, Sattin, Pelong, solid Silver Buttons, with a variety of other Goods, such as Pedlars use to carry, and it is probable, by several Circumstances, that the said Goods were carried over Hunter's Ferry, on Delaware, into the Frontiers of Pennsylvania, by some Person not immediately concerned in said Robbery (the two Persons suspected being apprehended and taken); therefore whoever secures such Goods, so as the Subscriber may have them again, shall have Fifteen Pounds Reward, or in Proportion for any Part of them, and Five Pounds for any Person that exposes the said Goods to Sale, if brought to Justice, paid by the Subscriber, living in Penn-street, Philadelphia.

John Woodside

The Pennsylvania Gazette, August 5, 1762

New York, May 19. We hear that on Monday Night Last, Mr James Carter of New-Jersey, who had inadvertently discovered to a mixt Company of Strangers that he had a considerable sum of Money about him was soon set upon in the street by several men who, as he made vigorous Resistance, bruised and wounded him in a cruel Manner and then robb'd him of upwards of 500 Pounds (which he had that day taken up in Interest to pay a debt for which he was Security) after which, on some Peoples coming to his Assistance, the Villains went off, leaving him an old hat instead of his own, which they took away; and, on Tuesday, a Person lately discharged from Gaol in this City was discovered with the said Hat, which having some

---

[13] A "hanger" was a short sword hung from a belt around the waist.

blood on it, and other causes of suspicion appearing against him, he was secured and known by the Persons he had robbed; and we hear is, with two or three of his Accomplices, now in Gaol. *The Pennsylvania Journal*, May 12, 1763

Several Robberies have been committed within a few Days past in Newark, Elizabeth-Town and Rahway. 'Tis said some persons are committed on Suspicion and 'tis hoped Justice may take Place. Mean While, this should caution People to be a little more careful, as great numbers of Stragglers, are about the Country. *The New York Gazette*, October 17, 1763

On Wednesday last, one Matthew Wright, a travelling Pedler, was robbed about two miles from Potter's Town in East New Jersey, by two Foot Pads, suppos'd to be Irishmen, of 45 Pounds in Cash and some Goods of considerable Value, after which they used him and his Horse very barbarously, by giving them several Gashes with their Cutlasses and then made off. *The New York Gazette or Weekly Post Boy*, September 23, 1754.

Other killings were not planned in advance but took place during a crime. Today, they are referred to as "felony murders", and often merit even harsher punishment that an other forms of homicide. That did not always seem to be the case in the 1700s. Witness for example:

On Thursday the 31st of December ult. Obadiah Wilkins, a Constable, having executed a warrant against one Crow, for debt, attended him to a neighbouring House in order to obtain Security --- - - but the Prisoner being disappointed, watched an Opportunity, and made his Escape to his Waggon, then in the Road, and drove away, which Wilkins discovering, called to him, and charged him to stop, being his Prisoner - - - This being disregarded, he pursued and overtook the Waggon, and Endeavoured to stop the Horse; but Crow still determined to proceed, told him if he did not desist he should drive over him - - - which happened immediately after, poor Wilkins being entangled in the Geers of the Horses. It is said the Wheels dragged him thirty yards, then run over and killed him, notwithstanding a Person present called out that Wilkins was under the Wheels, and did all in his Power to stop the Horses. I am informed the Jury of Inquest have brought in their Verdict, "An accident, owing to Crow's driving the Horses". *The New York Gazette Revived in the Weekly Post Boy*, July 2, 1750

We hear from Morris County in New-Jersey, that about ten Days ago one William Thorpe of that County, having assisted in bringing some Persons to Justice, for Breach of the Laws, they were so enraged at him, that they threatened Vengeance against him; of which the Justice getting Intelligence, he sent his Son to Thorpe to give him Notice. While the young Man was at Thorpe's House, the People came there to execute their Purpose, whereupon Thorpe got up Stairs in his Chamber with his Gun, and the others attempting to pursue him, he told them that it would be a their Peril to advance; but they disregarding that, pushed forward, whereupon he fired and shot one Dead upon the Spot and with his Gun, and the Assistance of the Justice's Son, beat off the rest. Thorpe then went and surrendered himself up to the Justice. We have not learnt the Name of the Person killed. *The New York Journal or General Advertiser*, March 3, 1768

Other deaths occurred during a time of extreme emotional distress. The following news accounts report the crime, an escape and a resolution that indicates that sometimes "mercy seasoned justice".

New York. We are informed from Whipany, in E. New Jersey, that about a Month ago, a Woman of that Place was committed to Newark Gaol, being charged by the Coroners Inquest with the Murder of a her Bastard Child, which was found, after diligent Search was made, with its Mouth most barbarously cram'd full of Leaves and its Hands fill'd with Leaves, gasping for Life. A Court of Inquest is to be held in June next at Newark, where She is to have her Trial for the said Fact. *The New York Gazette*, May 28, 1733.

Last Night broke out of the Gaol at Monmouth County at Freehold East-New-Jersey, one Eleanor White, who was under the Sentence of Death for the Murder of her Bastard Child, she is tall and slender, round faced, freckled with Black Eyes and Black Hair; had on Callimanco Gown striped with red, blue and white and a round-ear'd Cap; she is suppos'd to be gone towards Cohansie. She escaped with the Assistance of one Mary Bowman, Servant to John Williams, Gaol-Keeper, who is gone with her. The said Mary is a thick, short and fat Woman, pockfretten and of Brown Complexion, born in old England; had on a reddish brown Wrapper, a black Petticoat and blue Stockings. Whoever secures the said Women (especially Eleanor White) shall have Ten Pounds Reward and reasonable charges paid

by John Williams, Under-Sheriff
The Pennsylvania Gazette, April 24, 1735

Whereas I am informed that a Report is lately spread at Amboy and other Places to the effect following viz. That it is generally believed that I gave great sums of Money to the Governor, Chief Justice and Attorney General for the reprieving Eleanor White, now in Monmouth Gaol and condemned to dye for the Murder of her Bastard Child (as is said). . . . Therefore, I think it is my Duty is this Case to do what lies in me to undeceive the People and defeat the above Design. And in order thereunto, I hereby declare that the aforesaid general belief. . . is altogether groundless. For his Excellency was pleased to grant such Reprieve at the Petition of some of the Justices of Gaol Delivery for said County and above One Hundred and Forty Freeholders and Inhabitants of said County, without any Money being given or paid to the Governor, Chief Justice, Attorney General or any other Person whatsoever, for granting said Reprieve. And for the Confirmation that what I here publish is true, everyone that knows said Eleanor White and her very few Relations that she hath, knows them all to be very Poor and that no Money can be expected of them or her . . .

          Robert Lawrence
The American Weekly Mercury, February 11, 1735.

Other fatal assaults were the products of a deranged mind as the following attests:

As the following Account has not been in any of the publick Papers yet, I think it ought to be taken Notice of. It is really Truth, however improbable it may appear and was only discovered but a few Days ago. A farmer in the neighbourhood had two Servant Lads, one aged 11 Years, the other 17, who were commonly sent out to work together in the Fields. One Night on their coming home the Boy was observed to look poorly, and on being asked what was the Matter, answered that he durst not tell of it or it would be worse for him; but some of the House observing Blood about him, he was stript and was discovered to be in a most deplorable Condition, having the lower region of his Belly cut and skin'd off, and the whole covered with Ashes and Fat to prevent the Bleeding. On his Examination, he said that the Other had done it, threatening to kill him if he ever discovered the least Hint of it; that he had frequently used him very barbarously and kept him in continual Terror. On a Surgeon's being sent for, his Life was declared to be in Danger, when the other was committed to Jail, where he now lies, in order to receive his Demerits, if such can be possible. We don't learn that the little One ever gave him any Provocation for such usage, but that it proceeded from his own Wicked Heart. *The Pennsylvania Journal*, June 7, 1753

The detection and apprehension of murderers sometimes required information from other provinces and there the newspapers served to circulate the questions and bring back answers, as the following examples would indicate:

Whereas it appears by *The New York Gazette* of March 25, 1751 that William Jackson was murdered in February last. The said William Jackson was a Freeholder in Augusta County at Jackson's River in Virginia and left a Wife great with Child last Fall; He had when he left my House in Newark the 30th of November last, about 184 Skins of Wash-Leather, one Shirt marked "W.I." with white lett holes, his great Coat, Waistcoat, Breeches, and Hanger, as is described in the said Gazette right, the Horse that he had when he went away from us was of a ronish and sorrel Colour; as for his other Goods, I can't give any particular Account. It would be very agreeable to me, and no doubt to his Relations, to hear how the Trial went and what Effects are or may be found for the Widow and Heirs of the Deceas'd. This is to interest his Majesty's liege Subjects of South Kingston [Rhode Island], to be aiding by publick or private Letter, the which, if it comes to my knowledge, I shall be as expeditious as I can, to convey to the Widow.

Thomas Bows
The New York Gazette Revived in the Weekly Post Boy, April 15, 1751

At the Superior Court held here on the first Tuesday of this Month, Thomas Carter was convicted of murdering and robbing William Jackson Of Virginia for which Crimes he received he Sentence of Death and to be hung in Chains. Since his Tryal he has confessed the Facts and that he took from Jackson his Horse, 107 Deerskins, in Silver and Gold to the amount of about eighty dollars and about Forty Shillings Pennsylvania Paper money. Notwithstanding that he has spent and squandered away great Part of the Money and Effects, there is so much to be had yet, that it would be advisable for the Representatives of Mr. Jackson to take Letters of Administration in Virginia and either come in Person or send a Power to some proper Person here to secure the same. Mr. Bows is desired to inform whether Mr. Jackson had a wench with him or not.
The New York Gazette Revived in the Weekly Post Boy, April 22, 1751

Whereas Thomas Ageman, late of the City of Burlington, in the Western Division of the Province of New Jersey, has been missing ever since the 30th of March last, and no one hereabouts being able to give any account of him, has induced his son William Ageman and most of his neighbors, to be suspicious that he was murdered. These are to desire the readers hereof that, if they or any of them can give any account of the said Thomas Agemen, either living or dead, that if they would be so good as to communicate the same to his son William Ageman by directing their letters to George Eyre Esq. in Burlington, it will very much oblige him and his neighbors and likewise clear the person who is suspected to be guilty of the murder, who, upon examination, denies, the fact. He is a lusty man, if

living, about 80 years of age, a laboring man. *The Pennsylvania Gazette,*
February 13, 1753

*Aside from murder, there were a host of other crimes which the
colonists suffered and on which the papers dutifully reported. Perhaps, one
of the most embarrassing involved the burglarizing of the Colony's Treasury,
then located in Amboy, Capital of the Province of East New Jersey:*

One Hundred Pounds Reward

Whereas the Treasury in Perth-Amboy, was last night broke open
and Seven Thousand Pounds carried off. A reward of One Hundred Pounds
shall be paid to any one whatever that will detect or discover the Thief, by
me

Stephen Skinner

The New York Gazette and Weekly Mercury, July 25, 1768

Last Night the Office of the Treasurer of the Eastern Division was
broke open, and a Quantity of Money, in Dollars and Paper, stolen, to the
Amount of between Six and Seven Thousand Pounds. The Money was in an
Iron Chest, in which the Public Money, when cut from the Sheets and signed
by the Treasurer, is put. It appears that the Villains first broke open a
Scrutore, in which was some few Johannes[14] and some old Bills to the
Amount of about Thirty or Forty Pounds, which they took; in the Scructore,
they found the Key of the Chest, which was drwan to the East Window,
where it was opened, and the Money carried off. *New York Journal or
General Advertiser,* July 28, 1768.

*And, then there was the time that the Monmouth County
Commissioners themselves were victimized on their return from the
Provincial governmental seat at Perth Amboy.*

Redfords Ferry, March 10, 1724. These are to give Notice that the
Commissioners for the County of Monmouth in their Return from Amboy
to Redfords, at the Ferry House in the Night, had taken out of the Roome
they slept in, on of their Bags of 2011 Pounds, out of which Bag was taken
544 Pounds; but on the Munday following, they found all the Money but
half a book of Bills of 12 shillings and 15 shillings each, in all 100 Bills
from No. 22100 to 22200 of which all Persons are desired to be Carefull not

---

[14]   The colonies used French and Spanish coins as much. if not more. than English
ones.

to receive any such Bills, but to Apprehend and Secure any such Person or Persons who shall Offer to Utter them and they shall have as a Reward on Conviction of said Person or Persons the Sum of Five Pounds. And any Person that shall find, send, or bring, the 100 Bills to Mr. David Lyall, shall have a Reward of Twenty Pounds and no Questions askt. *The American Weekly Mercury*, March 3, 1724.

Rape was as horrible then as it is now. As the two following accounts indicate, the difficult burden on the prosecution to present proof that corroborated the victim's testimony and the male society's bias toward the accused often combined to produce results that would anger us today.

Burlington, November 10. On Friday last, at our Supream Court, came up on the Tryal of James Burnside, an Irishman, for a Rape on the Body of Anne Eastworthy, Widow of ----Eastworthy.

The said Anne Eastworthy, being brought into the Court in a Chair, depos'd, that going from Philadelphia in a Boat to A. Goforth's Plantation, she enquir'd for some Spinning, that the said James Burnside being in the Boat with her and several others, told her "he could help her to half a Year's Work", that afterwards, landing on the Jersey Shore, near Anocus about Dusk, she went with him in Hopes to get Work; but he led her through several Woods and Fields and at last into a Cow Pen, that upon her telling him "She would make him amenas if he could assist her", he told her "he desired nothing but a Night's Lodging", which as she said very much surpriz'd her; and thereupon he took her in his arms and ---[N.B. We omit those expressions which, tho' used in Open Court, we appehend may be offensive to the Ears of the modest Reader], that she struggled, resist'd and cry'd out bitterly, begging him for Christ's Sake not to abuse her but rather to kill her, saying "For Christ's sake, Man, do not abuse me thus but rather kill me"; that after he had ravished her, they walked on for some time, she being, as she said, in a miserable Condition, and in Fear of her Life, he asked her "whether she would talk of it or no and saying no", he ---- ravish'd her again; that they walked on further till they came to a House where the Good Man took her in.

The said Person depos'd that she came to his House about the same time before depos'd in a seeming weak condition, that she remained in his House two Weeks and upwards, weak and languishing. It was also sworn that the said James Burnside offer'd to pay for her keeping and to make it up with her.

The Prisoner made little Defence himself, but having Counsel allow'd by the Lenity of the Court, several Witnesses were called, particularly Mr. E. R. Price, who depos'd, that some years since, when he was Deputy to the Attorney General, the said Anne Eastworthy had sworn a Rape against one Hill at Salem, that she and her Husband being bound to prosecute, absconded and forfeited their Recognizances, upon which the Grand Jury brought in the Bill Ignoramus[15].

Titan Leeds, Esq. Sheriff, deposed, that having a Writ for the same Anne Eastworthy, he found her in Bed, that several people being in the Room, Discourse began about the aforesaid Rape and the said Anne declar'd "that if the aforesaid Burnside would come and marry her in her present Condition she was in, he should not be hanged or words to that Purpose.

This was confirmed by another Evidence and the Fellow had several appear'd to his Reputation, particularly his Master, who gave him the Character of an honest, faithful, civil Fellow and another Evidence who told the Court bluntly "If they wanted to be informed further, they might ask the Prisoner's greatest enemy in Court who has several Daughters with whom he used to keep Company."

The Counsel offer'd to prove that the said Anne Eastworthy had been an infamous Woman, but that not being allowed by the Court, after a Tryal of about four Hours, the Jury brought him in Guilty, Death.

The next Day the Prisoner being brought into Court to receive Sentence, his Counsel offer'd several arguments in Arrest of Judgment, and particularly that the Indictment was insufficient, by Reason that after the word "Ravish" the Words "against her Will" were left out; whereupon it was order'd that the Pleadings on both Sides should be put off till next Court and the Prisoner was remanded back and put in Irons. *The Pennsylvania Gazette*, November 10, 1729.

On Monday last Dennis Kilsaye, the Coachman of his Excellency Governor Franklin, who was sentenced to be hanged at Burlington, for a rape committed on a Girl about 15 Years of Age, was reprieved under the Gallows, upon the Recommendation of the Honourable the Chief Justice and sundry of the principal Inhabitants of that City, who were of Opinion that some Circumstances appeared to be in his Favour. *The Pennsylvania Gazette*, December 15, 1763

---

[15] A phrase, literally translated as "we do not know", which the Grand Jury would apply when it believed a crime had been committed but that it did not have enough information to indict.

On occasion, however, the wrongdoer was both convicted and punished, here in an appropriate manner.

We hear that one Cadry Leacy, who was advertised in our Paper of the 18th instant, as a runaway from Richard Lemon of New-Ark, New Castle County, was committed to Glouster Goal last week for murder. He passed through the Country as a dumb man and, about two weeks ago, stopped at a House on the Egg Harbour Road, the lower end of Glouster County, where he made signs that he was hungry, when the woman gave him food; the woman's husband being at work in the Cedar Swamps, it is said that Leacy wanted to go to bed to her but, she refusing, he killed her with a pitch fork; then he beat the Children, leaving the oldest one for dead, who has since recovered, and then made off. He, being pursued, was taken as committed as above. *Pennsylvania Journal*, February 1, 1770

Friday last Cadry Lacy was tried at the Supreme Court held at Glouster in New Jersey for the Murder of a Woman in that County of which he was convicted and received a Sentence of Death. *Pennsylvania Gazette*, April 19, 1770

Philadelphia, April 26. Last Saturday, Cadry Lacy was executed at Glouster and his body was sent, by the Order of the Chief Justice, to Dr. Shippeman's anatomical Theatre for Dissection.[16] *Pennsylvania Gazette*, April 26, 1770

Both the crimes of child abuse and incest appear to have existed in colonial times:

New York, August 31. We hear from Shrewsbury, that about a Fortnight ago, one Carrol of that Place, a Silver-Smith, was committed to Goal and still remains there for debauching his own daughter, a Girl not fifteen Years of Age, who has sworn that she is with Child by him and that this detestable Commerce has subsisted for above two years. *The New York Journal or General Advertiser*, August 31, 1769

---

[16] That also was the fate of the corpse of Peter Mennel, executed at Glouster for the Murder of his Master's daughter. His body was "delvered to the Surgeons to be anatomized." *The Pennsylvania Gazette*, Novemeber 8, 1770.

New York, September 25. We hear from Freehold, in New Jersey, that about ten Days ago, one Aaron Buck was committed to Jail there, charged with committing incest with his own daughter and also Uriah Carroll for the Death of his Servant Maid, a Coroner's Inquest having brought in Wilful Murder. *The New York Gazette or Weekly Post Boy*, September 25, 1769.

Saturday the 25th ult. a Dutch Boy, about 16 Years of Age, Servant to Mr. Lippincott, near Haddonfield, enticed his Master's Daughter (a little Girl about 9 Years old) when he ravished and murdered her and then buried her in a swamp. He is since taken up and committed to Glouster Goal. *New York Gazette or Weekly Post Boy*, September 10, 1770

There even was an incidence or two of arson. It is unlikely that insurance fraud was the motive for this crime. Perhaps, it was spite, an act of a competitor or that of a deranged man.

We hear from Newark, that on Monday Night Last, Schuyer's Copper Works, which were burnt about 7 years ago, were again destroyed by Fire, supposed to be by Design, as it was not known that any Fire had been lately used there. *The New York Journal or General Advertiser*, July 21, 1768

Another report on the same incident elaborated:

On Monday Night last, a very costly and valuable Engine for extracting Water out of Col. Schuyler's Copper Mines at Second River, unhappily took Fire, and that, together with the Buildings which inclosed it, entirely consumed. This is the second Time that Fire has consumed their Engine, and as it is of great Value and many Labourers had their chief Dependency on this Work, which they will now probably know the want of, the Damage will be very sensibly felt. It is unknown how the Fire began, but it is said, not to be without some suspicion of Design. *The New York Gazette or Weekly Post Boy*, July 25, 1768

Jail break, especially with the aid of others, was particularly bothersome to colonial peacekeepers because it struck at authority itself and the ability of Government to enforce its regulations:

Last Tuesday, about 9 o'Clock in the evening, the Turnkey of the Goal in this City, going to put a man in one of the rooms upstairs, the prisoners being twelve in number, six of which had been in irons, but had got them off, rose on the turnkey, knocked him down, and demanded the Keys or his life, on which he gave them the Keys; they pushed the other man down stairs and made their escape out of the door. Two of them returned the next morning, the others are not yet taken.

William Parr, Sheriff
The Pennsylvania Journal, December 18, 1766

All the Villains mentioned in our last to have broke goal are all taken up, except David Smith. [He] is aged 36 years, about 5'5 inches high, dark thin visage, his hair lately cut off, had on a light brown coat, red jacket and black stockings. He lately kept store at Reckless town New Jersey. . . .[He was] the person on whom the goods were found that was taken from some of the Inhabitants of this town last summer. *The Pennsylvania Journal*, December 25, 1766

New York, August 3. Tuesday Night last Ichabud Higgins, committed on Suspicion of Counterfeiting the Bills of Credit of this Colony, in Company of a Sailor and a Soldier, crept up the Chimney of the Room in which they were confined, let themselves down by the help of their Bed Cloaths into the Goal Yard and got clear off. *The Pennsylvania Journal*, August 6, 1761

New-Jersey, Monmouth County, February 7, 1767. Whereas by Virtue of a Warrant in his Majesty's Name, to me directed, I did this day arrest a certain Henry Killigrove, on suspicion of Felony, and also did take said Killigrove, at the suit of Robert and Esek Hartshorne, in an Action of Debt and Damage for Six Pounds Proc.

And whereas said Killigrove was rescued from me by, in a violent and Riotous Manner, by Thomas Kirk and Thomas Moore (alias Wilkies Tom) all belonging to the Liberty and Cluster Pilot Boats. Therefore any person who apprehends the above Henry Killigrove, Thomas Kirk and Thomas Moore and delivers them to me at Middletown, in the County aforesaid, for any Two of them the Sum of Eight Pounds, or for any one of them the Sum of Five Pounds, Money aforesaid. Witness my Hand.

Safety Bowne, One of the Constables for said Township
The Pennsylvania Journal, February 7, 1767

Horse theft in the 1700s, at least judging by the number of advertisements seeking the return of horses "that strayed or were stolen", must have been a common crime, like car theft today. The following is a typical notice, describing both the animal and the suspected thief. Notice that, just as a colonist would not be able to comprehend words like carburetor, white wall tires, or FM/AM stereo in a description of an automobile, we will find the detailed description of the horse and its equipment somewhat difficult to follow, as some of the everyday words then used by the colonists to design their principal mode of transportation did not survive in our working vocabularies:

Forty Shillings Reward

Borrowed by William Godfrey, and his wife, of the subscriber, to go seven or eight miles, on the twenty-fifth of April last, a dark roan horse, with a mealy nose, has several saddle spots, and a lump at the end of the saddle next the crooper; lops his ears when rode slow, goes heavy in his pace; when put on his courage is spry, trots smart and large, one of his hind ancle joints is thicker than the other, but this does not hurt his travelling, is surefooted, is about thirteen hands high; had no shoes on when taken away, had a switch tail, was not trimmed, but may be altered, branded H.S., and another brand under the other, upside down, not so plain as the H.S. on the near buttock, is nine years old; also had with the horse, an old side saddle, with a blue plush seat, and leather skirts, and a bridle almost new, one rein chewed.

The man is of a middle stature, thin pale face, has lost his upper teeth, except one, winks his eyes when speaking, is about fifty years old, brownish hair, had on a new pair of boots, and a new pair of worsted stockings; otherwise poorly dressed. His wife is short, round faced, and double chinned; borrowed at the same time a linsey petticaot with yellow and other stripes, but mostly yellow, the other part of her dress cannot be particulariz'd; she is a school mistress and handy with a needle. For securing the horse and giving notice to the owner, living in Knoulton township, in the County of Sussex, in the province of New-Jersey, so that the subscriber may have him again, shall have the above reward, with reasonable charges paid by

Philip Bellus

N.B. The last account of him was at the Great Swamp, at Tomkins tavern in Pennsylvania. *The Pennsylvania Chronicle*, May 23, 1768

Sometimes, the horse theft was on a grander scale, an undeniable criminal enterprise, as illustrated by the following:

New-Jersey and the County of Hunterdon, in Hanover, Township, May 1, 1732. John Haywood of full age, Deposeth: that on or about the 22nd Day of April last past, in the Forks of the North Branches of Rarinton

River in said County, one Benjamin Hillyard, late from Potowmack River in Maryland or Virginia but formerly of Piscataqua in New-Jersey, Blacksmith, took this Deponent aside and there spoke to this Deponent as followeth, viz. That one Timothy Burcham and others were d--ned Fools that they would not be persuaded to go with him, with whom they could get Money as fast as Heart could wish, then he added D--n it, I'le tell you how (pointing to some horses) he said, such would sell down in Maryland for 14 or 15 Pounds a Piece and that at this Season of the Year there were plenty in the Woods, being turned out to get Flesh against Ploughing Time and that he would take them and go back to the inhabitants of Maryland to sell them. And, if they did not sell amongst the English, he would take them back to the Indians and there they would sell for skins at a better Value, and that many new Plantations was settling towards the Head of Potowmack River, where a great Number of Negroes was to be had, Ten or a Dozen at a time and take them back to the French Indian Traders to sell them.

And that he would assure any one of them that would joyn with him in this Project, more than One Hundred Pounds in three Months Time and that it should be so nicely wrought (or carried on) that none should be suspected of doing any Wrong. And he also proposed to take this Deponent as a Partner in this Wicked Design, who absolutely refused. And this Deponent further saith that the said Burcham and John FitzRandolph, are absent from their Wives and Children and suspected to have been persuaded to undertake the aforesaid Project with the said Hillyard and further saith not.

Sworn before me John Budd, Justice
The American Weekly Journal, June 8, 1732

or:

New York, February,25. On Thursday last, some Persons who had lost sundry Things, having got intelligence that one Elizabeth Herbert, a suspected Person who came from Philadelphia, with a Man at whose House she lodged here, had gone off in a Boat with some Bundles for New Brunswick, they got a Pettiauger[17] and went after them. They came up with the Boat near Elizabeth Town Point, and on searching the Bundles, found most of the Things they had missed, whereupon they brought them both back and committed them to Jail.

They have been since examin'd and the Proof seems full against them. This woman was tried here a few weeks ago for stealing and would

---

[17] A small water craft approximately 30 feet in length.

have been burnt in the Hand but was begged off. There appears to be a Gang of them, tho' it's supposed these two are the Chiefs and 'tis hoped will meet with the Reward their Merits deserve. There is a piece of blue and white handkerchiefs found among the Goods supposed to be stolen for which no Owner has yet appeared and sundry other goods. *Pennsylvania Journal,* March 5, 1751

As the following indicates, horse thievery was dealt with considerably more severely than auto theft is today:

New York, June 10. We hear from Burlington that Two men were to be executed there on Saturday last for Horse stealing.
The New York Gazette Revived in the Weekly Post Boy, June 10, 1751

Philadelphia, June 13. The two Men that were to have been executed Saturday last, at Burlington, for Horse stealing, are both reprieved. One of them was reprieved some Days before the Time scheduled for his Execution; the other under the Gallows.[18] John Crow (who was lately reprieved under the Gallows by our Governour) is again in Jail here; he was taken at Glouster Point and had a Mare with him supposed to be stolen. *The Pennsylvania Gazette,* June 13, 1751

New-York, October 30. Last Week was held at Newark, for the County of Essex in the Province of New Jersey, before the Hon. Frederick Smyth, Esq., a Court of Oyer and Terminer and General Gaol Delivery when two persons were convicted of Horse-stealing and received the sentence of Death, viz.

James M'Carthy, a Native of Ireland, about 21 Years old; says his mother lived in Philadelphia; that he sometimes lived in New Haven, from whence he came last March, and passing through Elizabeth-Town, took a Horse, Saddle and Bridle, was followed, and apprehended at the Indian Queen, in Philadelphia, with the Horse, Saddle and Bridle.

John Morris, also a native of Ireland, aged 49 Years, took a Horse at Springfield, near Elizabeth-Town, in August last; was apprehended in Morris County with the Horse.

---

[18] Apparently, it was common for death sentences to be commuted at the last moment, it being thought the scare would discourage recidivism. Second chances were also given sometimes, but rarely third.

They both denied Stealing the Horses and said they purchased them from Persons travelling on the Road, to them unknown. They are to be executed on Friday the 31st Instant October. *The New York Journal or General Advertiser*, October 30, 1766

New York, November 6. Friday last John Morris was executed, pursuant to his sentence for horse stealing; but John M'Carty, the other man condemned at the same time, was reprieved by the Governor of New Jersey. *The Pennsylvania Gazette*, November 13, 1766

Rustling of livestock was also a problem and, ironically enough, was sometimes punished by branding:

Philadelphia, May 17. From Burlington we have Advice that one John Shores was tried at the Supreme Court, held there for stealing a cow, of which he was convicted and burnt in the Hand. *The Pennsylvania Gazette*, May 17, 1753

Sneak thieves seemed as prevalent as today, especially on the road and in the harbor as were "fences" for some of the snatched merchandise.

Thursday Night last, some Rogues got into the Cabin of the Boat of Soloman Davis, of Newark, whilst he lay asleep, and carried off upwards of Thirty Shillings in Money. *The Pennsylvania Journal*, October 12, 1752

New York, October 16. One Night last Week, the Boat of one Mr. Alexander Blair of Brunswick, lying in this Harbour, was robbed of Cash to the Value of Five Pounds; the Thief was next Day detected with the greatest part of the Money about him. *The Pennsylvania Gazette*, October 19, 1752

New York, September 3. On Monday Night, at the Albany Dock, the Cabin of a Sloop belonging to Egg Harbour, Levi Hosier, Master, who with two other men was asleep within it, was robbed of his Chest, which was carried out onto the Dock, broke open and plundered of his Clothes and 150 Pounds New York Currency.

He suspected one of his own People, named Norton, who being committed to the Goal, confessed being concerned in the Fact, discovered the Place where he had concealed the Money, and where it was all found and named a Seaman from a Vessel lying close by as his Accomplice, who he said had taken possession of the Clothes; the man was immediately taken up and committed to Goal, where both he and Norton now remain. *The New York Journal or General Advertiser*, September 3, 1767

New York, February 5. Last Tuesday Night, the Boat of Mr. Bain, of South River, in the Jersies, lying at the Old-Slip[19] in our Harbour, was robbed of nine pounds in Cash, a Check Shirt and a Knife. Barnabas Morgan, a Man who went in the Boat, being about the next Day, was suspected and Search being made, he was found with the Shirt on his Back and Knife in his Pocket, but he denies he took the Money; after Examination, he was committed to Gaol. *The Pennsylvania Gazette*, February 13, 1753

Philadelphia, November 13. On Sunday, a Man who calls himself David Smith, was brought to Town from New York, being concerned in committing divers Robberies in this City some time ago; it seems that he had taken a Store and resided some time in Reckless Town, New Jersey, where he conveyed the stolen goods, from time to time; but being suspected from his not knowing how to sell them, he thought proper to move off; he was, however, pursued to New-York, where he was taken up with a great Quantity of Goods, which are brought back and most of them have been owned by the different People, from whom they were taken; he was examined on Monday before the Chief Judge and committed to our Gaol; among the Goods were two marked Pocket-books, one with Silver Clasps, marked W. B. and William Burns worked at large thereon. *The Pennsylvania Gazette*, November 13, 1766

Sometimes, they would even steal the boat itself:

New York, June 25. We learn from Egg Harbour, about Ten or Twelve Days ago, a Vessel bound in there from Virginia, took up at Sea, the Boat advertised in this Paper last Week to have been taken from Mr. John Latham's Wharf, with only one Man on board and he almost starved to Death. He said that, as he had stole the Boat, he Purposed to carry her around into the Delaware River and there make use of her as a Passage Boat. For this voyage, he had laid in but little more provisions than a Loaf of Bread. *The Pennsylvania Journal,* June 28, 1753

---

[19] While the wharf has been gone centuries, its former location, filled in during the 1700s and early 1800s, still bears the name "Old Slip". It lies at the foot of Manhattan, on the East River side, just south of Wall Street.

Poaching, both in the forests and the oyster beds, were also serious crimes, at least as far as the landlord was concerned. In the following example, the land involved is today part of the Sandy Hook National Park. Size aside, it's appearance is unaltered since the days of this Notice.

Whereas Gastavus Kingsland, Yesterday Afternoon clandestinely shot a Hog upon Sandy Hook; and as the subscribers have frequently lost sucking calves, which they believe to have been stolen off Sandy-Hook. Therefore public Notice is hereby given, that any Person or Persons that shall presume for the Future to carry a gun or shoot on Sandy-Hook, without Liberty being first obtained from under their Hands, will be prosecuted with the utmost Rigour of the Law.

Robert Hartshorne
Esek Hartshorne

N.B. As the aforementioned Gastavus Kingsland, was in company with one Edward Collard, who it is thought was Confederate with him, said Collard is forbid to land or to dig Clams on Sandy Hook, as he will be looked upon as a trespasser as soon as landed.
The New York Journal or General Advertiser, August 11, 1768

Looting of shipwrecks along the shore were similarly illegal:

New York, April 8. We have Intelligence from the Jersies that some Men who belonged to one of the Vessels that attempted to carry off some of the Money belonging to the Spanish Wrecks at Ocacock in North Carolina, were last Week apprehended and committed to Amboy jail, as 'tis said, by Orders of the Government. *The New York Gazette Revived in the Weekly Post Boy*, April 8, 1751

One clever group of looters added the element of distraction and confusion to help aid them in the crime, as the following pair of accounts reveals:

New York April 20. The Schooner Delight, Captain Wallace, Master, from South Carolina for Philadelphia run ashore the 8th instant, in the Night at Little Egg Harbour; the Vessel and Cargo will be entirely lost, as the Men went on shore and left her to drive to Pieces; The Captain cannot be found, neither will the Men give any Account of him. The Register of the Vessel was in Captain Wallace's Name but the People say one Burns was then Master. *The Pennsylvania Journal*, April 23, 1761

Philadelphia, May 7. The extraordinary Account of the Loss of the Schooner Delight, John Byrne, Master, at Egg Harbour, was false in every Circumstance, except the Loss of the Vessel and the Cargoe. The Person who brought the Account first was one of the Villains who plundered that vessel. In order to give some Colour of Justice to their Proceedings, they alleged that she had been runaway with and, on this Pretence, apprehended the Captain for Piracy and the Murder of Thomas Wallace (the Owner) who they say was the real Master and had been killed by the Mate, who, with the People's consent, assumed the Command. *The Pennsylvania Gazette*, May 7, 1761

There were crimes against the Government back then, most often desertions but in one instance, a mutiny by a ship's crew resisting being impressed into the Royal Navy. How successful they were, we never learn:

Tuesday, 5th of August, at 10 o'Clock in the Morning arrived off Sandy Hook, the Ship Minehead, Captain Forrest, in eight Weeks from Lisbon, with Salt. The Ship of War, lying in that Road, sent a Boat to demand her Men; but on the refusal of the Ship's Company (who had seized all the Small Arms and who confined the Captain and the Officers and were determined not to surrender until the last Extremity) Signals from the Longboat were made for more Assistance, soon after which three more Boats were manned and come under the Minehead's Stern, sometimes discharging Small Arms and demanding Admittance but were still refused by the Men who had taken Sole Command of the Ship, which the Officers in the Boats knew as they were informed of it several Times, both by the Master from his Cabbin and from the Pilot on the Deck. Notwithstanding, the Ship continued to fire Grape-shot, Langrage[20], Twelve pounders &c., many of which lodged in her Wales, went through her Boltsprit and Main Top Mast, damaged her Sails considerably, killed one Man and wounded another. *The Pennsylvania Gazette*, August 14, 1760

There were also indirect crimes against the Crown, "economic" offenses, as there are now. Smuggling was one of them and the Government went to great efforts to curtail it:

---

[20] A form of irregularly shaped shot, designed to shred the adversary's sails.

Boston, September 19. The London Papers say that 16 armed cutters are cruising on the coasts of Essex, Sussex, Norfolk, Devon &c. in quest of the smuggling vessels; and orders are given to the Commanders of the other sloops and vessels not sailed, to proceed immediately to their respective stations to seize smugglers. And we hear that five of those vessels are to be stationed between Cape Sables and Sandy-Hook, as also a number to be kept cruizing off all the West India Islands. *The Pennsylvania Journal,* September 29, 1763

Another wrongdoing that threatened the economic health of the Provinces was counterfeiting. There was not a uniform currency in the Colonies during the 1700s. In addition to the English pound sterling, there were in circulation assorted currencies, both coins and bills, from other nations and each Province. In the beginning years, even indian wampum was used. One man, with a sufficient quantity of counterfeit notes could do a lot of damage:

Albany, New York. A certain Gentleman, who goes by the name of John Davis, alias Joseph Daniels, and lately brought into this Government a large Quantity of New-Jersey Bills of Credit, printed in England, was a few Days ago, apprehended in Orange County and committed to Tappan Goal, and upon searching, it was found he had about him not less than 3500 pounds of that Cash, all signed by himself, but he declared he never passed any of it. *The Pennsylvania Gazette,* March 27, 1766

Sometimes, a "ring" was involved, here on an international scale:

On the 14th Instant in the Morning , one David Willson and one David Wallace, were apprehended and committed to the common Goal of New York for Uttering Counterfeit Bills of Credit . . . of this Province and the Province of New Jersey. Upon their Examinations before the Mayor and other Magistrates, they confess they brought about Eight Hundred Pounds of that Money from Maryland. David Wallace ingeniously confessed that, about Four Months ago, he had brought about a Thousand Pound of the Counterfeit Money over in the Ship Richmond to Philadelphia from Dublin; that he had the said Money from Thomas Morough (whom lately lived at Elk River in Maryland) but was then in Dublin and that the said Thomas Morough told him they were Counterfeit Bills but he knows not who Printed or Signed them; that he was to have a third of the said Counterfeit Money for puttin it off. . . that the whole Counterfeit Money that was being made being Three Thousand Pounds or upwards; that the aforesaid David Willson was Employ'd by the said David Wallace to Exchange and put off the

Counterfeit Bills, for which he was to have Four or Five Shillings to the Pound. *The American Weekly Mercury*, March 16, 1727.

Therefore, vigilance was preached:

A Caution to the Publick

Last Saturday several counterfeit One Shilling Bills were uttered here.The Paper is pretty stiff and good and some of the Bills have an Impression of a Sage Leaf, ill done, upon their Backs. If these Bills are compared with the True ones, both being fair, many Variations may be observed both in the Signing and the Printing, as the counterfeits are a very bad Imitation of the True. Those who do not have both Sorts to look at together, may take notice, that the Figures that make the Ornament or Border at the Bottom of the False Bills, which have the resemblance of a Flower de Luce at Top and something more under, stand apart, which in the True Bills stand close; and that in the False Bills the first "I" in the word SHILLING, that ends the Bill is shorter than the last "I" in that Word; that the second "L" in the same Word is shorter than the first and that the "G" is longer than the other Capitals and made very open. *The Pennsylvania Gazette*, November 15, 1744

On Thursday last a New Jersey Man, tall and pock-fretten[21], paid ten Pieces of Eight[22] in a Shop in this City; and on Friday it was discovered that three of them were counterfeited; The Bulk, Impression and Letters are so well imitated that one would scarcely suspect them; they ring almost as other Pieces of Eight; the Colour nearly but not quite her same; but on cutting, they are almost as soft as pewter, and, on weighing they are 2 s. lighter than Pieces of Eight, which are the only sure ways we know of discovering them. This is published to put People on their Guard and that, if possible, the Authors of this Villainy may be discovered. *The New York Gazette Revived in the Weekly Post Boy*, October 9, 1752

Last Week a Jersey One Shilling Bill was passed in this City for Six Shillings, the Word One being cut out and the Word Six put in and the other

---

[21] Many colonists were scarred from bouts with small pox. See *Medical News infra*.

[22] This is the famous Spanish coin legendary in pirate tales. Also known as a doubloon or *real*, it could be broken into eight parts or "bits" to provide currency of a lesser amount. Curiously, it survives today in our expressions "two bits" or "four bits" when referring to a quarter or fifty cents piece.

parts of the Bill so defaced, as not to be distinguished on first Sight, but easily may be known on close Examination. As there may be more of the same sort, People are cautioned to beware of them. *The Pennsylvania Gazette*, October 12, 1752

Because there was no norm, counterfeiting currencies became a temptation to some. However, as it undermined commerce among the Provinces (and the trust upon which such commerce was predicated) between and among the Provinces, as well as being a theft in its own right, attempt were first made to discourage it by embarrassing the wrongdoers:

Perth-Amboy, November 1. At a Special Court of Oyer and Terminer, held at Perth-Amboy, on Wednesday, the 29th of October last, were tryed at the said Court one Anthony Adamson and William Scott for Counterfeiting Bills of Credit of this Province of New-Jersey and for uttering the same, who were found guilty of the Crime so charged upon them. And the Court gave Judgment against them as follows viz.

That you the said Adamson being taken into a Cart at the Prison Door, on Friday the last Day of October, and so Carted thro' the Streets of Perth Amboy with a Roap about your Neck, and that you be, about Eleven o'Clock in the Forenoon of the same Day, put into the Pillory and there to continue for an Hour and from thence carted with a Roap about your Neck to Woodbridge, to the Meeting-House of said Town, thence to the Square before Mr. Herds Door and to stand in the Cart for a quarter of an Hour, and that you have a Paper fixed to your Back and Breast, declaring your Offence, with one of the Counterfeit Bills fixed thereto, and from thence back to the Goal to remain until you pay the Fees and Charges.

The same Sentence was passed on William Scott, with this Difference, he was to be Carted to Piscataway and not to be inflicted on him until Saturday the 15th of November. *The American Weekly Mercury*, October 30, 1729

Apparently such wrist slapping did not help much and counterfeiting began to be treated more harshly when detected:

Amboy, May 18. On Saturday last, one Duncan Campbell stood two hours in the Pillory, according to his Sentence at the Supream Court of this county. To-morrow, he is to receive 39 Lashes of the Carts Tail and, on

Friday, 31 more. His Crime is Counterfeiting and Passing Pistoles [23]; he is to be sent to Monmouth County to receive another Trial on the same Account. *The American Weekly Mercury*, May 13, 1731.

When that did not work, the penalties got harsher. Poor John Stevens from Ash Swamp and Henry Yaeger from Trenton are cases in point:

New York, August 13. On Friday se'nnight[24] last came before the Supreme Court for this Province, the Trial of John Stevens, late of Ash Swamp in East New-Jersey, for counterfeiting the Bills of Credit of this Province and uttering them Knowing to be counterfeit, when the Jury, after a short Stay, brought in the Prisoner Guilty; and on Tuesday last, Sentence of Death was passed on him and he is to be executed on Friday se'nnight next, tho' we hear he complains much of a Hurt in his Right Thumb and it is tho't he will have it cut off for fear of a general Mortification. *The Boston Weekly Post Boy*, August 20, 1744

New-York August 27. On Friday last John Stevens of Ash-Swamp was executed here, according to sentence pass'd against him the 7th Instant for counterfeiting the Bills of Credit of this Colony and uttering them knowing them to be counterfeit; He dies penitent, but his crime was too well known for him to have pretended to extenuate it by any Speech from the Gallows; and as it was tho't he expected a Reprieve, it may be reasonably suppos'd he refrain'd making one till too late.

If some of our Neighbouring Governments would but act with equal Justice, it might be presumed those Pests of Society would be something scarcer than they are. *The Boston Weekly Post Boy*, September 3, 1744,

We hear from Trenton, that at the last Court of Oyer and Terminer &c. held there, one Henry Yaeger, being upon full and clear Evidence convicted of Counterfeiting the current Money of the Province of New Jersey, was condemned to die and accordingly was executed there on Saturday the 16th instant and that several more are apprehended and confined on Suspicion of being guilty of the same Crime. That the Government is determined to exert itself in detecting and punishing this growing Evil. *The Pennsylvania Journal*, July 28, 1748

---

[23] A Spanish coin worth about $4.00.

[24] Phrases such as "fortnight" and "se'nnight" puzzle many, when their derivations and meanings are really simple. "Fortnight" is a contraction for "fourteen nights" --or two weeks ago -- and "se'nnight" is a contraction for "seven nights" or a week ago.

One would expect murder and other heinous crimes to be punished by death. However, back in the 18th Century, it seemed to be the preferred sentence. Very often, the sentence was commuted at the last minute, literally at the gallows, in an effort to impress upon the defendant how close he came to eternity. It did not always work. An example involves John Crow, who, as already noted, was arrested in 1751 for horse theft, just after he had been spared at the Gallows by the Governor. We see him three years later in exactly the same predicament:

Philadelphia, May 30. Saturday last the notorious John Crow (who a few years ago was reprieved under the Gallows and had been several Times in Danger of being Hanged since) and one Chester, were executed at Trenton for House breaking. *The New York Gazette or Weekly Post Boy,* June 3, 1754

Most times, however, the death penalty was applied as ordered:

Perth-Amboy, January 14. On Saturday last a Negroe Man was tried here for Murdering a poor Man, one Thomas Cook, who was a Taylor by Trade and went about working at People's Houses. For the said Murder the Evidence against the Negro being very clear, altho he denied the Fact at his trial, but there appearing to the Court sufficient Proof that he was guilty of the Murder, he was condemn'd for the same and the Sentence prounced'against him that he Should be Burnt the Monday following which was then put in Execution, and he was then accordng to the said Sentence Burnt alive and confest'd the Fact before he was burnt. *The American Weekly Mercury,* January 14, 1730.

In the account of our last (under the New York head) relating to the apprehending of two ruffians, at St. Eustatia, a mistake was made in names, it being Nicholaus Johnson who was apprehended there, tried and condemned to the Rack for the Murder of Capt. Duryea, and Joseph Andres, who went off for Casco-Bay, on board of one Captain Strickney. He shipped himself it seems under the name of Joseph Saunders. . . . Nicholas Johnson confessed that he was the Man who murdered the Captain of a small French vessel and afterwards turned his wife and children adrift in a canoe at sea, near upon two years ago; and it thought, with some shew of reason, that he was the man who murdered a traveller about a year ago, between Woodbridge and New-Brunswick. *The Pennsylvania Journal,* December 25, 1766

Last Friday was Executed at Hackinsack a Negro for Poisoning 3 Negro Wenches and a Horse. *The Boston Weekly Post Boy*, June 4, 1744

Yesterday our Chief Justice passed sentence of Death upon 2 Criminals, one a Girl for the Murder of her Bastard Child, the other a Fellow for Horse Stealing. *The New York Gazette or Weekly Post Boy*, May 22, 1766

From Somerset County in the same Province, we hear, that a Negro Man about 19 Years of Age, was apprehended and committed to prison for ravishing a white Child aged about 9. 'Tis said he will be burnt alive. *The Pennsylvania Gazette*, December 14, 1744

A few days ago one Bourns, a private soldier belonging to the 44th regiment, was shot at Elizabeth-town for desertion. It seems he had been an old offender and saw three offenders shot for the same crime in Albany and at the same time he himself received 500 lashes, notwithstanding which he soon deserted again. *The New American Magazine*, February, 1758

Sometimes the punishments were less final, although barbaric by our standards two and a half centuries later.

On Wednesday last in Jamaica on Long Island, at a Special Commission of Oyer and terminer and Gaol-Delivery, before Roger Mompesson Esqr Chief Justice of this Province and New Jersey &c and others one Samuel Wood, late of Connecticut Colony, was indicted for feloniously Stealing Money and other Goods of one John Marsh. The witnesses for the Prisoner as well as those against him were Sworn and upon full Evidence he was found Guilty & burnt in the left Cheek, near the nose with the Letter "1". *The Boston News Letter*, April 23, 1704

A most peculiar report, almost comical at first, displays its own version of cruelty of our forebears --- the intentional infliction of frost bite upon those found guilty.

From Salem, they write that at the last Court, 4 Irish Men were found guilty of a Misdemeanor, having with others, chiefly Servants of that Nation, to the number of 15 or 16, been engaged in a foolish Conspiracy to make an Insurrection in order to seize that County, with an old Irish Trooper at their Head etc. They stood in the Pillory last Week, till their Ears and Fingers were nipt with Frost. *The Pennsylvania Gazette*, December 14, 1744

The concept of the prisoner having to pay for his food while incarcerated is also odd sounding today, although, as the following indicates, is was brutally the fact in the 1700s:

New York, September 14. A Person from Newark in New Jersey, gives us the following odd Intelligence; that one Sears, four or five years ago, having willfully shot and desperately wounded one of the Conservators of the Peace in the Borough of New Jersey, had been committed to the Newark Gaol; Before his Trial came on, he assigned over what Estate he had to some near Relation; on his Trial he was found guilty, and among other Articles of his Sentence, he was to find Security for his good Behaviour during Life; but he being of a very fractious and obstinate Temper, he could never get such Security. For some time his Relations supported him in Gaol, when, finding it too chargeable in their Imagination, they withheld their Supports; For some Time longer he was supported by the Charity of the Town, but they thinking it was not their Duty to do so, stopt their Hand also a few Months ago. Upon his being told those who had hitherto supplied him with Provisions would do so no longer, he voluntarily determined to fast Forty Days without Food or die. He persisted in the Resolution and all the Time he only took two coppersworth of Rum, and neither eat nor drink any thing else for Forty Days, in which time he was reduced to a perfect Skeleton and continued in a great Measure like a mere Lunatick. At the Expiration of the Time, which was but a Fortnight ago, he was prevailed with to take some Nourishment, but for the first Day or so, every Thing he took came up again, his Belly having grown almost fast to his Back. However, by the Help of some Medicines of lenitive Food, he is at last like to recover again after his long obstinate Fast, though he is very poor and low. *The New York Mercury*, September 14, 1767

Courts of the colonial period meted out justice, quickly and cruelly in comparison to courts today, as illustrated by the following docket.

On Wednesday, the 6th inst.at the Court of Oyer and Terminer and General Gaol Delivery, held at Salem, before the Honourable Frederick Smyth, Esq, Chief Justice of the Province of New Jersey, Bills of Indictment were found against the following Persons: Daniel Rice for Manslaughter, who was acquitted; Joseph Haynes, an Englishman, for a Misdemeanor, who confessed his Indictment and was sentenced to receive 39 Lashes at the Common Whipping Post, which was executed the next Morning; Haynes and one Andrew Ring (who since broke Gaol and escaped) were committed about the 6th of June last for breaking the Shop Window of Jacob Hollingshead, Watchmaker in Salem, and stealing three Watches. They, with several others, were, a few Days before, taken out of the Work-House in Philadelphia and carried into the Jerseys, to be sold as servants newly imported; James Weldon, an Irishman, for Grand Larceny, who confessed his Indictment and was sentenced to be burned on the Hand, which was executed accordingly. Weldon is the same Person who broke open the Stores of Messsrs. Test and Johnson and stole upwards of a 100 pounds in cash. 'Tis supposed that he has been guilty of several crimes before. *The Pennsylvania Chronicle*, May 11, 1767

However, the legal system's primitive, superstitious side can be seen in all of its ugliness too.

New York, October 1. The following extraordinary attestation of the Coroner of Bergen County was communicated by a Gentleman of such Credit as leaves not the least doubt of its being genuine.

On the Twenty Second Day of September in the Year of Our Lord, 1767, I, Johannes Demarest, Coroner of the County of Bergen of the Province of New Jersey, was present at a View of the Body of one Nicholas Teurs, then lying dead, together with the Jury, which I summoned to inquire of the Death of the said Nicholas Teurs. At the time, a Negro Man named Harry, belonging to Hendrick Christians Zabriskie, was suspected of having murdered the said Teurs, but there was no Proof of it and the Negro denied it. I asked him if he were not afraid to touch Teurs and he said No, he had not hurt him and immediately came up to the Corpse then lying in the coffin; and then Staats Storm, one of the Jurors, said "I am not afraid to touch him" and stroked the dead Man's Face with his Hand, which made no alteration in, and (as I did not put any faith in any of those Trials) my Back was turned toward the Dead Body, when the Jury ordered the Negro to touch the dead Man's Face with his Hand and then I heard a Cry in the Room of the People, saying "He is the Man" and I was desired to come to the dead Body; and was told that the said Negro Harry had put his Hand on Teurs Face and that the Blood immediately ran out of the Nose of the dead Man Teurs. I saw the Blood on his Face and ordered the Negro to rub his Hand again on Teur's Face; he did so and immediately the Blood again ran out of Teur's Nose at both Nostrils, near a common tablespoon at each Nostril, as well as I could judge. Whereupon the People all charged him with being the Murderer but he denied it for a few minutes, then confessed that he had murdered the said Nicholas Teurs, by first Striking him on the Head with an Ax and then driving a wooden Pin into his Ear, tho' afterwards he said he struck him a second time with the Ax and then held him fast until he was done struggling; when that was done, he awakened some of the Family and said Teurs was dying (he believed)

Johannes Demarest, Cor.

The New York Journal or General Advertiser, October 1, 1767

Crime can have a lighter side. Sometimes, it is a beloved character such as the legendary Tom Bell, who, in 1742, upon realizing he that bore an amazing resemblance to a popular preacher of the time, impersonated him at Sunday dinner tables and pulpits, stealing money and a horse in the process. So effective was his impersonation, that the real preacher was indicted and tried for the crimes committed by Bell. He was found not guilty, but not before two of his alibi witnesses, including the well known Rev. William Tennent, were also indicted for perjury. Involved in other scrapes with the law, his antics were followed by an eager readership:

Newport Rhode Island, January 13. Last Week the famous Tom Bell who landed here from Barbados in June last, having made the Tour of New England, New-York, New-Jersey, and Pennsylvania &c. returned here incog[25]. in order to redeem his fine Cloaths that were attached on account of the House he hired at Chelsea, but attempting to escape from a Person who had supplied him with Money &c he was taken and clapt in Gaol. He talks of publishing his Journal, on proper Encouragement, and says it will be very entertaining. We are assured that he has already (since he was here last) passed under the Names of Winthrop, DeLancey, Jekyl, Wendell and Francis Hutchinson. He brought this last from Hudson's River, a little below Albany, quite to this Town. The poor Wretch is in deplorable Circumstances and very much needs Compassion.

January 14. Tom has to Day sent out a Brief to beg Relief and promises an entire and universal Reformation. *The New York Weekly Journal*, February 15, 1742

We hear from the Jerseys that the famous Tom Bell being on the Pad hither, about 10 Days ago, was taken up and committed to Jail in Monmouth County. *The New York Weekly Post Boy*, September 17, 1744

Enlistment in the army often brought with it a pardon. So Tom Bell became a soldier --but, one wonders, for how long?

---

[25] i.e., incognito or not regognized

New York, September 15. We have Assurance that the noted Tom Bell is listed a Soldier, under Command of Captain Stevens, in one of the New Jersey Companies and is gone with them to Albany. *The New York Weekly Post Boy*, September 15, 1746

As much as Bell was idolized by the common man, another apparent fraud, a Richard Perot, was scorned by the populace, as the unfolding of the following accounts would suggest. First, the report of the crime is received and it seems a part of an existing crime wave.

New York, August 3. By the Philadelphia Post we have an account that last Wednesday Afternoon, Mr. Richard Perot, a West India Gentleman, now living at Elizabeth-Town, in returning from Philadelphia, was set upon by two Highwaymen, in the Woods called Penn's Manor, about two Miles and a half from Trenton-town Ferry, who bound him Neck and Heels and then robbed him of a Green Purse, wherein was 38 Pistoles, 5 Doubloons and some Dollars, together with two pairs of Ear-rings, two Neck-laces and two Solitares, all Paste set in Gold. They left him in that Condition where he was fond some time later by James Odear, who loosed him. One of the Rogues was mounted on a Bay Horse; with a brown Great-Coat behind him and had a large scar on his right Cheek; the other had a horse between a Mouse Color and a Bay and a Brown Great-Coat on. They talked Irish and were both well set lusty Men with ruffled Caps. We hear that Mr. Isaac De Cow narrowly escaped being robbed in the same Place and that the Inhabitants thereabouts have lost eight Horses within a Week past. *The New York Gazette Revived in the Weekly Post Boy*, August 3, 1752

The next account repeats the salient facts but then throws some doubt on Mr. Perot's credibility.

Philadelphia, August 5. We have an Account from Trenton that on Wednesday the 29th of July, Richard Perot was attacked and robbed by two Men on Horseback in the Woods between Trenton and Bristol, who took from him he says 38 Pistoles, 5 Doubloons and some Dollars and two pairs of Ear-rings, two Neck-laces, two Solitares, all set in Gold. He says they were well set lusty Men, one of which had a large scar on his right Cheek and talked Irish. They tied him up with his own Garter and so left him.

Upon examination of the above Account, it is generally believed that the Person bound himself up in order to impose upon People and that he was not robb'd. *The Pennsylvania Journal*, August 6, 1752

Unlike with Tom Bell and his escapades, the readership did not appear pleased with the antics of Mr. Perot:

To the Publishers of the Pennsylvania Gazette

At a Time when we of this Province have been so unfortunate as to have real Crimes of the most atrocious Kind committed amongst us, as appears in two late Instances, it behooves us to prevent the Publick from being imposed upon by the belief of such as, upon very good grounds, we may pronounce fictitious. Most People have heard a Report of a High-way Robbery being committed on a certain Richard Perot, in the Manor of Pennsbury, on the 29th of last Month . . . An Article in your Paper of August 6th, discrediting the Report of any such Crime being perpetrated, has produced another in the *York Gazette* of August 17, informing us that your Intelligence were evil-minded Persons, intending great damage to the said Mr. Perot, that the People of Philadelphia, hard hearted and incredulous, and no Way regarding his misfortune, had suffered two suspicious Persons, flush with Gold, to slip through their Fingers and escape.. . . but we may now venture to assert that the Evidence resulting from the following Facts (which are well . . .supported by Witnesses of unquestionable Reputation . . .) must convince every unprejudiced Person, that the whole was a Contrivance, tho' not cunningly enough laid, to answer some bad Purpose and it is but acting in Character for the Author of such a scheme to make a mighty Bustle and Stir, in order to persuade a general belief in it.

And first, from the Deposition of Mr. Patrick O'Hanlon. . . very strong presumptions shall be gathered that the whole Business was premeditated and that Mr. Perot had resolved upon a Place very proper, as he thought, for the Scene of the Robbery. The Deposition of James Adair . . . will speak for itself, only let it be observed that said Perot was on Horseback, with his Hands tied under his Hams, when Adair came up to him, tho', as he told him, he had been dismounted by the Robbers and left by them tied on the Ground. We do not say it was impossible for a Man in such a Situation, to recover the Back of an uncommonly tall Horse, which it is said Perot rode, but it must be allowed to be very difficult, and to require more Time perhaps than we can afford him for this Feat of Activity, as will appear by and by . . . But what will still greatly strengthen the Credit of our Side of the Quest is the Relation which Ennion Bristol, Esq. gives us upon his own knowledge:

" That on the 29th Day of July last, between the Hours of five and six in the Afternoon, as he was returning homewards, soon after entering the Woods, next to the Plantation of William Allen, Esq., he met two men travelling, one of whom he knew to be Mr. William Yard, of Trenton; after riding about three-quarters of a Mile farther, he met two young Gentlemen,

Sons of Mr. Morris and Mr. Powell, riding towards Trenton, with whom he made a Halt of a few Minutes. Parting from them, he had occasion to alight from his Horse, which delayed him some Minutes more; remounting his Horse again, in a few Minutes riding, he met a Stranger, whom afterwards, upon Recollection and by Description, he judged to be the Person pretending to be robbed; and that, in four or five Minutes afterwards, he met James Adair and his Wife in a Waggon, just at the Run of Water, commonly called Lambour's Run; that it was his Opinion, there being about 2 Miles Distance between the Place he met the first Company and James Adair, there was neither Time nor Opportunity for a Robbery as was pretended and, if any of the Rogues had been lying in Wait, he was more likely to become their Prey than any other at the Time, having Saddle-Bags behind him and travelling alone the contrary Road. *The New York Gazette Revived in the Weekly Post Boy*, October 2, 1752

Other witnesses came forward to cast even more doubt on Perot's story of having been robbed.

Bucks County, Pennsylvania. On the 15th Day of August, 1752, to wit, personally appeared before us, John Abraham Denormandie and Alexander Graydon Esquires, two of his Majesty's Justices of the Peace, for said County, James Adair, of the Falls Township, who being duly sworn &c. did declare and say: "That as he, this Deponent, was travelling in his wagon, between Bristol and his own House, on Wednesday the 29th Day of July last, between the Hours of Five and Six a clock, of same day, within a Half Mile of his own House, he came up with a man on horseback, whose name, he afterwards learned to be was Perot, who called to this deponent and begged him to unbind him, telling him he had been robbed; this deponent, supposing he only jested, replied that perhaps he might charge him with the Robbery, if he unbound him; that upon this deponent's asking his wife who was with him, what he had best do? For he believed that he was a Rogue, she told him to do as he pleased; that this Deponent then went out of his Waggon and found the said Perot sitting on his Horse, with his Hands bound under his Hams with a Garter, which, said Perot told him was his own Garter, wrapp'd several times about his Wrists, but without any Knot tied on it; that the Wrists were swelled by the Tightness of the Binding; that the said Perot, after he was unbound, seemed very weak and faint, or pretended to be so, and said he could not ride; but by the Assistance of a Foot Traveler, who then come up, this Deponent did help the said Perot into his Waggon and carried him to his House; that the said Perot told this Deponent that two Men on Horseback, which said Perot described, had robbed him of between thirty and forty Pistoles, Four Doubloons and some Jewels and Necklaces and that one of the Rogues had knocked him down from his Horse by a Blow on the Head, altho' this Deponent upon Examination could not discover any Sign of Hurt, Wound or bruise in the

Place where said Perot alleged he had received the Blow. And this Deponent further sayeth that on Wednesday, the 12th of the instant August, that said Perot came to this Deponent's House and desired him to go with him to Trenton and to declare before some Magistrates there, the condition that he had found the said Perot in on the 29th Day of July last; that accordingly this deponent did go with him before Theophilus Severns, Esq. in Trenton, where the said Perot did write a Paper which was read to this Deponent, but not so distinctly that he could apprehend the meaning of it; and, altho' this Deponent expressed an unwillingness to sign the Paper, yet he was solicited so much that at length that he was prevailed upon to sign it, but refused to swear to it; that afterwards this Deponent procured a copy of Same and now declares that such part of the contents of said Paper which contradicts this present deposition to be entirely false and further this Deponent sayeth not. *The Pennsylvania Gazette*, August 27, 1752

It was indeed the consensus of the populace that Richard Perot had made it all up:

We are well assured that Richard Perot, the Person who has lately made so much noise on pretence of being robbed in Penn's Manor, has turned out almost a second Tom Bell; but having attempted to play some Pranks here, a few days ago, he was discovered, whereupon he saw fit to decamp and on Thursday Night last went quite off. *The New York Gazette Revived in the Weekly Post Boy*, October 9, 1752

All of this Perot banging in the press, however, must have come as little consolation to John Jones, who was arrested --and we presume acquitted --for the robbery of Mr. Perot!

New York, August 27. We hear from Philadelphia that John Jones, who is committed to Jail there, as mentioned in the Philadelphia News, is suspected of being one of the Fellows who robb'd Mr. Perot in Penn's Manor. *The New York Gazette revived in the Weekly Post Boy*, September 1, 1752

Next to murder and other sordid crimes, newspaper readers, then as now, were drawn to reports of unexpected or mysterious deaths. There is nothing quite so sobering as to view death swoop down upon the unsuspecting. Many fatal accidents were reported in the news journals of the 1700s, reminding us that life has always been fragile. Death by drowning leads the pack, logically enough as the rivers and bays were the highways of the times, travelled by all types of craft and subject to sudden and foul weather and misadventure. Some of the accounts are dispassionate, indeed, rather matter of factedly reported. For example:

Philadelphia. The 12th Currant[26], 3 persons were drowned by the oversetting of a Wherry from Burlington hither. 5 other persons in it were saved. *The Boston News Letter*, April 9, 1704

Perth-Amboy, November 26. Last Saturday, our Ferry-Boat coming over from the other Side with 7 Men and 7 Horses, a Gust of Wind arose and overset the Boat, by Means where of 2 Men and 2 Horses were drowned. The rest were saved. *The Pennsylvania Gazette*, December 4, 1729

Philadelphia, January 25. On Wednesday last, one Samuel Burroughs and his Son being at our Market, in their way home to the Jerseys, broke thro' the Ice and were both drowned, the Father was taken up the next Day but the other is not yet found. *The Boston Weekly News-Letter*, February 10, 1732

Last Week, a Boat coming from Glouster to Philadelphia was overset by a Gust and a Woman with a young Girl were unfortunately drowned. *The Pennsylvania Gazette*, April 26, 1744

On Monday last, one John Tom, a Mariner, accidently fell over the Gunnel of a Wood-Boat near Robbins-Reef in his Passage from thence to Newark and was unfortunately drowned. *The New-York Evening Post*, November 14, 1748

---

[26] "Currant" and "Instant", used in conjunction with a date indicates the same month during which the report is being issued.

New York, March 14. On the 24th of February last, Mr. Samuel Ball of Newark, in New-Jersey, in crossing Hackinsack River, on the Ice, fell in with his Horse and Sleigh and was drowned. His Body was found the Sunday following and decently enterred. *The New York Gazette*, March 14, 1763

Saturday Noon, in a hard Squall, an Elizabeth-Town Boat in going up the Kills, took in such a quantity of Water of a sudden, that a Woman and Children said to be Germans lately arrived, were drowned in the Cabinn, before any assistance could get to them; the Husband with another Child, the Boatman and Capt. Lawrence with Difficulty saved their lives. *The New York Journal or General Advertiser*, January 1, 1767

Other reports of drownings were more sympathetic and detailed, perhaps the result of a first hand account being available.

Thursday last, the Wind blowing hard at West, and very squally, a Schooner from Philadelphia to Burlington, carrying too much Sail, was overset near that Place, whereby four persons out of seven were unfortunately drowned, viz. Peter Bayton, Esq., a considerable Merchant of this City, Mr. John Stapleford, a young Gentleman who serv'd an apprenticeship with him and had lately married his Niece, with a Dutch Man and Boy. Mr. Bayton and Mr. Stapleford were so well known and respected that this unhappy Accident occasions an Universal Concern. *The Pennsylvania Gazette*, March 1, 1744

New York, March 15. About Twelve o'Clock last Thursday, as one of the Staten Island Ferry Boats was coming over the Bay, with 13 Passengers and three Horses, by the Boat giving an unexpected pitch, (the Wind blowing fresh and a high Sea) the Horses fell astern, when they shipped so much water, that she sunk in a few minutes after, between Bedloe's and the Oyster Island[27], by which sorrowful accident, eleven out of the thirteen People, with three Horses, were drowned. Captain Benjamin Williams and Nathaniel Douglass, were taken up by a Boat that went to their Assistance, having held by the top of the Mast which remained above Water for a considerable Time. *The New York Mercury*, March 15, 1756

---

[27] Bledoe's Island is today known as Bedloe's and the site of the Statute of Liberty.

We hear from Middletown in New-Jersey that last Thursday Sen'night, a Boat loaded with Wood bound to New York, having sprung a leak soon after having sailed from thence, filled and sunk before they had any Notice of it; by which Means a Woman with two Children Passengers drowned; two White Men and a Negro got on the Top of the Mast, where they continued near 12 Hours, when happily a Perriauger coming by took them off. *The New York Gazette revived in the Weekly Post-Boy*, March 20, 1749

However, some of the drownings were dramatically depicted in Pulitzer Prize winning style:

New-York, August 19. Last Thursday a very sad Accident happened; one Mr. Brooks a Boatman, belonging to Brunswick took in several Passengers here, as Men, Women, and Children to the Number of 17 and accordingly proceeded on their Passage, but coming about in Jakeses Bay, she Miss-stay'd and, as she fell off again, the Wind suddenly filled all her Sails, and she being Light, having only two casks of nails in her Hold and they shifting overset her; there was one Mrs. Trebey and two of her Children drowned and also a High Dutch Woman, one Mary Moor with her Child being in the Water and striving to get to the Boat was sucked into the Hold by the Force of the Water that plentifully flowed in where she continued a Considerable time, but her poor Babey was drowned though she used all the Endeavours she could and kept it in her Arms for above two Hours after it was dead, but finding her Strength decayed she let it go. The said Mary Moor was in the Hold 14 hours, during which Time the Hatches, Scuutle, and Companion-Door were all under Water; but by Divine Providence the Boat Righted and she got out upon Deck and there remained till 2 o'Clock in the Morning, when the People went on board to Bale and Pump the Water out, and not thinking to find any Living Soul there, but as they came alongside, she called "I am not dead yet" at which they were all surprized; she said during her Stay in the Hold, she got her Hand in a Crack in the Seiling where she held and as the Vessel rowl'd the Water was some Times up to her Chin and some Times over Head. The other People that were saved were taken up by a Boat then in Company. *The New York Evening-Post*, August 19, 1745

At least one death by drowning resulted from an act of gallantry. Witness the fate of poor Lieutenant Perkins, truly an officer and a gentlemen, from the first report to the interment of his remains:

June 2. Monday last Lieutenant Perkins, of the Royal Irish Regiment, coming from Burlington in the Stage-Boat, unfortunately fell overboard, and was drowned, before any Assistance could be given him. *The Pennsylvania Gazette*, June 1, 1768

On Monday afternoon last, as the Burlington stage-boat was coming down the river, a young lady's hat blew overboard, which, Lieut. Perkins, of the 18th Regt. endeavouring to recover, by getting into a small boat, fell into the river and was drowned. His body has not yet been found. *The Pennsylvania Journal*, June 2, 1768

The Body of Lieutenant Perkins, who was drowned, as mentioned in our last, has since been taken up, and was decently buried on Sunday last, in New-Jersey, about six miles up the river. *The Pennsylvania Journal*, June 9, 1768

In fact, attempts to retrieve a lost hat caused more than one death:

We hear from Philadelphia that on the 10th Day of March, (being the Lord's Day) about 3 o'Clock in the afternoon, six Boys who went from thence in an open Boat Pleasuring; they designed to cross then River over to Glouster and in their way, one of them lost his hat overboard, and they, not understanding how to manager a boat, tack't about all of a sudden, endeavouring to get to the Hat; in so doing, the Boat overset and three of them were drowned and the other three were saved from perishing in the Waves (thro' the Divine Providence of God) by some Persons who went in Boats from the City to their Assistance. *The New England Weekly Journal*, April 1, 1728

New York, August 12. Tuesday Evening last, Thomas Clark, a Boatman from the Jerseys, returning from this City, lost his Hat in the Bay, and in attempting to recover it, fell overboard and was drowned. *The New York Gazette revived in the Weekly Post Boy*, August 12, 1751

Young boys and boats, a perennial source of tragedy, also accounted for some accidental deaths.

From Middletown in East New-Jersey, we hear, that a Boy about 9 Years of Age, was lately driven out to Sea in a Canoe & after some days found dead on the Long Island Shore, near Southhold, the Canoo not far from him; It seems he went with a Negro Man to fetch something from a Shallop that lay off at Anchor and was to hold the Canoo to her Side while the Negro went on board; but not being able to keep his hold, the Canoo separated from the Shallop; and being without Paddle or Provisions, 'tis tho't he perished with Cold and Hunger. *The Pennsylvania Gazette*, December 14, 1744

From Trenton we hear that on Friday the 21st past, two Lads, Benjamin and Severns Albertis, Brothers, going in a Canoe to fish near the Falls, the Canoe overset by running against a log and the latter was drowned, the other hardly escaping. Great Search was made for the Body on that and the three following Days, by a great Number of People in Boats and Canoes, but to no Effect, it being driven down, to the Surprize of many, as low as Burlington, and there taken up and interred on Monday. *The Pennsylvania Gazette*, July 4, 1745

New York, May 30. We hear from Hackinsack that the following melancholy Accident happen'd here on Sunday last, just after Sunset viz. a fine little Boy, who went to School there, about 8 Years of Age, (Son of William Livingston, Esq. of this City) proposed to one of his Companions to take a sail, (as he called it) that is to go in a Canoe on the little River at that Place. They went off together but the other Boy changing his mind and coming back, little Livingston went alone. He had been gone about half an Hour when he was missed and enquired for. On going to the Landing, his Hat was found on the Shore, and at a little distance his Body quite Dead lying in the Water, which was about 2 Feet deep. The Canoe was not put off, but it is imagined by some Accident he fell into the Water and thro' surprise was disabled from helping himself. *The New York Journal or General Advertiser*, June 2, 1768

Indeed, it would not be the first time that a lad's quest for excitement (and his disregard of a parent's instructions) led to his demise:

A few Days ago a melancholy Affair happen'd in the Township of New Windsor, in New-Jersey, a Farmer's Son, a Youth about eleven Years of Age, being ordered to lead a Horse to Water, but not to ride him, was a short time after found dead in the Fields near to a Fence and some of the Lad's Hair sticking to the Fence; 'Tis supposed he had mounted the Horse contrary to Order and was thrown and kill'd. The Coroner's Jury brought in their Verdict "Accidental". *The Pennsylvania Gazette*, December 10, 1741

We hear from Elizabeth Town, New Jersey, that on Saturday the 13th instant, the following melancholy accident happened near the Place, viz. a Boy of about 10 Years of Age, Son of Mr. Richard Townley, being sent on an errand, turned aside and stopped at a Meadow on the Way, to look at another boy who was mowing with a Sithe, a Business he was not used to, when he unwarily approached so near that the other was struck irregularly, reached him with the point of the Sithe, which penetrated the inside of the upper Part of his Thigh near the Groin, to the Bone, and beyond it, dividing the main Artery. Of this dreadful Wound, notwithstanding all the Assistance that could be given him, he bled to death in less than an Hour and before a Surgeon could arrive. *New York Journal or General Advertiser*, October 25, 1770

In fact, merely being at odds with one's father was suggested as the cause of one lad's early demise:

New-Jersey, October 4. Saturday Night the first of October, near 10 o'Clock, a genteel young Man at Rahway in East New Jersey, was flung off his Horse and killed. His death seems to be more dreadful as he had been for some time past at Variance with his Father. *The Promise of Long-Life is to obedient Children.* *The New York Gazette* October 17, 1763

Some reports of accidents remain as sad now as when they happened.

And on Monday Night last, the Barn of Mr. Steel, near Somerset Court-House, was burnt down with a considerable Quantity of Provender, etc. but providentially all the neighbouring Houses were preserved, tho' the Barn, I believe, was not twenty Feet from the Court-House, and said Steel's Dwelling-House - - - There were also several other Houses contiguous. In the Hurry and Confusion of the Occasion, a Negro Child, about six Months old, was smothered on a Bed, being covered over inadvertently with Bedding and other Goods.
The Pennsylvania Chronicle, January 11, 1768

New York, September 3. We hear from Woodbridge that on Wednesday last, a Child there, about two Years old, attempting to climb up a ladder, which leaned against a Haystack, he unhappily fell from thence upon a Scythe that lay at the Foot of it, and cut himself in so terrible a Manner a cross the Thigh, that he died a few minutes after. *The Pennsylvania Gazette*, September 6, 1753

We have the following Melancholy Account from Absecum on Egg-harbour, viz. That on the 7th of May past, at Night, Deborah the Wife of Nehemiah Nickerson and granddaughter of John Scull of that same Place, with a Girl of about 10 years of Age and a Negroe Boy attempted to come on Shore in a Canoe, from the Beach where they lived, but, as appears by all circumstances, they lost themselves in the Dark, and a great Storm happening at the same time, they put ashore at a small island in the Marsh, where their canoe driving away, they all three unhappily perish'd. *The Pennsylvania Gazette*, May 25, 1738

On occasion, tragedy was averted and the child was saved:

New York, May 14. We are assured from Woodbridge by an Eye-Witness, that on the 28th of April last, a Woman with her Child of about 15 Months old, being at a Neighbour's House, the Child, playing about the Yard, unnoticed fell into a Well without a Curb of about 18 Feet deep; the Parents, soon after missing it, hastened to the Well, when the Father, notwithstanding his Infirmities, ventured down and with much Difficulty got it out, after it having been in the water which was three Feet deep, and as cold as most wells are, upwards of ten Minutes; it being immediately shifted and kept warm, reviv'd, and is likely to do well. *The New York Gazette or the Weekly Post Boy*, May 14, 1753

Another source of newsworthy articles on accidents came from the workplace. In those days, most jobs involved manual labor and a great degree of risk from animals, machinery and the unexpected. For example:

Philadelphia, April 6. We hear from the Jersies of . . . two young Men carrying a piece of timber on their Shoulders were obliged to step backwards a few steps in order to turn, when the hindmost unfortunately striking his Heel against a Stump, fell on his Back and the end of the Piece lighting on his Breast kill'd him immediately. *The Pennsylvania Gazette*, March 30, 1732

Philadelphia, April 6. We hear from Burlington County that on Thursday last as one John Briggs was felling a Tree, a limb thereof fell on him and crush'd him to Death. *The Boston Weekly News-Letter*, April 13, 1732

We hear from Pompton in Bergin County, East-New-Jersey, that last Tuesday Evening one Nathaniel Fold, a Miller there, attempting to beat some Ice off the Water-Wheel in order to set the Mill a going, unhappily fell into the Water by the side of the Wheel, Head foremost as is supposed, he being found dead in such a Posture next Morning. *The New York Weekly Post-Boy*, January 2, 1744

June 16. On Tuesday last, a Boat coming here from Elizabeth-Town, belonging to Mr. Brunnel of that Place, having on board a Quantity of Timber, lying a Cross the Vessel, on which was a Negro Boy belonging to Mr. Chetwood of the same Town, a sudden Flaw of Wind heeled the Boat so much that the Timber with the Boy upon it fell overboard, and the Boy was seen no more, and as the Water where he felled appeared bloody, it is supposed he was crushed by the Timbers. *The New York Journal or General Advertiser*, June 16, 1768.

New York. We hear from Newark that the Son of Peregrine Sandvoord unhappily got his Fingers in between the cogg'd Rollers of a Cyder Mill, which drew in his Arm up to the Elbow, before he could be rescued by him that tended the Mill; they were obliged to cut off his Arm above the Elbow.

Also that one John Marsh in the mines[28], being about to blow off a Blast, that before he could shelter himself from the Explosion, it went off and bruis'd him very much and that there were some hopes of his Recovery. *The New York Weekly Journal*, November 5, 1739

New York, June 28th. From the County of Morris, in New-Jersey, we learn on the 7th Instant, a Lad going down into the Well of William Beard, of that Place, it caved in with him when he was 18 Feet down, but the Neighbours being called together, they got him out alive, altho' considerably bruised, after three Hours hard working and he is like to do very well.

From Roxbury, in the same County, we learn that last Wednesday Fortnight, a Man named Nathaniel Coleman, helping to raise a Grist Mill in that Place, fell down 18 Feet among a Number of Rocks and was very much bruised, but it is thought will do well. *The New York Mercury*, June 28th, 1762

New York, August 17. Monday Evening the 3d. Instant Mr. Phineas Dunn of Piscataqua, in New Jersey, fell off from a Gang of Hay

---

[28] The Schuyler copper mines, near Newark

into Rariton River and, before any relief could be had, drowned. He was a Man of a fair Character and truly lamented. *The New York Mercury*, August 17, 1761

We hear from Hackinsack that one John Benson in Company with some Ship Carpenters as they had fell a Tree, in falling the limbs of said Tree, loosened an old Stump that stood next to it and they sat down to rest themselves, the old Stump fell down and unluckily kill'd the said Benson on the Spot. He has left a Widow and seven Children. *The Boston Weekly Post-Boy*, February 13, 1744

Although it sounds quite incongruous to mention it today, a number of industrial deaths in colonial America were associated with the now vanished mining industry of the Province, especially in the Newark area.

New-York. From Newark, we hear that on Tuesday the 12 instant, one James Souther, being about to blow a Blast in one of the Mines, near to that Place, and having made his Fuze too short, or being too inadvertent to seek a retreat, some of the Fragments of the Rock struck him and broke and bruised him to that Degree that he expired within a few Hours. *The New York Weekly Journal*, January 25, 1742.

We hear from Newark that on Saturday the 26th of March last, one Malachi Vanderpoel unfortunately fell into one of the Mine Pits near that Place upwards of a 100 Feet deep, by which his whole Body was so bruis'd and many Bones broken that he died immediately. *The Boston Weekly Post-Boy*, April 11, 1743

While America of the 1700s was spared the slaughter on the highways of today, it, nevertheless, suffered at the hands of the automobiles' predecessors, the horse and "waggons":

We hear from Elizabeth Town that on Monday last one Peter Sineau was unfortunately kick'd to Death by a Horse.

The same Day, one Peter Garritson, of Hackensack was unhappily run over by a Waggon, which run over a Part of his Neck and Head, so that he expired immediately. *The Boston Weekly News Letter*, July 21, 1743

I take this Opportunity to acquaint you of several unfortunate Events that have happened lately in this Neighbourhood, which may of Service (by Way of Caution) to publish in the Pennsylvania Chronicle. They are as follows:

The same day as a man in Hopewell was driving a team, in jumping off his Waggon, he slipt, and the Wheeles went over and killed him. *The Pennsylvania Chronicle*, January 11, 1768

From Greenwich, in Cumberland County, New Jersey, we learn, that on the Sixth Instant, a Boy was killed, as he was taking a pair of Oxen from the Cart's Tongue, by the Team's suddenly taking fright. *The Pennsylvania Chronicle*, April 18, 1768

We hear from Morris-Town that on the 11th Ult., as one Peter Berry was riding down a Hill, his Horse stumbled, by which he was thrown down and the Horse falling on him instantly killed him. He was on the point of going to Ireland where it was said he had a 1000 pound sterling lately bequeathed to him.

And on the 18th which was the Saturday following, as David Correy was driving his Team, the Horses rode with Violence down the aforesaid Hill and by the Waggon giving a Jolt over a Stone, pitched him out, when the Wheels ran over his Head. He continued in great Misery till the Morning when he died. *The Pennsylvania Chronicle*, February 27, 1769

Guns, a necessity of the times, sometimes went off accidently, fell into the hands of children or were carelessly used, as attested to by this series of news reports:

Philadelphia, September 9. We hear from Cranbury in the County of Middlesex in New Jersey that one Daniel Parine taking his gun down (that his Brother had charged, unknown to him) and striking the Flint with his Knife in order to sharpen it, the Powder took Fire and the Gun went off and shot his Wife with a Bullet and seven Swan shot just above the Hip Bone. The Force of the Shot was deadened by her Quilt Petticoat so that the Bullet and Wadd was taken out but an inch in the Flesh near her Back. Her life was at first dispaired of, she being with Child and near her Time; but it is now hoped that her inwards are not hurt & that she may recover.
The Boston Weekly News-Letter, September 23, 1731.

Philadelphia, April 6. We hear from the Jersies of . . . a Man charging his gun smote the Breech on the Ground to settle the shot, which jarring the Lock, it gave fire and shot him dead. *The Pennsylvania Gazette*, March 30, 1732

We have the following deplorable Account from the Township of Maidenhead in this Province viz.

That on Thursday last as one Benjamin Drake, a Farmer at Hopewell and his Brother-in-Law, were viewing of a Fowling Piece a little Girl, Daughter to Drake, was carelessly playing with the Lock, unobserved by the Men, when the Piece went off and unfortunately shot the Father through the Breast and into his Arm, of which wound the poor unhappy Man languish'd till the next Morning, then died. *The Pennsylvania Gazette*, April 8, 1742

We hear from Elizabeth Town that the Hon. Col. Sir John St. Clair, Bart. died there last Thursday Week and was buried on Saturday Evening with all Military Honours.

Two Lads, being left together at a House during the Time of the Funeral, one of them got a Gun which was loaded and shot the other dead. *The New York Journal or General Advertiser*, December 10, 1767

We have a very melancholy Account from Hackinsack that on Friday last, a Negro Boy belong to Abraham Ackerman of that Place, taking his Master's Gun (as is supposed) thinking it not loaded, fired it off and thereby shot one of his Master's Children dead on the Spot and wounded a Negro Boy (his own Brother) in the Head that 'tis thought he can't recover; upon which he was immediately committed to jail. *The Boston Weekly Post-Boy*, May 2, 1743

And from Mount Holly we hear that last Week a young Lad who had been shooting Pigeons, hanging a Parcel of them over the Barrel of His Gun, they slipt down to the trigger, which was without Guard, and discharg'd the Piece against his Breast and kill'd him on the Spot. *The Pennsylvania Gazette*, March 20, 1740

We hear from Middletown in East New Jersey, that on Wednesday last, the Son of William Rodgers of that Place, returning from Gunning, told his father that he could not get the Gun off, who thereupon taking her in his arms, snapped her, when she suddenly went off and killed his Wife on the Spot. *The New York Gazette or Weekly Post Boy*, October 22, 1753.

As some Men were hunting last week in Glouster County, New Jersey, one of them took his Companion for a Deer, as he was coming through a Swamp and shot at him and wounded him so that he died on Tuesday last. *The Philadelphia Journal*, November 8, 1753

New York, December 15. We hear from Baskinridge, in New Jersey, that on Thursday the 4th Instant, as two Boys about 8 Years of Age each, one named Leonard, the other Ricky, were playing in the Shop of Brice Ricky of that Place, Leonard took up a Gun he had found at Hand, and after blowing into it, told his Play Mate that it was not loaded, when he cocked her, and drawing the Trigger, the former right before the Muzzle, the whole Charge, which was a Brace of Balls, entered his Body under his right Breast and went out through his left Shoulder Blade, of which Wound he immediately expired. *The New York Mercury*, December 15, 1755

New York, January 13. From Roxbury in Morris County, East New Jersey, we learn that a few Weeks ago, one John Velzer's Wife, having a pound of gunpowder in a Bason, and not dreading the consequences of going too near the fire with it, a Spark, it was supposed, jumping in the Bason caus'd an Explosion so great as to affect a Child who stood near it in such a Manner that it died soon after , whilst the Mother received little or no Damage thereby.
The New York Gazette or the Weekly Post Boy, January 13, 1755

The accidents were not limited to the civilian population, as the following news articles report.

Philadelphia, July 18. From Shrewsbury, we hear, that on the 5th Instant, being training Day at that Place, One of the Soldiers having his musket loaded with a hard Wadd on the Charge, in attempting to fire between the Legs of one Samuel Davenport, his fellow soldier, about 25 Years of Age, the Wadd struck his ancle Bone with such force that it was shattered and broke quite off; and a Day or two after the poor Man's Leg was cut off and it was greatly feared that he would lose his Life thereby. *The New York Gazette*, July 29, 1734

New York. Thursday last as Col. William Rickets of Elizabeth Town, with his Wife and Family, were going home from this City in his Own Boat, accompanied by some Friends, they unfortunately left their Burgee[29] flying at their Mast Head, and on their coming abreast of His Majesty's Ship Greyhound, then lying in the North River, a gun was fired from on board her, but they not apprehending it to be at them, took no Notice of it, on which a second directly followed; and the Shot passing thro' the Boat's MainSail, struck a young Woman, Nurse to Col. Ricket's Children, in the Head and kill'd her on the Spot; she had the Child in her Arms which happily received no Hurt. The Boat on this immediately put back to the City. And the Coroner's Inquest being summoned, and Evidences on both sides examin'd, they brought it in Wilful Murder. We hear that Capt. Roddam, Commander of the Greyhound, was not on Board his Ship at the Time.[30] *The Boston Post-Boy*, June 18, 1750

Some deaths are the unmistakable results of fist fights or horseplay gone wrong, the stuff of which manslaughter pleas are made. For example:

We hear from Rahaway in New-Jersey, that on the 27th of December last, a difference arising between two Lads about a Cock that had been shot at two Days before, one of them threw a Gouge at the other which entered in at the small of his Back and 'tis suppos'd touch'd one of his Kidneys; he was carried home and the Wound seemed not mortal, it was hoped that he would recover; but died the 8th Instant. The other Lad is taken into custody. *Boston Weekly News Letter*, February 10, 1743

We hear from New-Brunswick that last Week two men quarrelling together, about 4 or 5 Miles above that Place, one of them struck the other on the Head with a Carpenter's Iron Square, which fractured his Skull in such a Manner, that he died in three Days afterwards. We hear the other immediately surrendered himself. *The New York Gazette Revived in the Weekly Post Boy*, May 28, 1750

---

[29] A burgee was a flag of identification, usually triangular in shape, on vessels. Why it caused the Navy to fire on the smaller civilian vessel is unknown.

[30] The upshot of all of this was a trial, a finding of guilt against the offending sailor and then a pardon, probably an automatic one, as the accused was a member of the military. James Parks, the Gunner's Mate of the Man of War, who fired the Gun at Col. Ricket's Boat, was likewise tried and was found guilty of Manslaughter, but being called to Judgment, he pleaded his Majesty's most gracious Pardon, which being read and allowed of, he was discharged. *The New York Gazette Revived in the Weekly Post Boy*, August 13, 1750

A very unfortunate Accident happened last Friday, at Princeton; a little Boy about eleven years of Age went into a Taylor's Shop to inquire for some cloaths that were making up for him, when an Apprentice Lad told him he should have them in about an Hour and insisted upon him then giving him a Treat. This, the Boy refusing, the other began to tease him, upon which, more in Play than in Passion, having a Pair of Scissors in his Hand, he threw them at the Apprentice. And the Scissors unluckily turning in their Passage, the sharp point entered just above the Breastbone; in a Minute or two the Lad fainted and almost immediately expired.
The Pennsylvania Chronicle, September 25, 1769

We hear from Ringwood Ironworks in New Jersey that last Week a Fray happened among some of the Workmen of that Work, which continued some Time, by which one Man lost his Life and several were badly wounded. *The Pennsylvania Gazette*, June 25, 1767

Mother Nature, in the forms of poisons, wild creatures, and the elements, was responsible for a number of the accidental deaths reported.

Philadelphia, July 1. Yesterday two Men and a Woman Reaping in the Jerseys, it being very Hot, they unadvisedly drank Cold Water, whereof the 2 Men died immediately and the Woman's Life is despaired of. Also a Negro Man died very suddenly in this City by drinking Cold water. *The American Weekly Mercury*, July 1, 1731

Philadelphia, July 24. We hear from Penns-neck (in West New-Jersey) that a few days ago, Mr. John Redstrakes Son of about 3 Years old, his Servant Boy & Negro Woman, having eaten some Mushrooms, were all three taken with Swelling soon after they had eaten them and kept swelling till they died, which was not long after. *The American Weekly Mercury*, July 17, 1735

New York, April 16. We have an Account from Morris County in the Jersies, that about a Fortnight ago, a poor Man and his Son of about seven years of Age, being burning some old brush in the Swamp, found some Roots that looked like Parsnips, which they roasted and ate. Soon after returning home, they found themselves unwell and died both together in a few Minutes without any Token of Hurt. *The Pennsylvania Journal*, April 19, 1753

New York, August 6. We hear from Freehold that on Thursday the 26th of last Month, one Rachael M'Koy, went out in good Health to gather Huckleberries and, after being in the Woods some time, complained of being out of order, which increasing that night, she died the next Morning; it's supposed she was poison'd. *The New York Gazette or the Weekly Post Boy*, August 6, 1753

New York, June 4. Last week a young Woman, the Daughter of Adolf Brower, of Hackensack was bit in three different Places by a Rattle-Snake, as she was gathering Straw berries; the injected Venom operated so speedily that she died in a few Hours. *The Boston Weekly Post Boy*, June 11, 1739

New York, December 1. On Monday Evening, the 24th ult. escaped out of the Goal of Morris-Town, one Conner, who was found dead the second day after, in a By-path, about two miles from the Goal. The Coroner's Verdict was that he died of Cold; after which the Corpse was carried back to Gaol. *The New York Journal or General Advertiser*, December 4, 1766

Some deaths are destined to remain forever mysterious:

New York, June 25. Last Saturday the Body of a Man was found buried (scarcely covered) in a Field about a Mile away from Elizabeth Town, which occasions some Speculation in the Neighborhood. *The Pennsylvania Gazette*, June 25, 1767

Philadelphia, November 13. We are informed that ----Aldsworth, who lately kept the Sun Tavern in Burlington, is supposed to be drowned; he having been missing some time and his Hat found near a Creek Side two or three Miles from Town. *The Pennsylvania Gazette*, November 10, 1729

On Friday last was taken up a float in the river Delaware (between Philadelphia and Burlington) the body of a woman supposed to be drowned sometime last summer. She had on two strings of white wax beeds round her neck, cotton gown, good stays, black callimanco petticoat, white thread stockings and leather shoes. *The Pennsylvania Journal*, May 18, 1769

New York, August 13. We hear from the Jerseys that a Girl about 12 Years of Age was sent last Monday Se'nninght to look for a Cow and a Calf and that she has not been heard of since. The Neighbors have been for a Week in quest of her, but to no Purpose; they suppose they have found her Track, about 7 Miles off in the Woods and that she had eaten Huckle Berries, which it appears that she had vomited up again. *The New York Journal or General Advertiser*, August 13, 1767

Sometime last Week Mr. Aldsworth, mentioned in our Gazette (November 13, 1729) was found dead on the Jersey Shore, where he had probably been thrown up by the Tide. His Privities were eaten off and part of his under Jaw. *The Pennsylvania Gazette*, March 13, 1730

We hear from the Jerseys, that John Eves, who used the Philadelphia Market, went one Day last Week, to visit a sick Neighbour and returning home in the Evening which was dark and stormy, he lost his Way as is supposed and was found dead the next Morning in a Swamp; his Head was in some Water and the Bridle of his Horse remain'd over his Arm. *The Pennsylvania Gazette*, March 20, 1740

Last Saturday, a Poor Man who had been seen about the Bowery for ten Days before, was put in a Cart at the Request of the People of that Neighborhood in Order to be sent to a Magistrate for Relief, he appearing very Sick; but the Driver of the Cart, being a Boy, who did not find the Magistrate to whom he had been ordered to apply, at home he tipt up his Cart, near the Fresh Water, threw the Man out and drove off. The Neighbours coming up found the unhappy Man, who was dead, and having stopt the Boy, they made him carry the Corpse to the Work-House, where it was buried. The Coroner's Verdict was natural Death. The Deceased's name could not be known; all that we can learn of him is that he said he came from the Jersies, where he left a Wife and nine Children and that he was going to Boston where his brother lived in good Circumstances. *The New York Gazette or Weekly Post Boy*, May 8, 1766

The same Week, two men of that Place [Shrewsbury], Mr. Cook and his Son, who had gone from home with their guns and had been missing for five Days, were found drown'd, near the Shore, in water not more than a Knee deep. Each of them had a Bruise on the Forehead, over one of the Eyes, but whether by Accident or Design, or for what reason they went into the Water (they had no Vessel with them) was not known. *Supplement to the New York Journal or General Advertiser*, February 20, 1768

Those who have experienced a fire, especially within a dwelling, know full well its horror. This was true in colonial days, where candles, open hearthed fireplaces and wooden structures, carried with them the potential for sudden disaster. Witness the following accounts:

Philadelphia, December 2. We hear from the other side of the River that a few days ago, a House about 4 Miles back of Benjamin Wood's was burnt down to the Ground. The Man was abroad at Labour and the Woman gone to borrow a Sieve at a House about a quarter of a mile distant; she left two young children playing at the Door, and a third, the youngest, lying on the Bed. When she was returning, to her great Surprize she saw the House on Fire and ran to call her Husband, who came home with her but too late to save anything, tho' they could see all their three Children surrounded by the Flames and by no means to be delivered. 'Tis thought the two went in to fetch the youngest. A Bitch which had two puppies, carried one of them out of the House and 'tis supposed she endeavoured to fetch the other out also, her Hair being much singed. *The Boston Weekly News-Letter*, December 23, 1731

Philadelphia, January 23. We hear from Salem that a few Weeks ago the House of Samuel Smith sen., near that Place, was burnt down, occasioned by the Maid's leaving the Candle carelessly when she went to bed. Mr. Smith saved his Money and Writings and some Beds but the rest of the Furniture was destroyed and the Maid Burnt to Death. *The Pennsylvania Gazette*, January 16, 1735.

On the 14th Inst., the House of one Spenser in Salem County was consumed by Fire and two of his Sons (one about six and the other eight Years old) unhappily lost their Lives in the Flames, it being out of the power of their distressed Friends to save them. About a Week before, the House of one Cox, in the same County, was burnt to the Ground and one of his Children, a Son, also perished in the Flames. *The Pennsylvania Chronicle*, March 20, 1769

From Minisink there is advice, that on the 21st ult. three Children were burnt to death there. The Mother of them had Occasion to go to a Neighbor's House and left them shut up for fear of their getting out; but, while she was gone, her House took Fire and, before any Help could be got, the Children perished in the Flames. *The Pennsylvania Gazette*, September 28, 1752

New York, March 12. We hear from Elizabeth-Town in New Jersey that Mr. John May of that Place, and his Wife, going into one of their Neighbouring Houses, left a young Infant in Bed asleep, to the care of a Negro Wench who, 'tis supposed, looking carelessly around the Bed, with the Candle in her Hand, set fire to the Curtains, which soon communicated itself to the Blankets, and had not some People who were accidently going past, discovered the Fire, and took the Child out of the Bed (tho' much burnt), it must undoubtedly have perished in the Flames. *The Pennsylvania Gazette*, March 20, 1753

There were numerous <u>close calls</u>, where the inhabitants were lucky to escape with their lives:

We hear from New-Brunswick that a most terrible Fire has happened there which entirely consumed the Dwelling House of Mr. Philip French, a Gentleman of that Place, and all the Furniture &c belonging thereto, the People therein hardly escaping with their Lives and a Daughter of Mr. French's being forced to jump out a Window, two Story's high; how the Fire began is yet unknown. *The New York Weekly Journal*, February 16, 1741

New York, July 30. We hear from Brunswick that on the 11th Instant, the House of the Honorable Edward Antill Esq., near that Place, was accidently set on fire, by the Discharge of a Gun. It was not discovered by the People around the House until they were informed by those who came from the Meadows to their Assistance, which was just in time to save it. Five Minutes more would have been too late. The Roof and some other Parts were considerably damaged before the Fire was extinguished. *The New York Mercury*, July 30, 1764

We hear from Hackensack that the House and Barn of George Smith, was burnt down to the ground in a few minutes; lost all his Cloaths, Beds and Beding &c. and also a considerable Quantity of Wheat; the Fire broke out when the Family was all from home; at least one of the nearest Neighbours saw a prodigious Smoke, ran towards it he seeing the House and Barn all in a blaze, hoop's and Hollow'd but receiv'd no answer, so he Thought they were all consum'd in the Flames, but Providence had ordained it otherwise, for they were at a Neighbour's House about a Mile off. *The New York Evening Post*, February 17, 1746

Elizabeth-Town, March 1, 1763. Last Night about 12 o'Clock, a Fire broke out in the Dwelling House of Captain Hampton, of this Town, which would have been all consumed in a Few minutes, had not Mr. Hampton and his Wife been alarmed at the Fall of a large Looking-Glass in the common Parlour. At first sight, Mr. Hampton judged it past Recovery and was getting out his Writings and best Things in his Bed-Room, but his two young Daughters who Slept at the other End of the House, heard their Mother's Shreiks, run immediately out through the Entry, which was full of Smoke and Fire, but they had Resolution to attempt to save the House and in a little time called for their Father and raised the Negroes, who all came to their Assistance, and by their Means, the House was saved. The Fire began in the Mantle-Tree, occasioned by a new Fashioned Fire Place, being made in another, which cast all the Heat forward; the Parlour and the Room over it were consumed, with all the Furniture; Mr. Hampton got very much Burnt at first opening the Door. The saving of the House looks like a Miracle to everyone who sees it and it is hoped it will be a caution to all who make the new Fashioned Fire Places to take out all the Wood Mantle-Trees. *The New York Gazette*, March 14, 1763

New York, March 3. The following Melancholy Accident happened on Sunday the 12th of February last, in the South Ward of the City of Amboy, Cranbury. Between two and three o'clock, a Man passing the House of Mr. Joseph Rue of that Place, perceived a great Smoak issuing from some Part of the Roof, near the Kitchen Chimney, on which he went in, in order to alarm and assist the Family. He found little or no Fire on the Hearth, nor was the Chimney on Fire above, yet the Smoak increased, he could hear the Flames roar, and they presently burst out of the N.W. Corner of the Roof; the Wind being high at North West, which drove them full upon the rest of the Building, the whole was almost instantly in Flames. Mr. Rue and his Wife were both abroad and only some small Children at home;

the Fire spread with such Rapidity and Fury, that only a few Neighbours had Time to assemble and get out an inconsiderable Quantity of Goods, before the whole Building and all it contained, which were very valuable, were entirely consumed. *Supplement to the New York Journal or General Advertiser*, March 4, 1769.

The conflagrations consumed structures other than houses:

New York, October 25. We hear that the City Hall & Prison of the City of Perth-Amboy is burnt down to the Ground and the Prisoners forced to look out for new Quarters. *The New England Weekly Journal*, November 1, 1731

Williamsburg, March 16. We hear from Brunswick that about a Fortnight ago the Prison of the County was burnt down and a Man, who was in it a Prisoner for Debt, was burnt to Death. It is suspected that he set the Prison on Fire in the Hopes of escaping thereby; he was heard crying out for Help, but no Assistance came Time enough to save him or the Prison. *The Pennsylvania Gazette*, April 26, 1739

Last Friday Evening, the Roof of the Court-House at Glouster, took Fire, by a Spark from the Chimney, which greatly damaged the same; but by the timely Assistance of the Inhabitants, the Building was preserved. *The Pennsylvania Gazette*, February 4, 1768

New York, April 20. We have advice from Roxbury, in Morris County, East New Jersey, that in the Night of the 25th of March last, Mr. Constant King of that Place, Hatter had his Dwelling House and Hatters Shop, in which was a considerable Quantity of Fur, new hats &c. entirely reduced to Ashes by Accident. The major part of the Family had but just time to escape, with only such cloaths as they slept in; the wearing Apparel, Furniture &c being entirely consumed. The whole is valued at upwards of 500 Pounds. *The Pennsylvania Journal*, April 23, 1761

We hear from Perth-Amboy that the Jail of the County of Middlesex, in that City, took Fire on Thursday last, and all the Wooden Part thereof entirely consumed. It was built about two Years ago and the Person who undertook to do it, at the Charge of the County, unhappily being a Prisoner in it, there have been some suspicions hinted as if it was set on Fire on Purpose; but we believe without any just Foundation, except on Account of the Time, which was thus. On that Day, there was a Fair and a great Horse-Race at Woodbridge, which occasioned the greater Part of the Inhabitants of Amboy to be absent, so that on the Fire's breaking out, there were scarce any Person appeared to assist in quenching of it. This is the third Time that the County Jail in that City has been demolished by Fire, in our Memory. We don't learn that any Lives were lost on the Occasion. *The New York Gazette or Weekly Post Boy*, September 18, 1769

New York, May 21. We hear from Shrewsberry in New Jersey, that on the 19th of April last, the Fulling and Grist Mill of George Williams and Ebenezer Applegate were burnt down wherein there was above one hundred barrels of Flour and 1,000 Bushels of Wheat, besides a large Quantity of Cloath. *The New York Gazette*, May 21, 1738

We hear from Weselen in East Jersey that the Barn of Jurri Alfe took Fire by the Lighting and was burnt down to the Ground in 10 or 12 Minutes; the Barn was full of Wheat. *The Boston Weekly Post Boy*, August 6, 1744

We hear from Pechqueneck in East Jersey, that some Time last Week, the Barn of Mr. Peter Meed took Fire by the Lighting and was entirely consumed in a short Time. The Loss is considerable, for the Owner having most Part of his Grain in the said Barn. *The New York Evening Post*, July 22, 1745

Last Night about nine O'Clock, on board a Sloop from Egg-Harbour, loaded with Shingles, one Davis, Master, lying without the Great-Dock, a Fire Kindled, it is supposed under the Hearth, in the Cabin, burst out, and was got to a considerable height before discovered. It is said that most of the Things in the Cabin were destroyed, and the Vessel with several others and their Cargoes, were in great Danger, but by timely Assistance and scuttling the Vessel, the Fire was extinguished, after having done, it is supposed, about 50 Pound Damage. *The New York Journal or General Advertiser*, December 4, 1766

New York, February 26. Last Tuesday se'ennight, a Tanner's Bark-House at Lyons Farms, in Elizabeth-Town, having made a small Fire made in it to warm the People at Work, in the Evening the Master put it out himself, as he thought, with Snow, but when he got up in the Morning he found the Bark-House with a good Quantity of Bark, and upwards of 30 Hides in it, all reduced to Ashes and neither he nor any of his Neighbours saw or heard any Thing of the Fire. *The Pennsylvania Chronicle*, March 2, 1767

Princeton, March 9. Friday at about three o'clock in the afternoon, a fire broke out in Nassau Hall, but by the immediate and vigorous assistance of the students and the inhabitants of the village, it was extinguished without doing any considerable damage. It did not appear to have been owing to the heedlessness of any person whatsoever, but probably to a spark from the windward, dropping on the leeward side of the building, as it kindled in the roof where there was no communication with any of the chambers. *The Pennsylvania Journal*, March 16, 1769

From Barnegat, Little Egg-Harbour and country round about there, we learn that a very great fire happened in the Cedar Swamps, on the 20th of May last and burned with such violence that in a few Days Time, it rendered desolate Lands to the Extent of near thirty Miles, the Trees and ready cut shingles being entirely burnt into Cinders and most of the Inhabitants reduced thereby to meer Penury and Want. And it was with the utmost Difficulty that Hawkin's Swamp was preserved from the Conflagration, of which no account could be given how it first began. *The Pennsylvania Gazette*, June 12, 1755

Monday last a dreadful Fire happened at Newark, when the Barn, Stables and some Out Buildings, belonging to the Hon. David Ogden Esq., was entirely destroyed with every thing that was therein. They were thought to have been set on fire by some evil minded Persons. *The New York Gazette or Weekly Post Boy*, January 15, 1770

April of 1768 appeared to have been a terrible time in the New Brunswick area for fire. Witness the following:

April 18, 1768. Between the Hours of Twelve and one o'Clock last Wednesday, a terrible Fire broke out in the Dwelling House of the Widow Dilldine, in Brunswick, New-Jersey, which consumed the same, with the Dwelling House and Bake-House of Mr. John Van Norda, jun. adjoining thereto, in a very short Time. The wind being high, the Flames soon reached across the Street, and set fire to the House of James Nealson, Esq; which was also consumed, with his 2 Store-Houses, a Cooper's Shop, and Bolting House, wherein was a large Quantity of all sorts of Country Produce to a very great Amount. The Dwelling-House and Store of Mr. Peter Vredenberg, and the Widow Carmer's, were also burnt, as they adjoined Mr. Nealson's Buildings, with almost every Thing that was therein.[31] In short, the Loss is very considerable[32]. The Inhabitants, joined by the Military, used their utmost Efforts to extinguish the Fire, but the Wind being so very high, could effect it by no other Method than pulling down some Buildings in its Way, by which it was happily accomplished. Not one Person was hurt during the whole Affair. How the Fire began is not well known, but supposed to be occasioned either by some Sparks from Mr. Van Norda's Bake-House, or from the Chimney of the House of Mrs. Dilldine.

At the Time Mr. Nealson's Dwelling-House was on Fire, he with some of his Friends, were about two Miles out of Town at his Mills that were in Danger of being set a Fire by the burning of the Woods.

This City has been alarmed no less than 19 Times by Fire within the Space of about 20 Days. Mr. Bond's House between Newark and Elizabeth-Town and Mr. William Nicholl's House, and Barn, at Freehold,

---

[31] The houses were frame ones with cedar roofs.

[32] Another article puts Mr. Nealson's loss at several thousand pounds which included over 2000 bushels of wheat, many barrels of flour, a large parcel of Gammons and nearly a 1000 bushels of corn. A third report, which puts the loss at 8,000 pounds, praises his good virtue: "In him, the Distressed had always a sure Resource, and the County, a faithful Merchant." *The New York Journal or General Adviser*, April 21 1768

were burnt the same Day; and the House of John Johnson and William Burnet of Amboy, both took Fire the same Day also, but were happily extinguished, without doing any Damage.[33] *The Pennsylvania Chronicle*, April 25, 1768

The cold dry Weather we have lately had, has been attended with bad Consequences to many in the Country, by the loss of cattle etc but the usual Practice of burning of Woods and Meadows in the Spring, has been more so than usual; for we are assured, that near Mt. Holly, in Burlington County, three Dwelling-Houses and much Fencing have been destroyed by Fire on Wednesday last, besides other great damages: And in the Event has been detrimental to those who probably would have been out of reach of such Fires otherwise. *The Pennsylvania Chronicle*, April 25, 1768

The House of the Widow Martin, at Lebanan, in Essex [Hunterdon] County, New-Jersey, and the Durham Iron Works, near that Place, were burnt on the same day that the Fire happened at New-Brunswick. *The New York Journal or General Adviser*, April 28, 1768

---

[33] A house in Piscataway, belonging to Thomas Fitzrandolph, also caught on fire the same day, as did one in a "brew-house" in Mount Holly, that belonged to one Thomas Cooper. It also destroyed a barn and a blacksmith's shop. *The New York Journal or General Adviser*, April 21, 1768

New Jersey has 127 miles of coastline and thousands and thousands of ever shifting sand bars that lie offshore in shallow waters. The sudden summer squalls and the long, cruel gales of winter, smash the wary and the unwary mariner alike onto the sandbars. Then, as now, they were quick hitting, like the gust of unexpected wind that silently sneaks upon us then, suddenly, slams the back door with such sound that makes the startled jump from their skins. Such a storm much has been responsible for the following disruption and destruction of Atlantic shipping:

New York. Wednesday Night last, Captain Kip, in a Sloop from the Bay of Honduras, but last from Bermudas, endeavouring to come in here, was drove upon the South Side of the East Bank and bilged; the next Day, the Captain with some of the Hands got ashore in a small Boat, on Sandy Hook, and the Day following all the Rest; the Captain travell'd round and arrived here on Friday and the next Morning got a Boat and went down to the Vessel, but the extreme hard Weather prevented their saving any Thing but some of the Sails &c. and 'tis feared, now that the wind has got to the Eastward, that Vessel and Cargo will be entirely lost. Capt. Kip sailed from the Bay in October last, but coming on our Coast, met with such hard Weather as tore all his Sails to pieces, washed away his Cabose, stove his Boat all to pieces, and broke in several of his Top Timbers, which obliged him to bear away to Bermudas. He informs us that Capt. Riddel from this Port took up at Sea, one Brown from Egg-Harbour, belonging to Connecticut, who was reduced to the utmost Extremity and carried him to Bermuda; and that a Vessel from Anguilla was arrived at Bermuda and brought advice that upwards of 20 Sail of Vessels were arrived in the West Indies, that were blown off these Coasts, amongst which was the Ship Hawk, Capt. Bill of this Port. There were about 14 sail arrived at Bermudas, among whom was Captain Seymour bound from Antigua for this Port, and Capt. Bowen in the Brig Pelling, bound for Philadelphia, having lost all his Sails, and who having refitted at Bermudas, sailed in Company with Capt. Kip. He likewise heard that a Boston Snow and a Bermuda Sloop were lately wrecked on the Coast of Florida. *The Boston Weekly Post-Boy*, March 5, 1750

Press reports from New York, Boston and Philadelphia newspapers have identified almost a hundred of these shipwrecks along the Jersey Shore during the period 1705 to 1770. On some, the reports are sketchy and in installments as the groundings were seen only in the distance by other captains, not anxious to put their own vessels at risk for a better view. For example:

We hear from Cape May, that on Friday the 16th Instant, in the Evening, the Seneca, Capt. Wasborough, from Bristol, bound to this Port was drove ashore to the Northward of the Cape, bilged and fill'd with water, but the People all were saved. She had been out 14 Weeks. *The New York Weekly Post-Boy*, January 2, 1744

We hear from Cape May that the Schooner Prosperity, John Lee Master, bound from this place to Boston, was drove ashore there in the late high Winds, and 'tis thought can hardly be got off again. *The Pennsylvania Gazette*, January 1, 1745

Yesterday sen' night we had a violent Gale of Wind at East and North-East in which Capt. Dunbibin in a Brig from Cape Fare, and Capt. Dickinson in a Sloop from Jamaica was both drove ashore near Sandy-Hook; Capt. Dickinson is since got off and come up but it will be no small task to get the Brig off well; Abundance of small Craft were drove ashore and many of them lost. *The New York Gazette Revived in the Weekly Post Boy*, October 16, 1749

Philadelphia. Yesterday came Advice that the York, Capt. Gibson, belonging to Boston, but bound from Barbados to this Port with Rum &c. is ashore near Egg-Harbour, where the Vessel is lost, the Men and some of the Cargo saved. *The New York Gazette Revived in the Weekly Post Boy*, January 29, 1750

Philadelphia, January 25. The Ship Generous Friends, Captain George Ross, from Antigua to this Port, arrived lately in our Bay and prevented from getting up by the Ice, was proceeding to New York but unhappily run ashore near Great Egg Harbour, where it is feared she will be lost. *The Pennsylvania Gazette*, January 25, 1770

We have advice from Amboy that a Brig belonging to that Place, Thomas Crowell Master, bound inwards from Antigua, was cast away the 14th of last Month at 12 O'Clock at Night, in a hard Gale of Wind, near Barnagat; the Men saved their Lives, but the Vessel and a great Part of the Cargo lost. *The New York Gazette Revived in the Weekly Post Boy*, April 2, 1750

New-York, September 6. On Friday the 23d. ult. as Capt. M'Clean (who arrived here Yesterday Se'nnight) came by Barnegat, he saw a Snow standing toward the Land, so near the Shore that he could not speak with her; he imagined she was in Danger of getting aground; and we hear, from an Egg Harbour Man, since arrived, that on Saturday Morning he saw the said Snow aground, about 100 Yards to the Southward of Barnegat Inlet, upon the Bar, about a Mile from Shore. Her Gunwale was sunk very near to the Surface of the Water, and as the Winds have been easterly most of the Time since, and a large Swell, she is probably beat to pieces before this Time. Neither of the Vessels who saw her were able to get her any Assistance, or to give any particular description of her. She had, when she was seen aground, a Burgee Pendant at her Mast Head. As none of our Pilots choose to go so far to the Westward with an easterly Wind, we have not been able to find out what Vessel she is, but it is conjectured she is some stranger to this Coast. *The New York Mercury*, September 6th, 1762

Newport, Rhode Island, August 3. We hear that Captain Holway, in a Brig from this Port bound to Philadelphia, is cast away upon Barnegat. *The Pennsylvania Gazette*, June 24, 1762.

New London, October 29. We hear that a Schooner was cast ashore at Barney's Gut, near Egg- Harbour, the 18th Instant, said to be the Adventure, Ashcraft from St. Martins, of and for this Port, laden with Salt, but the Men were saved. *The Pennsylvania Journal*, November 18, 1762

We hear that a sloop, said to be from Teneriff, and a Schooner unknown, are ashore near Egg-Harbour. *The Pennsylvania Journal*, March 13, 1766

The Sloop Squirrel, Capt. Taylor, from Antigua, for this port, was cast away, in the storm on Sunday last, near Egg-Harbour; the People and the greatest part of the cargo are saved. *The Pennsylvania Journal*, April 10, 1766

Last Week, Captain Smith, bound to St. Kitts from this port [New York], was drove on the Point of Sandy Hook and 'tis feared will not be got off. *The Pennsylvania Gazette*, April 24, 1766

Some of the press reports are chilling, reminding us of the killing wrath of nature:

New-York, December 24. On the 19th instant, the Private Ship of War call'd the Castle Del Key of 130 Tons, 18 Guns. Capt Otto Van Tyle Commander[34] Sailed from Jackques Bay (about 10 Miles from hence) and in going down to Sandyhook with an easy Gale of Wind, She struck upon the East bank and stayed there. They sent some of their men on Shoar in their Canoo for boats to assist them but that night a hard Gale of Wind Sprung up between W. and N.W. and Froze very hard. The Ship began to fill with Water. A Sloop and large Boat was sent down, but it Friezing and blowing so hard, they would not venture to relieve them for fear of running the same fate of being a ground and so Froze or Drowned. The next Morning the Gale continued hard all day and the men were all alive upon the Decks and in the Shrouds, the Sea beating over them. And on Fryday morning, the Wind abating a Boat went on board and found . . . the Captain and all the rest being Froze and Drowned; there were 145 men on board when She Sailed who all perished but 13 & 132 dyed in this deplorable manner. Here are Widows Lamenting the loss of their Husbands and Parents their Children. 'Tis said about 80 or 90 of the men were English, Scotch and Irish and the rest of Dutch Parentage, most born in this Country. *The Boston News-Letter*, December 31, 1705

New York, January 12. On Friday, the 2d. instant, a sloop, belonging to this place loaded with oysters, from Blue-Point, between Plumb and Coney Island, three miles from shore, about sun-set, sprung a leak . . . . The People to save their lives made for the nearest land, but the wind being fresh at N. and a strong Tide of Ebb, it was between twelve and one before they could reach it. The weather being severely cold, the men were frost bitten and half a leg deep in water in the cabbin, when the vessel struck the shore which she did, between the false and the true Hook. . . . The People with great difficulty got to Land, in their skiff, and to the Light-house, but the vessel soon beat to pieces and everything was lost . . . . There were three Men on board, Henry Minck, Master, to whom the vessel belonged, John Hancock and Henry Steel, all belonging to this city, who have lost all their effects. *The Pennsylvania Journal*, January 15, 1767

---

[34] How close the line between pirate and privateer must sometimes have been. Eight years earlier, this same Captain Van Tyle had been arrested and imprisoned as one of the members of the pirate band of the infamous Captain Kidd.

New York, October 30. The Sloop Live Oak, Capt. Foy, of this Port, inward bound from Santo Domingo, in thick fogg Weather, had the Misfortune to run aground on Squan Beach, a little to the Westward of Shrewsbury Inlet and having 2600 Bushels of Salt, some large Logs of Mahongany and a considerable Sum of Money on board, in about nine Hours she beat to Pieces, by which melancholy Accident the following Persons were drowned viz. Richard Foy, Master; John Campell, Supercargo (a promising young Gentleman of an amiable Character, Nephew to Mr. Jacobus Van Zandt, Owner of the Vessel); John Haynes; Henry Williams, John Sample; and John Lahay, Seamen; John Abbit, James Sands; a German and his Wife; another married Woman with her Daughter of 18 and her Son of 9 years old, Passengers; and a Negro Boy belonging to Campbell. The Mate, Robert Hog, with Joshua Marriner and Cornelius Thompson, Seamen, got ashore on some of the Plank of the Vessel, as did also a German, Husband to one of the Woman and Father to the young Woman and Boy that were drowned on the Bows.

The Bodies of the Captain and Mr. Campbell, as also of 10 more, were taken up on the Beach and are decently buried. *The New York Gazette and Weekly Mercury*, October 30, 1769.

New York, October 26. On Sunday last a Messenger from Shrewsbury came to Town with the following melancholy Account viz, that on Friday Evening last, the Wind being Southerly and moderate, and the Weather having been some Time foggy and thick, the Live Oak, a fine large Sloop, belonging to Mr. Jacobus Van Zant of this City, Merchant, Capt. Foy, Master, from Spanish St. Domingo, bound into this Port, being nearer the land than they imagined, had the Misfortune to run aground on Squan Beach, a little to the Westward of Shrewsbury Inlet, where the Vessel, being deeply laden and a large Swell from the Sea, setting right on the Beach, in a few Thumps, the Vessel went all to Pieces and was entirely lost with all her Cargo, which was very valuable consisting of Sugars, Mahogony &c. and upwards of 20000 Dollars in Specie; and of the People, 4 only escaped with their lives, viz. the Mate, two Seamen and a Spanish Merchant who were cast upon the Beach, where they found themselves next Morning, but could give no Account how they got there. They were terribly bruised and mangled, especially the Merchant who was stark naked, had his flesh miserably torne, and, by lying so long in the water, turn'd pale, resembling that of a dead corpse and scarce any skin left on his Back. The rest of the People, 14 in Number, were all unfortunately drowned, among whom was

Mr. Campell, Super Cargo of the Vessel and Nephew to Mr. Van Zant. . . also the Family of the unhappy Spanish Merchant (consisting of his Wife, his Son, about 8 Years of Age and his Daughter, a young Lady of about 16 or 17) who is, by this distressing Stroke of Providence, at once deprived of all his Fortune and Family. . . *The New York Journal or General Advertiser*, October 26, 1769

From Great Egg-Harbour we learn, that on the 11th Instant the Wreck of a small Sloop came ashore there, with her mast and rigging hanging to her; her Quarter stove in; 7 Barrels of Hogs Lard and one of Pork were found in her and she appeared to have been loaded with Wheat; no Person on board; Nor Papers to be found. It is thought the people had been put to great straits, having cut up their blankets to caulk the Decks. It is also said some Tobacco in barrels were found on the Shore. *The Pennsylvania Gazette*, September 28, 1769

New York, December 26. On Saturday Night about 12 O'clock arrived in a pilot boat from Sandy Hook, Eliphalet Neal, late Master of the Schooner Felicity, from Piscatawy [New Hampshire], bound to North Carolina with Rum &c. Nath. Rand, Mate, and supercargo, Wm. Thresher and Paul Randell, foremast men, who gave the following account. They left Piscataway the 1st Instant, had bad weather and contrary winds, till they passed the Vineyard; On Monday the 16th had hard gales which obliged them to lie to, most of the Time till Thursday when it grew moderate, almost calm. Friday afternoon made the Highlands off the Neversinks, about three or four leagues distant; at 7 discovered a leak, which gained upon them 6 inchs in less than ten minutes, though the pumps were going. They then got out the boat and had only time to take a few cloaths and a compass before the Vessel sunk to the water's edge, a large swell driving out to sea. They left the Vessel at about 11 o'clock, got ashore near Sandy Hook, sent out a pilot boat to search for the vessel, but found only the binnacle, a Caboose and sugar box so that probably the Vessel had sunk. *The Pennsylvania Journal*, February 2, 1769

Some shipwrecks, became the subject a series of brief news flashes, from their first sighting to their ends. Witness the fate of the Sally:

June 6. Yesterday a Sloop came up from Great-Egg Harbour, the Master of which says, that last Saturday Morning he saw a Ship ashore at Little-Egg Harbour, with all her sails loose. *New York Gazette and Weekly Mercury*, June 6, 1768

The Ship Sally, Captain Rankin, in 7 Weeks, from Newry, for this Port, is ashore off Little Egg Harbour. *The Pennsylvania Journal*, June 9, 1768

June 13. The Ship mentioned in our last to be ashore at Little-Egg Harbour, proves to be the Sally, Capt. Rankin, from Newry, bound for Philadelphia. *New York Gazette and Weekly Mercury*, June 13, 1768

June 20. The Sally, Rankin, from Newry, for Philadelphia, mentioned in our last, to be on shore at Little Egg-Harbour, is gone all to Pieces. *The New York Gazette and Weekly Mercury*, June 20, 1768

Even in the days of yore, some shipwrecks would spill pollutants into the Ocean:

Philadelphia. We have advice that a Brigg loaded with Pitch and Tar, without Masts or People, is drove ashore at Squan. *The Pennsylvania Journal*, October 26, 1752

New York, December 4. On Monday the 13th of last Month, the Schooner Charming Peggy, Alexander Sloan Master, bound in here from Cape Fare, with 237 Barrels of Tar on board, was drove ashore in a Violent Gale of Wind at East, on the Outside of Sandy Hook. The Vessel was lost, but the Men and Cargo saved; the Captain afterwards hired some small Vessel to bring up the Cargo to this City and arrived with it last Week. *The Pennsylvania Journal*, December 6, 1752

The identities of some wrecks were never known; they sunk in silence and were covered by the sand. Still other wrecks were noted, but soon forgotten. A few others, however, seemed to have the knack of remaining newsworthy in the colonial press. Consider, for example, the following report on the Ellis:

Saturday, the first Instant, the Ship Ellis, from London, bound for Philadelphia, was cast away on Abequon Beach and one Mr. Wilson (lately appointed Comptroller of the Custom House at Amboy) and one of the Seamen were drowned. As soon as the Vessel struck, great part of the Cargo was thrown over board to lighten her, most of which drove ashore. The Ship with Part of the Cargo will be lost. *The New York Gazette or Weekly Post Boy*, March 13, 1766

The Ship Ellis, Capt. Egdon, from London for this port, with dry goods, was drove ashore at Abescomb Beach, in a hard gale of wind, on the first instant. Soon after her masts were carried away, and she fast aground, the Captain, Charles Willson Esq, appointed Collector of His Majesty's Taxes at Amboy, and a sailor of the name of Wilson, got into the boat to try for shore, but the fast breaking from the ship, the boat soon overset, the two Willsons were drowned, and the Captain with much difficulty got on shore; the remainder of the people stayed on board that night and in the morning, the tide being very low, they easily got ashore. The vessel is entirley lost, the goods all damaged and some of them lost, being thrown overboard to lighten the vessel.

Last Saturday night; one of the sailors of the above ship was stopped at the Ferry opposite the City, with a waggon load of the goods, which he had plundered and was bringing to this city. He has since been provided with a secure lodging, and storeage for his goods. *The Pennsylvania Journal*, March 13, 1766

By his Excellency, William Franklin, Esquire

Captain General and Governour in Chief and over his Majesty's Provinvce of New Jersey, Chancellor and Vice Admiral in the same &c.

A Proclamation

Whereas it is represented to me by Mr. Richard Footman of the City of Philadelphia, Merchant, that the Ship called the Ellis, whereof Samuel Richardson Egdon was Master, did lately in a violent storm drive ashore on Abescomb Beach in the County of Glouster in this Province, whereby the Vessel was lost; that some part of the cargo by the care and vigilance of the master is landed, and the owners of said vessel have suffered damage from some evil and wickedly disposed persons plundering and secreting part of said cargo. And Whereas such practices are highly criminal and tend to reflect dishonour on his Majesty's government of this Province, these are therefore in his Majesty's name to charge and command all Justices of the Peace, Sheriffs, and all other civil and military Officers within this government, that on this or any future occasion, they do to the utmost of their power assist and protect all persons under the misfortune of shipwreck in saving and securing the goods and merchandizes in such wreck contained and that the said civil officers do apprehend and commit (or cause the same to be done) to the gaol of the respective Counties, all and every person or persons found plundering or stealing any of the effects belonging to said vessels or cargoes, and to search any places that prove to be suspicious, for any goods or effects so plundered or stolen, as they will answer the contrary at their peril.

Given under my Hand and Seal at Arms, at Burlington the eighth day of September, in the Sixth Year of His Majesty's reign, one thousand seven hundred and sixty six.
By His Excellency's Command
William Franklin
The Pennsylvania Journal, March 13, 1766

A certain Richard Richards, alias Richardson, who came passenger in the ship Ellis, Capt. Egdon from London (lately cast away on Absecom Beach in New Jersey) did when in England, as likewise since his arrival in this city, put on and assume the dress and appearance of one of the people called Quakers, and so far succeeded as to impose on several humane benevolent persons in London, for which end he there took, as is supposed, a false affirmation and by many notorious falsehoods and artful stories prevented his being taken and brought to justice. *The Pennsylvania Journal*, April 10, 1766

Last Week a Sloop from Egg Harbour, brought up to Town, a small Bundle of stamped Paper, that had been found in the wreck of the Ship Ellis, lately cast away on her voyage from London for Philadelphia, at Absecom Beach, as mentioned in a former Paper. As soon as it was known, they were seized by the Sons of Liberty and purified at the Coffee-house last Friday, before a Thousand Spectators.[35] *The Pennsylvania Gazette*, April 10, 1766

The wreck of the ship Ellis as she now lies on Absecomb Beach, near Egg Harbour; and it is believed that sundry things of value belonging to said wreck may yet be saved, especially at this moderate season; it is hoped that those who are acquainted with her situation will give their attendance. *The Pennsylvania Journal*, May 22, 1766

A mystery envelops the vessel or vessels named Nancy. Are the following reports about one, two or three ships? Note that the ships are described differently (one a "brig", two "snows"), different masters names (York, Kerr and Carr) different dates of shipwreck a month apart, but is that inaccurate reporting or remarkable coincidence?

Saturday last, in a violent gale of wind, the Brig Nancy, Capt. York from Jamaica, for this port, was drove ashore at Great Egg Harbour, the sails, the rigging and most of her cargo will be saved.

When Capt. York went ashore, he saw a ship close in with surf, which he thinks must have gone ashore; and it is reported that a schooner is ashore at Barnagat. *The Pennsylvania Journal*, March 6, 1766

The snow Nancy, Walter Kerr, Master, mentioned in our last, left Bristol the 17th of January and King Road the 3rd of February following, bound for this port. About the beginning of March they fell in with the Sloop Ann, John Jones Master, of and from Rhode Island, bound for Jamaica, but being in great distress, Capt. Kerr took said Jones and his people on board the snow and proceeded on his voyage until the 5th inst. when he got soundings in 25 fathom water at 6 o'clock in the evening, and by observation had that day he was to the southward of Cape-Hinlopen and stood a N.W. course until 12 o'Clock, when he laid the snow to in 15

---

[35] The Sons of Liberty, a network of persons throughout the Colony, angry at the Stamp Tax imposed by the Parliament in London on many aspects of colonial life, such as newspapers, court proceedings etc., engaged in demonstrations such as this throughout the colonies. They were successful in forcing a repeal of the hated tax, a victory which whetted the appetite for greater independence.

fathom water. . . . At four o'clock in the morning she struck on Hereford Barr, about seventeen miles to the northward of Cape-May, being carried thither, as is supposed, by a strong current, for the captain and others on board judged they were on the Overfalls in the mouth of our Bay and endeavoured, by filling the sails, to press her over, but soon found their mistake by feeling the land very near to them. On this some of the people, contrary to the captain's orders, cut away the masts and others got into the boats, cut the gripes and the sea soon washed them overboard, then cutting or slipping the fasts drove to the shore where four men landed viz. Hutchinson, the carpenter, Magnus Sinclair, John Gowens and John Stansbury, which were all that were saved out of twenty eight persons, for the wind blowing a violent hard gale by this time, at N.E. and N.E. and by N., no assistance could be given them from the shore, the vessel unfortunately heeled off to the sea, which broke over her 30 feet high and the distressed people obliged to continue on her deck until 4 o'clock in the Afternoon, hanging on by the Quarter deck rails and upper gunnel &c as she lay on her beam ends; 0 but at low water they made a raft and, as is supposed, all got on it, expecting the tide of flood to drive them ashore, the raft came there well secured; and a hen coop lashed to the upper part, with their cloaths stuffed in it, coming ashore underneath the raft, shewed it had overset and the people all perished; twelve of their bodies have since been found and decently buried, The persons drowned by this unfortunate wreck are, Captain Walter Kerr, John Oliver, his mate, ... Fortesque, an apprentice and five others of the ship's crew. John Jones, Master, Andrew Mason, mate, John Brown, David Muttony and Peleg Wood, all of the Sloop Ann, taken up at sea. Captain William Willson, his wife and child, Captain John Corser, Mr. Robert Smith (a young lad brother of Revd. Doctor Smith of this place), the Revd. Mr. Willson, the Revd. Mr. Giles of New York, Mr. Mott, a tanner of Connecticut, and the master and two mates of a Rhode Island brig, that was sold in Bristol, names forgot. No letters or papers have been found and very little of the vessel or cargo saved; upon the whole, the circumstances of this Affair make it one of the most melancholy losses that ever happened on this coast. *The Pennsylvania Journal*, March 20, 1766

By an express arrived yesterday from Cape-May, we have the following:

I am persuaded the following lines will relate distress and sadness to you. However, I am bound to rehearse and to tell you that on the 6th of this Instant, on Hereford Bar, which is about 4 leagues N.E. of the pitch of the Cape of Cape May, the poor unfortunate Snow Nancy, Capt. Carr from Bristol, was, by a violent gale of wind at E.N.E. forced on shore and has become a forlorn wreck, which proved a watery coffin to all, except four persons, who only escaped out of a crew of 27 in number, the captain and the mate are of the drowned and some others of note and distinction. Many of their dead bodies are drifted on shore, and some goods also.

Humanity would teach me to exert myself and use the utmost of my care, which I purpose to do without any other license 'til I receive further orders or see some of you; by all means let some interested person or persons come down immediately on sight hereof, with the bearer; the dead I shall keep till the bearer returns and not suffer to be cramed into the sand . . . I saw them, poor hearts, in the height of their distress, where wind and sea had no pity, but could do no more than regret and sympathize with my fellow mortals, while overwhelmed with calamities in the raging waves.
The Pennsylvania Journal, April 10, 1766

The wreck of the snow Nancy, as it now lies on Hereford Bar, near Cape May, where the said snow was cast away; and as it is believed that the said snow may be got off by those who can attend to it in warm weather, the npurchaser will probably find himself possessed of a very good bargain.
The Pennsylvania Journal, May 8, 1766

The 1700s were as an exciting period of history as ever existed, although to the citizens of the time of this rural, agricultural land, life undoubtedly often must have seemed uneventful. The exceptions to the routine, undoubtedly viewed with horror back then, are today the stuff of which that Hollywood movies are made: pirates, indians, land riots, slave insurrections, and the birth of a Nation.

During colonial times, New Jersey's long coastline periodically suffered the assaults of pirates and enemy privateers. Pirates, of course, despite sometimes being romanticized by history, were outright scoundrels, multi-national outlaws that preyed on unprotected shipping. The concept of a privateer, on the other hand, was, in theory, similar or that of the posse or, here, naval militia. Seeking adventure and the premium pay that risk merits, honest men would crew the better merchant ships and attack the shipping of a specific enemy, invariably the Spanish or French. Today's privateer sometimes became tomorrow's pirate. Witness the following incident that demonstrates the edge of the law on which some privateers defiantly operated.

New-York, May 19. Last Saturday arrived here Capt. Roswell in the Privateer Trinton from her Cruize; as soon as she came in the Hook the Man of Wars Barge went on board and prest 16 of his Men and so came up in the Harbour.[36] Mr. Brant the Pilot, was a going on board of the Transport Ship with Provisions and the Insign belonging to one of the Companies of Soldiers was on board of the pilot Boat; the Privateers seeing him took him to be Captain of the Man of War, they immediately manned their Barge and row'd after the Boat took her and ran her aground and used the officer very base, by braking of his Sword and threw the Hilt in the River; had it not been for some Gentlemen that was present during this Action and told them it was not the Captain of the Man of War, they would have brought him aboard the Privateer and kept him till such time that he sent the Men on shore that was Prest; but finding their mistake let them go again, and seemed to be sorry for what had happen'd.
The New York Evening Post, May, 19, 1746

England had declared war in 1702 against the French because of the claims of Louis the XIV to the Throne of Spain, a potential Catholic

---

[36] The British Navy would "impress" sailors off British merchant ships and compel them to serve of the Men of War, a custom, understandably enough, usually resented by the unwilling recruits.

England had declared war in 1702 against the French because of the claims of Louis the XIV to the Throne of Spain, a potential Catholic alliance that would threaten England. Known as the War of the Spanish Succession, it lasted over a decade, until the Peace of Utrecht in 1713. During it, the Jersey coast was at continual risk of being attacked, plundered and burned. The following account from the summer of 1704 tells of the narrow escape of a British Captain (although his vessel had to be abandoned to the enemy along the way) from a French Privateer's lurking off the tip of Sandy Hook:

Amboy, June 29. On Wednesday last by an Express from Monmouth sent to his Excellency my Lord Cornbury, we were informed of a French Privateer that lay at Sandy-hook, who the night before had landed 24 men at Neversinks & plundered two Houses; upon which news Cap. Hamilton ordered a strict Watch to be kept here to prevent a surprize; & on Thursday night several Gentlemen came here viz. Messeurs Philip French, Glencross, Gordon, Richards, & Cap. Perkins, who were Passengers on board of Cap. Sinclare that came from London & were that morning about 4 o'clock standing a long the side of the Hook when they saw this Privateer whom they thought to be an outward bound Vessel from New York. The Privateer fired two shots at them, having English Colours out; Cap. Sinclare endeavour'd to get from him and run his Vessel on shore, but the Wind prevented; a man upon Shore pull'd off his Shirt & made signs that the Privateer was a Rogue, upon which those gentlemen got into the Boat and escap'd and took in Cap. Sinclare who was extremely ill & landed at the Highlands of Neversinks where was a strong guard, his Mate staid on board with some of the Seaman endeavouring to get the ship within the hook but could not and so jumpt into the water, he & Capt. Perkin's Son and swam on Shore when within Pistol Shot of the Privateer. *The Boston News Letter*, August 7, 1704

This same French Privateer was probably responsible also for the following chase scene, in which the escaping captain from the incident above and another victim so frighten the Royal Council in New York that it charters a Dutch Privateer to go out and take the Frenchman, evidently without success:

New York. On 20 Currant, Simon Pasco, from Antigua bound hither was taken by a French Privateer of 14 Guns, 120 men off of the Capes of Delawar lat. 45. The Privateer belongs to Bordeaux, unloaded at Martinico and there fitted out. Cap. Davy is Commander; they took a Barrel of Sugar and a Hogshead of Rum out of the Sloop, her Guns and Arms & then burnt her with all her Loading, notwithstanding Mr. Pasco offered three hundred pounds for her Ransom; afterward said Privateer Chas'd Mr. Sandiford bound hither from Carolina, who got into Sandy hook before him.

On the 25th, The Privateer came into an anchor at Sandy-hook and there took Eleazer Darby in a Sloop from Boston bound to Philadelphia; next day they took a Wood Boat & two slaves and that night gave Mr. Pasco and his men liberty, who about ten a clock got up to N. York.

On the 27th early in the Morning the Privateer took Capt. Sinclare, so soon as Mr. Pasco came with the news the Gentlemen of Her Majesty's Council met and sent for Capt. Claver Commander of the Dutch Privateer and proposed to him to go out and take said Privateer, at least to take the prize which we deem to be the Sinclare, who offered his services and in two hours sailed with 150 Men and 50 Men on board his Sloop and said day [would] come up with the Privateer and her Prize, but returned the 28th without effecting anything. And on the 29th, Capt, Claver man'd off new again; Capt Evertson and Capt Penniston in two Sloops are gone well man'd a second time in pursuit of the Privateer. *The Boston News Letter*, August 7, 1704

Yesterday our 3 Privateers return'd without seeing or hearing of the French Privateer at the same time came in a Brigateen from Nevis, who on the last of July, 8 leagues off Sandy Hook was taken by the French Privateer and Ransomed for 400 pounds St. Thomas Mony & say that the Privateer is gone for Tarpolin Cove, having sent Cap. Sinclare's Ship with 15 men to Martinico two days after they took her. *The Boston News Letter*, August 7, 1704

The next summer -- 1705 -- was also a period of privateer activity off the Jersey Coast:

New York. On the 16th Capt.Outerbridge and some of his men came to Town and relate that on the 3rd Instant he sailed out of Sandy-hook bound for Jamaica loaded with provisions and was taken by a Privateer from Martinico about 150 Leagues off and that his Sloop (with Mrs. Antill and her children who were Passengers on Board) is sent to Martinico.

That on the 14th Instant the same Privateer came to Sandyhook and in the Night sent up her Boat to the Narrows with the design to take Capt Potter who was then Loaden at the Watering place bound for Nevis; but the Boat could not find him; about 10 days before they took a small Sloop belonging to one Godfrey of this Town, loaded with Pitch and Tarr which they burned; one Reynolds was Master of her and 'tis said sides with the

French and is a Pilot to them on this Coast and has informed them of our vessels expected and Outward bound; The Privateers perceiving they were discovered, Capt Outerbridge and his men and Godfrey persuaded them to land at Sandyhook, which they did and afterwards stood along the shore to the Southward. Yesterday News was brought that they had landed in East New-Jersey a little beyond Neversincks and had burnt two Country Houses. On Sunday the 10th Instant, the Cettey Privateer, Capt Bond for England via Virginia and 2 Sloops sailed out of Sandy-hook and happily mist this Privateer. *The Boston News Letter*, June 18, 1705

Sometimes, however, the good guys caught up with the bad guys, but, unfortunately, not always decisively:

On the 2d Instant early in the Morning Her Majesty's Ship the Triton's Prize Sailed out of Sandy-hook and that night about 10 0'clock she met with a Ship 20 Leagues S & E. off the Hook, and kept her company all night and early in the morning engaged her, being a French Privateer of about 150 Tuns, she had ten ports a side and full of men, thought to be no less than 150 or 200 men. The Triton's Prize out sailed her and intended to run very close upon her and give a Broadside, but the Privateer prevented her by giving the first Broasdside and Volley of small Shot, whereby we had 4 men kill'd and 5 or 6 wounded, besides Capt. Davies who was shot just behind the Ear, and with the Fall, bruised himself very much upon the edge of a Shot Case, that rendered him unserviceable for some Hours, which gave the Enemy a great advantage, yet notwithstanding, the Fight was bravely maintained and a great many Broadsides given, the Privateer made a running fight and the Triton's Prize every now and then upon the Chase came up with her, gave her a Broadside of Round and Partridge. Several of the Frenchmen were seen to fall to the Deck, Part of his Gunnel and Sp'r-sail Yard found swimming. At last, the Gale slacking, the Enemy threw some of their guns overboard and row'd away and the Triton's Prize returned to Sandy Hook to repair her damage. And Yesterday put to sea again, being very well man'd and Capt. Davies well recovered; if that unhappy shot had not hit Capt. Davies, the Privateer had certainly been taken. *The Boston News-Letter*, June 9, 1707

Consider how much havoc and panic one small enemy sloop could cause:

New York. There is one small French Privateer Sloop, Commanded by Capt. Crapo (who was upon this Coast about two years ago) that at about the 24th of March last came from Martinico, having 72 Men on Board, who has taken four prizes between Sandyhook and the Capes of Virginia viz. On the 7th of April last, the Sloop Seaflower, Henry York, Master, belonging to this port and bound from Antigua to Virginia, out of which the Privateer took some Rum, Sails, Rigging &c. and then sunk her; and a few days after a ship from Leverpool bound to Virginia, whom the Privateer sent to Martinico, the Prisoners of both vessels being 25 in number they put on shore; The third was Rolland in a Sloop bound hither from Madera, whom he took bout 14 days ago, a few leagues without Sandyhook; and 5 days after he took another ship from Leverpool bound to Virginia which Prize he also sent to Martinco and the Prisoners he put ashore in East Jersey last Wednesday evening; the same day he sprung his Boom in chase of Capt. Francis Jones from Nevis and Bermuda that is arrived here, whom the Privateer followed within a League of Sandyhook; yesterday Capt. Rolland and some of the Prisoners came to Town and gave up this Account and do believe she is gone towards Fishers Island and Block Island to get water and fish their Boom and that he will endeavour to take another Prize and then to go to Port Royal to Refit and Man, having but 40 white men and 15 Negroes left on Board. *The Boston News-Letter*, May 3, 1708

The "cat and mouse" game between the privateers and the forces of protection was eagerly reviewed by the readership of the Colonial Papers:

One Barker in a Sloop from Nevis and Lathrop in another from Boston are arrived here. On Friday morning a fishing Boat, 12 Myles from Sandy Hooke, was chas'd by a Privateer Sloop, but she got into the Hooke and gave notice thereof to Her Majesties Ship Hector, whom she met under Sayle going out with several Outward bound Vessels. Some Boats came up since who say they saw the Hector in chase of her but we have heard nothing further. We believe it to be the Privateer who took a Sloop off the Capes of Delaware on the 18th Instant that was bound from Philadelphia to Barbados. *The Boston News-Letter*, May 26, 1712

'Tis reported in Town that some in New-Jersey saw the Hector Man of War in chase of a Privateer, who to escape her, ran into Shoal water and that the Captain then had Man'd one of the Sloops under his Convoy and took the Privateer, which we heartily wish it may be so, but it wants Confirmation. *The Boston News-Letter*, June 2, 1712

A privateer without a war became a pirate and the cessation of the war between England and France did not bring relief from the terror of attacks from the sea.

New York, June 17. On the 11th Instant arrived here Capt. Mead from Virginia and a Sloop from Exuma, Beson Master; they were both taken by the Pirate Sloop commanded by Paul Williams and plunder'd. They took from Mead, Holland's Duck, Rigging, Wearing Linen and other Goods to the value of 150 pounds and from the other Sloop (which belongs to Bermuda) two Negro Men and two great Guns. They also took a Sloop and a Briganteen Outward bound from Philadelphia, the first bound for Surranam, the other to the Western Islands or Lisbon; they took from the Sloop about 30 Barrels of Flower &c. and from the other four Vessels such Provisions and other things as pleased them. A Saylor of this Town and an Indian of Gardiner's Island, who were wounded aboard the Pirate in the Scuffle at Sandy Hook (and who were Prisoners on board) were sent ashore in Mead; the Saylor who discovered that Jeremiah Higgins, who had been Boatswain of the Pirate for some time, was put ashore while they lay at Sandy Hook and that none dyed of their wounds in that Scuffle but that there remained on board 36 or 37 Men, two whereof were Artists and 15 or 16 of them Negroes and Molattoes. *The Boston News-Letter*, June 17, 1717

Philadelphia, July 26. On Sunday the 22d arrived a small Sloop Jonathan Swain, Master, from Cape May, by whom we have Advice that a Pyrate Brigantine and Sloop have been cruising on and off both our Capes for Above Three Weeks. They several times sailed up the Bay Ten or Twelve Leagues and on the 8th Instant brought a large Sloop down with them, which they took up high in the Bay. That Night they anchored in the Bay, about a League and a Half off the Shore, beat Drums all Night and seemed to be very full of Men. What vessels they took we do not yet understand, none of the Prisoners being set on Shore. Our Trade is entirely stopped by them, no vessel daring to go out and all took that offer to come in. They were both seen on Thursday last cruising about their old Station, not fearing disturbance from the Men of War, who, by dear Experience we know, love Trading better than Fighting. No vessel has arrived here for a Week past, except Hargrave in the Sloop Little Joseph who sailed from hence two months ago for the Island of St. Christophers, but was taken by the Pyrates three times and rifled of most of her Cargo, so that she was obliged to return back. *New England Courant*, July 30, 1722

The 1740s found us at war with Spain and France and more, it appeared, the aggressor than the victim, at least in the first year of the war:

Newport, Rhode Island, February 1. Capt. Thomas Seabrook, Master of the Brigg Orange of Perth Amboy, arrived here the 27th of January past from London, in 12 Weeks Passage and now ready to sail with the first fair Wind for New-York, who informs that he spoke with a Ship off the Capes of Virginia, who informed him that the Diamond Man of War had taken a Spanish Ship as a Prize of considerable Value and had on board 74000 Pieces of Eight besides other valuable Commodities. *The New England Weekly Journal*, February 5, 1740

New York. Last Week arrived at Amboy a Sloop from Jamaica, by whom we have the agreeable News, that Capt. Warren after his Arrival there went out on a cruise, when he had the good Fortune in a few days to meet with a rich Spanish Sloop. *The New-York Weekly Journal*, December 1, 1740

But the tide seemed quickly to turn, with the result that the colonists recruited even more privateers:

New York, May 25, Last Week came here several Persons who had been taken by the Spaniards, some of which had been carried to Havannah, others were taken up along this Coast about ten Days ago; one was a large Sloop from Virgina, laden with Beef, Pork and Indian Corn, bound to New York or Amboy. By these Men we are advised that five Privateers, viz. three Sloops, a Snow and a Schooner sailed from Havannah for Augustine where they landed some Men and Provisions. After which they came upon our Coast, where the Successes of one of them (a Sloop) has been so great that she has taken as many Prizes as she could mann and is returned to the Havannah having first given their Prisoners (who were 43 in Number) a small Sloop to put them on shore, several of which have landed at Sandy-Hook and are come up to New York and the Sloop with the rest of the Company are gone for Rhode-Island and Boston. The other three Privateers are still on the Coast viz. two Sloops and a Snow and to be sure the Schooner is not far off; What success they have had since these Prisoners left them is uncertain. But on Saturday last, by a letter from a Gentleman at Rockaway on Long Island, we are informed that the two Sloops and a Snow (which we may suppose to be these Privateers) were seen off that Place, standing backward and forward between that Place and the Hook. And we are informed that the two Sloops are poorly manned, but the Snow is tolerably well fitted and has upwards of a 100 men on board.

We are now fitting out here by Subscription two good Sloops (Privateers) to look after these Spaniards. Our Assembly being now seated, have voted four hundred pounds towards the Charges of these two Sloops; they have likewise voted that every Man who should happen to lose a leg or an Arm or otherwise disabled, on this Occasion, shall have Fifty Pounds; and we hear by Act of Parliament our Privateers are to be paid Twenty Pounds Sterling, and which is to be paid without delay, for everyone on board a Spanish Privateer. It is to be hoped that these two Sloops will give a good Account of the Dons. We are now beating up for Volunteers and it is to be wished that every one who has the Interest of the Province at Heart and the Prosperity of its Trade, will lend a Helping Hand and contribute (in his way) to so good a Design. *Boston Weekly News-Letter*, June 4, 1741

Saturday last the Marlborough, a fine Ship, designed for a Privateer, was launched at Burlington and will be fitted out with all Expedition. *The New York Weekly Post Boy*, November 12. 1744

New York, July 11. Wednesday last came into this Harbour from Elizabeth Town where she was built by John Dally of this City, the Privateer Ship Sturdy Beggar. She is double decked and was purposely built as a Privateer, to cruize against his Majesty's Enemies. The Conveniences for her Men are large and commodious, which will greatly contribute to keep them healthy and is justly esteemed the best Ship of War belonging to this Port. She is to be commanded by Mr. Robert Troup, who often last War distinguished himself in a particular and brave Manner. She is to mount twenty 9 Pounders on her Main Deck and Six 4 Pounders on her Quarterdeck and will sail in order to intercept the Martinico and Cape Fleets, by the 15th of August. All Gentlemen Sailors and others, who have a Mind to make their Fortunes, may repair on board said Ship, where they will meet with kind Treatment from the Captain and Officers. *The New York Mercury*, July 11, 1757.

Philadelphia, May 14. We hear that the Warren Privateer, Capt. Katter, is to sail tomorrow or next day on a Month's cruize, between the Capes of Virginia and the Neversinks, to guard our trade from the Enemy's Privateers, who have chased several vessels lately near the Capes; she is fitted out by a Subscription among the Merchants of the City. The Men have three pounds Bounty Money and are to share all prizes. *The New York Gazette Revived in the Weekly Post Boy*, May 18, 1747

New-York, August 10. On the 5th Instant arrived at Sandy-Hook, two private Vessels of War, fitted out by the Colonies of Connecticut and Rhode Island to protect their Trade. *The New York Evening Post*, August 10, 1747

Boston. Yesterday arrived here Capt. Vanclew in a Sloop from the Jerseys, who put into the Vineyard at Old Town Harbour, from whence he sailed on Monday last, who informs That on Last Saturday a large French Ship, suppos'd to be about 200 Tons burthen was brought into Holme's-Hole, by Capt. Potter in one of Rhode Island's Privateers and that he heard she was laden with Fish and Salt, suppos'd to be a Banker[37]. *The Boston Weekly News Letter*, September 20, 1744

New York, November 29. Yesterday Morning a Seaman belonging to the Privateer Brig Mars, Capt. Wright, for this Port, came up in one of our Pilot Boats from Sandy Hook, where he left a French Prize Snow, belonging to the said Privateer, Capt. Sinnott of this Port and a St. Kitts Man, which they took about a Month ago, as well as 7 others at the same Time, being part of a Fleet of 25 Sail, under Convoy of a 40 Gun Ship, bound from Cape Francois for Old France, all loaded with Sugar and Indigo that the day after the above mentioned 8 Prizes were taken, the Privateers, still keeping sight of the Remainder of the Fleet, they fell in with Commodore Keppel who took them all, with the 40 Gun Ship, and carried them to Jamaica. Four of the Prizes are hourly expected here. *The Pennsylvania Gazette*, December 2, 1762.

and the colonists had their failures:

Friday last Capt. Waddel arrived here from the Bay of Honduras, who informs us that, on Wednesday Morning Last, he being about 12 Leagues from Sandy Hook, off Barnagat, and in sight of Land, saw a Ship standing in, supposed to be bound hither, and sometime soon after he saw a Sloop in Chase of the said Ship and about Ten O'Clock the Sloop came up with and fired a Shot at her, upon which the Ship directly struck and lay to awhile till he supposes the Sloop boarderd her; soon after they both put about and stood off to Sea. Capt. Waddel made the best of his Way to the Hook, where he arrived on Thursday Night; and his Majesty's Ships the Launceton, Capt. Warren, and the Gosport, Capt. Ellis, both lying there, the former waiting to Convoy some outward bound Ships off the Coast and then to proceed on a Cruize and the latter going Convoy to a Vessel with military Stores for Georgia; Capt. Waddel informed them of the aforementioned Affair, whereupon Capt. Warren immediately ordered his Ship unmoored that Night, and on Friday Morning at Day-break, he set sail in quest of them, leaving

---

[37] A vessel that fished the Grand Banks, off Newfoundland.

Orders for Capt. Ellis to take care of all the outward bound vessels before mentioned.

And on Saturday Night Capt. Long in a Brig from Curacoa arrived here, who says, that he saw a Sloop in Chase of a Ship the same day as Capt. Waddel, which he believes was the same, and adds that he was apprehensive he should himself have been himself chased if the Sloop had not been diverted from him in the pursuit of the Ship. *Boston Weekly News-Letter*, June 30, 1743.

Philadelphia, Yesterday came up to Town one of our Pilot Boats with 4 men lately belonging to a Sloop bound from Virginia to New-York, Constantine Hughes, Master, which was drove on Shore on Monday last on Cape-May by a Spanish Privateer Sloop, which Sloop had taken a few days before 2 of our Pilot Boats, one of which they manned with thirty hands & sent up our Bay, above Bombay Hook, where they landed on Sunday last and to the Plantation of Mr. Edmond Liston and took away 4 Negroes and everything else that they tho't they wanted to the Value of about 200 Pounds from whence they went to another Plantation and took a Negro, but the People shutting the Door upon them, they fir'd at them and shot a Woman thro'th the Thigh, and in the Evening, they went dowen to the Bay again, where meeting with another of our Pilot Boats, they stripped her of all her Sails &c and on Tuesday Morning she was seen going out of the Capes looking for the Privateer Sloop, having one of our Pilots on Board, and they told the last Pilot they took that they had taken 13 Vessels on our Coast, four of which they sent home and sunk and burnt the rest. *The New York Evening Post*, July 20, 1747

There were also a number of close calls, where the prey escaped and lived to tell his tale to the press.

New York. April 10. We hear from Amboy that a Ship which arrived there last Week brings Account from the Bay, that two Ships and a Brigatine were smartly chased by three Perriagoes, that the Ships being favored with the Wind & good Sailors got clear but the Brig was necessitated to Fight; during the engagement one of the Perriagoes got so close under the Brig's Counter that two of the Spaniards got into the Cabin Windows, but not unperceived, for one of the Hands went down and killed them both before they could get into a posture of Defence; there were but four of the Spaniards left in the large Perriagoe to row her off. *The New-England Weekly Journal*, May 2, 1738

New York, August 3. Last Saturday arrived here Captain Hughes from Virgina, who informs that, on the 13th of July being off Cape May, he was chased by a small French Privateer so near the land that he was forced to run her ashore and quit her; the privateer came along Side of the Sloop, broke open the Hatches and began to throw some of her Cargo overboard and by that means got her off. Next Morning, Capt. Hughes came down and saw her under sail; soon after, another Vessel hove in sight, they all left the Sloop to go after the other; he, seeing this, got a small craft with some more Men besides his compliment, went on board, hoisted Sail and is safe arrived. *The New York Evening Post*, August 3, 1747

New York. There are letters from New York of the 30th of May last that give an Account of a Sloop belonging to New Jersey that was taken about that time off of the Capes of Virginia by a Spanish Privateer of 4 Guns and 70 Men, belonging to St. Augustine, who, a few Days before, had taken a Vessel from London, bound to South Carolina. The Spaniards put three Frenchmen on board the said Sloop and left the Mate and one more Englishman and ordered them to follow the privateer; but the Night coming on and proving very Dark, they soon lost sight of one another. The Frenchmen, who were none of them Navigators, ordered the English Mate to sail towards St. Augustine, upon which he and the other Englishmen attempted to carry the Vessel to some English port, which brought on a Quarrel, wherein the three Frenchmen were too many for the two Englishmen; however, the former were very Civil and gave the latter good Quarters. The next Day the Wind blew hard and obliged them to go to the northward, whereupon the Frenchmen agreed to put in at this port, where the English have an opportunity to return the Civilities they had received. *The American Weekly Mercury*, June 9, 1720

Apparently, true to the concept that business must go on despite a war, the American merchants and the enemy privateers reached an arrangement that, if the merchant ship were seized, a representative of the owner on board could contract with the privateer as to the worth of the vessel and cargo and agree to pay that sum, if permitted to complete his voyage. The Privateer would take someone a willing hostage, who would be ransomed when the owner fulfilled his bargain and paid the stipulated amount. The privateer would give the Merchantman a pass to show the other privateers who might capture them that they were in fact already "seized" and should be permitted to resume their voyage. Often, it did not work that way as the following indicates:

We find two letters (published in the Boston Papers) dated Bayonne Prison, August 17, last, that Arthur Edmond and John Dalley had been long confined there as Ransomers for the Vessels on board which they were taken; and had often wrote to the Merchants and Owners of said Vessels but received no Answer or Relief. The former was a Passenger aboard the Sloop Little Molly (belonging to Joseph Mains, Merchant, in Barbados) Richard Albany Master, loaded with King's Provisions, bound to Martinico and on the 3d Day of July, 1762 taken and ransom'd for 1600 Spanish Dollars, for the Payment of which he remains confined. The other (John Dalley) sailed from Elizabeth-Town, in the Sloop Two Friends, (belonging to Messrs. Woodruff and Galf of that Town), John Dorrington, Master, bound to St. Thomas, and, on the 17th of August 1761, was taken and ransom'd, for the Payment of which Ransom he is now a Prisoner at Bayonne aforesaid. *The Pennsylvania Journal*, February 2, 1764.

Two weeks later came the following response from the Captain of the Sloop Good Friends, explaining why John Dalley was still a captive in the French Prison and how it was not the fault of the Owners for leaving him there:

On the 5th of August 1761, I sailed from Sandy Hook, Master of the Sloop Good Friends, bound to St. Kitts, loaded with Lumber and Provision. . . On the 17th, we were taken by the French Ship commanded by Jaquez Ammile, bound to Marseilles, of whom I ransomed the Ship and Cargo for 1725 Dollars and the above John Dalley went Ransomer. On the 22d, we met with two other French Privateers, belonging to Martinico, who, after detaining us 12 Hours and taking from us 18 kegs of Bisquit and 2 Firkins of Butter, on sight of my Ransom Bill, let me go. On the 8th of September was taken by another French Privateer commanded by Capt. Del Caprongere, from Martinico, who refused to allow my Ransom Bill, tho' I had 9 Days good on it and sent me into Port St. Peiers, where I was confined in close Goal till the 29th of October and on the 30th was sent to Guadaloupe. While I was at Martininco, the Vessel and Cargo were sold and I was informed by an Officer of the Admiralty that I could not have a copy of the Condemnation because my vessel and Cargo were contested between the Factors of the Vessel of whom I ransomed and the Privateer who sent me in. When I was in Guadaloupe, I attested the above and made a proper Protest, a Certificate whereof (made before John Cruger, Esq. Mayor of the City of New York) was delivered to the Mother of John Dalley, in order to be sent to France.

This being a true State of Facts, the Vessel and Cargo having become an entire loss to the Owners, they do not think by the Laws of War, the said John Dalley can be detained a Prisoner as Ransomer of their Sloop, especially as they have been advised by Atwood Cowman, Mate of the said Sloop, that when at Martinico, some time since, he was told that the factors of the first Vessel had received the Full of the Ransom Bill, by Order of the Court of Admiralty of that Island.

John Dorrington

The New York Mercury, February 20, 1764

Indian Attacks along the Frontier

When the first Europeans arrived, the Atlantic coastline from the southern portion of Long Island down to the Virginia Capes and inland for hundreds of miles was the domain of a tribe of Indians who had named themselves the Lenni Lenape, meaning in their tongue, "the real people". They were a peaceful nation and, aside from an incident or two, like the following, relations between the Indians and the white settlers were generally good:

Pompton, September 3. A few Days agoe an Indian arrived here from Pechachquelly, who gives an account that some Time since several Indians had seized a Boy belonging to Solomon Jennings, supposed to be the noted Outlaw, whom they stript and whipt with Hickery Switches; Solomon, being then on his return homewards and hearing the Boy lament, hastened to rescue him and in his Way got a Stick of Wood somewhat like a Handspike, with which he assaulted the Indians and struck one of them on the Forehead so he split his Scull and the Indian died on the Spot. Another of the Indians made at Solomon with a Knife and job'd him in the side under his ribs and the other job'd a Knife into the upper Part of his Shoulder, upon which Solomon took to his Heels, for he perceived one of the Indians running for his Gun; he had not gone far before the Indian shot at him running, the Bullet graz'd along his Neck and under Jaw and took off the Skin all the Way. He escap'd, though very narrowly. *The New York Weekly Journal,* June 10, 1734

Cape May, July 17. Yesterday, the Coroner's Inquest viewed the Body of an Indian Man, said to be killed by Joseph Golden, an English Inhabitant here. Isaiah Sites being present and seeing the whole Difference, gave his Evidence at the Inquest, the Substance whereof was that Golden, having hired the Indian, along with another Indian Man and Woman, to pull some Flax, was to give them three quarts of Rum for their Labour, with which they got Drunk and quarreled with Golden, who then bid them to be gone from his House, but they refus'd going and gave him ill Language, whereupon a Quarrel ensued and many blows passing on both sides, Golden got a small Stick or Cudgel to drive them away, but the two Indians fell upon him and got him down, beat him very much and twisted his Neck so that he seemed in Danger of his Life; Sites endeavoured to Part them; at length, Golden, (with Sites help) got on his Legs and then took a larger stick in his hand to defend himself, bidding the Indians to keep off; but one of them coming violently at him, he struck him on the Head, knock'd him down and he died without speaking a Word more; It appearing that there was no difference between Golden and the Indians before that sudden Quarrel and that they had put him in fear of his Life, before he struck the blow, the Coroner's Inquest found it Manslaughter. *The Pennsylvania Gazette*, August 2, 1736

The colonists were careful to buy title to the lands from the Indians, although at token prices. The Crown was also anxious to appear open handed, with the law equally applied to both white and indian. Indian chiefs were prosecuted for murder of settlers and settlers were prosecuted for the murder of indians.

Perth-Amboy, June 23. This Day was held a Special Court for Trying of Wequalia, an Indian King[38]; he was found guilty of the Murder of John Leonard, late of this Place, and accordingly received a Sentence of Death in the presence of a great number of Christians and about 20 Indians, the latter of which was all well pleased at the justness of his Sentence and says that he had his Deserts; he should have received a Reward like this a long time ago for the Murdering of several of them. And the Interpreter being (two Days before the Tryal) in the Company with three other Indian Kings, who were attended by 50 other of their most Principal Men, the said Interpreter desired to know of them what they intended to do for said Wequalia or whether they had any Message to send by him or not, to whom, after they had by themselves considered of the Affair, they said "We have thought of this Matter and desire you will tell Wequalia, that we neither have, nor intend to do, any thing in this Affair; it is he who wronged the English, not us, and therefore he must himself make them Satisfaction without expecting any Assistance or hearing any more from us.", which Message the Interpreter faithfully delivered unto the said Wequalia, at his Tryal not having an Opportunity to do it sooner, and, on Friday next, he is to be Executed at this Place, whose wretched example we hope will deter all his Indian Spectators from committing any acts of the like kind. *The Weekly News-Letter*, July 13, 1727

New-York, August 21. We have an Account from New Jersey that a number of Indians are come to the Plantation of the late King Wequalia (who was executed for the Murder of Capt. John Leonard) in order to Crown a New King in the Room of said Wequalia. *The New England Weekly Journal*, August 28, 1727

---

[38] In 1709, Wequalia, then a Sachem, had assisted the British in recruiting Indians from the Jersey region to battle the French in Canada.

A murder and robbery was lately committed near Minisink, New-Jersey, on the body and effects of an Oneida Indian, who had come to trade there, supposed, by one Robert Simonds or Seaman, who was taken up and confined in Sussex goal, but was rescued, and has since fled. Governor Franklin has issued a Proclamation, offering a reward of One Hundred Dollars for apprehending said Simonds. *The Pennsylvania Journal*, April 17, 1766

By his Excellency
William Franklin, Esquire

Captain General and Governour in Chief and over his Majesty's Province of New Jersey, Chancellor and Vice Admiral in the same &c.

A Proclamation

Whereas I have received information from one of the Principal Officers of the County of Sussex, that a most inhuman Murder and Robbery has been lately committed near Minisink on the body and effects of an Oneida Indian, who had come to trade there and had behaved himself soberly and discreetly and that one Robert Simonds, alias Seamon, has been charged with the same and was on the second day of April Instant committed to the common Goal of the County aforesaid, from whence he was rescued in the Night of the same Day about ten o'clock, by an armed Mob of twenty five Men. And whereas it is the indispensable Duty, and for the Honour of every Government to punish the Perpetrators of such atrocious crimes, committed against the Laws of God and Man and in manifest Violation of the solemn Treaties subsisting between his Majesty and the Indians, which have hitherto been inviolably kept by them with respect to the people of this Colony. And, as the Murder and Robbery aforesaid may greatly endanger the Peace and Security of the Frontiers and introduce all the Horrors and Calamities of an Indian War, I do therefore strictly charge and command all Officers, civil and military, within this Colony (particularly those residing in the County of Sussex) to use their utmost endeavours to take, and in goal secure, the said Simonds, alias Seamon, and such other person or persons whom they have sufficient reason to suspect guilty of the aforementioned Murder and Robbery or of the Rescue of the said Simonds, alias Seamon from the Goal and, on their commitment, to raise and keep a sufficient Guard to secure the Goal from being broke open or the Prisoners rescued. And in order to encourage his Majesty's liege subjects to exert themselves in the Pursuit and apprehending the said Simonds, alias Seamon and every Person or Persons concerned in the Murder and Robbery aforesaid, I do promise that the Person or Persons who shall, after the date hereof, apprehend the said Simonds, alias Seamon or any Person guilty in the Murder and Robbery aforesaid, shall, upon conviction of the Offender, receive from the Treasury of this Province, ONE HUNDRED DOLLARS reward. And I do likewise in the most earnest Manner recommend it to the Inhabitants of this colony, to behave with Kindness, Humanity and Justice to such Indians who shall visit the Frontiers in a Friendly Manner, as such a Conduct will have a tendency to perpetuate the Blessings and Advantages of Peace.

Given under my Hand and Seal at Arms, at the City of Burlington, in said Province, the fifteenth day of April, in the Sixth Year of His Majesty's reign, Anno Domini one thousand seven hundred and sixty six.

By His Excellency's Command
                    William Franklin
Charles Read, Secretary
The Pennsylvania Journal, April 24, 1766

Burlington, in New-Jersey, July 3. A Horrid Murder was last Week committed near Moore's Town, in the County of Burlington, on the Bodies of two well known Indian Women of that Neighborhood, supposed from strong Circumstances to have been perpetrated by two Men travelling to New York. One of the Persons is apprehended and confesses he was present at the Murder and gives the following Description of his Companion; that he is a Scotchman, about 18 or 20 Years of Age, wears his own Hair, light coloured, has no Beard, but a white Down on his Chin; one Leg sore and thereby is lame, a pair of whitish Stockings, one of which was stained with the Blood of the Indians, a whitish short Coat or Jacket, old leather Breeches, old shoes, too large for him, of Calf-skin with the Grain out and remarkable high Quarters. He says his name is James M'Kinsey and that he was a servant to a Scotch Officer, killed at Pittsburgh and that he was travelling to New York to his Master's Widow. And, as some of the Inhabitants have seen the Person now confined in Company with such a Man, and they travelled very slow, it is hoped that the Person above described may be apprehended and for the doing of which the Government will make suitable Satisfaction. The Inhabitants of this and the Neighbouring Provinces are requested to use their utmost Endeavours to apprehend a Person suspected of having committed a Murder, attended with many marks of Cruelty and Barbarity. *The Pennsylvania Gazette*, July 10, 1766.

On Thursday last James M'Kinsey, the Person mentioned in our Gazette of the Tenth Instant, as being suspected of the Murder and Robbery of two Indian Women near Moore's Town, in the Jerseys, was taken up here [Cumberland County], and examined before the Mayor of the City; and, altho' he did not confess that he was guilty of the horrid Deed, yet as he said it was done by James Annin, who was in Company with him and now in custody, as one of the Murderers (and who, we hear, told exactly the same story with respect to him, M'Kinsey) he was immediately sent to Burlington Goal. *The Pennsylvania Gazette*, July 17, 1766.

At a court of Oyer and Terminer, held at Burlington on Wednesday the thirtieth day of July last, came on the trial of James Anen, aged 54 years, and James M'Kenzy, aged 19 years, on an indictment for the murder of two Indian women, named Hannah and Catherine, who had long resided in the neighborhood of the place where the murder was committed. It appeared by their own examinations and by the testimony of credible witnesses that they had been on the western frontier of Pennsylvania and Virginia, but that their first acquaintance began in Philadelphia; that they came to Moorestown in the County of Burlington on Thursday the 26th of June last, about noon, begged for charity and obtained relief; that, while they were eating their dinners, the two Indians who were murdered came to the place where they were and that the youngest of the men gave them abusive language; that the Indians went off and rested by the wood near the side of the road; that one of them was possessed of a clean shift & the other of a new piece of Linen that they had that day got; that about two o'clock on the same day, James Anen sold the shift and James M'Kenzy the piece of new linen and a blanket about two miles from Moores-town; that they were parted by accident and that many people had seen the Indians laying in view of the road and had supposed them asleep, till Sunday, the 29th of June, when two persons perceived a stench, and on going near the bodies, found that they were dead; whereupon the coroner was called, whose inquest found them to be murdered by persons unknown. On this alarm the two persons were suspected and pursued. James Anen was apprehended and committed to the Goal at Burlington and the other advertised from the description given by Anen, and in a few days taken up by the Order of the Mayor of Philadelphia and sent to Burlington. The examination of the prisoners, taken before they had the opportunity of seeing each other, was read and by each examination it appeared that they went to the Indians with the intent to ravish them, if they should refuse their offers; each acknowledged that he was present at the murder, but charged the giving of the stroke on the other, and also acknowledged the taking of the goods; in this they persisted at the bar. The jury soon found them guilty and they received the sentence of death.

On Friday noon they were hanged at the gallows. They continued denying the fact and charging it on each other. The elder declared he thought it a duty to extirpate the heathen, and just before they were turned off, M'Kenzy, the younger of the men, acknowledged that one of the women, on receiving the blow from Anen, struggled violently, and that he, to put her out of her pain, sunk the hatchet in her head, but that they were both knocked down by Anen. The youngest of the squaws was near the time of delivery and had marks of shocking treatment which the most savage nations on earth could not have surpassed.

A few of the principal Indians are Jersey were desired to attend the trial and execution, which they did, and behaved with remarkable sobriety. *The Pennsylvania Journal,* August 7, 1766

This dying Leni Lenape chief had a nobility of character about him (matched by a disappointment in his sons) that was captured, like a modern day snapshot, by the colonial newspaper.

Philadelphia, January 19. The following is the Speech of an Indian King, named Oppekhorsa, who died lately in the Jerseys, spoken just before his Death to his Successor. The Gentleman, who, by letter, communicated this to us, makes the following remarks thereon: "You will therein find a true greatness of Soul, worthy of a King and a deep Sense of unshaken Honesty & a Humility, which even Christians might boast of, with many other Beauties of Sense, couch'd under strong Rhetorical Figures, dictated by pure Reason and simple Nature alone."

The Speech

My Brother's Son,

This Day I deliver my Heart into thy Bosom and would have thee love that which is Good and keep good Company and to refuse that which is Evil and to avoid bad Company.

Now, in as much as I have delivered my Heart into thy Bosom, I also deliver my Bosom to keep my Heart therein; therefore, always be sure to walk in a good Path and never depart out of it; and, if any Indian should speak any Evil of Indians or Christians, do not joyn with it, but look to that which is good and joyn with the same always. Look at the Sun from the Rising of it to the setting of the same. In Speeches that shall be made between the Indians and the Christians, if anything be spoke that is evil, do not joyn with that, but with that which is good. And, when Speeches are made, do not speak first, but let all speak before Thee and take good Notice what each man speaks and when thou has heard all, joyn with that which is good.

Brother's Son,

I would have thee to cleanse thy ears and take all Darkness and Foulness out, that thou may take notice of that which is Good and Evil and then to joyn with that which is Good and refuse the Evil; and also to Cleane thy Eyes that thou may see both Good and Evil and, if thou see any Evil, not to joyn with it, but to joyn that which is Good.

Brother's Son,

Thou has heard all that is past; now I would have thee stand up (he means by standing up to be resolute) in Time of Speeches and to stand in my Steps and to follow my Speeches, which I have said before thee, then what thou dost desire in Reason be granted thee. Why shouldst thou not follow my Example in as much as I have had a Mind to that which is Good; therefore do thou also the same. Whereas, my son Sheoppy and Swampis were appointed Kings in my stead, and I understand by my Doctor that Sheoppy secretly advis'd him not to cure me and they both being with me at John Hollingshead's House, there I myself saw by them, that they were more given to Drink than to take Notice of my last words, having then had a Mind to make a Speech to them and to my Brethren the English Commissioners, therefore I have refused them to be Kings after me in my stead and have chosen Thee Oppekhorsa, my Bother's son, to be King in their stead to succeed me.

Brother's Son, I desire thee to be plain and fair with all, both Indians and Christians, as I have been; I am very weak; otherwise I would have spoken more. *The New England Weekly Journal*, March 1, 1732

It was only in the latter half of the 1700s that New Jersey began to have Indian problems, attacks by Indians from New York and Pennsylvania, excited by the French as a tactic in their ongoing wars with England. These were not Leni Lenapes, but Iroquois.[39]

---

[39] By this time, New Jersey's native American population had already been decimated. In 1758, all title to New Jersey lands had acquired from them in exchange for 3,000 acres in a Burlington County reservation, named Brotherton. By then, only sixty members of the tribe were still left. In 1802, they left Burlington and moved to a region near Lake Oneida in New York, near New Stockbridge. They joined another band of Indians but this did not prevent their numbers from continuing to dwindle to about forty. They moved again to Wisconsin, near Green Bay, along the Fox river where they had bought some from the Menomonie Indians. Finally, they moved to Oklahoma, where their descendants of the Leni Lenape can still be found.

The fall and winter of 1755 and the spring of 1756 signalled an onslaught of indian raids that were to last all summer and even spill over to 1757 and 1758. Witnesses these war dispatchs from the frontiers of north western New Jersey, including a series regarding the Moravian Settlement of Gnaden-hutton:

Extract of a Letter from Sussex County, in New Jersey, dated November 26, 1755

Sir,

To my great Sorrow and Grief, I must acquaint you with the melancholy Situation we are in, surrounded by a great Number of cruel and barbarous Enemy, as it is certain, two Nights ago the Town called Gnaden-hutton of the Moravians is burnt down to the Ground and all the People barbarously murdered and only three escaped, two Men and a Boy, scarce twenty Miles distant from us. And last Night there was one House burnt down six Miles from us and by all Reports the Enemy is of great Force and we are weak in number. And it is unknown to you how our Country lies exposed to the barbarous Enemy, as I suppose, we lay sixty Miles on the Frontiers, exposed to the Enemy. Therefore, I beg you will not fail so that we may stop their entrance into this part of the Province. For, if we are cut off, it will give them great Foothold in this Province. Pray let your proceedings be with speed, for we are weak in number and scarce of Arms and Ammunition. Pray acquaint his Excellency of our Melancholy Situation. And this by Expression great haste conclude,
> your dutiful and obedient friend to serve
> Abraham Van Campen

The New York Mercury, December 1, 1755

Since our last we have received the following extract of a Letter from Easton, in Northhampton County, dating the 27th ult, relating to the Cutting off the Moravian Settlement at Gnadenhutton: "The Affair at Gnadenhutton is really very affecting; while the People were at Supper, the Indians, about twelve in number, as some say that had the good Fortune to escape, were about the House and in a very rude manner demanded Admittance, which the people were very unwilling to allow them; however, at length, a Lad rose from the Table and opened the Door and immediately an Indian fired into the House, which lightly grazed along the Lad's chin and killed one of the Persons at the Table, whereupon a most sad and lamentable Cry was heard all over the House. One Woman ran out of doors and they forced her back; some attempted to run upstairs but were torn down again; In short, they killed five in the House, who were all burned and consumed in the Flames. One Man that got out of the House was shot in the Back and also had three or four Blows in his Body by a Tomahawk; him they also scalped. . . The Dwelling House, Meeting House and all their Out-Houses were burnt to Ashes, with all the Grain and Hay, all the Horses and more than forty Head of fat Cattle for the use of the Brethren at Bethlehem and other Settlements. . .

The following is the Substance of an Affidavit made by Moses Totamy, an Indian Convert to the Christian Religion, who bears the character of a sober, honest and conscientious Person, before Mr. Justice Anderson, of New Jersey, to wit, that on or about the 22d of November last that he was informed by Isaac Stille and some other Indians that an Indian Lad named Jemmy came down from Queycake to the Forks of Delaware, where his Mother and one Joe Peepy and Wife and some other Indians there resided and gave them Notice that the Gap of the Mountain was then open and would remain so all the next Day, to give a free Passage for all the Indians in that Neighbourhood to return to their friends at Neskopecka but that, if they refused, this Invitation, they would meet with the same, nay worse, treatment than the white People; that great Numbers of the Alleghany, Shawanese, Mohawks, Tuscarora's and Delaware Indians had divided themselves into Companies under their proper Officers and were determined to destroy the Back Inhabitants of Pennsylvania, particularly the Minisinks, Forks of Delaware, Tulpehocken and Swatarrow, all in one Day and that the Moravian Settlement of Gnadenhutton would be first cut off; that the Indians of the above Nation had become so numerous at Neskopecka, Wioming and Shamokin that they were not to be counted and that more were coming daily to them; that thereupon the Lad, Jemmy's Mother, his Father-in-Law Amos and Joe Peepy went with him to Neskopecka. . . . and that the Deponent, upon the Credit of the above Report was removing his Family from the Forks to Trenton for Safety. *The Pennsylvania Gazette*, December 4, 1755

Last Saturday Sen'night, the People of New Providence in the Western Part of the Borough of Elizabeth, hearing fresh Reports of the Designs of the Enemy upon the Settlements in the Forks of Delaware. . . immediately set out and the next Day arrived at Easton where they found the People in the utmost Consternation and Distress as they had just received Intelligence of a Body of 1500 French and Indians within 60 Miles of them. . .and that they have killed great Numbers of People. And the People at the Forks have good Intelligence that the Enemy are determined to make a Descent on them before the light Nights of this Moon are past. A Friend Indian who deserted them says they say among themselves: "Now is the Time. The Barns are full and the Cattle are fat." *The New York Mercury*, December 15, 1755

The Country all above Easton for Fifty Miles, is mostly evacuated and ruined, excepting only the Neighbourhood of the Depuys five Families, which stand their Ground. The People are chiefly fled into the Jerseys. Many of them have thrashed out their Corn and carried it off with their Cattle and best Household Goods; but a vast deal is left to the Enemy. Numbers offered half their Corn, Cows, Goods, etc to save the Rest but could not obtain Assistance enough to move them in time. The Enemy made but few Prisoners, murdering almost all that fell into ther Hands of all Ages and both Sexes. *The Pennsylvania Journal*, January 1, 1756

Elizabeth Town, January 22. This Day arrived an Express from Captain Salnave, at Col. Van Camps, the Purport of whose Packet is that on Tuesday last the Captain discovering a Fire over Delaware at one Depuys, he crossed the River with about twenty five of his Men and, when he came up, found the House beset by upwards of fifty Indians, all busy in setting fire to it and murdering the Inhabitants; notwithstanding the Inequality of the Number, he engaged them so warmly that in a few Minutes Time he oblig'd them to give Way. . . and [they] directly took to the Woods, from whence Captain Salnave soon routed them and pursued them over the Mountain, observing the Enemy to carry off their Dead on Horseback, whilst he had but one of his Men wounded and not one killed. When Capt. Salnave entered Depey's House he found two Men killed and three wounded besides 18 or 20 other Persons, Men, Women and Children, all of whom would inevitably been reduced with the House to Ashes[40] had not the Captain and his Men opportunely come to their Relief. *The New York Mercury*, January 26, 1756

We also hear from Goshen that the Inhabitants of a Place called Little Britain in New Jersey, near that Place, to the Number of 70 Men, gathered together on Monday last and went out with their Arms and 7 Days Provisions against the Indians, determined to kill and destroy every one that they met. *The Pennsylvania Gazette*, March 11, 1756.

New York, March 29. About two Weeks ago, the Barn of one Westfall, at Minisink, was burned by the Indians with 24 Cows, 9 Horses and about 400 Bushels of Wheat. *The Pennsylvania Journal*, April 1, 1756.

We have advice from Sussex County New Jersey that the House of Mr. Anthony Swartwout was attacked about the 21st of May. The Wife of said Swartwout was found shot dead with a Bullet thro' the Back and three

---

[40] A subsequent news account indicates that the Indians tried a second time a few weeks later to burn down the same house and that time were successful.

Children were found a little distance from the House, with their Heads split open with a Hatchet, but none of them were scalped; and that Anthony Swartwout and the other of his Children are missing, supposed to be carried off by the Enemy.

We have also advice that the house of Capt. Hunt in Hardwick Township in Sussex County was burnt about the same Time and a white lad about 17 Years of Age and a Negro Man, who had the Care of the House are both missing and several Indian Tracks were seen. *The Pennsylvania Journal*, June 3, 1756.

New York, June 7. About a Fortnight ago, the House of one Capt. Hunt, at Paulin's Kills, 25 miles above Black River, in New Jersey, was burnt by the Indians and Hunt's Brother and a Negro Man are missing and are supposed carried off or cruelly murdered by the Savages. About two or three Days after, the House of one Swartwout, near Paulin's Kills also, was burnt by the Indians. Swartwout himself and three Children are missing and his Wife and two Children are killed. A Ball went through the Woman's Back and lodged in her Breast and the Throat of one of the Children was cut quite across. 'Tis imagined this Murder was done in the open Day, as none of the People were scalped, perhaps owing to the Temerity of the Indians lest they may be surprized unawares; and by the Children being found with Dead Flowers in their hands, which 'twas supposed they must have been gathering a few Hours before. As this Murder has been perpetrated several Miles nigher the Inhabitants of New Jersey than where the Forts have lately been built, upwards of 60 Families at and near Paulin's Kills have removed down towards Amwell, in order to avoid the Danger they seemed exposed to by their cruel bloodthirsty and latent enemies. *The New York Mercury*, June 7, 1756.

Philadelphia, June 24. We hear from the Jerseys that on the 12th Instant, four Officers, with 25 Men each, set out from Paulin's Kill toward the Great Swamp, in Search of Indians and they returned on the 19th, after burning four Indian Towns, one of which was the Shawanese Town, over the Sasquehanna, but they all appeared to have been deserted some Months past. They brought six Horses in with them. *The Pennsylvania Gazette*, June 24, 1756

Perth Amboy, August 19. We have certain Accounts from the Northern Frontier of this Province, that on Thursday last, Abraham Vanaken, Esq., a Justice of the Peace of the County of Sussex, was shot through the left Arm and had one of the Fingers of his Hand shot off by an Indian who had concealed himself in the Cellar of an old House in one of

Vanaken's fields; and as he was driving his Team loaded with Grain, his Daughter who had been helping him being on Top of the Load, the Indian fired upon him; upon which Vamnaken called to his Daughter to jump off the Load and to run for her Life. The Girl on leaping down happened to fall and the Indian was going to dispatch her with his Tomahawk, which the father perceiving, wounded as he was, made to the Indian with his Pitch-fork and saved his daughter from the Stroke. And Vanaken's Son, coming with his Gun at the same time the Indian fled, and when he was got to the End of the Field, they saw two other Indians join him but they all ran away. This was done within a Mile of Cole's Fort, upon Mahakamack River, near Delaware. Justice Vanaken lay so ill of his wounds that his Life was in great Danger.

We have a further Account from the same Place that on Friday last, three Men, to wit Gerardus Swartwout, eldest son of Major Swartwout, Samuel Finch and Peter Westphalen, were found murdered and stipt quite naked and Swartwout and Finch scalped by the Indians, some miles higher up the River Mahakamack and within the Province of New York. *The Pennsylvania Gazette*, August 26, 1756

Last Thursday Morning, about a Mile on the West Side of the Wallkill, two men were fired upon as they were in the Field at Work by a Party of Indians, but missed them; . . . two of the Indians set off to catch them, but, as they ran different courses, they both escaped and that Night got safe to their Neighbours. This day it is reported by some Minisink people that Major Swartout is carried off by the Indians. He went last Week to a Place called Besha's Land, to fetch some horses he had there, and not returning in the Evening, they found one Horse shot in the Field, and his throat cut, and ten taken away, but can hear no further of the Major. *The Pennsylvania Journal*, August 26, 1756

New York, September 6. We hear from New Jersey, that on Sunday Night, the 29th last past, 3 Men arrived at Elizabeth Town in a poor, weak and starving Condition, to wit, Thomas Sherby, Benjamin Stringer and John Denite, who had been prisoners among the Indians and were almost naked, having only old Indian Blankets about them to cover their nakedness. They made their escape from the Indians at a Place, called Jenango or Venango, an Indian Town, situate near the Head of the Sasquehannah and were 32 Days in the Woods, during which Time they suffered great Hardships for want of food and were obliged to eat Rattle Snakes, Black Snakes, Frogs, and such vermin and sometimes they could find nothing to eat for days together. The first settlements they made where they found any Inhabitants was the upper Fort, upon the Delaware River in New Jersey, called Cole's Fort, and from thence they were sent under a Guard to Elizabeth Town for fear that the White People should annoy them, they looking more like Indians than Christians, being very swarthy and their Hair cut by the Savages after the Indian fashion and dressed only in Indian Blankets. Springer says he was taken prisoner the 22nd Day of May last, when being at work at one Anthony Swartwout's in Sussex County New Jersey about ten o'Clock in the Morning, two Indians attacked the House and shot Swartwout's wife dead on the Spot. They the seized Swartwout and Springer and three of the Indians drove Springer away with a Negroe, who they had taken the Night before at Capt. Hunt's in the same County, making them run all the way, until they came to the River Delaware, which they crossed on a Raft of Rails, about 8 Miles above Col. Van Campen's. When they got about a Mile and a Half into Pennsylvania, they waited in the Bushes for the two Indians that were left with Swartwout and his Children; and in about an Hour and a Half, the two Indians came to them with only two of Swartwout's Children, a Girl about 12 Years old and a Boy about 9. These Children told Springer that the Indians had killed three of the Children of the House and had killed and scalped their Father about 7 Miles from the House, near a Brook, where they likewise killed their little Sister and threw her inn the Brook. The Indians then carried Springer, Swartwout's two Children and the Negroe to the Indian Towns where they dispersed them about. Hunt's Negroe told Springer that young Hunt, Brother to Captain Hunt, who was also taken Prisoner with him, was killed by the Indians in endeavouring to make his escape from them. This is the first intelligence we have had of the Swartwouts and his Children and of young Hunt and his Negroe, since they were missing in May last, when Captain Hunt's House was burned to the Ground.

Sherby says he was made Prisoner at Juanita, in Pennsylvania, by six Indians at the House of Daniel Williams in December last, when Williams himself was killed and Sherby and Williams's Wife carried into Captivity. Denite was taken Prisoner in the back Parts of Maryland by 7 Indians, in May last, as he and another were splitting rails, who were both carried into Captivity. They were all three taken care of at Elizabeth Town and a Collection was made for them to cloath them and to enable them to travel to their several Places of Abode. *The Pennsylvania Gazette*, September 8, 1756

Elizabeth Town, June 10. Last Sunday morning three Indians who were fed the Day before by a Person from Hyndshaw's Fort, fired upon 8 Men and 2 Women in a Scow going over from our Fort in Walpack, to Hyndshaw's Fort. They killed Stosel Demak, wounded his Wife tho' both Thighs near the Knee, thought to be Mortal, and her Sister through the Side, grazed the Ribs. On Wednesday, some Indians called to our Men at Cole's Fort, to come out, but only being a Serjeant and 7 Men, they refused. The same Evening, the Indians were heard on the Hill near Hyndshaw's Fort, which is opposite to Walpack. *The Pennsylvania Journal*, June 23, 1757

New York, July 25. Monday last came to Town in 31 Days, from Niagra, two young men, one named Peter Luney from Virginia and the other William Phalps, an Apprentice to Joseph Wright of this City, Shipwright. The latter was taken at Oswego, the 11th of May, 1756, in Company with Charles Carter of Philadelphia and James Flanagan and Lewis Dunning of New Jersey, cutting Timbers for the Vessels then building on Lake Ontario and informs us that Dunning, being wounded by a Shot from the Indians and unable to keep Pace with them in their March, they killed and scalped him, on their Way to Niagra, where they arrived in four Days after being taken; that Carter and Flanagan were soon sent to Montreal, but one of the Indians adopting him as a Son, he was obliged to go with him to their Country, where he remained all Summer and was used extremely well by them. *The Pennsylvania Journal*, July 28, 1757

New York, September 12. Saturday last, one John Cotes, who lately lived in Conojohary, In Albany County, passed by here in his Way to New Jersey; but first gave the following Account viz. that some Time last Week there were 46 Persons carried off by the French and Indians from the German Flats . . . that Numbers of the (pretended) Friend Indians were seen among the Enemy, that the Inhabitants were all moving away . . . and that the Enemy, it was thought, consisted of some Hundreds, pillaging and ravaging the Country and captivating or scalping all they come across, Cotes himself being one among the Fugitives. *The Pennsylvania Gazette*, September 15, 1757

Extract of a Letter from Lieutenant Rickey, dated at the Head Quarters, on the Frontiers of New Jersey, November 17, 1757.

" Sir, I have the melancholy News to tell you that your Friend John Doty was killed, scalped and butchered in a Barbarous Manner yesterday, within two Miles of the Fort, as was likewise Serjeant Mahurin. There was a Soldier with them, all on Horseback, when five Indians in Ambush fired, killed the two and shot thro' the Soldier's Great Coat, when he immediately got down. One of the Savages ran toward him with a Tomahawk but the Soldier fired his Piece and stopt him, then took up Doty's Piece and snapped it (for by Doty's fall he had hurt the Lock), however he kept it presented until he mounted and rode off. This alarmed the People but as of yet we have discovered nothing more than the usual marks, a Quantity of Blood. The Soldier is positive he killed one of them. The Inhabitants on the whole Frontier are so terrified that they are moving, the rest gathering together and stockading themselves in the Best Manner they can." *The Pennsylvania Gazette*, December 1, 1757

Extract of a Letter from Capt. Jonathan Hampton, dated the Headquarters, on the Frontiers of New Jersey, May 17.

Yesterday, I was at Nominack Fort at Minisink when I examined the Wife of Nicholas Cole and her Son Jacob, about ten years old, who said that the Day before, about Two o'Clock in the Afternoon, thirteen Indians rushed into the House, her Husband being from Home, when they immediately pinioned the old Lady and tomahawked her Son in Law, 18 years old, lying asleep on the bed, dragged her out of doors, where lay her eldest daughter, aged 13, a Boy, aged 8 and her youngest Daughter, aged 4 Years. They were all scalped and the poor helpless old Woman saw the infernal fiends run their spears into her gasping and dying infant. They afterwards rifled the House, then carried her and her Son Jacob off.. . . As four [of our soldiers] were going to one Chamber's, they heard the Indians coming down the Hill into the main road to cross the Delaware, when one of the four firing on them, the Indians immediately fled, giving a Yell. The Woman they led with a String around her Neck, the Boy by the Hand, who both finding themselves loose made their escape along the Road and happily met at James M'Carty's. . . The Woman says they [the Indians] could talk English and Dutch and she is assured one is a White-man. . . *The New American Magazine* for May, 1758

New York, June 12. The Beginning of last week four People were killed by the Enemy, at Cole's Fort, on the Frontiers of New Jersey, and by the great number of Beds found in the Woods thereabouts, 'tis imagined there are not less than an Hundred Indians on the East side of the River. *The New York Mercury*, June 12, 1758

New York, August 28. The 11th Instant Jacobus Middah and his Son were fired upon by the Indians in a Field near Cole's-Fort on the Frontiers of New Jersey: The Boy was killed on the Spot and Middah died a few Minutes after he got into the Fort.

And last Friday Week, a Woman was killed and two others carried off by the Indians also, within a few Rod of Gardiner's Fort on the Frontiers of New Jersey likewise. *The New York Mercury*, August 28, 1758

Finally, a truce was negotiated among a number of Indian tribes and the Royal Governors of Pennsylvania and New York, which kept the peace, at least along the Jersey frontier, for a few years.

New York, November 13. This day his excellency the Governor returned from the treaty at Easton, which he had been attending with the governor of Pennsylvania, near three weeks. There were present at the Treaty five hundred Indians, about two hundred of which were chiefs and warriors and of thirteen different Nations, namely, the eight Confederate Nations viz. the Mohawks, Onondaga, Senecas, Oneidas, Cayugas, Tuscaroros, Nanticokes and Conoys, now united into one; and the Tuteloes; and five Nations dependent upon the Confederate, viz the Delawares, the Unamies, Minisinks, Opings and Mohegans. There were also present two Indian Messengers from the Indians settled on the Ohio, who brought a message in writing signed by fifteen chiefs of the Ohio indians, expressing their desire to have peace with the English and their intention to accede to this treaty.

The conferences were carried on with great harmony. The Indians solemnly promised to return all the English prisoners. A message was sent to the Ohio Indians, accompanied by two English officers, a chief of the confederates and several other indians, informing them what has been done at this treaty and inviting them to accede thereto. And peace was formally ratified by a large peace belt, which was delivered by the two governors to the confederate chiefs and by them handled round to all the Indians present.

In the course of this treaty, his excellency our governor satisfied all Indians that had or pretended to have any claim of lands in the Province of New Jersey except English or private rights. And releases there of were executed and acknowledged in the presence of several of the chiefs of the confederate nations, who attested the same m and were afterwards published in open council; and his excellency governor Bernard gave a large belt to the confederate chiefs, to be a perpetual memorial that the Province of New Jersey was now wholly discharged from all Indian claims. *The Pennsylvania Journal*, November 16, 1758

This, however, did not solve all the problems as the French continued to encourage Indian attacks elsewhere in neighboring New York, which impacted Jersey settlors and soldiers alike. In fact, the terror caused by the

*indians resulted in the Governor's issuing a proclamation, terming the
Delawares "enemies, rebels and traitors" and declaring war on them.
Rewards were offered: $150 for capturing a male over 15 alive; $130 for
killing a male over 15 and producing his scalp; $130 for capturing any
woman and men under 15 alive; $150 for rescuing a captured colonist;
friendly indians were advised to move to interior and ferrymen were enjoined
from taking any indian over either the Delaware or Raritan rivers. In at least
one instance reported in the press, this proclamation resulted in four white
mens' killing the wife and children of a friendly indian so as to get their
scalps to turn in for the reward.*

*Because the Indians were encouraged by the French, who were
Catholic, anti-papist news accounts helped sway the colonists' hates and
fears:*

From Albany we learn that a French Priest, named Picquet, moved on
with the Enemy to Oswego, till just before they began the Attack, exhorting
the Men to do their Duty and advising them to give the English no Quarter.
The Pennsylvania Gazette, July 26, 1759

*In the summer of 1763, there was another period of border warfare
with the Indians. Much of the fighting happened in New York but Jersey men
were among the fighters and the fighting extended to the New Jersey frontier.
Things did not go well for the British colonists in the early days of the strife.*

New York, October 3. Extract of a Letter from Niagara, dated
September 16, 1763. "I have just time to tell you that we arrived safe at
Niagara the 13th Instant, delay'd much at Lake Ontario by hard Gales and
Storms of Rain; next day had an Express from Little Niagara (a Post above
the Falls) that our Convoy, with the Team employed to carry Provisions to
Lake Erie, was attacked; we sent off from our Fort a Reinforcement
immediately, consisting of a Major and about 70 Men, which was followed
by a Captain and 50 Men, an Hour after to support them. The Whole of the
Indians amounted, to the best count, about Three Hundred, divided into two
Bodies, one of which, the most inconsiderable, was that which attacked the
Convoy, the other lay in Ambush about 2 or 3 Miles nigher our Post, near
the carrying place and possessed themselves, of a most advantageous Piece
of rising Ground near the Road, to intercept Succours. On the first hearing
of the firing by the Convoy, Captain Johnston and three Subalterns marched
with about 80 Men, mostly Gage's Light Infantry, who were in a little Camp
adjacent; they had scarce Time to form when the Indians appeared at the
above Pass. Our People fired briskly on them but were instantly surrounded
and the Captain who commanded mortally wounded the first Fire. The two

Subalterns were soon after killed, on which general confusion ensued. The Indians rushed in on all Sides and cut between Sixty and Seventy Men in Pieces including the Convoy. Ten of our Men is all we can learn has escaped. They came through the Woods yesterday. From the many Circumstances, 'tis believed the Senecas has a Chief Hand in this Affair. I wish our Affairs at Detroit will not suffer by this, as all the Oxen and Teams on the Carrying Place is destroyed and the Horses missing, which 'tis thought were driven off by the Indians. Our Reinforcements came up too late to save them so they returned that Night and next Day march'd and buried all they could find; most of those that came in are wounded; we are in a pretty situation. . .

Another letter from Niagara, the same Date as the foregoing

"Most of the Provisions that were on our Sloop that was cast away on her Voyage to Detroit was saved and the People under the direction of Capt. Montesor intrenched themselves; Capt. Cochran, with 900 Men, was sent from hence to succour them and take the Command. The Indians attacked Capt. Montesor in his unfinished encampment, and after killing him three Men, were repulsed. The 12th Instant, Capt. McLeod, of the 80th, with 10 Officers, 200 Men, 2 Scows, 20 Batteaus, set off in Order to join Capt. Cochran, whose entrenchment was at the Catfish Creek, 12 Miles from the Mouth of the River . . . The 13th in the Morning, a Party, with a Sarjeant, 20 Oxen & 16 Horse were sent off, and with them Capt. Thomas Johnston, of Amboy, and Mr. Stedman, our Sutler. . . . At ten 0'Clock, Stedman returned on Horseback and said that about three Miles from the Landing, between two Bridges, in a Thicket, Sixty Indians, all naked, attacked the Party to which he belonged and killed all but himself; and in deed on burying the Dead, we found that he had not deviated far from the Truth. Lieutenant Campbell, who commanded at the Landing, hearing the Firing, took part of two Companies . . . in order to succour our People, but he was soon also attacked, in a Situation so disadvantageous to him, that his Men could not do their Duty and in a short time the whole Party, save Two, . . . were either killed or taken; we imagine Mr. Campbell made a noble Resistance with a few of his People, as his Body, with several others, were found lying together. On making a Computation of the Loss, it was found that Lieut. Campbell, Lieut. Frazier and 78 Men of the Light Infantry, with Lieut. Rosco of the Artillery, Capt. Johnston of New Jersey, Lieut. Dayton and 8 Drivers are missing and also supposed to be killed, as we have reason to think that the Indians made no Prisoners. . . . All the Oxen are killed, but no Horses, that we know, the Enemy having carried them all away. *The Pennsylvania Journal*, October 7, 1763.

On Tuesday last we received the following melancholy Advice from Northampton County viz. that on Sunday the 16th Instant, the Laghowexin Settlement, on a Branch of the Delaware betwixt Wyoming and the Minesinks, was cut off by the Indians, when nine People were killed and four wounded, one of which and two Boys had got into Upper Smithfield. That on Thursday last a Party of the Enemy rushed into a House in Allemingle Township and tomahawked the Man, his Wife and four Children and a fifth is said to be missing. And that on Saturday the following Persons were killed in a Flat going over to the Jersies, viz. Stephen Brink, Garret Brink, Esther Brink, Peter Vangarda, Benjamin Raur and a Negro Woman; Jacob Shoemaker and Samuel Guin missing. These People had moved their Families into the Jerseys, but had come over to milk their Cows, and were on their return back again when the Enemy fired on them.

And from Sussex County in the Jerseys, we learn that the Indians have been seen in different parts thereof. *The Pennsylvania Journal*, October 27, 1763

Indeed, so poorly were things going for the colonists that it was necessary to appeal to God and Country for inspiration:

When we hear continually of the Depredations of the Indians upon the English and every Government silent about either Revenge or Resentment and no Encouragement given to endeavour to chastise these Savages, will it be a Transgression to inquire what is become of British Spirit? Or is it really from a Christian Temper of Forbearance? Would to God this was indeed the Cause. *The New York Gazette*, October 17, 1763

These indians were no less fierce because they were eastern indians, as the following dispatch, reports and letters from the front all confirm:

An Extract of a Letter from Capt. Bowers of Hanover, dated the 6th Day of November, at the Head Quarters, twelve Miles above Col. Van Camp's, on the River Delaware, on the Frontiers of the Province of New Jersey.

"Sir,

I arrived here with my Detachment of 90 Men, by Order of his Excellency William Franklin, Esq. &c, where I found 150 Persons, Men, Women and Children, who were driven to this Station by the Cruel Savages of the Wilderness; of these 50 at least lodge every Night in one small

Room, in a very uncomfortable, confus'd Manner; in the Morning, they throw what Bed and Covering they have out of Doors in one Heap, which in a Sort resembles the Chaos before the Elements were separated from one another. These poor People, it seems, if ever there can be such, are the most proper objects of our Commiseration, for they have been compelled to quit their *little all*, their Provisions, their Corn, and in short, their whole Dependence, to be Devoured and Consumed without any Hope of Security. What can ever animate a Christian to unsheath the Sword and Bathe the same in Blood, if the Distress of his Brethren by Reason of the inhuman Cruelty of Savages will not? And what will not the Noble and generous deny himself of that he may rescue such innocents as are daily presented to our View? Every Time I see these piteous Objects, and hear there Lamentations, methinks I feel something within that makes me uneasy without Revenge. Two Indians were seen on their Side of the River Yesterday, by Capt. De Pue, to which he was qualified. And what will be the Final Issue of this Troublesome Indian Affair is yet in the Womb of Providence. O may God grant Repentance to his People that his Anger may be turned away, that we perish not.

I am, Sir, yours &c.
Lemuel Bowers

The Pennsylvania Journal, November 17, 1763.

Philadelphia, December 1. From Sussex County in New Jersey, we have Intelligence that on the 17th Inst. Capt. Wesbrook, with 11 more of the Militia, went over to the Pennsylvania Side, in order to bring off some Cattle and Effects which were left there by Persons who had deserted their Habitations, that at about three Miles from the River they were attacked by a Body of Indians, who killed Capt. Wesbrook, William Cartwright, Andreas Decker, Nathaniel Carter, and one Duncan; that Six others escaped to Nominac and a Person of the name Whealand is missing, supposed to be carried off, to give an Account on the Situation of the Forces on the River; that a Party of 150 Militia, immediately upon hearing news of this Disaster, went over to Pennsylvania to bury the dead, who found the bodies of five of our Men most inhumanly butchered and an Indian shaved and dressed in the Mohawk Manner, who was killed in the Engagement. The white men they brought off and buried and scalped the Indian[41]; that the Party of Indians was thought, by the Persons engaged, to be upwards of 40 in Number and 'tis imagined they were apprehensive of the alarm spreading and therefore made a precipate Retreat, as they did not carry off the Indian that was killed and left the following things behind them, near the Place of Action, viz. about the Quantity of a Waggon load of smoaked Beef and Pork, 12 pounds of Tallow, 2 French Guns, a Mohawk Indian Cap, 1 Blanket, 2 Belts of

---

[41] The scalping was apparently done by the brother of one of the slain men.

Wampum, a Scalping Knife, Looking Glass, Leggings, Moquasens &c.; and that it is the opinion of the Inhabitants on the New Jersey Frontier in general that this Party was on their way to that Province and that, if they had not been met as they were by Capt. Wesbrook's Party, they would have created great Damage that Evening among the Inhabitants on that Frontier, which it would have been out of the Power of the Guards stationed there to have prevented. *The Pennsylvania Gazette*, December 1, 1763

Our assurance from Upper Minisink, East New Jersey, is that on the 15th of November last Capt. Silas Park, with 23 Volunteers, set out from that Place to go to Cosheckton, on Delaware River in order to bury the Dead lately killed by the Indians and to bring off such of the effects of the poor People that left such Place, as could be found; on the 21st, the Captain with all his Men safely returned to Minisink in high spirits, having been to said Cosheckton, buried five Persons found dead there, brought off all the Cattle and Swine they could find, saw no Indians but say that on the Day they left the Place, they heard sundry guns fired on the other side of the River, supposed to have been fired by the same Party of Indians that did the Murder lately committed upon the Road, near a Place called Lacawse. The said Captain could not pursue them by Reason of the Great Quantities of Snow, it being at that Time Knee deep. *The New York Gazette*, December 19, 1763.

Danger ---for both sides --- lurked around every corner and both settlor and Indian had better have his weapon handy:

New York, December 19. The Week before last, an Inhabitant of Minisink, being a Hunting for Deer, on the West Side of Delaware, fell in with a single Indian. They espied each other almost in an instant, immediately tree'd and after exchanging several shots the Indian imagined he had wounded his Antagonist and rushed in upon him with his Tomahawk; but the White Man, after receiving two desperate Wounds from the Indian, knock'd his Brains out with the end of his Musket, cut his Head off and brought it home in Triumph. *The New York Mercury*, January 2, 1764

Even the friendly indians were frightened of being caught in the middle or blamed for the actions of others:

New-York, January 16. The horrid Massacre committed upon the Conestogoe Indians, settled in Lancaster County, though under the immediate Protection of the Magistrates, having greatly alarmed the other Indians (who at their own request were lately removed from Frontiers of that Province and settled, by Order of the Government on the Province Island and other Places, near to the City of Philadelphia) and filled them with Apprehensions of the Fates of the Conestogoes. We hear they are Desirous of returning to their Friends, or former Habitations, and that, on their Application, the Government appointed them Guides and directed their Route thro' the Province of New-Jersey and New-York, giving them Recommendatory letters to those Governments for Safe Passage and Assistance, with which, they, 140 in Number, immediately set out and proceeded as far as Elizabeth-Town, New-Jersey. But it is reported that, no previous Notice having been sent to this Government, Messengers are sent, by Remonstrance, to prevent their Entrance into it, and if they persist to give immediate Notice. Many People apprehend fatal consequences should these Indians at this Time, under such well grounded apprehensions and with such shocking Ideas of Justice, Humanity and Protection they may expect in an English Man's Government, return and Mix with the indians now at War with us.

We are told that the above Party of Indians are now at Amboy, under Escort of a Party of Highlanders. *The New York Mercury*, January 16, 1764

The folks safely back home greeted the returning soldiers as heroes:

Two Days ago, Capt. Montour arrived with some of his Party at Johnson-Hall and brought the Scalp, &c. taken some Time since. The Indian scalped was a Head Warrior, Nephew to the Squash Cutter, Chief of all the Delawares. Capt. Montour brought with him likewise, a lad named Emanuel Stover of Rariton, New-Jersey, taken last Year at Wioming, with 6 others, by the Delawares; and a Delaware who went to Johnson-Hall, on the 20th Instant, under some specious Pretence, was on Discovery of his Villainies, apprehended. *The New York Mercury*, May 7, 1764

New York, November 28. Thursday last, Col. Croghan, Commissioner for Indian Affairs under Sir William Johnson, arrived at this City, from the late Congress, in his way to Virginia. He has brought with him, one Lewis Andrews, who was a Soldier in the Jersey Force, and taken in the year 1763, by the Indians, near Lake Erie, in his way to Detroit and had been kept Prisoner among the Senecas ever since. He says they used him tolerably well and, at the late Congress, happily got releas'd and is now returning to his Friends near Burlington. *The New York Journal or General Advertiser*, December 1, 1768

Slavery was a horrible, inecusable institution. As men in servitude will seek liberty at any cost, the colonial masters were always frightened that the slave population would some day rise in revolt. It had happened before. There had been a slave conspiracy in New York in 1712 which resulted in the deaths of nine whites, the wounding of five hundred slaves, the suicide of six others and the arrest of more. Of those arrested, twenty one were executed by being burnt alive, broken on the wheel or hanged alive in chains. Six were reprieved and pardoned.

New Jersey had similar fears and several "conspiracies" were uncovered, although credible proof was not always of prime concern at the time to the authorities:

We have Advice from New York of the 21st of January last that in Summerset County in East New Jersey, on Raritan River, there has lately been a conspiracy among the Negroes there to Murder the English and to assemble together in a Body and make their Escape to settle themselves in some new Country. About 30 of the Conspirators have been apprehended, one of them hanged, some had their Ears cut off and others were whipped. Several of them had Poison found about them. *The Weekly Rehearsal,* February 11, 1734

One reader purported to know what caused these slave revolts and his letter of explanation was published for all to note:

Mr. Bradford:

The letter from Burlington printed in Franklin's Gazette, insinuating that the late rising of the Negroes in the Eastern District of New Jersey was occasioned by the Paper's lately published in the Neighbouring Province, the Authors of which he is very free with, I having been present at some of the Examinations of those Negroes, think it necessary to give the best account thereof I can in order to warn all Masters of Negroes not to be too careless of their own Safety, with respect to their Slaves, which now begin to be numerous, and in some of our colonies too much indulged, and by some particular Persons rather encouraged in their Vices, than put under a due Regulation and Subjection. It appear'd upon examination that Coll. Thomas L----d keeps at some Miles distant from his dwelling House, Negro-Quarters (as they are called) who provide for themselves, which Quarters have become a Randevouze for the Negroes and proved a Pest to the Neighbourhood by encouraging the Neighbours' Negroes to steal from their

Masters both Beef, Pork, Wheat, Fowles &c. where with they feast and junket at those quarters and have at times met in great Companies. It was at one of these Meetings that their Design of Rising was agreed and some time since fully resolved by some hundreds of them, but kept so private amongst themselves that there was not the least appearance or suspicion of it, till the Negroe of one Hall at Rariton, having drunk too much, accosted one Renolds on the Road and told him that the English-men were generally a pack of Villains and kept the Negroes as Slaves, contrary to a positive Order from King George, sent to the Governour of New York, to set them all free which the said Governour aid intended to do but was prevented by his Council and Assembly and that was the reason why there now subsisted so great a difference between the Governor and the People. Rennels was surprized at the freedom and independence of this fellow & told him he was a great Raskel to talk in that manner. The Negro answered that he was as good a man as himself and that in a little time should be convinced of it.

This was the first occasion of Suspicion of a Negro Plot. And, upon Rennel's Information on what this Fellow had said, he & another Negro was taken up, Tryed, Condemned, and One Hanged; Hall's Negro made his escape and is not yet taken. Upon this Examination and Tryal it appeared that the Design of these Negroes was this. That so soon as the Season was advanced that they could lie in the Woods, one certain Night was agreed on, that every Negro in each Family was to Rise at Midnight, Cut the Throats of their Masters and Sons, but not meddle with the Women, whom they intended to plunder and ravish the day following, and then set all their Houses and Barns on Fire, kill all the Draught Horses and secure the best Saddle Horses for their flight towards the Indians in the French Interest.

How easie this Design might have been put into practice, if it had not been discovered, I leave everyone to judge, and how very necessary it is for every Colony to make proper Laws and Ordinances for their own Security and against the Attempts of these Barbarous Monsters (by some so much indulged), I would also have each and every one of us to remember and not forget the great Calamity and Disolation in the City of New-York some years since, by the Negroes rising there and murdering many good innocent People and, had it not been for his Majesty's Garrison there, that City (in all likelihood) had been reduced to Ashes and the greatest part of the Inhabitants Murdered. The late Massacre perpetrated by the Negroes in the Island of St. John's, the very great head they have come to in the Island of Jamaica and the general Melancholy Apprehensions of his Majesty's Subjects in the West-Indies, gives too much room to fear there is some great Fatality attends the English Dominion in America from the too great Number of the unchristain and barbarous People being imported and then by some too much indulged in their Vices. *The New York Gazette*, March 25, 1734

The spring of 1741 apparently brought with it another foiled plot, this one among the slaves in Bergen County:

New-York. From Hackensack in Bergen County, East New Jersey, we hear that on Fryday last seven Barns were burnt, the Eighth was on fire several Times, but saved by the diligence of the Neighbours; it is almost past Suspicion that they were fir'd by a Combination of Negroes, as one was taken (as is said here) as he was putting fire to one of them. *New York Journal,* May 4, 1741

New York, May 4. We hear from Hackinsack in New Jersey that last week Seven Barns were willfully set on Fire and burnt down and the Eighth was three times endeavoured to be served the same but happily escaped. One Negro Man was taken on the Spot and several strong Circumstances appear against him. The People thereabout are greatly alarmed, and keep under Arms every Night, as well as at New-York. Its said the first Day of this Month was the Time appointed for New-York to be burnt. *The Boston Weekly Post Boy,* May 11, 1741

Trouble popped up again among the slave population, across the Hudson River, in New York City, just a few weeks later.

New York, June 29. The indefatigable Vigilance of our Magistrates is hardly to be expressed; there now being 11 Negroes capitally convicted and about 100 in Goal. Several Whites are impeached and committed, one of them is an Irish Romish Priest, and it is supposed that more White Persons will be found concerned in said Plot. The Blacks began to confess and agree generally in their Confessions that each was first too kill his Master and then to Destroy as many Whites as possible, and even since the Discovery of their Plot, they proposed to put their hellish Design in Execution, but were deter'd by the Military Watch. Three Negroes have lately been burnt at Hackinsack in New Jersey for burning of seven Barns. A Military Watch is yet kept there both Day and Night. *The Boston Evening-Post,* July 6, 1741

The slaves' poisoning their masters and mistresses seems to be what the colonists feared most.

Philadelphia, March 7. We hear from Trenton that two Negroes were Last Week imprison'd on the following Occasion. 'Tis said that they were about to perswade another Negroe to poison his Master and to convince him of the efficacy of the Drug which they had presented him for that purpose and the security of giving it, let him know that Mr. Trent and two of his Sons, Mr. Lambert and Two of his Wives and sundry other Persons were removed by their Slaves in that Manner. This Discourse being overheard, they were apprehended and 'tis said have made some Confession. But as the Persons above mentioned died apparently of common Distempers, it is not fully credited that any such method was used to destroy them. The Drugs found on one of the Negroes was Arsenick and an unknown kind of Root. *The Pennsylvania Gazette*, February 28, 1738

Philadelphia, June 8. We hear from Burlington that two Negroes found guilty of practising Poison, by which they had destroyed sundry Persons, were executed there last Week. *The Boston Evening Post*, June 19, 1738

New York, March 7. We hear Bergen in East Jersey, that on Friday Last, several Negroes belonging to that Place were apprehended and committed to the County Goal in Hackinsack upon the evidence of some of their Fellow Slaves of having poisoned their Masters and Mistresses a few months ago and of which they died not long since. It is thought from this Commitment that some other Schemes of Villany will be discovered, the Negroes in that Neighbourhood have lately assembled more together oftener than usual. And the discovery of this was owing to some Ill Will which one Negro had against another. *The Pennsylvania Journal*, March 10, 1757.

The word "riot" today evokes images of destructive civil insurrections by a mob of "have nots", the disenfranchised, who want a say in society, egged on by malcontents with less noble motives. But, riots are not new in America. There were labor, racial and political riots in this century and draft riots during the Civil War. And there were riots in colonial America. The major issue then was land. Who owned it? Was it the rich man who had probably never seen it but who had a deed claiming title from some Duke, who had gotten a patent from the Prince, who had been given it by his father, the King --usually at a profit for each in line? Or was it the squatter who had worked the land for a generation or the good faith purchaser who had bought it from another whose title was now in doubt? Many of those who lived on the frontiers of northern and western Jersey, where this conflict was the greatest, were the Scotch -Irish, a group of clannish, hard drinking, quick shooting refugees from Ulster in northern Ireland, a failed settlement of lowland Protestant Scots in the Catholic celtic Ireland. They moved with the frontiers, from Jersey, to Western Pennsylvania, then to Appalachia, Kentucky, Tennessee, into Texas, Arkansas, Oklahoma among other wilderness area. They were the Daniel Boones and the Davy Crocketts, the "hillbillies" of Kentucky and the proud defenders of the Alamo in Texas. They were not easily controlled and they moved on frequently, when civilization with its regulations appeared.

The first riot reported in the New Jersey by the Press was in 1735 and it compelled the Royal Governor to issue a Proclamation condemning the act:

By his Excellency
William Cosby

Captain General and Governour in Chief and over his Majesty's Provinvces of New York and New Jersey and the Territories thereon Depending in America, Chancellor and Vice Admiral and Colonel in his Majesty's Army in the same &c.

A Proclamation

Whereas I have received information upon Oath that one Duncan Oguillon and one John Collier, were on the second Day of July last past, severally put into the Possession of the Dwelling Houses and Plantations lately in the Possession of John Parks and Thomas Smith, late of Hopewell in the County of Hunterdon, by Daniel Coxe Esq., who then had Possession of said Dwelling Houses and Plantations, delivered unto him by Bennet

Bard, Esq., High Sheriff of the County of Hunterdon, by Virtue of a Writ of Possession to the said Sheriff, directed and issuing out of the Supream Court of this Province of New Jersey; and that in the Night between the Thursday and Friday following, divers persons unknown, to the Number of Twelve or more, being all disguised, having their Faces besmeared with Blacking and Armed with Clubs and Sticks in their Hands, did in an Insolent, Violent and Riotous Manner, break into and enter the said respective Dwelling Houses and did Assault, Beat and Wound the said Duncan Oguillon and John Collier and other Persons then in the said Dwelling Houses and them did with Force & Arms violently amove and turn out of Possession, Cursing, Swearing and Threatening in a most outrageous Manner that they would Kill and Murder the said Daniel Coxe, Esq. in Defiance of all Law and Government.

To the End therefore that the said Audacious Offenders may be brought to condign Punishment, I have thought fit by and with the Advice of his Majesty's Council to issue this Proclamation, hereby promising his Majesty's most Gracious Pardon to any one of the Offenders, who shall discover one or more of their Accomplices so that he or they may be brought to condign Punishment. And as a further encouragement to any one who may detect so unparalleled and insolent an Outrage, I do hereby Promise to Pay to the Discoverer the Sum of Thirty Pounds, Proclamation Money, within one Month after any or either of the Offenders shall by his Means be convicted of the said Offence.

Given under my Hand and Seal at Arms, at Perth Amboy, the twenty-second day of August, in the Ninth Year of His Majesty's reign, *Anno Domini* 1735.

God Save the King

The American Weekly Mercury, August 21, 1735

Witness the following accounts of land riots in Newark two hundred and fifty years ago and wonder whether history repeats itself.

We have just received the following Account of a very extraordinary Riot at Newark on Thursday last viz. The Day before one Nehemiah Baldwin with two others were apprehended there by Order of the Governor in Council for being concerned in a former Riot and committed to Jail; In the Morning one of them offer'd to give Bail and the Sheriff for that purpose took him out in order to carry him to the Judge; but on their way thither, a great Number of Persons appeared armed with Cudgels, coming down from the Back Settlements, who immediately rescued the Prisoner in a very violent Manner, contrary to his own Desire; upon this the Sheriff retreated to the Jail, where he raised 30 Men of the Militia, with their Officers, in order to guard it; but by two o'Clock in the Afternoon the Mob being increased to about 300 strong, marched with the umost Intrepidity to the Prison, declaring if they were fired on, they would kill every Man; and after breaking through the Guard, wounding and being wounded, they got to the Jail which they broke open, setting at liberty all the Prisoners they could find, as well as Debtors as others, and then marched off in Triumph, using many threatening Expressions against all those who has assisted the Authority. Several of the Guard as well as of the Mob were much wounded and bruised and 'tis thought one of the latter is past Recovery. What may be the Consequence of this Affair is not easy to guess. *The New York Weekly Post Boy*, January 20, 1746

The Crown was appalled at the action and Governor Lewis Morris, in a speach before the General Assembly promised that:

His Majesty's Attorney General will lay before you an Account of a great Riot, or rather Insurrection, at Newark. This was a natural consequence of one that was some time before that; and, although I did what by Advice of his Majesty's Council they judged at that time sufficient to put a Check to an Evil that had been too great a Probability of growing bigger and to prevent its doing so, yet (as appears) it was without the Effect intended. So open and avowed an Attempt in Defiance of the Government and in Contempt of the Laws, if not High Treason, make so nigh Approaches to it, as seems but too likely to end in Rebellion, and throwing off His Majesty's Authority, if timely Measures be not taken to check the Intemperance of too licentious Multitude; I therefore recommend this matter to your most serious Consideration. *The New York Weekly Post Boy*, March 31, 1746

God too appears to have the side of took who took their legal title from the lawful authority. The chain of command and the duties of the citizen in turn was set forth as follows:

Mr. DeForest:

Hoping the following Lines will be of some benefit to the Public, I desire you give it a Place in your next Paper.
from your humble Servant,
Layman

I think it necessary at present to speak a few words on the first seven Verses of the 13th Chapter of Paul to the Romans. St. Paul's Words in these seven Verses are so very plain and conspicuous that they need but little Explanation. I shall a little open the first Verse and the rest I hope will be clearly understood.

1st. Verse "Let every Soul be subject to the higher Powers, for there is no power but of God. The powers that be are ordained by God." This Text divides itself into three parts.

1st. That it's every Christian's Duty to be subject to the Higher Powers, that is, to the present temporal Authority or the Laws of our country that are now in force.

2dly, "For there is no Power but of God" That is, all temporal Government that is established in any Country is of God, tho' its done and acted by Men, yet it's by God's Permission and Appointment.

3dly, "The powers that be or the present powers are Ordained of God" . . . By this we may plainly see that we are not to Dispute how the supreme Magistrate came by his power or whether he has a Lawful Right or not; but whoever has got the Government in their Hands, it immediately becomes our Duty to be subject, that is, in all things that are not contrary to our Duty to God and, there, we may say we ought to obey God rather than Man.

2d Verse "Whosoever therefor resisteth the Power resisteth the Ordinance of God and they that resist shall receive to themselves Damnation."

By this it is evidently clear that whosoever resisteth any Officer, even the lowest Officer, that comes lawfully in the King's or supreme Magistrate's Name and Authority, resisteth the Ordinance of God and they that resist shall receive to themselves Damnation.

. . . .

Now beloved Brethren, seeing the resisting of the powers that we live under is so great a sin, what shall we think of those who live under the best and mildest Government in the World, who have always been protected in their Lawful Rights and Privileges, according to the known good laws of the Land and Nation to which they belong? And only because they can't have a litigious Case tried just according to their own Humour and their own will, be it right or wrong, . . . will rise up in rebellion against the powers that be by raising of Mobs, become guilty of Riots, beating the Officers of the present Government when they are upon their lawful Duty, breaking open Jayls, setting fellows at liberty, gathering in great numbers with Clubs, beating down all that oppose them, turning poor people out of their possessions and standing in Defiance of all Laws and Government, trusting to their great Numbers to protect them in all their Villainy.

. . . .

I accuse no particulars; if there be any that find the Coat does fit them, they are welcome to wear it. *The New York Evening Post*, August 3, 1747

However, someone spoke on behalf of the mob and raised issues that a Revolution thirty years would advance even further.

Mr. Parker.

As several of your late Papers have been almost filled with Matter relating to the Proprietors and their disputed lands in New Jersey, I desire you'd give the following short Piece a Place in your Paper, for altho' it was not written designedly, yet it may fully serve as an answer thereto (and 'tis without any &c's) and which, tho' it not be Law, yet 'tis Equity and Reason, and therefore ought to be Law, as 'tis Better than any Law without reason, viz.

No Man is naturally intitled to a greater Proportion of the Earth, than another; but tho' it was made for the equal Use of all, it may nonetheless be appropriated by every Individual. This done by the Improvement of any Part of it lying vacant, which is thereupon distinguished from the great Common of Nature and made the property of that Man, who bestowed his Labour on it, from whom it cannot afterwards be taken, without breaking thro' the Rule of Natural Justice, for thereby he would actually be deprived of the Fruits of his Industry.

Yet, if Mankind who was designed by the Almighty to be Tenants in Common of the Habitable Globe, should agree to divide it among themselves into certain Shares or Parts, the Contract will be by binding by the Laws of Nature and ought therefore to be inviolably observed. Such a Division has been attempted by the Treaties made between the several Princes and States of Europe, with Regard to the vast Desert of America. But each Prince stipulated, or ought to be understood to have stipulated, for the general Benefit of the People under his Government and not for his particular Profit. The Kings of England have always held the Lands of America, ceded to them by Treaties, in Trust for their Subjects, which Lands, having lain uncultivated from the Beginnings of the World, were therefore as free and as common for all to settle upon, as the Waters of the Rivers are to all to drink of. Yet to prevent the Confusion that would follow on every Man's being his own Carver, Governor's were from time to time appointed by the Crown to parcel out to the Subjects as much Land as each could occupy. But the Mischief of it was that the best Parts and most commodiously situated have been granted to a few Particulars, in such exorbitant Quantities that the rest of the Subjects have been obliged to buy it for their use, at an extravagant Price, a Hardship that seems as great, as if they had been put under the necessity of Buying the Waters of the Rivers. *The New York Weekly Post Boy*, June 9, 1746

One letter to the editor -- editorials would not appear in the popular press until after the Revolution, their role being filled by these "letters" -- took a wise halfway position between wanting liberty but not wanting to draw the Crown's attention or ire:

On reading the *New York Evening Post*, No. 141, I find a Discourses by Mr. Layman, on the first seven Verses of St. Paul to the Romans, showing the Danger and sin of resisting the Powers that be or the present Government. Tho' he mentions no Time or Place, yet he certainly points at the present New Jersey Rioters, who have run on to a great height and still going from bad to worse (as if they had no remorse) which is to be feared will bring Destruction on themselves, both to Soul and Body and it will be a singular Providence if the innocent don't at last suffer in same Measure with the Guilty.

It is an old Maxim "The strictest laws is the greatest Oppression." And it may happen so sometimes in some intricate Cases and there are so many tricks and advantages to be taken in the Law, whereby an innocent Person may suffer and I don't doubt but some of these poor people has suffered very much. If I am rightly informed there are some very industrious, hard laboring People in both the Eastern and Western Divisions of New Jersey that have bought their land and paid for it, once or twice, and some three times, and now they expect to loose it at last.

There are Grievances and Oppression or Misfortunes, call them how you please, that is too hard for Nature to bear. But all that are guilty in these Riots are not in this case for most of them have no title to land at all and the rest but Blind ones.   . . . .

Doubtless the Indians have a just Right and may justly Keep others off that wouldn't buy. But had not the King got a good right also by virtue of Discovery to dispose of to whom he pleases of his own subjects, born in his Dominions. So that none has a right to hold by Indian Title, till they buy of the King also or from those whom the King sold to. And whoever will pretend to hold lands alone, without any regard to the King's Patents, ought to be looked upon as enemies to his Majesty.

     . . . .

Tho' I am neither Proprietor, Lawyer or Phisicia, nor any way by interest concerned, yet I shall venture to give a little advice in this case. It is an old and true saying "Take away the Cause and the effect will cease". . . Let some reasonable and easie proposals be made to those that are the real Sufferers with a prudent mixture of Lenity and Justice and let everything be carried fairly; and then it is hopeful with a little wise Management, these warm Resentments will cool and be forgotten. And those that are the Advisors and Ringleaders in the Club, they would do well to consider speedily of some method to keep their own Necks out of the Collar. . . . I am not going to Justifie them in the least for their wicked Rebellious behaviour, for except they repent and forebear such doings, I don't see how they can expect any Favour or Protection, but to be treated as common Enemies and Rebels to the present Government. . .

Now Gentlemen, you that are so warm in the Club Affair, I shall only ask you one civil Question, how would you like it to have three or four thousand Soldiers sent over as a standing Army to be Quartered upon you? *The New York Evening Post*, September 7, 1747

Those charged with leading riots were sometimes saved by further civil disobedience. Others seemed to want to get caught.

We are informed from New-Jersey that one of the Heads of the Rioters having been committed to Goal at Newark, a Number of these People came to the Goal on Monday Night last and let him out and he afterwards made his Boast that a strong North-West Wind blew the Door off the Hinges and he walk'd out of the Prison as Paul and Silas did.[42] *The Pennsylvania Journal*, December 13, 1748

New York, April 20. We have advice from Perth Amboy that one of the reputed chiefs of the Essex Rioters, having appeared there at the Supreme Court last Month, as an Evidence of a Land-Trial, he was apprehended and committed, but some time later was admitted to Bail. He then returned home but in a few days came back again and surrendered himself Prisoner and discharged his Bail. And on Monday Morning last, upwards of 200 Men, well mounted, appeared on the Skirts of that City, when about 30 of them left the Company and went to the Jail, where without further Ceremony, they set the Prisoner free and then rejoined their Party again and returned peaceably back from whence they came. *The New York Gazette revived in the Weekly Post Boy*, April 20, 1752

---

[42] The reference, of course, is to early Christian preachers of the Gospel, who were imprisoned for spreading the Word of God, then released by His Grace.

New York, October 2. We hear from Newark that on Tuesday last, Amos Roberds, one of the Chiefs of the Jersey Rioters, was committed to the County Jail. This Man was a few years ago indicted in the Supreme Court for High Treason, which Indictment still lies against him. And Samuel Nevil, one of the Judges of the Supreme Court, going the Circuits to Morris-County, attended by a great Number of Magistrates and Gentlemen, Roberds had the Imprudence, or rather Impudence, boldly to intrude into their Company and Presence, as if in Defiance of Justice; whereupon he was immediately ordered into Custody and committed to Jail.

The New York Gazette revived in the Weekly Post Boy, October 2, 1752

The year 1770 brought more riots. According to a lengthy report in The New York Gazette and the Weekly Mercury for January 22 of that year, the riots ensued after years and years of litigation had gone against those claiming to have purchased good title from the Indians in favor of those who claimed title from the Crown. Despite threats to burn down Newark, mobs of self viewed disenfranchised citizens and arrests of the mob's leaders, violence was minimal and damage limited. The leaders, who stood trial and were convicted by a jury of freeholders, were fined.

New York, March 1. We hear from Newark that a Court held there last Friday last for trial of sundry persons concerned in some late riotous proceedings, on account of a dispute between the provincial proprietors and a number of inhabitants, claiming under the purchase of Indian titles, when one of the rioters was fined one hundred pounds and several others in lesser sums. *Pennsylvania Chronicle*, March 5, 1770

There were other acts of civil disobedience, including what today would be described as extensive criminal conspiracies. At other times and in other places, these activities might have been criticized by the press and society alike as criminal mob behavior. However, because of the popularity of the movement, the actions of the law breakers were reported sympathetically -- even triumphantly -- by the papers of the time. The best example of this involves the famed Sons of Liberty, the network of common citizens throughout colonial America that resisted the overreaching of the English Parliament and which allowed a people to experience both their collective strength and their desire to be left alone.

To the Printer

Sir, you are desired by a number of your New-Jersey Customers to give the following Account a Place in your next Paper which will oblige them and particularly your humble Servant

D.S.L.

Woodbridge in New Jersey, 31 December, 1765. On Saturday last, the 28th Instant, the Sons of Liberty of this Place and the Parts adjacent had a Meeting here, and not sufficiently assured that Mr. Coxe of Philadelphia, who was appointed Distributor of Stamps for New Jersey, had resigned that Office, they deputed and instructed two of their Number to wait on Mr. Coxe, with a Letter, praying a satisfactory Account of his Resignation. Instructions were forthwith made out and delivered to the deputies, together with a Letter to Mr. Coxe which were as follows, Viz.

Instructions given by the Sons of Liberty to their deputies to Mr. Coxe, who is appointed distributor of stamps, for the Province of New-Jersey.

First. We command and strictly enjoin it upon you, upon pain of our high displeasure, that you do immediately, with the greatest expedition possible, repair to the house of Mr. Coxe, our stamp distributor, in Philadelphia or elsewhere, and into his hands deliver our letter, praying his resignation, according to the tenor of said letter &c which, if he complies with, you are to bear the same to us and in the name of every Son of Liberty in the Province of New-Jersey, to return him your thanks therefor.

Second. Upon Mr. Coxe's refusal, we command you to return immediately and make report to us of the same.

Third. We command and strictly enjoin it upon you, that whether said Mr. Coxe resign his commission &c or not, you do treat him with that complaisance and decorum, becoming a gentleman of Honour.

Copy of a Letter to Mr. Coxe

Sir,

Whereas you have been appointed to the odious and most detestable office of distributor of Stamps for the government of New-Jersey, and whereas the former resignation (said to be yours) is no way satisfactory to the inhabitants of same, We the Sons of Liberty in said Government hereby desire your resignation, in as ample form and manner as possible, expressly and solemnly declaring, upon the veracity of a gentleman and man of honour, that you will never, directly or indirectly, yourself or by deputies under you, ever distribute said stamps or be any ways accessary in putting said Act in force in the government aforesaid; whereby you will not only endear yourself to the inhabitants but prevent such matters as may be taken through necessity to oblige you to the same. And whereas it is publicly reported and generally believed that you have already nominated and appointed deputies under you, to distribute Stamp Papers in said Government, whereby we are and shall continue to be in the utmost danger, by reason of said declared enemies to their country, notwithstanding your said resignation. Now, Sir, we desire and insist that you, without reserve, acquaint us of all such deputies (if any there be) that they may be dealt with in a proper manner. It is expected that you do, in the presence of our deputies, comply with every one of our aforesaid requests and deliver the same (signed by yourself) to them to be brought to us. If Sir, you refuse our very reasonable request, it will put us to the trouble of waiting upon you, in such a way and manner, as perhaps will be disagreeable both to yourself and us, which we hereby notify you we shall do on Saturday the fourth of January next and it is expected you will then be ready to answer us.

Sons of Liberty in East New-Jersey

This Day, the 31st of December, the Deputies returned and reported that they had waited on Mr. Coxe at his house in Philadelphia and delivered the letter aforesaid; that after reading it and being informed of their business, they were treated with the utmost civility and respect both by him and by his Lady and he delivered to them in writing the following Copy of his genteel and ample Resignation, viz.

I do hereby resign into the hands of the right honourable the lords commissioners of his majesty's treasury, the office of distributor of stamps for the province of New-Jersey. Witness my hand and seal, this third day of September, in the Year of Our Lord 1765.

William Coxe (seal)

Sealed and delivered in the presence of
William Humphreys
Tench Tilgman
The Pennsylvania Journal, February 13, 1766

We hear from New-Jersey that the gentlemen of the law in that Province met last Thursday at New-Brunswick, to consider the propriety of resuming their practice, which they have discontinued since the 1st of November, where they were waited upon by a deputation of the Sons of Liberty, who expressed their uneasiness about the suspension of law proceedings and it was decided by a majority of the lawyers then convened "that they would resume their practice the 1st Day of April next, whatever accounts may be received from England or sooner if earlier intelligence arrives of the determination of Parliament respecting the Stamp Act" . . . which being communicated to the deputies who then attended, they appeared to be satisfied therewith. And at the Same time deputies from the Sons of Liberty of the County of Hunterdon, waited on Mr. White, prothonotary of that County, with a request that he open his office to transact business as usual, who received them politely and they received assurances that the office should be opened the first day of April.

We likewise hear from the same quarter that a certain person being dunned for a debt, he gave his creditor to understand that as there was no law, he would not pay him, whereupon the creditor seized him by the shoulders and called out "here is a man that wants stamps!" He was in a little time surrounded by a number of people who would make a sacrifice of him, who dar'd to take the advantage of the distressing situation of his Country, had he not immediately paid the money and made an acknowledgment of his fault. *The Pennsylvania Journal*, February 20, 1766

A large Gallows was erected in Elizabeth-Town last Week with a Rope already fixed thereto, and the inhabitants there vow and declare that the first Person that either distributes or takes out a Stamped Paper shall be hung thereon without Judge or Jury. *The New York Gazette or Weekly Post Boy*, February 27, 1766

We have certain Intelligence from Elizabeth-Town, in New-Jersey, that the Magistrate and Lawyers carry on their Business in the Law as usual without Stamps. *The New York Gazette or Weekly Post Boy*, February 27, 1766

We hear from Cumberland County, West New Jersey, that the courts there were open and all business went on without regard to stamps.

We are assured that the Court of Sussex county, in New-Jersey, was opened last was opened last week and business transacted as usual without regard to stamps. *The Pennsylvania Journal*, February 27, 1766

We have certain Intelligence from Elizabeth-Town, in New-Jersey, that the Magistrates and Lawyers carry on their business in the Law as usual without Stamps. The same is done in many other Places, viz. in some Parts of Carolina, Virginia, Maryland, Pennsylvania, New-Jersey, and the Massachusetts, in which last place, New Jersey &c. they intend, whether the

Stamp-Act is repealed or not, in a few Weeks, to proceed in all Kinds of Business, without regard to any unconstitutional Acts; and in the Governments of New-Hampshire, Rhode Island, St. Christophers, Antigua, &c. all Kind of Business in Courts &c. is already got into its usual Course, without Stamped paper. *The Pennsylvania Gazette*, March 6, 1766

At a Meeting of the Sons of Liberty of the Township of Piscataway, in the County of Middlesex, and Province of East Jersey, the 11th of March, 1766

It was unanimously Resolved

I. That we will cheerfully to the utmost of our Power, defend all our just Rights and Privileges, as they have always been heretofore allowed us.

II. That we oppose all Attempts to deprive us of our Rights and Privileges as Englishmen and therefore will at all Events oppose the Operation of that detestable Thing called the Stamp Act in this Colony.

III. That we will in all Cases behave ourselves peaceably, and as far as our Influence extends, will preserve the publick Peace so far as that may be done without suffering any Imposition on our just Rights and Liberties.

IV. That we will by all Means within our Power, assist and protect all the Officers of Government of this Colony, who act consistent to their Duty and the Good of the Public.

V. That we will always hold ourselves in Readiness and with the utmost Cheerfulness assist any of the Neighbouring Provinces in Opposing every Attempt that may be made to deprive them and us of any of those Rights and Privileges we have heretofore enjoyed as Englishmen and therefore do hold most sacred.

And, lastly, that we do bear true Allegiance to his Most sacred Majesty, King George the Third, acknowledge him as our rightful Sovereign and will at all Times faithfully adhere to his Royal Person and just Government and heartily oppose every Attempt to injure his Person, Crown or Dignity. *Supplement to the New York Gazette or Weekly Post Boy*, March 27, 1766

Too often, we associate newspapers only with "bad news", the accidents, crimes and tragedies that, unfortunately, have always been part of the fabric of life. To be sure, the colonial newspapers portrayed plenty of that. But, amid the news accounts were public notices revealing neighbors doing what was right for each other, from a son voluntarily honoring his dead father's wishes, although at great expense to him, to neigbors helping out a fisherman who had lost his boat and livelihood to a storm, to other citizens assuring, with their pocketbooks, that a young freed slave boy would not re-enslaved.

After all this was a society that placed an emphasis on virtue in mankind:

To the Printer of the Pennsylvania Chronicle:

The letter sent to me some months ago without a name or signature, dated from Mansfield, in Burlington County, New-Jersey, contained an instance of greatness of soul, which deserves publication; and the reason for its being hitherto delayed was, that I might be fully assured of the truth of the fact, and having lately seen several persons of credit from that way, who tell me it is to be depended upon, I now give it in my correspondent's words:

"An early settler in this neighborhood, acquired a large estate --- he had five farms or plantations and as many sons; and for each son he intended one of the places, and his mind in that respect was well known in the family; he however neglected to get his will reduced into writing, and died without one, so that the English laws, in regard to descents, take place in this province, the whole landed estate became the property of the eldest son.[43] This he knew, and tho' he had then a family of children of his own, he, without hesitation or delay, ordered deeds to be drawn and cheerfully executed them, to convey to each brother the plantation designed for him by their common father. The name of this just man was William Black and, as he has been deceased several years, it is hoped that the mentioning of it can

---

[43] This is the English law of Primogeniture --i.e., the estate was passed on its entirety to the eldest son. Girls would be provided dowries but no property and younger sons would have to leave and seek careers in the military, or in a profession such as the law or with the Church. In the United States, an estate, unless there is a will to the contrary, will be divided among the decedent's spouse and children in a fashion equitable to all.

give no offense to any body, nay, rather may it not be called a tribute due to such virtue, and the more necessary as his private way of living prevented him from being much known and his religious profession from directing any marble monument to be erected to his memory.

The opportunities of shewing such disinterested acts of justice, such proofs of real goodness, beyond the obligations of human laws, happens to few, and when, those to whom the trial is permitted, acquit themselves with honor, the recital of their conduct affords great and heartfelt joy to the best of mankind, and even such as are too selfish and degenerate to have behaved thus in the like circumstances, cannot but outwardly applaud those who have done so.

Atticus

The Pennsylvania Chronicle, January 11, 1768

Major Pullene, and Mr. Kelly, have been kind enough to collect a Sum of money for the Relief of Moses Sears, a Poor Man, that lives in the Highlands, who lost his sloop in the late Storm, by which Accident, himself and Family were real Objects of Charity. The Money is lodged in the hands of the Mayor, for the Use of said Moses Sears. And we are desired by the Major, to give this Notice of it, that the poor Man may have the Money, whenever he will call for it. *The New York Mercury*, January 11, 1768

Whereas Isaac Johnson, formerly of the City of New-York, Shop-Keeper, but late of the Nevesinks, deceased, did, by his Will, set at Liberty a Molatto Slave, called Thomas Jackson, and provided Security to render his Manumission effectual, but the Bond given for that purpose hath been destroyed and an unjust Attempt lately made to sell him at Vendue, which induced certain Persons from Motives of Humanity, to indemnify the City or Place he may reside in, whereby his freedom is perfected. These are therefore to caution all Persons against purchasing the said Thomas, if he should again be offered to Sale. And Threats having been thrown out by Persons claiming the Estate of Isaac Johnson that they would dispose of the said Thomas beyond the Sea, all Masters of Vessels are prohibited from carrying him off, as they will answer it at their Peril, the Persons who have taken him into their Protection being resolved to procure him Justice. He is about 14 Years of Age, five Feet high, of slender Make, born in this Country and can read and write. *The New York Gazette*, July 18, 1763

Not all the good news was somber. Reports on parties, celebrations and other __fun__ gatherings could be counted on to draw some interest, although the intensity of the festivities varied, as today, with the personalities of the participants. For example:

Mr. Parker,

Please insert the following Relation in your next Paper and you'll oblige three of your readers: G.D., E.S., and E.G.

On Friday the 17th Instant, at Night, some young Men of us at Newark, being minded to make ourselves merry with dancing, one of our Company, E---r G---y dressed himself in Woman's Cloaths; and while we were in our Jollity, there came in one D---d B ---L, Son of Major B---l. (who calls himself a Great Man) and who soon grew very busy with and inquisitive to know who the suppos'd Woman was; some said her name was Miss Sarah and others Miss Sally; and B---l was so taken with her that he must needs be hugging and kissing her; whereupon she invited him out to dance but he refusing, she applied to another, with whom having danced fell a kissing again, but the Great Man being angry swore the D---l was in her, d---d her for a Strumpet and swore he would beat out her Brains; for he had an honest wife at home. Upon this G---y stept out of the Room and putting on his own Cloaths returned to the Room again. B---l immediately informed him of the whole Affair and wished he had been there to see the woman, who was not then to be found; and G---y appeared desirious also. But some Time after, the Great Man being acquainted with the Frolick was so enraged that he arrested poor G---y for Assault and Battery, and thro' the great Wisdom of the Justice, recovered 13 shilling 4 pence Damages. From which we learn the great Danger of innocent jesting with such a Great Man. *The New York Gazette revived in the Weekly Post-Boy*, March 20, 1749

Newark (in East Jersey) Jan 1, 1762. Monday last, the anniversary of the Festival of St. John the Evangelist, was observed here by the Antient and Honourable Society of Free Masons. They walked in regular Procession from the Loge to Church, where an excellent Sermon was preached, by the Reverend Mr. Brown, from 1st Peter, Chapter 15, 16, 17 verses. After Church they returned back to Dinner, accompanied by several of the Clergy and the Magistrates and concluded the Day in decent Mirth. *The New York Mercury*, January 11, 1762

New Brunswick, in New Jersey. On receiving the Advice of the Surrender of Quebeck, the Capital of New France, to his Majesty's Forces the 17th ultimo, the same was observed here on Monday Evening the 15th Instant with a Feu De Joie, Illuminations and every other publick Mark of Hearts overflowing with Joy and Graditude, for this most signal Acquisition and Addition to his Majesty's Dominion in North America, which God grant may continue. *The New York Mercury*, October 22, 1759

There were Notices of get togethers for the town people and the country ones.

-139-

We hear that the Committee, appointed by the American Philosophical Society, held at Philadelphia for promoting Useful Knowledge, to observe the Transit of Venus, which happened on Saturday last, having distributed themselves into three classes, the Rev. Mr. John Ewing, Joseph Shippen Esq., Doctor Hugh Williamson, Messieurs Thomas Prior, Charles Thomson and James Pearson, observed at the public Observatory; on the State-House Square, the Rev. Doctor William Smith and John Lukens, Esq.; Messieurs David Rittenhouse and John Sellers, at Mr. Rittenhouse's Observatory, at Norrington; and Mr. Owen Biddle at the Light-House, near the Capes of Delaware. The Weather was extremely favourable and the Observations at the three several Places, were compleated greatly to the satisfaction of the Observers. *The Pennsylvania Chronicle*, June 5, 1769

Trenton, April 7, 1766. The Members of the Trenton Library Company are desired to meet at the House of Isaac Yard, in Trenton, on the 14th Day of this instant April, at Two o'clock in the Afternoon, to choose a Treasurer and Directors, and make their Sixteenth Annual Payment, agreeable to their articles. And it is expected the Company will order the shares of the Delinquents to be disposed of, the Members are requested generally to attend. *The Pennsylvania Gazette*, April 10, 1766

The Spring Fair will be held at Princeton, on Wednesday and Thursday, the 20th and 21th Instant. *The Pennsylvania Chronicle*, April 4, 1768

While religion was a source of grace and enlightenment, public preaching provided a form of beneficial social entertainment, guaranteed to gather crowds:

On Sunday last the Reverend Mr. Whitefield preached twice at New-Brunswick to about 7000 People, and collected 42 pounds 10 shillings Currency which is about 26 pounds Sterling, for the Orphans in Georgia, Mr. Tennent also preached between the Sermons, and there was great Meltings in the Congregations. On Monday, Mr. Whitefield was to preach at Woodbridge and Elizabeth Town. On Monday Evening at 5 o'Clock he is to preach at the Meeting House at Amboy. On Tuesday morning at 10 o'Clock at Mr. William Tennent's new Meeting House at Freehold, where a Collection is to be made for the Orphans aforesaid. On Thursday the 15th Instant, he is to proceed to Lewis-Town and is to preach at Dover and some other Places by the Way, of which Notice is to be given. The Sloop is to meet him at Lewis-Town; meanwhile if any person is pleased to Contribute Provisions or Goods for the Orphan House, they may send the same to Mr.John Stephen Benezel, Merchant in Second-street. *The American Weekly Mercury*, May 1, 1740

The Reverend Mr. Tennent preach'd at the several Places mentioned in our last, and on Friday last he preach'd in the forenoon at Mr. Morehead's Meeting House and in the Evening at Dr. Colman's; on Saturday last in the Afternoon at the Rev. Mr. Webb's Meeting House; on the Lord's day in the forenoon at Mr. Morehead's Meeting House, and in the Afternoon at the Work House in the Common, and in the Evening at Dr. Colman's Meeting House where was a vast crowded assembly and several hundreds were forced to go away, not being able to get into the House; yesterday, he preach'd at the Rev. Mr. Gee's Meeting House; this Evening he is to preach the Lecture at Dr. Colman's Meeting House and tomorrow in the afternoon he is to preach a Lecture at Mr. Webb's Meeting House. *The New England Weekly Journal*, December 2, 1740

Last Night, the Rev. Mr. Whitefield returned hither, after an Excursion of 9 Days into the East Jerseys, during which he preached 4 times at Cape May, once at Cedar Bridge, once at Woodbury and three times at Greenwich to a very large and affected Auditories. He purposes, God willing, to preach Tomorrow Evening at the New Building and to continue so doing till Tuesday Evening when he intends to take his Leave. *The Pennsylvania Gazette*, September 11, 1747

Note that all the preachers were not men!

Philadelphia, November 17. Since our last, Mrs Rachael Wilson, an eminent Preacher among Friends, who lately arrived here, in Captain Falconer from England, set out by land for South Carolina . . . She preached several times in this Province and New-Jersey, to the great Satisfaction of thousands of well disposed People of all Denominations. *The Pennsylvania Gazette*, November 17, 1768

The right to vote was limited, often to property owning men alone, but that did not detract from the entertainment value of elections. As the following brace of accounts indicates, two things have not changed in politics: dirty tricks and long standard speeches from veteran officeholders that say little.

City of New Brunswick. By our Charter we are to choose Aldermen, Common Council, and other Offices, the second Tuesday in March in every Year and that by a Majority of the Votes of the Burghers and Freemen of said City, being the inherent Privileges of all English Subjects. But, in our last Election, the Bell was rung but once, whereas it used to be rung twice on all such Occasions; the Election opened before Noon and adjourned to the Afternoon, that the People might have time to assemble; but in our last we were deprived of our Privileges, the Election called before Noon, Aldermen and Common Council chose in a Quarter of an Hour, the Poll shut only by J--- R---, J--- A---, K---H---, J---H---, H--- M---, and Baby, in a clandestine Manner. When the People assembled at the proper and usual Hour, the Election was over. This is designed for the Benefit of the Publick, that they may guard against all arbitrary and clandestine Proceedings, such as we met with in our last Election in the City of New-Brunswick.

R.R.

The New York Gazette Revived in the Weekly Post Boy, April 17, 1749

Milstone, New Jersey, June 21. Yesterday came on our election, and continued by adjournment to this day, when Hendrick Fisher and John Berrien, Esqrs. were elected representatives from the County of Somerset; The election was carried on with the greatest coolness and good order; no reflecting nor abusive words were heard during the whole election. After the pole was closed in favour of the above gentlemen, Mr. Fisher addressed himself to the people in the following words:

Dear Friends and Gentlemen Voters.

Press'd with a due sense of gratitude, for the repeated and distinguishing marks of your sincere respect for my person; the honours you have conferred on me are very obliging; trusting your delicate and most tender concerns again into my hands, is really affecting; by this you not only approve of my former, but pledge your honor to my future conduct. I am at a loss for words on this renewed occasion, to express the grateful sentiments of my enlarged mind; I must therefore content myself, returning you my humble, most hearty thanks, and refer the proof of my sincerity and this assertion to my future acts. Permit me, nevertheless, at this time to congratulate you on the promising appearance of your numerous and tender offspring, treading in the patriotic steps of you their aged parents, a prospect more agreeable, as patriotism in many places at this time, is become a martyr; very sensible I am to my inferior abilities to many in this county, but as to real satisfaction and sincere delight in promoting your best interest, and preserving your civil and religious rights, I except none.

Having spent a considerable part of the appointed number of my days, in the public service, and am now arrived at that period, which would have made it very agreeable to have spent the remainder of my moments, in a more inactive and retired life. But on considering the distressed circumstances of the province, and the repeated solicitations of my friends, I have consented once more to stand your candidate, which, however, in all probability will be my last. God grant, that it may be for your interest, and his glory; and, which will be the sufficient reward of

Your very obliged and most
Humble Servant
Hendrick Fisher

Which address, the people very thankfully accepted. In testimony whereof, gave three huzza's. After which Mr. Berrien gave a handsome treat to those who were willing to accept it.

N.B. It appears by the poll, taken at this election, the freeholders in the county of Somerset are increased more than double the number since the first electing of Mr. Fisher in 1739.
New York Gazette or Weekly Post Boy, July 4, 1768

The source of the good feelings could be a Birth Announcement, either on an individual basis:

We hear from Rockyhill, New Jersey, that a Woman there was delivered a few Days ago of two Girls at Birth and who about ten months before had been delivered of three Boys, all which are now living and like to do well. *The Boston Weekly Post Boy*, June 4, 1744

From Northampton, in Burlington County, we learn, that on the 5th Instant, Jane the Wife of John Mullen, of that Place was delivered of three Female Children, at one Birth, and are all likely to do well. *Pennsylvania Gazette*, March 22, 1770

or *collectively*:

We hear from the Raritons in New Jersey that within about six weeks past, three Women in those Parts have been deliver'd of eight children, all alive and well. As those Parts yielded a good Number of Soldiers sent to Carthagena[44], they seem to be in great Forwardness to replenish their Loss. *The Boston Evening Post*, December 17, 1750

---

[44] A war against Spain, much of the fighting in which took place in the Islands of the Caribbean.

Hunterdon County in New Jersey, July 9. To give an instance of the Health, Constitution and Fruitfulness of our North American born People, there is one Daniel Robins, aged about sixty six Years, born in North America, and is now living in the County of Hunterdon; he is so Strong and Healthy that he hath lately travelled oftentimes forty Miles a Day rather than ride an easy Horse. He is the Father of thirteen children, Eleven of which are married, and by them he has Sixty Two Grandchildren, born in less than Eighteen Years Time, which, with his other Children, makes Seventy Five Persons besides Eleven Sons and Daughters in Law, so that, though he is but half the Age of Jacob, when he went down to Egypt, yet he has more Children and Grandchildren than Jacob then had, and with a more remarkable Blessing, he never lost Child nor Grandchild, Son-in-Law or Daughter-in-Law in his Life. And said Daniel Robins, with everyone of his Children, GrandChildren, Sons-in-Law and Daughters-in-Law have their Health, Perfect Senses and Limbs. Thus, it appears that said Daniel Robins has successfully kept and fulfilled that Great and necessary Commandment of "Multiply, be Fruitful and Replenish the Earth" in this Wilderness Country. *The New England Weekly Journal*, July 30, 1733

On the other end of the spectrum of life, old age, even an obituary, if the life had been long, completely and virtuously lived, could bring a smile:

Trenton, January 11. Last Friday died here Sarah Furman, a Widow, about 97 Years of age[45]. She was born at Fairfield, New England; her Maiden Name was Strickland; her first Husband's Name was Roberts; her second Husband's Name was Furman. Such was her Conduct in every Station of Life that she obtain'd from all her Acquaintance the reputation of a good Christian. Her helpless Old Age, attended with twelve Years Blindness, was rendered easy to all about her by her Patience and Resignation. She left a Numerous Off-spring of her own Body, viz.

```
Children - - - - - - - - - - - - - - - -   5
Grand Children - - - - - - - - - - - -  61   (living)
Great Grand Children - - - - - - - - - 182
Great Great Grand Children  - - - - - _12
```

In all 260

The Pennsylvania Gazette, January 27, 1742

---

[45] This means that Mrs. Furman must have been born in 1645, within the first quarter century of the colonization of New England.

A Negro Woman, belonging to Mr. Clement Hall, of Elsenborough, in the County of Salem, New-Jersey, lately died there, aged upwards of 120 Years. *The Pennsylvania Chronicle*, May 11, 1767

The beginning of August last left this Life at Pilesgrove in West New Jersey, Mr. Mounce Keen, aged 105 Years and 8 months. He was born of Swedish Parents at Chester, Pennsylvania and always enjoyed his Health and Understanding well, till within the last few Years of his Life. About three Years before his death, he rode alone three miles and Home again. *The Pennsylvania Gazette*, October 11, 1770

The Governor of the Province, by Proclamation, selected holidays for special occasions, one the spirit of which we continue to observe today:

His Excellency, the Governor of New Jersey has issued a proclamation appointing Thursday the 22d of November next, to be observed as a day of Thanksgiving throughout the province for the signal successes of his Majesty's arms over his enemies. *The New American Magazine for October*, 1759

Wednesday the 28th of November next is appointed by the Government of New-Jersey to be a Day of publick Thanksgiving throughout that Province. *The Boston Weekly News Letter*, November 2, 1750

Two celebrations, only five years apart, depict the growing sense of independence among many of the colonists.

Perth Amboy, January 26. This Day his Majesty King George IIId was proclaimed in this City. In the Morning, the Militia of the County of Middlesex, Horse and Foot, came into Town, and about Twelve o'Clock his Excellency the Governour, attended by the Gentlemen of his Council, repaired to the Court House preceded by the Justices of the Peace of the County of Middlesex, the Mayor, Recorder, Aldermen and Common Council Men of this City, with their proper Officers, where his most Royal and Sacred Majesty was proclaimed, in the Presence of the Governour and the Council, amidst the joyful Acclamations of a numerous Audience of this and the neighbouring Counties. The Troops of Horse and Detachments from the

Regiments of Militia of this County lined both Sides of the Way to the Court House. In the Evening, there were Illuminations, which concluded with all the Demonstrations of Joy, usual upon such Occasions. *The Pennsylvania Gazette*, January 29, 1761

We hear from Philadelphia that on Wednesday the 21st Instant, his Majesty King George the Third, was proclaimed here. . . On the same day a considerable number of Merchants and other Gentlemen of this City repaired to the New Ferry House, to an elegant Entertainment, provided on the Occasion, where they drank his Majesty's and all other loyal Healths, together with his Prussian Majesty, Prince Ferdinand, Prince Henry and all the brave and gallant Generals, Admirals, Officers, Seamen and Soldiers in his Majesty's Service &c. &c. under the Discharge of seven Brass Cannon at every Toast; The Anthem of God Save the King was admirable well sung, with the Chorus, by the Company with Heart and Voice. The whole was conducted with great Decency and concluded to the entire Satisfaction of every one present. *The New York Mercury*, February 2, 1761

On Saturday last, on Account of the Glorious News of the Repeal of the Stamp-Act, an elegant Entertainment was prepared in the City of Burlington, at which his Excellency the Governor and the principal Inhabitants of the Place were present, when the following Toasts were drank viz. The King, The Queen, and Royal Family, the Parliament of Great Britain, the present worthy Ministry, The Governor and Province, the glorious Mr. Pitt, Lord Cambden, Lord Dartmouth, General Howard, Colonel Barre, Doctor Franklin, Trecothic and Hanbury, Friends to America on this and the other side of the Atlantic. May the Stamp Act be buried in Oblivion. Increase to the Manufacturers of Britain and Prosperity to the Agriculture of America.

The city was handsomely illuminated; Bonfires were lighted and other Demonstrations of Joy were shewn and every thing was conducted with the greatest Order and Decorum. *The Pennsylvania Gazette*, May 29, 1766

As the fifteen toasts at the withdrawal of the hated Stamp Tax suggest, celebrations, then, like today, often meant alcohol, which in turn sometimes meant fun or rowdyism:

November 6. We hear from Westchester, that at the Fair held there last Week, a Man from the Jersies, drank in two hours, 17 Quarts of Cyder and Two Quarts of Rum, and to keep it down, eat only 100 Cakes. *The New York Gazette and Weekly Mercury*, November 13, 1769.

New York, December 7. We hear from Crosswicks in West-New-Jersey that some time ago two Brothers quarrelling, the one bit off the other's Ear. It is supposed they had been too free with liquor.
The Boston Weekly News-Letter, December 30, 1731

But, more often than not, the news reports relating to alcohol were of tradegies:

Philadelphia. Last week came to Town five Indians from the back Parts, having done their Business and being on their return home yesterday, at Germantown they met an old Indian from the Jerseys, and after drinking together, they quarrelled and shot the old Man, on which the others were secured and brought to Town last Night. *Pennsylvania Journal*, August 22, 1751

New York, May 28. Last tuesday Evening, Thomas Martin and Gilbert King, both of this City, having been at a tipling house in Elizabeth-Town, in returning to their lodging, Martin grew noisy, and being reproved by King for it, he started up and suddenly stabb'd him in the Breast with a Pen-Knife; a Surgeon was immediately sent for and, apprehending the Wound to be Mortal, Martin was committed to Jail. But we hear that on Thursday last there were some Hopes of King's Recovery. *The Pennsylvania Journal*, May 31, 1753

New-York, January 16. We hear from Little Egg-Harbour, that in the time of the late Snow Storm a little before Christmas, three young Swampmen, who lived in one Cabin, two of the Brothers named Smith, carried a Bag of Corn each to a Mill, about 8 Miles from their Residence, and while their Grists were grinding, they went to a Tavern at a small Distance from the Mill, where having drunk pretty freely, they returned to the Mill in the Evening, took their Baggs on their Backs and went off with Design to go home. The next Morning, one was found dead in the Snow and his Bag nigh him, with an Appearance as if he had struggled to get his Bag from the Ground. Some Distance another was found in the Snow, with some Signs of Life. He was taken to a House and means used for his Recovery but to no Purpose. The other had made a shift to get to an old Cabin and had tried to make up a Bed with Leaves but the Cold overcame him so that he was froze to Death also. *The New York Gazette or Weekly Post Boy*, January 16, 1769

Last week a corporal belonging to the 22d regiment, was found hanging upon a tree in the woods near New Brunswick. He was much esteemed by his officers for his good behaviour. No other reason can be assigned for his committing murder upon himself than gaming. It seems that he had lost about five pounds at cards, which affected him very much and he was observed to be melancholy the evening he disappeared.

Drunkeness and gambling are the two principal springs that give motion to all the disorders committed by soldiers. And I would have all retailers of spiritous liquors seriously to consider what an absurdity as well as an iniquity it is, first to administer to them such pernicious potions as must certainly deprive them of their reason and then complain of the outrages they commit in its absence. These retailers do an injustice to the Publick by turning loose such madmen of their own making, to terrify and insult his Majesty's peaceful subjects. They do an injury to their own officers, by making them uneasy upon hearing these complaints and putting them to the disagreeable necessity of punishing the offenders; and they do injury to the poor fellows themselves by not only bringing them to the halberds, but often to an untimely end and may therefor be justly esteemd accessaries before the fact. *The New American Magazine*, February, 1758

On Sunday the 3d of this Instant July, about 2 a'Clock in the Morning, one John Thompson, an aged Man, who lived in this Town of Salem in New Jersey, who was very Poor, but very subject to drink Rum, had been drinking Rum the fore-part of the Night till he was Drunk or very near it, and being got in a Passion with his Wife, told her, he would pack up his All and go to Carolina; and, thereupon he took a Bundle of Things in a Wallet, or Bag, and went to the Wharffe at the lower end of the Town, and by endeavouring to get into a Cannoe (a Vessel he had chosen to make his Voyage in) accidentally slipped off the Wharffe into the Water and was drowned.

He had a Son drowned near the same place, about two Years ago, in the like condition of being drunk with Rum.

This, and the like, often prove the Consequences of excessive Drinking, which, tho' however frequent such things come to pass, yet nevertheless People will not be deterred from the immoderate Use of strong Liquors. This certainly bespeaks want of due Conduct in the Use of Things, a Defect too frequent amongst Mankind, which is, I think, a perfect Blot in that Escutcheon of Reason annexed to the Fabrick of human Bodies." *The Pennsylvania Gazette*, July 14, 1737

Despite some busy ports and an active fishing industry, New Jersey, as with the other Provinces, was primarily an agricultural society. Its eastern and southern counties helped feed the New York City and Philadelphia markets. Its western side bordered on the frontier, especially in the earlier years. The more west one went, the more wilderness it became.

Descriptions of these early farms, called "plantations" in those days, both in the northern as well as the southern colonies, can be found in early advertisements for their sale or lease. Today, they would be the envy of the even the wealthiest:

To Be Sold

A Plantation in Shrewsbury, New Jersey, containing about 440 Acres, upon Rumson Neck, well Timber'd, it Fronts Northerly on Navesink River, Southerly on the South or Shrewsbury River, both Rivers Navigable; there is plenty on it both of salt and fresh Meadow; several Acres of Clover is yearly Mowed; there is at least 50 Acres more may be put to the same Use if Clear'd. There is on it a good new House, with a large Stone Cellar under it, a Barn and Orchard and the Fences generally in good Repair. There is about 100 Acres cleared; the Land is good for both Winter and Summer Grain and Hay enough may be had on the Premises already to maintain 30 Milch Cows, with other stock answerable yearly. It lately was purchased by Mrs. Mercy Stilwell deceased and ordered by her in her Will to be sold by her Executors, namely Catherina and Elizabeth Stilwell, of whom a good Title to the same will be made to any Purchaser. *The New York Evening Post*, August 10, 1747

There will be Exposed to Sale, by way of Vendue, to the highest bidder, the Plantation that Isaac Stelle now lives on, near Allens-Town, within Two hundred Yards of Nathan Allens Mill, in the Jersey's, on the 3d of June next. Containing about Five hundred and fifty Acres, Two hundred and fifty whereof is Clear'd and in good Fences; well run-over with English Grass. There is on said Place a large Dwelling-House, Barn, Out-Houses and Stables, an Orchard of about 300 Apple-Trees, there is also good Meadowing on said place. . . *The American Weekly Mercury*, April 30, 1730

Monmouth, New Jersey, April 2, 1764. By Virtue of a Writ of *Fieri Facias* to me directed, against the Goods, Chattels, Lands and Tenements of John Tunison, I have seized and taken a Tract of Land, containing 240 Acres, lying and being in the Township of Middletown, near the High Lands of the Neversinks, whereon is a good Dwellling House, Barn &c., with two bearing orchards on the same, being pleasantly situated on Shrewsbury River, within about two Miles of Black Point, with Fishing, Fowling, Oystering &c. within 80 Yards of the Door, where Boats daily pass and re-pass to and from New-York. The Land good for Wheat, Rye and Indian Corn, which tract is to be sold by Way of publick Vendue on Monday, the Fourth of June, next, on the Premises aforesaid, between the Hours of 12 and 5 o'clock in the Afternoon, by me

John Taylor, Sheriff
The Pennsylvania Gazette, May 17, 1764

Livestock, especially horses and cattle, were vital to this rural life and, not unexpectedly, advertisements regarding them are often found in colonial papers. Steeds of proven worth were offered as studs, even outside their own provinces, as bloodlines were expanded[46]:

To cover this Season at Perth-Amboy, at Ten Pounds Proc. each Mare for the Season, the Brown Horse FALSTAFF. He was got by OLD CADE, out of a well bred Mare, and is the Stoutest Horse of Cade's get. *The Pennsylvania Gazette*, March 25, 1762

To cover Mares the ensuing Season

At Robert Rhea's in Freehold, near Monmouth Court House, East-New-Jersey, at three pounds Jersey Proclamation for each mare; the famous black Horse called FREDERICK, Imported two years ago from England. He is full fifteen hands high, and is allowed by good judges to be the most compleat made horse in America. . . . He was got by a son of Hobgoblin's, out of Lord Godolphin's golden-lock mare. His dam was the famous Fire tail mare, belonging to Mr. William Croffts, of Suffolk. Good pasture for mares and proper care taken of them, at one shilling and six pence per week.

N.B. As sundry persons in Pennsylvania have expressed a desire of sending mares to said horse, if they could have convenient opportunity, these are to inform them or any others that will bring their mares to Philadelphia

---

[46] The Dutch, who had minimally colonized New Jersey before the English, apparently had a poor stock of horses. Efforts was thus made by early colonists to improve the American breed, especially with English lines.

by the first day of May, that they shall be sent down to the horse without any expence to them, more than the ferriage and the grain upon the road, and when they have done with the horse, shall be returned to Philadelphia in the same manner, accidents excepted, by applying to John Rhea in Market Street, opposite the Indian King Tavern. *The Pennsylvania Journal*, April 17, 1766

New Jersey, April 4. As sundry Gentlemen, in and out of Philadelphia, are desirious of raising Colts out of the celebrated English Hunting Horse, called Frederick, that is kept for covering Mares in Monmouth County, East-Jersey, they may have the opportunity of sending Mares to him at the 15th of May, by applying to Robert Baines, at Mr. Rhea's Stable, in Church Alley, any time before the said Date and no Expense will attend them, but the Ferriage and eating upon the Road, and the Mares will be returned to them again, when done with the Horse (Accidents excepted). The Price for covering for the Season will be Eight Dollars and eighteen pence per week Pasturage for the Mares to be paid at their Return, or they may have their Mares warranted to be with Foal for Five Pounds, and if they do not prove so, the Money will be returned upon Honour. *The Pennsylvania Gazette*, April 20, 1769

For Covering this Season
The Horse ROEBECK

To be kept by the Subscriber, at Mountholly, New Jersey, at Fifteen Shillings the Season, Twenty-five Shillings a Colt, or Five Shillings a single Leap; he is a famous well made Horse, a good Sorrel, with Blaze and Snip; three white Feet, about fifteen Hands high, rises eight years old this Spring, an excellent Trotter and came of good Country Breed. *The Pennsylvania Gazette*, April 3, 1763

West New-Jersey, April 1, 1766. The Horse Swan Covers Mares this Season. He is a jet black, with one white foot, a small Star, and a Snip, full fifteen Hands High, an exceeding gay, bold Carriaged Horse, a fine Trotter, and swift Pacer, full half blooded and very handsome. The Price 20 Shillings the Season each Mare, to be paid to the Subscriber, living in Wood's Town, Salem County.

Jechonias Wood
The Pennsylvania Gazette, April 10, 1766

THE RAVEN

A very fine three-Quarter blooded Horse, 14 Hands 3 inchs high, a jett Black with a Star and a Snip, one white Foot, rising 7 Years Old this Grass, a very easy Trotter and as handsome perhaps as any Horse upon this Continent, covers this Spring for a Pistole a single Leap, or Two Pistoles Leap and Trial and two Shillings to the Groom, paid at the Stable Door; Mares will be taken good care of by Abraham Chattin, Woodbury Creek, Glouster County, West New-Jersey. *The Pennsylvania Journal*, April 7, 1763

Aside from advertisements for stud service, the early press passed along "horse news" from saddle sales to alerts regarding equine disease:

To Be Sold, three doors below Mr. Leary's livery stables, in Leary's street, a variety of New Sadlery Ware, Among which are ladies hunting saddles, with handsome housing fring'd; Burking's hunting do[47]. with doe skin seats, full welted hog skin do. plain hunting do. chair do. and two neat race saddles; they are all made of the best rivetted trees from Elizabeth-Town. *The New York Journal or General Adviser*, May 5, 1768

We hear from Shrewsbury, in New Jersey, that upwards of forty Horses have lately died in that Township very suddenly, of a Disorder not known here before. They are seized with a trembling of their hind Legs and die almost immediately. It was observed that the Dews in that Part have been very copious and the Grass in the Morning would almost be covered with Spider's Webs and it was supposed that some pernicious Quality in that Dew or those Webs and small Spiders taken in with their Food, might have occasion'd this Mortality. But five exceeding fine Horses, belonging to Mr. Allen of Philadelphia, who was lately at Shrewsbury, tho' they were kept in a Stable and not put to Grass at all, were all seized with the Disorder, four of them died and the fifth is not yet recovered. Some of them were opened and their Livers were found to be much swell'd and inflamed. No certain method of Cure has been discovered. But it is tho't that some had received Benefit from Bleeding and spreading Tar upon their Breasts and about their Nostrils and keeping some in their Mouths, spread upon Rags or Tow tied around the Bitts of their Bridles. *The New York Journal or General Advertiser*, September 17, 1767

---

[47] "do." means "ditto" or the same thing

-152-

Extract of a Letter from Cohansy in New Jersey, dated September 28, 1767

We have the dreadfulnest Havock among our Horses with the Distemnper that was ever heard of; by the most reasonable calculation, I do not think that Two Thousand Pounds would repair the loss to this one County; it has taken off all of our best Horses and Colts and left nothing but Hackneys behind. *The Pennsylvania Gazette*, October 8, 1767

Extract of a Letter from a Correspondent at Princeton, October 28, 1767

The Distemper that has been so prevalent among Horses in the neighbouring Parts, begins also to rage here, tho' I do not hear that it has yet proved fatal to any. The People however are under some uneasiness lest it should prove as mortal as it has been in many other Parts of this and the adjacent Provinces. *The Pennsylvania Chronicle*, November 2, 1767

Boston, January 18. The Mortal Distemper, which lately prevailed among the Horses at New-York, New-Jersey, Pennsylvania etc is now very prevalent in this Province. *The New York Journal or General Advertiser*, January 28, 1768

Cattle also were integral to the colonial farm and news of them is found in the news journals of the day:

Working Oxen

To be sold, by Edward Antill, at his Seat near New Brunswick, four or five Yoke of working Cattle, of different Ages, from 8 to three years old; they are fit for Service, being in Good Heart and full Flesh'd, they are fed upon good Hay and Corn. *The Pennsylvania Gazette*, March 4, 1762

To Be Sold by John Forman, near the Court-House, at Freehold, Monmouth County, Two Steers, Six Years old this Spring; one has been measured, he is nine feet and one inch from the Middle of his Forehead to the Extremity of his Rump; he is nine Feet and one inch Thick and is something better than 17 Hands High; the other is not much inferior to him. They have been fed in the best Manner than they could have been ever since they were between Three and Four Years old; they have had as much Indian Meal as they could eat and the best Clover Hay, green Wheat, and the best Clover Pasture that could be glad for them since the first Beginning to feed them. Fatter nor larger Cattle has never been seen or raised in the said County before. Any Person that has a mind to buy said Cattle, may apply to the aforesaid John Forman and they shall have them reasonable. *The New York Gazette*, February 28, 1763

We hear that there was killed the Week before last at Elizabeth-Town a Steer, which had been there in keeping by Robert Ogden, Esq. about 9 Months, weighing, Beef, Hide and Tallow, about 1700 Weight. This Steer was bred by Doctor Lewis Johnson of Perth Amboy. *The New York Gazette* March 14, 1763

To be Sold by the Subscriber In the County of Cape May and Province of New Jersey, a Number of Fat Cattle, consisting chiefly of Oxen and Steers, fit for Slaughter.
     Jeremiah Leaming

N.B. There may be a large parcel of Grassfed Cattle bought in the said County, of different People besides him. *The Pennsylvania Gazette*, September 6, 1770

Philadelphia, March 27. Wednesday Last, an Ox was Kill'd by Joseph Stinrand and Sold in our Market, the four quarters of which weighed only 477 pound, but the clear Suet about one of the Kidneys weighed 53 pound, that about the other 22 pound and the Gut-Fat or Tallow 38 pound. So much Fat in so small a Creature, particularly about one Kidney, is reckoned a very extraordinary Thing. It was raised and fattened at Shrewsbury in East Jersey. *The American Weekly Mercury*, April 14, 1735

New York, June 4. A few Days ago, the extraordinary Size of a Calf of 3 Days old, belonging to Mr. Joseph Van Martyr, of Middletown, in New Jersey, induced him to weight it, when he found the weight to be 98 lb. *The New York Journal or General Advertiser*, June 4, 1767.

Notice is hereby given to the Ladies and the Gentlemen that the Subscribers intend to kill a Steer, which was raised in Springfield, New Jersey, the like never before killed in America. It may be seen, *gratis*, at George Wolpper's in Race Street, a few doors above Fourth Street, on the 20th instant; and, notwithstanding that there have been several fine Cattle killed heretofore, yet none of them was like this, either for Largeness or

Fatness. Notice will be given when he will be killed and weighted; those who are pleased to favour us with their Custom, it shall be greatly acknowledged by their humble Servants, George and Benjamin Wolpper, standing at No. 45. *The Pennsylvania Gazette*, March 15, 1770

On Saturday Morning the Steer mentioned in our last to be killed by George and Benjamin Wolpper was weighted at Stall No. 45 in our Market, as follows, viz. the four Quarters 1394 lb., rough tallow 225 lb. and the Hide 126 lb., in all 1745lb. *The Pennsylvania Gazette*, April 5, 1770

A Correspondent from New Jersey informs us that a few Weeks ago a pretty extraordinary Affair happened in his Neighbourhood. A Ram broke into a Pasture among some Oxen, one of which he attacked, and after several parries between them, the Ram drew a few Steps back and ran with such Violence at the Ox, that the latter dropped down and died instantly. *The New York Gazette and Weekly Mercury*, October 24, 1768

This last account was quickly used as the basis for a political comment:

A Correspondent who dates his letter at Burlington, writes us, that the Encounter between the Ox and the Ram, mentioned in the Chronicle Extraordinary of October 26, Page 340, wherein the former was slain on the Spot, happened in that Town before a Number of Spectators and adds this Quere: Whether it might not be well to train a Regiment of these Gentlemen and send them to the Assistance of the Boston Men, for I think the Regiment that has arrived there may be justly taken for Government Bulls. *The Pennsylvania Chronicle*, November 7, 1768

Swine also were important agricultural products worth some bragging:

Philadelphia, Dec. 18. 'Tis said that a Hog was lately killed near Burlington that weighted 518 lb. *The New England Weekly Journal*, January 6, 1736

Philadelphia January 24. Last Week the large Hog bred in New Jersey, which was kept here some time for a Show, was killed. He measured (when dead) from his Nose to the End of his Tail 8 Feet and 4 Inches. He was not so fat as was expected and weighted but 574 pounds, when singed and dressed. *The Boston Evening Post*, February 20, 1738.

One Day Last Week a Hog that weights upwards of 850 lbs. was brought to Town, alive, from New Jersey. Those who have seen him think he is the largest Creature of the Kind ever raised in America. It is said he will be sold, next Market Day, for the Gratification of the true Lovers of fat Pork. *The Pennsylvania Chronicle*, December 7, 1767

Sheep also became popular sights in colonial New Jersey pastures. They had their admirers. Some seemed to be genuine shepherds, anxious to protect their flocks:

Our inclinations are different as our Faces, mine have let me to the Care of Sheep. . . The Public is certainly much interested in the fleecy Flock. . . Legislatures have thought Sheep an object worthy their Notice. . . The Assembly of New Jersey enacted several laws for their Preservation, but those laws being only temporary have now expired. By the last Act of that Province, among other things, a Tax of one Shilling was laid on the first Dog kept in any Family and two Shillings on every other; this Fund was appropriated to make good the Damages done by Dogs killing Sheep.

Amintor
Supplement to the Pennsylvania Gazette, September 10, 1770

In reading the Supplement to the Pennsylvania Gazette, I was met with a Piece, signed *Amintor*, which was so agreeable to my Mind that I could not but rejoice when I read it and should be glad if it might not be a Means of making some Provision for the Safety of our Flocks in the Jerseys. I must confess that I was sorry when I heard that so useful a Law as that which laid a Tax on Dogs was expired and come to an End. Is not taking the Tax off Dogs, an Encouragement for many People to raise and keep more than are really necessary? And Dogs, when they get several of them together, are more apt to do Mischief than where there is but one by himself.
[Continuance of the tax] is the Case with many more, if not the Greatest part, of the Farmers in New Jersey.

One Objection I have heard against the Dog Tax is that it amounted to a great deal for the Hunters, who keep Hounds, to pay; but, may we not say with Amintor, to tax the mischievous Pleasures of Mankind, cannot be thought unjust or impolitic?

A Jersey Man
The Pennsylvania Gazette, September 17, 1770

I agree with *Amintor* and the *Jersey Man*, that the Tax upon Dogs has been found beneficial in the Province of New Jersey. The only Objection I have to it is that the Sums raised did not pay all the Damages done, but I doubt not that our honourable Assembly will not only revive the Dog tax at their next session but will also make the tax two Shillings a Dog, instead of one.

A Grazier

New York Journal or General Advertiser, September 27, 1770

But sheep also meant business, both <u>short term</u> in generating profits, but also <u>long term</u>, creating jobs and a manufacturing capability and thereby lessening the colonies' reliance upon England.[48] Indeed, the following writer had visions that foresaw the industrial revolution of the northeast and the end of a principally agrarian society.

Sir,

A Farmer in New Jersey gives the following genuine Account of the Profit he made on his Sheep in one year, which please to communicate to the Public, as it may induce others to follow his Example.

In the Fall of 1769, he had 46 Sheep; the Common Rate in that season is 8 shillings per Head [which equals] 18 pounds, 8 shillings.

In May of 1770, he had a 136 pounds of wool which he used sold at 2 shillings [which equals] 13 pounds, 12 shillings.

He has sold or used in his Family 8 Weathers[49] at 15 shillings is [which equals] 6 pounds.

---

[48] One of the industries that far seeing colonists were trying to encourage domestically was the manufacture of cloths and woolen products. The availability of wool was essential to that effort:

As a further Specimen of the Practicability of manufacturing our own clothes in this country, we can assure the Public of the following persons in Woodbridge in New-Jersey, making in their respective Families, within the Year past, both woolen and linen of their own raising, the Quantities following, viz. Mr. Isaac Freeman, 599 Yards, Mr. James Smith, 567 Yards, and Mr. Nathaniel Heard, 414 Yards.

The New York Journal or General Advertiser, January 21, 1768

[49] a castrated ram

He has sold or used in his Family 4 Ewes at 8 shillings [which equals] 1 pound, 12 shillings.

His Stock now remains 56, value at 8 shillings as above [which equals] 22 pounds, 8 shillings.

Which gives a profit of 25 pounds, 4 shillings on 18 pounds 12 shillings. The winter was uncommonly open so that they required very little fodder, hardly any besides Corn Stalks in February and March to the heavy Ewes and in Summer a Fallow of about 45 Acres, kept them to the First of September, except about three Weeks. Another Farmer in this Neigbourhood who kept 60 Sheep last Winter, sold this summer 14 Weathers for 15 pounds fifteen shillings so that his Profit must have been greater, but have not the particulars.

We might expect that self interest would be a sufficient motive to Farmers to increase their Stock of Sheep, as they are indisputably more advantageous than any other Article they can go upon and much less Trouble. It is also of the highest concern to the Public, for it is not doubted that if we had double the Quantity of Wooll, that it would be all manufactured. Now every pound of Wooll of 2 shillings may be worth 8 shillings. Therefore, a Farmer who increases his Stock of Sheep, besides the great gain to himself, will highly benefit the Country for reckoning each Sheep, will yield 2 1/2 pound when made up will be worth 20 shillings of which 15 shillings will be clear gain to the Colony.

The County of Hunterdon in 1768 had in all nearly 20,000 Sheep. Suppose them to be doubled, which might very well be if they kept fewer useless Horses and plowed fewer worn out Fields, this would yield 50,000 pounds of Wooll and would be worth 15,000 pounds besides paying for the Wooll, for all the Expences of Spinning, Weaving and Dressing is our own Labour, except a little dying stuff. But suppose we reckon the County of Hunterdon together with the twelve other Counties, should each increase their Sheep only 5,000, this would make an Addition of 65,000 in the Colony, the Wooll made up would be worth 43,750 pounds besides paying the Farmer. What a large annual Sum, would thus be saved or gained to the Colony and how worthy the Attention of the Public?

The Farmer who gives the above Account has already increased his Flock of Sheep to above 100 and, although four times as many as used to be kept on his Farm, he further intends to add to this Number.

In this Backsliding Age, the only effectual Remedy against Importation, that Bane of our Country, would be for the Northern colonies to increase their number of Sheep, which, together with raising flax, will put the Materials in our Hands of being a Rich and Powerful People. For, if we take to Manufacturing, it will keep our wealth at Home and our People together who are now scattering over this wide extensive Continent to remote Wildernesses, where they live slothful indigent lives and are lost to the Community. However much better might they live by improving the old Lands, settling Towns and increasing our Manufactures. This would be establishing more Wealth than Mines of Gold and Silver or an extensive foreign Trade. Are not Spain and Portugal Poor, tho' they are the Masters of the Richest Mines in the World? And what advantage is Trade to us, while we export Provisions or raw materials and import superfluities? *New York Journal or General Advertiser*, September 20, 1770

The Papers also published other information important to those who worked the colonial farms:

As the best time for transplanting of Apple-Trees and indeed of any Trees natural to this Country is now approaching, that is at any Time between the Fall of the Leaf and the Setting in of Winter or hard Frosts, as has been found by the Experience of curious and judicious Persons, These are to inform the Publick that any one wanting young Apple Trees fit to transplant into an Orchard may be supplied with a sufficient Number of such Trees by Edward Antill, living near New Brunswick, at Nine Pence per Tree if chosen, or six Pence per tree if taken by Row, as they stand in the Nurserys; they may be easily transported by Water. *The New York Gazette Revived in the Weekly Post Boy*, October 29, 1750

A Gentleman from Trenton favoured us with the following Account of a most remarkable Increase in a Gentleman's Garden there, viz. a single Grain of Rye produced 69 Ears, which contained 4800 Grains. *The Pennsylvania Gazette*, July 9, 1767

The Daucus or Wild Carrot that is found on my Farm grows in a moist loamy rich Soil, that has been in Tillage once every three or four years, for these Hundred Years past, having been an old Indian Field.

If anything here is omitted, that may be judged necessary for the more ready finding the desired Plant, upon information either from thyself or any Person discovered, shall readily give any further Description that may be desired. And am

Thy Friend
Robert Hartshorne
The New York Journal or General Advertiser, August 13, 1767

This is to give notice to all persons that the Subscriber, now living in the Jerseys, has a Quantity of Garden Seeds to dispose of viz. Charlton dwarf pease, dwarf marrowfat, the common dwarf, the early horspur, the Spanish marat, the green oston, the white and brown sugar pea, the rich marrowfat, the bush pea, the Windsor beans and all sorts of kidney beans, with all other sorts of garden seeds, the best of their kind. The customers may be supplied at a covered stall, at the upper end of the Jersey Market, north side, or at Caleb Hewes's, Hatter, a few doors down from the New Printing Office, where customers may depend upon good usage by

Richard Collins, Gardiner

N.B. Any Person that has a Boy that inclines to learn the art and mystery of a gardiner, may apply as above. *Pennsylvania Gazette*, March 8, 1770

These are to give Notice that on Wednesday the 26th of this Instant October, at the Borough Town of Trenton, in the County of Hunterdon in the Province of New Jersey, will be held and kept a Fair, in the selling and buying and all Manner of Horses, Mares, Colts, Cows, Calves, Steers, Hogs, Sheep, and all other Cattle, Goods, Wares and Merchandizes whatsoever. Which said Fair will be held and kept the same Day above mentioned and Two Days next following pursuant to a Clause in a Charter of Privileges, lately granted to the said Borough for that Purpose. *The Pennsylvania Journal*, October 3, 1745

New York, October 17. The Public are hereby informed that from good Intelligence, received from the Back Country, a large number of fat and store Horn Cattle, Horses and Swine, will be offer'd for sale at Newark on Wednesday, the 19th of October inst., being the day appointed by a late Advertisement, for the opening of the annual Cattle-Market, in that Town, and to be continued on the Thursday and Friday following, when and where all Persons may be supplied with the above mentioned Cattle and Swine. *The New York Gazette and Weekly Mercury*, October 17, 1768

Whereas many Inconveniences frequently attend the Sale of Horses, Horn Cattle, Sheep, and Swine, for want of some publick convenient stated Market or Fair, where Sellers and Buyers might meet for that Purpose. And as the Town of Newark, from its vicinity to New-York, and other circumstances attending its Situation, is by many, esteemed a most Proper Place for such a Cattle Market, it is the Request of a Number of the Inhabitants of New-York and New-Jersey, that Publick Notice is hereby given, That on the Third Wednesday in October next, and on the Thursday and Friday following, and on the same Days yearly, and every Year thereafter, will be opened and held at Newark aforesaid, a publick Market, for the sale of all kinds of horses, fat and Store Horned Cattle, Sheep and Swine, and for no other Purpose whatsoever (except it be for the Sale of the Products and Manufactories of the Country.) Proper Officers will attend for the Preservation of Decorum and Good Order. Newark, August 16, 1768 *The New York Gazette and Weekly Mercury*, August 22, 1768

Whereas Richard Collings, Gardener, once of the Northern Liberties, for some Years past has not followed raising of Garden Seeds, as he formerly did, by reason of a removal to the Jerseys, and not having his Ground properly cultivated for that Business, he now gives public Notice that for the last two Years, he has taken care to procure an Assortment of the best Garden Seeds, Pease and Beans of all sorts and begs the Favour of his former customers to apply to him, at his Stand, at the upper End of the Jersey Market, Philadelphia, on the North Side where they shall be kindly used. *The Pennsylvania Gazette*, March 2, 1760

Stolen out of Daniel Cooper's Corn Field, opposite to Philadelphia, a Corn Harrow; it was payed in the Spring with a Coat of Pitch; it has a Knee fixed along the Middle of it, fastened down at the fore End with a Bolt and Key; it has handles fixed on the Top, not unlike to Plow or Wheelbarrow handles, to work with it; it contains 35 Iron Teeth; it has in the fore End of the Knees two Holes, one above the other, for the Clevis Pin to go through; as also was taken away, at the same Time with it, a Clevis Plow, fixed to the head of same (it is supposed that the above described Harrow was taken away by Water). Whoever will give Information to the Owner, so that the Harrow may be had, and the Thief detected so that he may be brought to Justice, shall have Forty Shillings, as reward for the same, from

Daniel Cooper

The Pennsylvania Gazette, August 10, 1769

The forests of the Province contained much game, some, like the mountain lions, snakes and bears, dangerous to the colonists. Witness the following accounts:

Philadelphia, January 13. On Monday senninght was killed near Shrewsbury in the Jerseys a monstrous large Phanter, the like never seen before in these Parts. Its Legs being thicker than a that of a Horse, with a Body proportionable and the Nails of its Claws longer than that the middle Finger of a Man's Hand.

It seems that the Indian who killed him was creeping up on the Ground, in order to have a Shot at a Buck, but hearing the rustling of leaves

It seems that the Indian who killed him was creeping up on the Ground, in order to have a Shot at a Buck, but hearing the rustling of leaves behind him accidentally saw the Panther a few yards off, just ready to leap upon him, he thereupon instantly fires and, luckily, with 4 or 5 Swan shot, hit him in the Head and Killed him. The Indian received a considerable Reward for the Service from the Liberality of the neighbouring People. *The New England Weekly Journal*, February 23, 1730

Philadelphia, May 13. There has lately been killed near Mount Holly, in the Jersies, the largest Bear that has been known in these Parts; his Forehead measur'd two Spans wide, his Leg just above the Foot as big as could be well grasp'd with both hands after the Skin was off, and tho' exceeding lean, he weight'd upwards of 300 weight. There has been another of the same gigantic size seen about the same place. *The Pennsylvania Gazette*, May 6, 1731

Near Colt's Neck in Monmouth County, New Jersey, a few Days ago, three or four men dug out of the Side of a Hill, from whence a fine Spring issued, Fifty-two large Rattle Snakes and Nineteen Black Snakes, all twined together in one Bunch or Knot. The cold Weather prevented them, from making any resistance, though the Rattle Snakes were so lively as to be able to rattle prity briskly. They cut the Heads of the Rattle Snakes off and then Skin'd them. The Digging was purposely after them, as a great Number had been seen near the Spring the Summer before. *The New York Mercury*, February 2, 1761

Other prey was not as threatening. However, that did not seem to lessen the vengeance with which they were pursued.

New York, December 11. We are desired to let the Public know that the New Jersey Men will not be outdone by those of New England, in so virtuous an Act as killing those destructive Vermin called Squirrels. For it is said that a whole Town of the latter assembled and killed about 1600, whereas about thirty eight men of the former, from the Towns of Morris and Mendem (not one Quarter of either) in one Day killed 840. *The New York Gazette and Weekly Mercury*, December 11, 1769.

In this pristine setting, there must have wonders of nature that, we, hundreds of years later, find hard to believe:

Upper-Freehold, September 7. Yesterday one Thomas Deacon, a Servant to Robert Lawrence and a Boy of about 11 Years of Age, coming from Meeting together, heard their Dog (who for Fashion sake had been at Meeting) bark very much, sent the child to see what was the Matter, who running back told him, it was two great Bucks, fast together by the Horns. The Man with much difficulty cut both their throats, their Horns being so locked together that the several have tried to part them, since both their Heads are cut off, but find it cannot be done without breaking or cutting of them. *The American Weekly Mercury*, September 2, 1731.

We hear from Hopewell in the Jerseys that on the 4th past, two Bucks were observed fighting near the New Meeting House there, one of them extraordinary large, supposed to be a Roe-Buck, the other small and of the common sort. In company with them was a Black Doe, who stood by to see the Engagement. The small Buck proved a full match for the great one, giving him many violent Punches in the Ribs, but in the height of the Battle, they fastened their Horns so strongly together that they were not able with all their Strength to disengage and in that condition were taken. The Doe retreated into the Woods, but being pursued with several Beagle Hounds, she was taken also alive and they have put her and the large Buck into a boarded Pasture, hoping to have a breed, if the Sizes are not too unsuitable. This is the second Brace of Bucks that have been caught by the Horns this Year. Had they not better put 'em quietly in their pockets? *The Pennsylvania Gazette*, October 7, 1731

From Shrewsbury in East New Jersey, on Saturday the last Day of December, 1726. Theophilus Longstreat of Shrewsbury in the County of Monmouth, aged near Sixty Years, he met with seven Swans flying over a Meddow who shot down Six of them at one Shot, such a Shot was never known amongst us. *The American Weekly Mercury*, February 14, 1727.

Nature was unspoiled in those earliest years, as the following description of property along the Delaware River suggests:

There are great variety of Fish that are caught on the River, which affords a great deal of Diversion in Trouling and Angling the whole Spring and Summer and in the Fall and Winter Seasons there is great Plenty of Duck and other Water Fowl. *The Pennsylvania Journal*, July 12, 1759

The first settlers often fought among themselves for the rights to the beast of the forests and the fish of the streams and seas:

Whereas some Persons have of late entered in to the Park of me the subscriber Johnn Schulyer, on New Barbadoes Neck, in the County of Bergen, and have there shot and killed some of my Deer in the said Park.

These are therefore to forbid all Persons to enter into said Park, or to carry a Musket or Firelock on any of my inclosed Lands or Meadows without my Leave first obtained for so doing, under the Penalty of being prosecuted with the utmost Rigour of the Law.

I hereby also promise to give a reward of Ten Shillings to any one who shall inform me and prove any Person's going armed with a Musket or Firelock into said Park, without my Leave as aforesaid.
And also a Reward of Three Pounds to any Person who shall inform me and prove so as to convict any Person of Killing or Shooting at any Deer in said Park without my Liberty being first had and obtained as aforesaid.

John Schuyler
The New York Gazette Revived in the Weekly Post Boy, December 4, 1749

New York. We are informed that last week some People belonging to this City went a Oysterin near Amboy, a party of their Men came off in a Canoe well armed and asked what business they had to come and fetch Oysters on our Beds? They answered in a surly manner what was that to them, they immediately fired on them, kill'd two and wounded one, the Men's Names are not known as yet. *The New-York Evening Post*, November 21, 1748

Whereas on Monday Night last (June 14) some malicious Person was at the Pains to carry a large Rock of 4 or 500 Weight and place it in the middle of the Fishing-ground where I draw my Seine. The chief Person suspected is one N.P. living near Trenton, he having told three credible Persons, that I catched so many Fish as spoiled his Trolling and had asked one or two to lend a hand in placing a large Rock Stone in my Way, that he would lay it in such a Manner, that when I went out with my Seine it should run under the Rock, and then the D----l could not get it out , and that he would carry it out in a Flat, on a Platform, or Board, so as to let it down easy, with the Edge upwards, just as he would have it. Accordingly, the next Day, going out with my Seine, found such as Rock as that Person described, and two more with it, which tore my Seine and did me considerable Damage, besides losing the most promising Part of the Season. And as the Place where I fish is no Man's particular Property (being almost in the

Middle of the River and free for any Person) to prevent others from meeting with the like Obstructions, have thought it proper to publish the same, with a Reward of Five Pounds, to anyone that will impeach either of the Persons concerned in this base Action so as he or they be brought to Justice.

Edward Broadfield[50]

New York, March 19. By an Act lately passed in New Jersey, any Person seeing another carry a Gun over any inclosed Land, not his own, by Information against him, obliges him to Pay 5 Pounds and to be bound over to his Good behavior, one Half to the Informer; and, in case of failure, to be dealt with at the Judge's Discretion. In Consequence of this Act, we hear, a few Weeks ago, a poor Fellow, in East New Jersey, was taken in the Fact and brought to a Justice. The Justice was accordingly obliged to give Judgment, but the poor Fellow, Gun and all, was not worth Half the Money, the Justice was at a Stand what to do.; at last determined him a Whipping of Thirty Lashes, and as the Informer was entitled to Half the Fine, very judiciously ordered him to receive one Half the Lashes. *The Pennsylvania Gazette*, March 27, 1753

The clean waters and abundance of wildlife gave rise to industries which flourished briefly before devouring themselves:

We are told that the Whale Men catch'd six whales at Cape May and twelve at Egg-Harbour. *The Boston News-Letter*, March 17, 1718

On the 25th of February last, there were two whales killed at Cape May, the one is ashore on Cape Island and the other on the upper end of the Cape, on the East Side; 'tis supposed they will yield about 40 Barrels of Oil each; the one was three years old and the other a Yearling; the whale men are in hopes of killing more, for they have lately seen several more on the Coast, near the Cape. *The Pennsylvania Gazette*, March 11, 1736

Philadelphia, April 23. We hear from Cape May that they have taken Six Whales there this Spring. *Pennsylvania Journal*, April 23, 1752

New York, December 11. Last Saturday, a dead Whale 45 Feet 9 inches long and 9 Feet thick, was found floating in our Bay, by a Jersey Boatman and has since been towed over to the Jersey Shore. *Pennsylvania*

---

[50] Edward Broadfield appears frequently in the news papers of the 1760s. His business was the catching, curing (by pickling) and sale of sturgeon. He appeared to be constantly fighting with --or complaining about the ethics -- of his competitors. Upon his death, his widow Margaret took over the business and ran it with the same whine.

New York, September 4. We hear that on Tuesday last, Mr. **Abner Hetfield**, of Elizabeth-Town, and another Man, being out fishing, discovered a whale swimming about, near Coney island, on which soon after it ran ashore, and before it could get off, they came up and killed it with a rusty sword that happened to be on board the vessel. We are told that Mr. **Coffler**, at the Ferry, opposite to this City, on Long Island, has bought it for 30 pounds and that it is now brought up to that Place. It is said to be 45 feet in Length and that, if cut up, it would produce about seventy barrels of Oyl. *The New York Gazette or Weekly Post Boy*, September 4, 1766

New York, October 29. We hear from Amboy that 2 Whales were seen near that Place about a Fortnight ago but, before any Persons properly skilled could be got, they had disappeared and are thought to be got back to Sea. *The Pennsylvania Gazette*, November 5, 1761

Natural fish kills were a phenomena in the unpolluted 1700s as well as today:

We have Advice from New Brunswick, that on Monday Morning last, Abundance of dead Fish appeared floating down Rariton River, which increased till next Day, when Numbers of them were drove ashore and began to putrify; and 'tis imagin'd that, if the Inhabitants do nor speedily take Measures either to burn or to bury them, they may cause such a Stench as may produce Disease. 'Tis conjectur'd that the excessive hot Weather of the Day before has occasioned their Destruction as we have since heard that many died at the same time in Elizabeth Town Creek. *The Boston Weekly Post-Boy*, July 3, 1749

On occasion, the sea also threw up menaces and mysteries:

Burlington, August 11. Saturday and Sunday last, a Shark judg'd to be near 10 Foot long was seen swimming up and down in the River near this City. *The Pennsylvania Gazette*, August 7, 1736.

New-York. We are credibly informed that some Days ago a Fish was found dead ashore near Harsimus in New-Jersey, opposite the back of this

City, having a head nearly resembling that of a Man, with some Hair on it. It was first discovered by a young Man, who observing the Crows very busy at it, went to view and at coming Home told his Father; but the Father thinking it was only the Effect of an idle Imagination, took no further notice of it till some Days after, when some other Persons going that way, also perceived it and were much dismay'd at it; but not yet thinking it was worth their while or else being afraid to meddle with it, they let it lye some Days longer, by which Time the Crows had almost entirely carried off all the Body except the Bones, which, 'tis said, about the Breast and Ribs, very much resemble the human Anatomy, but as it draws to the Tail ends very much like a Fish. This strange Phenomena has occasioned no small Speculation all over that Part of the Country, as well as in some parts of this City; however, we are told that it has been since discovered, or at least thought to be, only a Porpoise with his Snout eaten off; but whether a Porpoise has Ribs resembling a Man's or anything like hair on its Head must be submitted to those who are better acquainted with the Dissection of Fishes than we dare pretend to be. *The New York Weekly Post Boy*, January 27, 1746

The mystery of the next account is whether the author of the "follow up" piece to the first report was poking sarcastic fun at the press and its audience:

New Brunswick, July 6. This Day a Porpois was taken and killed in this River, above the Still-House which drew together a great Number of Spectators, while some in Boats, Canoes &c formed a Line across the River, in order to keep him in, and to prevent her Escape to deeper Water and more Sea-Room; others had their Guns to fire upon her, whenever she'd rise. This continued for several Hours, till at last after having received several Wounds in the Body, was shot thro' the Head, which did her Business. She measured 8 Feet and a half. These are rarely seen so far up; whenever it so happens, they seem to be lost. *The New York Gazette Revived in the Weekly Post Boy*, July 10, 1749

Mr. Parker, As the following further and more complete Account in Relation to the strange Adventure at New Brunswick of taking a Porpois &c may be entertaining to your Readers, I desire you'll give it a place in your Paper

J.S.

After this Fish was actually taken and killed, a great Dispute arose to whom the Benefits of the Oyl which should be tried out, should belong. Some were of the Opinion that every Person who had been at taking the Fish should have an equal share, whilst others objected and said that, altho' that was a Rule among Hunters, yet it was not so among Fishermen; others were of an Opinion that it belonged to the Person who gave it the Mortal Wound for which he earnestly contended. In the meantime, a third Method was proposed, and that was, the Fish was to be tried up by Persons to be appointed for that purpose, for which they should be first paid out of the Mesne Profits, and the Residue should be applied to the Relief of the Poor, which was unanimously agreed to and so the unhappy Dispute ended. The Fish was accordingly tried and afforded three and a half Pints of Oyl, which I hear they offer to sell at the rate of 12 shillings per gallon. Something further remarkable is that this same Day Capt. Collins arrived here in a Scow, in three weeks from the Shipyard, two miles below this Town, who brings advice, that on his Passage here, he was surprized by seeing in the Water, a strange Animal, which, from the Description he gives, is judg'd to be a musk-rat. *The New York Gazette Revived in the Weekly Post Boy*, July 31, 1749

The above might have been written in jest. But, clearly the wealth of the waters was often the subject of fighting:

The late Seizure of sundry Boats belonging to New-York, made by Persons appointed to put in Execution the Act of Assembly made for the Preservation of Oysters within the Province of New-Jersey having occasioned a Great Clamour and Reflection against the Inhabitants of this Province [New Jersey] . . . [t]he Proprietors of the Province of New Jersey are said to be legally vested, under the Crown, with a Right (among other things) to all Fishings in all the Rivers to the Westward of the Channel from Sandy Hook to Hudson's River. I suppose the Fishery of Oysters passed in that Grant. . . .

The occasion of putting this Law into execution is this. Several Boat-Men in Boats belonging to New York, provided themselves with chosen men, small Arms, Powder and Bullets &c. in direct Opposition to the Law, did gather large Quantities of Oysters from the Beds within the Bounds of this Province, where Captain Hews (one of the Commissioners) accidently being with a White Man and a Negro, saw these Men transgressing &c., he thereupon manfully attacked, entered and seized the Boat of one John Cannon, who was called their Commodore, and was fastened to another, in which there were 15 Men, accoutred, as is before set forth. After his receiving many blows, they knocked him overboard, but he recovered himself and seized the Boat of one David Provoost, another of Jacques Dennis and a Pettiauger of Alderman Romer and brought them into Amboy, but Commodore Cannon and one William Cook got clear and hoisted a Flag of Defiance (as they called it) and dared the Jersey Men to attack them (as by their Message). Capt. Hewes pursued them and, Cook running aground, Hewes came up with him. Hewes resisted with six Men and presented their Fire Arms to Capt. Hewes (who had not any with him) but, not being daunted thereat, he enter'd and seized Cook's Boat, but in the Engagement two of our Men were knock'd overboard and had like to have been drowned and two others of our Men wounded to the Scull. One of our Men who were knocked overboard, being got upon Cook's Deck again (and before he had recovered his Senses) took up a Cutlass and struck Cook upon the Head, which was the chief Wound the New-York Men received, who then surrendered their loaded Arms, one of which was loaded with Nine Swan Shot . . .

Being landed at Perth Amboy, they were treated civilly but conducted before the Mayor and other Magistrates, who upon Complaint and Proof of Facts committed against the words and intent of the Law, could do no less than commit them, but they remained in the Court House, without any Restraint of Lock and, on the 3d and 4th Day, they were all bayl'd out and the whole matter accommodated with the Persons who, by the Act, had the right to the Seizures, by the Mediation of almost every one who was on hand and the like was done in behalf of the Owners of the two Boats and Periauger, who all (before they left Amboy) acknowldg'd their transgressions and the reasonable treatment they have met with. . . . *The New York Gazette*, March 22, 1736.

Finally, in addition to its rich soil and abundant pasture, its streams and coastal waters, its forest full of wildlife, the Province of New Jersey also had another resource, minerals. Mining is not something we associate today with New Jersey. Yet, it was back in the colonial era, especially iron mines. The production of iron was an essential of colonial survival and New Jersey became the leading producer of it until the Revolution. This was bog-iron, not the deep red ore of the Great Lakes region.[51] It is found in swamps and flooded woodlands throughout the province and, once extracted, had to be purified in the furnaces and forges of an "iron works", of which Jersey had many.

The newspapers also indicated that copper was another mineral that was early mined in the Province:

---

[51] Bog iron is a hydrous peroxide of iron containing 40% metallic iron. It was formed by a complex process that transferred, by means of percolating ground waters, the iron in the greensand and other cretaceous formations of a hundred million years ago to the decayed vegetation that lay in woodland swamps and pools. Gradually, sometimes in fewer than twenty years, these deposits, mixed with other mud, dried out and hardened into thick ore beds, which could be effectively mined and refined.

These are to give Notice to all Persons who may have the appearance of Copper, or other Mines, on their Lands and not inclined to go with the Work themselves that John Johnston of Perth Amboy and Company will hire the Land of the Owners and give them One Sixth Part of the Produce of the Mine, clear of all Charges, and in Eighteen Months, or sooner, will be obliged to provide Miners and go on with the Work.

You may direct your letters to Dr. John Johnston in Perth Amboy and Time and Place will be appointed to meet in Order to agree concerning the above Proposal.[52] *The American Weekly Mercury*, February 20, 1722

Philadelphia, January 16. We hear from Rocky Hill in the Jersies that a very Valuable Copper Vein of Six Foot Square is very likely found there. *The Pennsylvania Gazette*, January 16, 1753

---

[52] This interest was apparently caused by the discovery of copper in Belleville, near Newark.

In colonial days, the relationship between man and woman had many of the same aspects to it, both pleasant and unpleasant, that it does today. Happiness, harmony and a life of love were undeniably the goals of marriage. The following news article, styled in the form of a letter between friends, presented colonial America's view as to the desirability of enduring marriages:

Mr. Parker,

Please to give the following Letter a Place in your next Paper and believe you will not disoblige the Publick by obliging your constant Reader &c.

A Letter to a Gentleman from his Friend, July 7, 1752

Sir,

As you are a known and peculiar Votary to a State of Celibacy, I judged it would do you no disservice to acquaint you of a late Occurrence, which sufficiently evidences, that after the most mature Consideration, some of our wisest and best Men, do prefer the Endearments of the Nuptial Bed. About eight Days since, the Rev. Mr. Aaron Burr, President of the College of New Jersey[53], was married to a Daughter of the renowned Mr. Jonathan Edwards[54], late of Northampton. She is a young Lady of about Twenty-one; her Person may be called agreeable, her natural Genius seems to be sprightly, and, no doubt, is greatly improved by a virtuous Education. In short, she appears to be one every way qualified to make a Man of Sense and Piety happy in the conjugal Relation. As to the Courtship or Marriage, I shall not descend to Particulars . . . I hope, Sir, that this Instance both as to Matter and Form, will have its genuine Influence upon you, and, as well, bear a Part in convincing you, that Wedlock is incomparably preferable to the roving Uneasiness of the Single State, as to direct you, when you are chusing your Mate, that instead of acting the modern Gallant, wisely, to

---

[53] Today, Princeton.

[54] A famous preacher of the times.

imitate the present Example and so have the Honour of being another, who, in this Day of Degeneracy, has endeavoured to restore Courtship and Marriage to their original Simplicity and Design. I am, Sir, &c.

Philogamus[55]

The New York Gazette revived in the Weekly Post Boy, July 20, 1752

In fact, there is some suggestion, matrimony being such a desired status, that, in the very earliest days of the Province and under very limited circumstances, a Court could even order some couples to partake of it:

Mr. Goddard,

Upon reading the History of New-Jersey, lately published, I observed in the summary of the first laws made in the Eastern Division of said Province, one very singular article "That Fornication should be punished at the Discretion of the Court by Marriage, Fine, or Corporal Punishment." I called this singular, but upon recollection, I have been told that there was a law of same Import in the early Times of Pennsylvania. Whether the Records of Proceedings of any Court, under either of these laws, are now to be found, I do not know, but fear that, if there are, that the worthy Judges who presided, may have omitted entering the Reasons on which they founded their discretionary Judgment. If Minutes properly entered and kept of this Kind, could be Exhibited to the Public, I fancy they would be esteemed as great Curiosities in the Literary Way, as any Thing found in Herculaneum[56]. *The Pennsylvania Chronicle, February 23, 1767*

But most marriages were voluntary and eagerly anticipated. Newspapers published wedding announcements back then too, although the information stressed within them differed somewhat than that of today:

New-York, June 21. Friday Evening last John Smyth, Esq. of Perth-Amboy, was married to Miss Susanna Moore, of this Place, Daughter of the late Col. Moore, a Lady possessed of many eminent Virtues and of a graceful Person. *The New York Mercury, June 21, 1762*

---

[55] This Greek "name" translates as "lover of marriage".

[56] Herculaneum was a Roman city that had been buried in ash from the eruption of Mount Vesuvius in 79 A.D., perfectly preserving the city and its culture. Herculaneum became a window through which the educated person of the 1700s, an admirer of the Greek and Roman republics, could view these civilizations.

Burlington May 21, 1768. On Thursday last was married in this City, Mr. William Dillwyn, to Miss Sally Smith, Daughter of John Smith, Esq; a young Lady possessed of every Accomplishment requisite to render the married State happy. *The Pennsylvania Chronicle*, May 23, 1768

On Thursday the 26th of May, the reverend Mr. Beach of New Brunswick was married to the amiable and accomplished Miss Nancy Van Winkle, a lady whose shining virtues and sweet disposition must render the marriage state truly happy. *The Pennsylvania Journal*, June 9, 1768

New York, May 1. Last Thursday Capt. Archibald Kennedy Esq. was married to Miss Nancy Watts, Daughter of the Hon. John Watts, Esq. of this City, a young Lady of great Merit, with a handsome Fortune. *The New York Gazette and Weekly Mercury*, May 1, 1769

The desire to wed can be a life long want, as the following obituary suggested:

Elizabeth Town New Jersey, January 23, 1764. Last Friday departed this life Miss Mary Eldrington, an Old Virgin in the 109th Year of her Age; she was of an ancient Family, born at Eldrington-Hall, in Nurthumberland, Old England and was, on the next Day, decently interred in St. John's Church yard, at Elizabeth-Town. It is remarkable that, notwithstanding her great age, she was desirous of getting a Husband before she died and, not two years since, nothing would offend her so highly as to tell her she was too old to be married. *The Pennsylvania Journal*, February 2, 1764

There is one report of a breach of promise to marry lawsuit between a rich man and a young woman that was allegedly conditioned upon his present wife dying:

New York, July 26. We are informed that a Cause of a very singular Nature is coming on to be tried in the Supreme Court of New Jersey, wherein a young Woman is Plaintiff and a Gentleman of Fortune Defendant: for Breach of a Promise of Marriage made in Writing to the Plaintiff by the Defendant, in the Life Time of his wife, since deceased, to be contracted with the Plaintiff after the Death of the Wife, provided she would continue in her single State until such Contingency might happen. Which the Plaintiff in her Declaration sets forth she has done, pursuant to and in Virtue of the Defendant's Promise and Assumption as aforesaid and, by reason thereof, has lost her Marriage. The action is laid for 3000 Pounds Proclamation Money.[57] *New York Journal or General Advertiser*, July 26, 1770

Then as now, reports of May-December marriages that could raise both eyebrows and snickers:

We hear from Crosswicks in New-Jersey that last Week an Old Man of 82 Years of age, was married to a brisk young Girl of twenty one. *The Boston Weekly News-Letter*, April 11, 1745

Other news reports, bordering on being ribald, brought smiles, if not grins:

We hear from the Head of Timber Creek in the Jerseys that a Woman there has lately had Five Children, all born alive, within the space of 11 Months, by two Husbands. *The Pennsylvania Gazette*, January 18, 1739

Middletown in Monmouth County, October 26th. The Wife of one John MacKenster was brought to Bed of three Girls and all likely to live, being her first children and she upwards of 40 Years of Age, the Neighbouring Women of all Ages, both far and near, come Daily to see them; and it is thought there will be some great Discontent among the Marry'd Women that their Husbands can't perform the same piece of Manhood. *The New York Weekly Journal*, November 12, 1739

Annapolis in Maryland, June 4. About a fortnight ago there happened in Frederick County in this Province, as comical a Wedding as we remember to have heard of. A Couple, with their Guests, having obtain'd a License, came to the House of a reverend Clergyman, late in the Evening, after he had been in Bed some time with his Wife, and desired to be married; he, willing to oblige them, got himself up and dress'd himself in order to perform the Ceremony, but the Bridegroom, having imbibed a Notion that if he married a Woman with anything, he should be obliged to

---

[57] The unique legal issue probably had something to with the argument that having a "back up" wife, in the event the present one dies, is contrary to public policy and should not be enforced, even if there were an otherwise enforceable agreement in writing to that effect.

pay all her Debts, and not otherwise, and as she came from the Province of New Jersey, he was doubtful about her Circumstances, the obliging Bride, to remove all incombrances, stripp'd to her Buff and two Women held a Sheet between her and the Clergyman, while he performed his Office. But, she having forgot her Cap at undressing, in the midst of the Ceremony it came to her Mind, she took that off too and flung it on the Bed and was married to her Spouse, if not in her Wedding Suit, then in her Birthday Suit; After the Ceremony was over, the Bridegroom put on her one of his own Shirts to cover her. This Account the Reader may perhaps look on as improbable and untrue, but he may be assured, it is a certain and naked Truth. *Pennsylvania Journal*, June 18, 1752

But marriages broke up in colonial times also and then the hateful fighting began. The basic human emotions have not changed in the last two centuries but what is different now is that a woman has rights and equality that were unthinkable in the 1700s. For example, a woman had no property rights in pre-revolutionary times, other than an interest in the real estate their husbands owned, an interest, called dower, that, as a practical matter, merely gave the widow a place to live out her days when the husband died first. Merchants were entitled by law to look to the husband for payment of any obligation incurred by wife, since, the assumption was, she could not pay it as, being a married woman, she normally would have no property of her own. When a couple separated, the law required the husband to alert the "world" that he no longer was responsible for his wife's debts, thus cutting off her credit and, hence, options, as well as protecting his assets. The notice was usually printed in a newspaper in a prescribed form.

Whereas Elizabeth Burtonstand, alias Ashton, the Wife of Benjamin Ashton of Glouster County in the Province of West Jersey, hath lately eloped from me, her Husband, without any Manner of Provocation; now, in order to prevent her, the said Elizabeth, contracting Debts in my name, I give this Publick Notice that I will not pay any Debts whatsoever, which she shall or may, after the Date hereof, contract. Given under my Hand, this first Day of July, 1758.

Benjamin Ashton

The Pennsylvania Gazette, July 6, 1758

Whereas my Wife Anne Davis, alias Ward, of the Town of Newark has eloped from my Bed, and absented herself from Cooking and Eating with me; I forewarn all Persons whatsoever to entertain or trust her in any Shape on my Account, as I will pay no Debts of her contracting.

Ebenezer Davis

The New York Gazette and Weekly Mercury, July 31, 1769

Occasionally, however, the husband felt compelled to improve upon the standard form notice and add some details, thus provoking our curiosity for more!

Amwell, province of West New Jersey, May 16, 1768. Whereas Ruth, the wife of John Corwine, hath been eloped from him ever since September last, and doth refuse to return to her husband, and be in her duty as a lawful wife, but hath joined with other men against him, to the great damage of him and his children, and hath run him considerably into debt: And further to inform the public that notice hath been given in December last, forewarning all people from trusting her upon his account; which advertisements have been privately taken down. I do hereby forewarn any person or persons, whatsoever, of trusting her upon my account, and of harbouring any of the goods which she hath taken with her, upon their peril; therefore I shall pay no debts by her contracted from December last; nor from the present date hereof.

John Corwine

The Pennsylvania Journal, May 19, 1768

Whereas Mary, the Wife of Gabriel Poneo, of the Township of Evesham, in the County of Burlington, hath and doth most intolerably and unjustly misbehave herself to her said husband, strolling about from house to house; these are to desire all persons not to trust said Mary, for he will pay no debts she shall contract. *The Pennsylvania Gazette*, November 16, 1749

Whereas Bathsheba, Wife of Nicholas Dally, of Bound Brook in East New Jersey, by reason of Age and Infirmity, growing silly, attempts to run her Husband into Debt, to his great Detriment. This is therefore to forewarn all Persons whatsoever from trusting the said Bathsheba upon his Account, for he will pay no Debts she shall contract from the date hereof. *The New York Gazette revived in the Weekly Post Boy*, November 13, 1752

Whereas Deborah, the Wife of John Farnsworth, late of Philipsburg, in the County of Sussex, West New Jersey, hath for some time behaved herself to me in a shameful and unbecoming manner, did on the 16th day of October, elope and abscond from her bed and board to the house of a certain Nathan Levy, a Jew, in the aforesaid town of Philipsburg, shop keeper, and privately took with her considerable of my effects and says she likes the said Levy better than me and that she intends to live with him, as he will maintain her as a gentlewoman. I have waited on Mr. Levy respecting the affair, from whom I have received no other satisfaction than insolent language, threatening me to let her have credit on my account of the amount of 50 pounds or whatever sum he sees cause and says he will oblige me to pay the same if I am not very silent in the matter &c. These are therefore to forewarn all persons from trusting her on my account, as I will pay no debts of her contracting from the date hereof and also to forewarn all persons from harbouring her or detaining or secreting my goods, on pain of being prosecuted as the law directs.

John Farnsworth

The Pennsylvania Journal, November 5, 1769

Freehold, Monmouth County, New-Jersey: January 25, 1768: Whereas Eleanor, Wife of Subscriber, hath eloped from him and run him considerably in Debt, besides pilfering from him a valuable Sum of Money and sundry Effects of Value and continues to strole around the Country with a certain Highland Tinker, who calls himself John M'Donall (who it is probable was an accomplice in the aforesaid base Conduct) and passes for his Wife, and he has Reason to fear that she will run him farther in debt, takes this Method of requesting all Persons, not to trust her on his Account, for he will pay no Debts of her contracting, after the date hereof.

William Orchard

The Pennsylvania Gazette, March 10, 1768

Whereas Sarah, the Wife of Israel Folsom of Piscataway, in East New-Jersey, eloped from her Husband's Bed and Board and thereon her Husband posted her, forbidding all Persons to trust her on his Account; But said Sarah came to his House on Saturday the 14th Instant and stayed all Night and went off again the next Day, refusing to stay with him; therefore he again desires no Person to trust her on his Account,[58] she being eloped and continues so.

Israel Folsom

The New York Gazette revived in the Weekly Post-Boy, February 20, 1749

There is even an instance of a wife posting such a notice about her husband, although its legal value must be suspect:

---

[58] Under the common law, adultery could be forgiven in a legal sense by the husband cohabiting with the wife again, with knowledge of her infidelity. Thus, Mr. Folsom, probably on the advice of legal counsel, was telling the world here that, even if he had spent the night with his wife, it was not a reconciliation, that she had left again and that no one should give her credit on his account.

Whereas John Quackinbush, late of the City of New Brunswick, Cooper, hath eloped from his Wife, and left his Bed and Board, and, contrary to all Reason and Christianity, hath, contrary to the Laws of Nature and Justice, to stroll about, keeping bad Company, stripped her of her Goods and Bedding, that she has nothing to subsist upon. Therefore these are to inform the Publick that the said Mary forewarns any Person or Persons whatever trusting him, for she will pay no Debts he shall contract, from the Day of the Date hereof, as Witness my Hand, the 31st Day of August, 1762.

Mary Quackinbush

The New York Mercury, September 6, 1762

Occasionally, the notice drew a reply from the wife, giving her side of the story. Then, like any family squabble, the husband sometimes felt compelled to get in the last word and submitted a rebuttal. Now, the neighbors know everything! Witness the exchange between the Dunlaps of Pile Grove:

Whereas Elizabeth Dunlap, Wife of James Dunlap of Pile-Groves, in the County of Salem, in the Province of New Jersey, hath lately eloped from the said James Dunlap her Husband; these are therefore to forewarn and forbid any Person to trust her the said Elizabeth for any Goods or other Things whatsoever, for that her said Husband will pay no Debt or Debts contracted by her after the Date hereof. *The American Weekly Mercury*, March 25, 1742

Whereas James Dunlap of Pile-Groves, in the County of Salem, in the Province of New Jersey, by an Advertisement lately incerted in the American Weekly Mercury and in the Pennsylvania Gazette, did publish the Elopement of Elizabeth Dunlap and forewarned all Persons to trust her for any Goods or other Things &c.

These are therefore to certify all Persons whom it may concern that the Contents of the said Advertisement as to the Elopement of the said Elizabeth is utterly false; for the said Elizabeth never Eloped from the said James Dunlap her Husband but was obliged in safety of her Life to leave her said Husband because of his Threats and cruel Abuses for several Years Past, repeatedly offered and done to Her and that she went no further than to her Father's House in the said County, where she has resided ever since her departure from her Husband and still continues to reside. And the said James Dunlap, having a considerable Estate in Lands in the said County, which the said Elizabeth is informed he intends to sell, as soon as he can, she therefore thought proper to give this Notice to any Person or Persons that may offer to buy, that she will not join in the sale of any part of the said lands but that she intends to claim her thirds [or right of *dower*] of and in all the Lands, the said James Dunlap has been seised of and possessed of, since their Intermarriage, let whosoever may, purchase the same.

Elizabeth Dunlap

The American Weekly Mercury, June 17, 1742

Whereas in an Advertisement in the publick Gazette, the Wife of James Dunlap of Piles Grove had caused to be published that she had not eloped from her said Husband in the Manner that was set forth in his Advertisement, some time ago published in a Gazette and was endeavouring to set forth her Innocence therein and that she went from her said Husband and Family by reason of his Abuses, Threats and Menaces, which Endanger'd her Life, and had also in the said Advertisement made known that as her said Husband was possessed of a considerable Estate of Lands in the County of Salem and that he intended to make Sale thereof, she gave Notice that she would not join in any Sale therein but would claim her Maintenance and Right of Dower in the said lands. In answer to which the said James Dunlap thought it proper to certifie that the Contents of the said Advertisement, made and published by the said Elizabeth, is intirely False and Spurious for that she had actually Eloped from him and went from his House and Family unknown and took sundry of his Goods, and after her Elopement took up Goods from a Store on his Credit and so continues her Absence; and as to any Threats, Menaces or Ill Usages that she pretended to have received from him, it is an utter Falsehood for sundry Persons who lived in the Family, on their Examinations to that point, positively proved the Contrary.; and as to his Intent of making Sale of his Lands, there is not one Word of Truth therein for he has actually Leased the same to several Persons for 3 Years, this is what he can prove & every other Matter alleged herein & to do himself Justice publishes this. And if anything more appears in print hereafter by her or her Friends, the said James Dunlap will be obliged to publish other Matters for his Justification. *The American Weekly Mercury*, August 12, 1742

And the one between the Moores of Woodbridge:

These are to give Notice that Deliverance Moore, the wife of James Moore of Woodbridge in New Jersey is eloped from her Husband's Bed and Board; wherefore all Persons are desired not to credit her on her said Husband's Account, for as he is not obliged by Law, so neither will he pay for anything she takes up during her said Elopement, dated the 18th of July, 1734.   James Moore

The New York Gazette, August 26, 1734

Whereas James Moore of Woodbridge has advertised in this Gazette, as well as by Papers sent to me and posted up, that his Wife Deliverance has eloped from his Bed and Board. These are to Certifie that the same is altogether false for she has lived with him above eight Years under his Tyranny and incredible Abuses; for he has several Times attempted to Murder her and also turned her out of Doors, shamefully abusing her, which is well known to the Neighbours and Neighbourhood in Woodbridge. *The New York Gazette*, September 9, 1734

The Perkins of Burlington

Whereas, Elizabeth Perkins, Wife to me the Subscriber, of the Township of Willingburg and County of Burlington, hath not only eloped from my Bed and Board, but otherwise behaves in a very unbecoming manner toward me; and, as I am apprehensive, from what I have already experienced, she may endeavour to run me into Debt I am obliged to take this public Method to forewarn all Persons from trusting her on my Account, as I am determined I will not pay a single Farthing of her contracting from the Date hereof. . .

Joseph Perkins

The Pennsylvania Chronicle, August 17, 1767

Joseph Perkins of the township of Willingburg and county of Burlington, my graceless husband, having maliciously advertised to the world, that I hath eloped from his bed and board, run him into debt and otherwise behaved in a very unbecoming manner towards him, I am obliged to take this method solemnly to declare that those charges against me have not the least foundation in truth, which can be easily made to appear and were entirely occasioned by my refusing to assign over to him the little interest that I have, that he may squander it away in disorderly company, as he has done the greatest part of his own, and my declining to entertain and encourage the infamous guests he frequently brought to his house, where, amidst the most notorious scenes and disorder, I often met with treatment which would have shocked a savage of the Ohio, which at last obliged me to fly to my mother's house in this city, which I unfortunately left, as the only sanctuary I could expect to find from his persecutions. . . . *The Pennsylvania Chronicle*, August 24, 1767

Philadelphia, January 16. Whereas Louisa, the wife of William Leddel, has eloped from her husband's bed and board, these are to forewarn any persons giving credit to the said Louisa, for he will pay no debts she shall contract.

William Leddel

The Pennsylvania Gazette, January 16, 1753

Philadelphia, January 23. Whereas the subscriber, wife of doctor William Leddel, of Elizabeth-Town, was advertis'd in this Paper last week as having eloped from her husband's bed and board, which is known by the major part of the people in said Town to be false, she hereby gives notice that the reason for leaving him was that her life was in danger from the ill usage she received from him, that he kept another woman by whom he had two children, and, after having spent Four Hundred and Fifty Pounds Sterling of her money, obliged her to leave his house. *The Pennsylvania Gazette*, January 23, 1753

Wife beating obviously was an evil then, as now. Interestingly, organized community efforts, albeit curious ones, were taken in Elizabeth, perhaps on behalf of the Mrs. Leddels of that town, to prevent such deplorable conduct:

We hear from Elizabeth-Town, that an odd Sect of People have lately appeared there, who go under the Denomination of Regulars; there are near a dozen of them, who dress themselves in Women's cloaths, and painting their Faces, go in the Evening to the Houses of such as are reported to have beat their Wives, where, one of them entering first, seizes the Delinquent, while the rest follow, strip him, turn up his Posteriors and flog him with Rods most severely, crying out all the Time, "Woe to the Men that beat their Wives." It seems that several Persons in that Borough (and tis said some very deservedly) have undergone the Discipline, to the no small Terror of others, who are any Way conscious of deserving the same Punishment. 'Twere to be wished that, in order for the more equal distribution of Justice, there would arise another Sect, under the Title of Regulatrixes, who should dress themselves in Men's Cloaths and flagilate the Posteriors of the Scolds, Termagants &c. &c. *The New York Gazette revived in the Weekly Post Boy*, December 18, 1752

At first, their vigilante justice, brought a favorable response from the community and discouraged further wife abuse:

Mr. Parker,

As I understand you are a Native of New Jersey, I doubt not therefore that you are a Lover of your Country and, as such a one, I now address you and pray that you give this a Place in your Paper, which will not only oblige me but all the Good Wives that have the Misfortune to have bad Husbands in this Province.

You must understand, Sir, that I have for some years past borne, with uncommon Patience, the Lashes of an ill-natur'd Husband, who constantly made it a Practice to stay at a Slop Shop[59], till he had drowned his Senses in Rum, his Darling Delight, and then poor I must stand clear, for the merciless Wretch would spare neither my Tea Cups or Saucers to throw at my Head, besides whipping of me; but I must do him the Justice to acknowledge that he always had compassion on the Rum glasses, which stood close by them, but tho' we have had but two of those glasses for Eight or Ten Years, yet they have lived to see as many dozen of Tea Cups and Saucers broke over my Head, for he says if I can't drink my Tea out of those glasses, I shall go without, which I had rather do, for I should imagine I would be drinking Rum instead of Tea and I think he need not be so hard upon me, for they did not cost him a Penny, but his destroying of them has brought me so low that I have no more Apparel than I at present have on and I will have Tea Cups and Saucers if I pawn my very Shift for I must own I love Tea as well as he loves Rum.

Besides, Sir, I have two little Children a boy and a Girl, who while their Father was of whipping me, were frightened of such a degree (for fear of losing their Dear Mother) as would make them fall in fits in each others little arms, while I could not afford them the least Assistance and they might have then have died before he would have given them any. Was not this hard, Sir? Ah, cruel hard, not only to use me so inhumanly but to be so void of Bowels to those little Ones, that derived their Existence from him! And, he would tell me, when I dared to complain, that Man had the Government given him over Woman, but I don't imagine his Authority to be so extensive as to impower him to Beat her Brains out without Rime or reason, and as often as I read my Bible (my greatest Delight) I never yet found that Adam ever whipped his Wife, tho', I must confess, she richly deserved it.

---

[59] a tavern

My Case being happily nois'd abroad induced several young men to discipline him. These young Persons do stile, or a stiled, *Regulators* and so they are with Propriety, for they have regulated my dear Husband and the rest of the Bad Ones hereabouts, that they are afraid of using such Barbarity. And I must with Pleasure acknowledge that, since my Husband felt what whipping was, he has entirely left off whipping me and promises faithfully that he never will begin again, which I have reason to believe, for there never was a better Harmony existing between Man and Wife, than there is at present betwixt us and we are as happy as we were in our Courting Days. And he does with Pleasure Own (as does myself) that he is under infinite Obligations to those Persons before hinted at and is so generous as to say, that if they had not done what they did, he might unhappily in his Anger whipped me into Eternity.

I doubt not that all the World will agree with me (especially those of my sex and those that have any regard for them) that it is a most brutal action for a Man, who Nature has endowed with superior Strength to a woman, to exercise such Severity over her. While I say brutal, I do injustice to the Brute Creation for they shew more Compassion and Tenderness than such Monsters do.

Tho' there are some afraid of whipping their wives for fear of dancing the same Jigg, yet, I understand, they are not afraid of making Application in order to have those Regulators indicted; and, if they should, it might discourage them for the future to appear in the Assistance of the Innocent and Helpless; and then, poor wives who have the Misfortune to be lockt in Wedlock with bad Husbands, take care of your tender Hides, for you may depend upon being banged without Mercy.

I am, Sir, your most humble Servant
Prudence Goodwife
The New York Gazette or Weekly Post Boy, December 31, 1753

However good intentioned the Regulators were, their early efforts against wife abuse landed them into deep trouble, as vigilante conduct often does.

New York, January 15. We hear from Bound Brook that one William Daniels, near that Place, having beat his Wife some Time last Week, which he had frequently done before, she left him and went to reside with a Daughter she had at some Distance, and on Monday last a Number of persons who are termed there *Regulators* went to Daniels and, taking him out of his Bed, whipp'd him very severely; they then left him to himself and the next Morning he was found dead in his Bed. *New York Gazette or Weekly Post Boy*, January 15, 1770.

New York, January 25. We hear from Piscataqua, in New Jersey, that about 10 Days since, three men that lived near Bound Brook, named Harris, Buskirk and Howell took the Liberty of flaggellating a certain William M'Donald, who lived near that Place, for having some Words with his Wife, to such a Degree that he died in less than 24 Hours thereafter. Howell we have heard has fled, but Harris and Buskirk have surrendered themselves to Justice and are now confined in Brunswick Gaol. *The New York Journal or General Advertiser*, January 25, 1770

Divorce was not an acceptable termination of a marriage in colonial America[60] so society approved a type of separation or living apart as long as it was understood that the townspeople would not have to support either of them. Witness the unfortunate mistake of Daniel Barlay and Elizabeth Waters and how they undid it:

New York, November 25. We hear from Kingston in East New Jersey, that on Sunday the 10th of this Instant, in the Evening, after having been twice published the same Day, Daniel Barlay, aged 68 Years, was married there to Elizabeth Waters, aged 78 Years. The first had been a widower 8 Months and the other a Widow 35 Years. The Ceremony was performed with the utmost Solemnity before a very crowded Audience. *The New York Gazette revived in the Weekly Post Boy*, November 25, 1751

Mr. Parker,

In your Paper, Numb. 462, we had an account of the Marriage of Daniel Barley and Elizabeth Waters, solemnized on the 10th of November last, in this Town, which Couple have ever since lived in happy enjoyment of each other, for the most part, until the 9th of this Month, when, by consent of both parties, in the Presence of a Number of Spectators, after

---

[60] Nor was bigamy, as the following advertisement for a runaway servant illustrates.

Run away from the Subscriber, living in Shrewsbury in the County of Monmouth and the Province of East New Jersey, the 30th of April, a Man about five Foot five or six inches high, round faced, a very straight limbed fellow, about thirty Years of Age, named Thomas Howell. Merica Bourn, a Woman, has left this Place in order to marry him, which will be his third Wife, if so she may be called, the first being living and [he] was branded in the Hand for marrying the second. . . .

Stephen Tallman, Jun.

The New York Journal or General Advertiser, May 11, 1769 No. 1375.

Note the name of the other woman, "Merica Bourn". Obviously, it is some type of word play on "America born", a rare description in a land where most were born abroad.

having given security never to be burdensome to each other as likewise for their Loyalty while absent, parted, never to meet again in the State of Matrimony. What the Cause was, we know not, but, some that pretend to know, say they had not courted long enough before Marriage. *The New York Gazette revived in the Weekly Post Boy*, March 16, 1752

Clearly, however, no matter how long they had lived apart, they were still married and the husband was responsible for the wife's necessities of life:

Whereas I, the Subscriber, of Connecticut Farms, in the County of Essex, in the Province of New Jersey, and my wife Hannah (some Times calling herself Hannah Willis, the Relict of Isaac Willis, deceased), have by Mutual Consent lived separate and apart from each other for some Years past; and now by the Suggestion of some evil minded Persons, my said Wife has run me considerably into Debt, these are therefore to forbid all Persons whomsoever, trusting or crediting her the said Hannah on my Account, as I am determined to pay no more Debts of her contracting, from the Date hereof.

Reuben Cherry

The New York Gazette and Weekly Mercury, April 17, 1769

Not all marriages are terminated in living apart. Mary Ashford was accused of taking matters in her own hands, a charge she challenged with an interesting explanation:

Whereas it has been for some years past, maliciously and spitefully reported by John Hewes of Rocksiticus, New-Jersey, that I, the Subscriber, had made away with or destroyed my Husband Thomas Ashford of the same Place, which report, altho' notoriously false and wicked, has been greatly to my Hurt and Damage; My Husband, having designed for England, did go with Capt. Hylton from New York, as the following Certificate will testify, since which I have had no other Account of him.

Mary Ashford

I do hereby certify that one Thomas Ashford, of New Jersey, did go with me in the Ship Queen of Hungary, for London in the year 1745, when I was taken by a French Privateer and carried into St. Maloes; that the said Ashford was very sick there and sent to the Hospital, where I have reason to think he died. As Witness my Hand in New York, Dec. 28, 1750

Ralph Hylton

The above can be attested by several People in New York, if need be. *The New York Gazette Revived in the Weekly Post Boy*, December 31, 1750

Another did it more directly:

Samuel Corrlas of Shrewsbury is now in our Gaol for killing his Wife with a Gun. *The New York Mercury*, May 11, 1761

A gentleman from Hackinsack also ended his marriage, although his wife was not his victim:

New York, April 5. Last Thursday one Mr. Lesyear, of Hackensack, in New-Jersey, happening to have some high Words with his Wife, went out of the House in a Passion, and shot himself thro' the Body of which Wound he instantly died. It is said that they had lived very discontented together for some Time before. *The New York Mercury*, April 5, 1762

Jealousy, especially the insane type, was responsible for at least one gruesome termination of a marriage:

Burlington, October 19. The following are all the circumstances we have been able to collect, relative to the inhuman murder committed last Friday, at the Lake, about 25 Miles from Glouster in the Jersies. About 4 o'Clock in the Morning, the Man (a Person in good Circumstances) got out of bed and went upstairs to a Negro Wench and inquired after some Leading Lines, telling her that he intended to have a Butcher in the House that Day; he then went down Stairs and shot his Wife with some Buckshot, which not immediately killing her, the wound being in the Shoulder, he beat her Brains out with the Butt End of the Musket. The Report of the Musket alarmed the Negro Wench, who directly sprang out of a Window, one Story high, rushed in the Room where she saw her Mistress wallowing in her Blood; she forced the Musket out of her Master's Hands and ran to the first Neighbour's House, seven Miles distant, whom she informed of this dreadful Affair. When they came to the House, they found the woman lying as the Negro had left her and, tracing a Track of Blood into the Barn, they found the Man hanging. The unfortunate Wife had prepared a Quantity of Butter, two Bucks etc, to bring to the next market in Philadelphia and had managed a Dairy of 40 Cows. Jealousy, we hear, was the Occasion of this fatal Affair. The Man bore the Character of being very desperate and had attempted twice before to shoot his Wife. *The Pennsylvania Chronicle*, October 23, 1769

Sometimes the jealously was betweensuitors for the same woman and the results tragic. For example:

A few days before Christmas last, a very valuable Negro named Caesar, belonging to the Widow Furman, in Colt's Neck in Monmouth County, New Jersey, was found dead at some distance from his home and, being conjectured to have died from some accident, was buried. But soon after, a neighbour informing that he had heard great Cries of Murder near the Place where the Negro was found and that he would have gone to the Assistance of the Distressed except that a very large Mill Pond lay in the Way which he could not cross. The Negro was taken up again and both his legs were found broke and his neck dislocated. Whereupon further search was made and a the place of the Out Cry was found many marks of Caesar's struggling with his Adversaries and several plain tokens of his having been hung from a low Limb of a Tree. It seems that Caesar had made his Addresses some Time to a neighbouring Wench, who received them kindly and they were to be married at Christmas, but another Fellow, who also addressed the Wench, not being received well, and jealous of Caesar and having several Negro friends, it is thought that Caesar was waylaid and murder'd in that Manner and this suspicion is corroborated by a Person's having heard an Old Wench tell Caesar a few days before, that if he continued to visit that young Wench, he would not live to see Christmas. Several Negroes have since been taken up, on the Account, and 'tis thought the truth will be discovered so that poor Caesar's Antagonist is likely to be found in a worse State than the Dog in the Manger.[61] *The New York Mercury*, February 2, 1761

Some few disputes however resolved themselves and the couple reconciled:

Whereas I, William Carter, of Trenton, Hunterdon County, some time since advertised my Wife Phebe Carter in this Paper, this is to inform the Publick that as we are on good terms again and have agreed to live together, our dealings will be the same as heretofore. *The Pennsylvania Journal*, November 18, 1762

But most couples of troubled marriages did not live happily ever after and the gold medal winner in the "get back even" contest will have to remain anonymous [except to those neighbors who heard the screams!]:

We hear from Shrewsbury, in New-Jersey, that the Week before last, one Mr.------ of that Place, being plied by strong Liquor by three Females, till he was much intoxicated, they then proceeded very deliberately to deprive him of his Manhood by C--------n, which they effectually performed. The Crime he was charged with, was for depriving his Wife of

---

[61] The Dog in the Manger refers to the fable about the dog which kept possession of something for which it had no need, solely so as to deprive another of it who had the need.

Favours that he bountifully lavished upon his Neighbours. The Operators were his Wife, his Wife's Mother, and one other Woman. He is in a fair Way of recovering, and the Women are all in Custody. *The Pennsylvania Chronicle*, April 18, 1768

It is very difficult to envision the strides that have been made in medical knowledge and health care since colonial times. What we take for granted today was either unknown or just being probed back then.

For example, small pox was not only a killer but it scarred the survivors for life. In over 15% of the notices seeking the return of runaway servants, deserters, escaped prisoners and thieves are descriptions like "pock mark'd" or "pox fretten", reflecting how many of the survivors of this disease were permanently scarred by it. An outbreak of small pox was to be feared and efforts, even primitive inoculations, were taken to avoid its spread through the population.

Burlington, April 18. At a Petty session of the Peace, held for the County of Burlington, at Burlington, the 16th Day of April, 1731, it was consider'd that Fairs generally occasion great Concourse of People, from the most adjacent Places, and that at present it was not Meet for keeping the Fair at Burlington, as usual, by reason of the great Mortality in Philadelphia and other Parts of Pennsylvania, where the Small-Pox now violently Rages. Therefore, to prevent, to the utmost Power of the Justices of the said Sessions, the further spreading of so Epidemical and Dangerous of a Distemper, and more especially, for that the approaching Heat of Summer may be more malignant and fatal, it is Ordered that May Fair next be, and hereby is, Prohibited to be kept in the said Town of Burlington and all Persons are hereby strictly required to take Notice hereof accordingly as they will answer for their Contempt at their Peril. *The American Weekly Mercury*, April 15, 1731.

New York, January 11. We are informed that the Small-Pox spreads very much in several Parts of this province and in New Jersey also. And that at Amboy, New Brunswick and the adjacent Places, many have been inoculated and none have died but have had, and at present have, the distemper very easy. *The Pennsylvania Gazette*, January 11, 1732

New York, January 18. By a Letter from a Friend in Jamaica, on Long island, dated the 9th Instant, we are informed that in and about that Town, there have been Inoculated with the Small Pox, about One Hundred and Sixty Persons, that not one of them has died, save one Foster Waters. *The New England Weekly Journal*, February 27, 1732

Whereas the Small-Pox is in our neighbouring Province of Pennsylvania and, particularly, in the City of Philadelphia, has been for some time last past, very Brief, and has occasioned a great Mortality amongst the People inhabiting the said City and Province; and, according to information, the said Distemper has not as yet entirely ceased to Rage; and whereas the Justices and Freeholders of the County of Salem, being this Day convened, pursuant to an Act of Assembly of this Province of New-Jersey, have thought fit to make an Order and to Advertise the Publick that (as they are under some Apprehensions that the Persons intending to come from Pennsylvania and from the City of Philadelphia, as accustom'd, to our Fairs here and may casually bring down that Distemper and may perhaps occasion it to spread amongst the People in this Province) no Fair will be Held or Kept at Cohansey nor Salem in May next, of which the Persons concerned are desired to take Notice.

By Order of the Justices and Freeholders, Salem in New Jersey
Dan. Mestayer, Clerk to the Justices
and Freeholders
The American Weekly Mercury, April 7, 1737

By 1770, however, progress had been made in both determining the cause of small pox and preventing it, as suggested by the following:

Inoculation

George Pugh Surgeon, lately arrived from Jamaica acquaints the Public that he was the first Person who introduced the Suttonian Method of Inoculation for the Small Pox in that part of the West Indies, where he has been instrumental in almost eradicating that loathsome Disease. He now proposes carrying on that Branch of his Profession, every Spring and Fall in Elizabeth Town, New Jersey, where he has opened a Commodious House for the Reception of Patients. Any Person, Family, or Company, desirous of being inoculated by him at New York, Philadelphia or elsewhere, may depend upon his strictest Care and Attendance to conduct them through the Small Pox, and upon Terms agreeable to their Circumstances, and what may justly be added with little Loss of Time or Hinderance.

N.B. The Poor, properly recommended, will be inoculated gratis.
The New York Journal or General Advertiser, June 21, 1770

The above advertisement was followed by a list of Plantations in Jamaica, each with 400 slaves on average, whom Dr. Pugh had inoculated without the loss of a patient.

Concern for infectious were not limited to small pox. Measles and plagues from abroad were equally to be feared.

Philadelphia, March 11. The Measles begin to spread in our Town; it was brought hither from Salem in West-Jersey, where it proved very mortal. *The Boston News-Letter*, March 15, 1714

On the 22nd arrived Gerrard in 20 days at Amboy from Barbadoes. Letters from thence say that Island is very sickly and that a great many die of the Sickness. *The Boston News-Letter*, June 28th, 1714,

On the 7th Currant arriv'd here the Port Merchant, Capt. Baker from London, who sayl'd the 15th of August; she is gone to Perth Amboy in New Jersey to load stayes of the Dimensions of Hamburg, the Trade to that port having failed by reason of the Plague. *The Boston News-Letter*, October 18th, 1714

Remedies --- and a Practioner for each -- abounded for all sorts of ailments. Witness the following:

Advertisement

In a few days will be published "Observations on that vulgar disease called the Throat Distemper", with Advices as to the method of Cure. . . . The above letter has been perused by several of our ablest Physicians who have expressed their Satisfaction in the Author's Account of the Phenomena of the Malady and his method of Cure. *The Boston Weekly News Letter*, August 14, 1740

Philadelphia, January 27. We are inform'd that, at Crosswicks in West New Jersey, divers Persons have lately died of a Distemper of the Throat and that the Distemper prevails there. We are therefore desired to publish the following Remedy (which has proved successful) for the advantage of those who may hereafter be visited with the like Distemper. Take some Honey and the sharpest Vinegar, with Allon dissolved therein and let the patient often gargle it in their Throats, or, if they be children, then take a feather and dip it into said Liquor and so wash their throats. *The New York Weekly Journal*, February 9, 1736

I have seen in your publick Gazette an account of a very surprizing Distemper prevailing in some Parts of this Continent, especially in the Eastern Parts . . . And having had some late news that this Distemper still prevails and no remedy can be found, which makes me (out of pity to my fellow creatures) willing to communicate of my Judgment and Experience, for the Distemper has been and is now very brief among us, but, I believe, that not one of sixty Dies thereof. What is used is as follows: First, be sure that a Vein be opened under the Tongue, and if that cannot be done, open a Vein in the Arm, which must first be done or else all other means will be ineffectual. Then take Borax, Allum and Bole Armoniack, powder'd and mix'd with Honey, to bathe or annoint the Mouth and Throat and lay on the Throat a Plaister of Unguintum Dialthae. To Drink, give a Decoction of Devil's bitt or Robins Plantain, with some Sal Prunellae dissolved therein, as often as the Patient will drink. If the Body be costive, use a Clyster agreeable to the Nature of the Distemper. I have also known many other things used, especially a Root, called Physick Root, filaire or five leaved Physick, also a Root that I know no name for only Canker Root, but be sure to let Blood and that under the Tongue. We have many times made Blisters on the Arms but that has proved some times dangerous.

From your faithful Friend and Servant

N.H.

The New York Weekly Journal, March 8, 1736

New York, December 2. We hear from Elizabeth-Town in New Jersey that several Mad Dogs have infested that Neighbourhood within these few Weeks past; some of which had been killed before any Mischief was done, but that a Girl had been Bit by one of them which had flung her into that terrible Condition, which all Accounts agree is common to those bit in Europe. As these are the first that ever appeared in these parts, it has much alarmed the Inhabitants as has also occasioned the following Letter and Recipe's being sent to the Printers:

(part of a letter from Alexander Reid, Esq. to Dr. Wilmot)
London Nov. 5, 1745

Dear Sir,

As your Zeal and Abilities for promoting the Good of Mankind are my principal inducements, they must be my only apology for troubling you with the following Account of what I know concerning the internal Use of Musk in large Quantities.

About 15 Years ago, I learned in China, that the Tonquinese had an infallible cure for the Bite of a Mad Dog, and being very desirous of possessing such a valuable recipe, I was two or three years after favoured with it by the late Mr. Hart.

They take the best Musk, about sixteen Grains, of the purest native Cinnabar and finest Vermillion, each about twenty four Grains, and having reduced them separately to impalpable Powders, mix and administer them in about a Gill of Arrack (Rum will answer the end as well) which, in two or three Hours, generally throws the Patient into a sound Sleep and Perspiration. If not, they repeat the dose and think the Cure certain. *The New York Gazette revived in the Weekly Post Boy*, December 9, 1751

Margaret Powell, living at Mrs. Elbertson's in New Street, New York, hereby gives Notice that she undertakes the Cure of all Rheumatic Pains, Sore Legs and Cataracts of the Eyes, but above all the Canker, either in the Nose, Mouth or Throat of ever so long standing or to whatever Height the Disease might have run. She has lately made a Cure of an obstinate Canker in the City of New Brunswick. *The New York Gazette or the Weekly Post Boy*, August 5, 1754

Just imported in the Nebuchadnezer, a choice assortment of Medicines, calculated for Practice in the Country, from the Hall in London. They are quite fresh and allowed to come from the most eminent Hand, subjected to the Inspection of the Royal College of Physicians; to be sold very cheap by Charles Scham Leslie, M.D. at his House at Connecticut Farms, a few Miles from Elizabeth-Town in the Jersies. The said Dr. Leslie intending to deal in the future in that Branch of Business will always take care to have fresh assortments from London and to give the usual Credit, tho' now he proposes for cash to sell 20 per cent cheaper that shall appear from any Invoices or Bills of Parcels, for the same kind of Medicines in any trading place in America, where Practioners are served at second-hand. *The New York Gazette revived in the Weekly Post Boy*, August 3, 1752

The subscriber begs leave to inform the Public, that he was bred to the practice of Physic and Surgery, and has had more than thirty years of experience, the last seven of which he served in the Pennsylvania Hospital, attended to all the administrations of medicine and chirurgical operations in that infirmary, during the whole time.

George Weed

The Pennsylvania Chronicle, August 21, 1769

The Subscriber begs leave to inform the Public, that he has removed from Burlington to the City of Philadelphia, in Almond Street, a few doors from the Blue Bell, on Society Hill, where he proposes to practice all Branches of Physic and Surgery. He undertakes particularly to cure, with small Expense and Pain to the Patient, Cancers and Wens, without cutting them, the King's Evil, venereal disorders, without Salivation; Rupture,

Strangury and Stone; and as he has had great Experience and Success in all the above Diseases, he hopes, by the Divine Blessing, to be able to give Relief to any distressed Persons, afflicted with them, that shall apply to him. He takes Patients into his House and boards and lodges them, if desired.

Thomas Wire

The Pennsylvania Gazette, June 18, 1767

When necessary, personal endorsements as to the effectiveness of the treatment or the healer, accompanied the advertisement:

The Calamity of Diseases being incident to every Species of Being, has employed the Time and engaged the Searches of many Men into such Things as might prove Antidotes to the several Disorders and to endeavour at such Applications as would totally eradicate each Distemper; and that their attempts might be more effectual, the Animal, Mineral and Vegetable Creations have been consulted and a union of them all rendered conducive to answer the Purpose of recovering decayed Nature and Restoring Health. Any one that is inflicted with Gravel in any Manner or Degree, that there is prepar'd by Doctor William Clark in Freehold, East-Jersey, an Oil, which has not only given Relief but by continuing of it for some Time, has so eased me of that dreadful Disorder that I am now capable of doing any Business, when that before I was not able for to go on any Occasion of my Affairs. The Vertue and Efficacy of which Oil, in the Cure of the above mentioned Distemper, will be made evident by my own Words, if questioned by any Person, upon Enquiry; when ever I found the Disorder coming upon me, I took about fifteen Drops which gave me present Relief. Any Person that requires further Information by applying to the said William Clark shall be informed of Persons that has made Tryal of the above Oil.

William Clark

The New York Gazette Revived in the Weekly Post Boy, January 8, 1750

Doctor Stork

Surgeon and Oculist to Her Royal Highness the Princess Dowager of Wales

Acquaints the public, that he is to continue in Philadelphia till the latter End of February next; such as are in need of his assistance may apply to him at his Lodgings near the New-Meeting House on Arch-Street.

We the Subscribers are induced, not only in Gratitude to Doctor Stork, but likewise for the Benefit of the Public to communicate the

Recovery of our Sights from Blindness by his Operations . . . This is to certify that I Thom Roberts of Hopewell, near Trenton, being deprived of sight for two years, was by Dr. Stork restored to it again. *The Pennsylvania Journal*, January 21, 1762

There were well intentioned quacks, of course.

Daniel Goodman, living in Arch Street, in the City of Philadelphia, Baker, (being a Seventh Son) hereby gives notice, that for a number of years past, in England, New-Jersey and Pennsylvania, he hath cured divers persons afflicted with the King's Evil, by using no other means or remedies than by stoking the part affected with his hand[62]; therefore any person or persons affected with the disorder, by applying to him, may be relieved in like manner. And as he doth the same from a principle of humanity, and not with any lucrative views, any person or persons will be cured without fee or reward. *The Pennsylvania Chronicle*, June 13, 1768

We are informed from Prince-Town in the Jerseys, that a certain Person (who we are told also lives near the Yearley's Ferry in this Province) has very lately turned Occulist and tried his Skill upon several in that Place; but his Successes has not yet gained him any Credit. It seems that his Operations have turned out contrary to the desire of his Patients, for instead of Restoring their Sight, he intirely takes it away. This effect his Experiments have had in particular on Mr. Benjamin Randolf, who before this blind Occulist had any thing to do with his Eyes, could See; but now he is quite Blind and in great Pain. It is hoped that People will take Caution by this who they suffer to meddle with their sight and not employ those who will put out both their Eyes to make them see so clearly. *The American Weekly Mercury*, October 2, 1735

But professional physicians were being instructed in the fledgling medical schools in courses of study, not totally unknown to today's medical students.

---

[62] The disease, strikingly called the *King's Evil* for some unknown reason, is better known in medical circles as *cervical lymphadenitis* or *scrofula*. Tubercula in nature, it is characterized chiefly by swelling and degeneration of the lymphatic glands, especially around the neck area. It is rare in the United States today because of the elimination of tubercle from the milk and the prevention of mass infections in childhood. Heliotherapy --getting outside in the sun -- was a traditional method of treatment but, not surprisingly, none of the tomes consulted mentioned Daniel Goodman's treatment of stroking the lesion with his hand.

College of Philadelphia, June 21, 1768. This day, which may be considered as having given birth to Medical Honours in America, the following gentlemen were admitted to the Degree of Bachelor of Physick; viz Messrs ... Jonathan Elmer of West Jersey, John Lawrence of East Jersey....

Agreeable to the rules of the College, these gentlemen previous to their admission to a degree, had diligently attended the lectures of the several professors of Anatomy, the Materiae Medica, Chymistry, Theory and Practice of Physic, and the Clinical lectures in the Pennsylvania Hospital, in which (as well as in the Languages and the necessary branches of Natural Philosophy) they gave the most satisfactory proofs of their proficiency, both in their private and public examinations. *Supplement to the New York Journal or General Advertiser*, July 16, 1768

Whereas Anotomy is allowed on all Hands, to be the Foundation of Physick and Surgery, and, consequently, without some knowledge of it, no Person can be duly qualified to practice either. This is therefore to inform the Publick that a Course of Osteology and Myology, is intended to be done some time in February next, in the City of New Brunswick (of which notice will be given in this Paper as soon as a proper Number have subscribed to it). In which Course, all the human Bones will be separately examined and their Constructions and Dependencies on each other demonstrated and all of the Muscles of a human Body dissected, the Origin, Insertion and Use of each plainly shewn &c. This Course is proposed to be finished in the Space of a Month by

Thomas Wood, Surgeon

Such Gentlemen who are willing to attend this Course are desired to subscribe their Names as soon as possible with Mr. Richard Ayscough, Surgeon at New York or said Thomas Wood at New Brunswick, paying, at the same Time, Three Pounds, Proc. and engaging to pay the said sum of Three Pounds more, when the Course is half finished.

N.B. If proper Encouragement is given in this Course, he proposes to go soon after thro' a course of Angiology and Newrology and conclude with performing all the operations of Surgery on a dead Body, the Use of which will appear to every person who considers the Necessity of having at least seen them performed, before he presumes to perform them himself on any living Fellow-Creature. *The New York Gazette revived in the Weekly Post Boy*, January, 27, 1752

New York, June 29. On Sunday last was performed at Newark, the operation of Lithotomy[63], on a youth of about 8 years of age, before several very eminent gentlemen in the practice of Physick and Surgery, by John Jones, one of the principal Surgeons of this City. The largeness of the stone and the dexterity with which it was extracted was sufficient indications of his judgment in manual operation and met with the cordial approbation of all the Gentlemen present. The symptoms are as favorable toward a recovery, as can be expected, from the severity of so dangerous an operation. *The Pennsylvania Chronicle*, July 6, 1767

Likewise, practicing physicians formed associations and medical societies designed to improve their profession in the eyes of the public.

Mr. Gaine,

A Number of the Practioners of Physic and Surgery in East-Jersey, having form'd themselves in a Society, for their mutual improvement in their Profession, and other good Purposes; and as their Meetings may cause some speculation among the Inhabitants where they reside, they though it proper to insert in your Paper the Laws and Constitution whereby their Society is governed, as well as obviate any Misrepresentations which may arise from Prejudice or Mistake, as to convince their Employers that this Scheme is designed to be of Publick Utility.

Narrative of the Rise and Establishment of the New Jersey Medical Society

The low State of Medicine in New Jersey and the Many Difficulties and Discouragements, alike injurious to the People and Physicians, under which it has laboured, and which still continues to oppose its Improvement in Utility to the Public, and its advancement to its native Dignity, having for several Years past engrossed the Attention of some Gentlemen of the Profession and occasionally been the Subject of their Conversations, it was early last Winter determined to attempt some Measure for rescuing the Art from that abject Condition (not to say worse) into which it seemed too fast to decline.

To this End, a Legislative Interposition appeared in the first place

---

[63] An operation to remove a stone from the bladder.

to be desired, and an Application to that Favour was proposed; but in this it was necessary to have the concurrence of the principal Practioners and as many other Persons of Weight and Influence as possible; a voluntary Association, therefore, of such Gentlemen of the faculty who might approve of the Design, was next projected; A Society of this kind it was thought, besides considering of a proper Application to the Legislature and promoting it most effectually, could in the mean Time take such Measures as were of immediate Importance and form such voluntary Regulations as would greatly conduce to the Usefulness and Honour of Medicine and, should the Legislature in their Wisdom think it not expedient to interfere, might, to a great degree, answer the purposes of a more authoritative Establishment; not to mention, whether under Law or otherwise, a Medical Society well conducted would naturally confer Credit on the Profession and ever be of the highest Advantage, both to the Public and to the several Members. With these good Views, the annexed Advertisement was inserted in the Mercury.
The New York Mercury March 2, 1767

The Members of the New-Jersey Medical Society are desired to remember, that their next stated General Meeting will be on the first Tuesday in May next, at the House of Mr. William Hick, in Princeton, and, as some very important Affairs respecting the future Establishment &c of said Society will be then taken into Consideration whereby its benevolent Intentions may be more fully answered, it is expected every Member will make a Point of attending, and should not absent himself unless something very extraordinary should interfere.

Those Gentlemen of the Profession who have not joined are again invited, and for the above Reasons, it would be extremely agreeable to the Society that as many as possible would attend the ensuing General Meeting.
Moses Bloomfield, Secretary
The Pennsylvania Chronicle, March 28, 1768

Today, we take for granted our knowledge, even as lay people, about the causes of sudden deaths, due to strokes, heart attacks, brain damage, even blood poisoning which, several centuries ago, perplexed the ordinary colonist.

On Tuesday Evening, November 25, about Ten o'Clock, Thomas Bates of Hanover was found lying on the Road near Hanover Church, groaning as in great agony but speechless, was carried to the nearest House (from which he had rode off from after Eight O'Clock the same Evening) where, after tossing in Pain for some Time, he expired. The Coroner returned a Verdict that "he died by a Fall from his Horse, having received a mortal Contusion on one of his Temples." *The New York Journal or General Advertiser*, December 4, 1766

New York, March 26. On Saturday Sennight, in the Morning, Henry Moore Esq. of Cranbury, supposed to have fallen from his Horse, was found speechless and soon after expired. *The Pennsylvania Chronicle*, March 30, 1767

We are inform'd that about the beginning of last Month Mr. Thomas Wood belonging to New Jersey rode through New-London seemingly in perfect health, but when he got a few Miles from that Town, was taken with a numb Palsey and fell from his Horse; he was taken up and carried into a House and all possible care taken of him; he lived about two weeks, without speaking one word and then dyed. *The New-York Gazette*, February 25, 1734

Perth-Amboy, April 4. On Tuesday last dyed Mr. Robert Atkins, Merchant; he went to Bed very well and was found Dead in the Morning. *The American Weekly Mercury*, April 2, 1730

We hear from Middletown in New Jersey that one Johannes Lystrum of that Place, 66 Years of Age, was found dead in his Bed in the Morning, being hearty and well the Night before. *The New York Mercury*, March 1, 1756

We have an Account from Perth Amboy that on Tuesday Evening last two Seamen belonging to a Brig in that Harbour, being at a Tavern, one of them took occasion to boast of his Bravery, which the other resenting a little, they agreed to walk out and make a Tryal of Skill at Boxing, which having exercised a while, they were parted and came in and drank Friends where the Person who had boasted of his Strength, died a few Minutes after. We hear the other has since made off. *The Boston Weekly Post-Boy*, December 25, 1749

From Salem we hear, that on Monday Evening last, Israel Porter, who was a strong lusty Man, came Home from his Labour and, sitting down, called for his Cup of Cyder, but had scarce taken his Draught before he started out of his Chair and dy'd in about two Minutes. *The Pennsylvania Gazette*, October 9, 1729

We hear from Cohansey that a few days since, John Miller and his Son, being about ready to load a Cart with some Wood, the said Miller fell down with a stick in his Hand and call'd to his Son to help him up, because he was struck blind. His son helped him up, but he died presently. *The Pennsylvania Gazette*, March 11, 1736

Burlington, October 2 Last week a sad Accident happen'd here (in the Manner following, viz.). An Apprentice Boy belonging to one Joshua Barker, after having done his usual Work with his Master, was desired by his Sister to assist her in carrying in some Wood, which the Youth freely did, chose to tarry with his Sister all Night, and in the Morning return'd pretty early, which nevertheless exasperated his Master so as to Chastise him with a Horse Whip in such a manner as not to give him Time to Answer for himself. But at length, the Lad getting the Door on him, ran down Stairs, his Master pursuing him close, ketch'd him in the Entery and used the same Crualty as before, until he was so much tir'd that he fell down Dead on the Spot, with his Horse Whip so fast Clinch'd in his Hand as to cause trouble to his Neighbours to clear him of it. *The New York Evening-Post*, October 7, 1745

On Saturday Sennight, in the Morning, Henry Moore Esq. of Cranbury, supposed to have fallen from his Horse, was found speechless and soon after expired. *The Pennsylvania Chronicle*, March 30, 1767

Extract from letter from Amwell, New Jersey, Oct 17, 1768. On Wednesday the 5th inst. a melancholy Accident happened here. On the afternoon of said Day, Captain Daniel Reading . . . and two other Gentlemen, each with his Fowl-ing Piece, charged with small Shot, went out . . . in the Pursuit of Game in the neighbouring Woods. And they having discovered a Squirrel on a tree, one of the Gentlemen presented, but the Object moving, he took down his Piece, and, as he confidently thinks, half cocked it. Whilst they were walking about the Tree in order to discover again the Game, the Gun of the Gentleman . . . accidentally went off and Captain Reading . . . unhappily received the Charge in his right arm, rather above the joint of the Elbow, which not only lacerated the flesh and fractured the Bone where it struck, but broke it off short, a little above where it entered. With much difficulty he got Home, in most excruciating Pain, which continued for some Days. Skilful Surgeons were immediately called to his Relief, who willing, agreeable to his own Desire, and that of his Friends, to use their utmost endeavours to save his Arm, did not proceed to an Amputation. Little or no Fever ensued, and after a few days, the Pain abated and the Wounded Part began to suppurate. But notwithstanding many flattering Symptoms of a favourable Issue, yet, on the Morning of the 15th instant, he unexpectedly and suddenly expired, without any visible

Mortification in the Part, unless livid and blackish streaks, under his wounded Arm and on that Side might be judged Indications of it. *The Pennsylvania Gazette*, October 27, 1768

New York, June 26. The Wife of a Labouring Man in Dye Street, who, to all appearances went to bed well on Tuesday Night last, was found dead in her Bed the Morning after, occasioned, its imagin'd, from the great Effects the Thoughts of her Husband's enlisting as a Soldier, had upon her. It seems that the Man had left for some Time before and had not gave her Notice where he was gone to. And the first Appearance he made was that very Evening, in order to take his leave of her, he being one of the New Jersey Recruits. She has, we are told, left three young Children behind. *The Pennsylvania Journal*, June 19, 1755

The 10th of May last, as the son of Thomas Ward, a Boy about 10 years old, of the County of Bergen and Province of New Jersey, stood on a Rock fishing for Trout, in Long Pond River, near Ringwood, a large Wild Cat, supposed to be on the Limb of some Tree near the River, jumped on his Head and he, being much frightened, fell into the River with the Cat with him, when he was scratched and bit in so dismal a Manner that it was with the greatest of Difficulty that the Boy could extricate himself out her Claws, but at length both being much fatigued, he seized his Antagonist by the throat, dragged her on shore, and there with stones, beat out her brains. The Lad then went home, the Doctor being sent for; he had his wounds dressed which were all healed up in a few weeks and he seemed quite well to the 20th of June in the Morning, he was suddenly taken with pains all over his body, but complained most of the places that had been bit and was in such an Agony that Day and Night, that next Morning he ran to a Neighbor's about two Miles distance and told them that their House and Barn, the Road and himself were all on Fire. He was sent from thence home and about Sunset on the 21st of June, he died quite mad, being just six Weeks from the time he was bitten by the Cat. After his decease, the Marks of the Wounds where he had been bit turned very black. *The New York Mercury*, August 4, 1760

There were evidences of mental illness present in the provinces, ranging from merely eccentric behavior to violence, extreme depression and suicide:

Four miles from Burlington, a recluse person who came a stranger, has existed alone, near twelve years in a thick wood, through all the extremities of the seasons, under the cover of a few leaves, supported by the side of an old log and put together in the form of a small oven, not high or long enough to stand upright or to lie extended; he talks Dutch, but unintelligibly, either through design or from defects in his intellects, 'tis hard to tell which; whence he came or what he is, no body about him can find out; he has no contrivance to keep fire, nor uses any. In very cold weather he lies naked, stops the hole he creeps in and out of with leaves; he mostly keeps in his hut, but sometimes walks before it, lies on the ground and cannot be persuaded to work much, nor obliged without violence to forsake this habit, which he appears to delight in and to enjoy full health. When the woods and the orchards afford him no nuts, apples or other relief as to food, he applies now and then for bread to the neighbourhood and, with this, is quite satisfied; he refuses money but has frequently been clothed by charity; he seems to be upward of forty years of age; as to person rather under the middle size; calls himself Francis. *The Pennsylvania Chronicle*, December 28, 1767

Philadelphia, February 15. We hear from the Jersey side that a Man near Sahaukan being disordered in his Senses, protested to his Wife that he would kill her immediately, if she did not put her Tongue in his Mouth. She through Fear complying, he bit off a large piece of it and taking it between his Fingers threw it into the Fire with these Words "Let this be for a Burnt Offering." *The Pennsylvania Gazette*, February 8, 1732

Last week, a Servant Man was found hanging in the Woods in Newtown Township, Glouster County, who, 'tis thought, has hung there since September last, when he ran away from his Master. *The Pennsylvania Gazette*, January 16, 1753

On Tuesday last an Apprentice of one Robert White in Shrewsbury, being Corrected by his Master, went home to his Parents who lived near and told them he would drown himself and took his leave of his Father. His Mother went with him to his Masters; by the way, he told her that what he had he would give her and informed her of what he had in his Pocket-Book and some small debts that were due him. His Mother told him that, if his Master abused him, he should go Complain to the Justices and they would discharge him, at which he smiled, signifying that was not to be compared with his own way of discharging himself. When he came to his Master, he threatened that he would beat him the next morning to prevent which the Lad rose early the next Morning, took a Rope and a Stone about sixteen Pound Weight and went out in the River in a Canow and, tying one end of the Rope to the Stone and the other with a running nuse about his neck, jumped overboard and drowned himself. *The American Weekly Mercury*, September 2, 1731

Philadelphia, January 23. We hear from Burlington County, in the Jersies, about a Man about 80 years of Age, who had been in a bad State of Health for some Time, and at Times delirious, cut his Throat, on the 11th instant, in so terrible a manner that, notwithstanding immediate Help was got for him, he died soon after. *The Pennsylvania Gazette*, January 23, 1753

Last week a corporal belonging to the 22d regiment, was found hanging upon a tree in the woods near New Brunswick. He was much esteemed by his officers for his good behaviour. No other reason can be assigned for his committing murder upon himself than gaming. It seems that he had lost about five pounds at cards, which affected him very much and he was observed to be melancholy the evening he disappeared. *The New American Magazine*, February, 1758

On Tuesday Morning the 6th of November, a young Man, genteelly dressed, shot himself in the Church Yard at Burlington. He had arrived at Philadelphia from Ireland about three Weeks before and had not been in Burlington above a Day or two. He attempted to shoot himself with a Pistol the day before but was prevented by the People of the House where he lodged. The Coroner's Inquest sat upon the Body and brought in their Verdict, *Felo de se* [64]. He accomplished this unnatural act of suicide in the following Manner. He had procured a short Fowling Piece loaded with large Duck shot and raising himself upon a grave in the Churchyard, he fixed the muzzle under the left side of his Breast and, with the Ram Rod forced the Trigger, whereby the whole charge entered his Body and (it is supposed) shattered his Heart to Pieces, for he expired immediately. By a Letter found in his Pocket, wrote to his Father, his name appears to be James McNamara and that he left Ireland upon some Family discontent. *The Pennsylvania Gazette*, December 27, 1759.

From Woodbury Creek, on the other side of the River, we hear, that on Sunday Night last, a servant man belonging to one Tateman got out of Bed about Midnight, and telling a Lad he slept with that he was going on a long journey and should never see him more, he went in to the Orchard and hung himself on a Tree. But it seems that a Rope broke in the Operation and, towards Morning, he found himsaelf alive upon the Ground to his no small surprise. He then went and hid himself in the Barn, among some Straw, for several hours, while his Master and the rest of the Family were searching and enquiring after him to no Effect. At length, having procured a better Rope, he hanged himself again in the Barn and was there

---

[64] Literally meaning to commit a crime upon oneself -- i.e. suicide.

accidentally found by the Maid in the Afternoon. When he was cut down, there appeared no sign of life within him, nor were any means used to recover him. But, by the time the Coroner and his inquest were got together and come to view his Body, he was up on his Legs again and is now living. *The Pennsylvania Gazette*, August 27, 1730

On Friday last a Negro Woman belonging to Mr. M'Myers was passing to Newark, in Mr. Congar's Boat, somewhat disorder'd in her Senses, she suddenly sprung overboard, and notwithstanding the utmost Endeavours of the People on board to save her, and although she was a considerable time in the water before she sunk, the Wind being high and unfavourable, they were unable to recover her and she was drown'd. *New York Journal or General Advertiser*, September 20, 1770

About two Weeks ago, one John Leek, of Cohansie in West New-Jersey, after twelve months's Deliberation, made himself a Eunuch (as it is said) for the Kingdom of Heaven's sake, having made such a construction upon Mat. XIX,12. He is now under Dr. Johnson's Hands and in a fair way of doing well. *The Pennsylvania Gazette*, October 28, 1742

Mental disease of some type clearly was behind the following murder in the "French Quarter" of Perth Amboy:

Perth Amboy, August 26. Yesterday one Paul Weebear[65], a Frenchman who has been in this Province about 14 Years, was committed to the County Goal by Mr. Justice Nevill, for the Murder of one John Poquet, a French Prisoner at Matchiponix, in the Southern Ward of this City. It appeared that Weebear had been robbed of some money and on Sunday last in the Afternoon, he came to Poquet and charged him with the Robbery, who denying it, Weebear immediately stabbed him in the belly with a long pointed knife, without the least Abuse given him by Poquet, who died of the Wound on Monday Morning. *The New York Mercury*, September 1, 1760

Philadelphia, October 30. On Saturday last Paul Oubert was executed near Perth Amboy for the Murder of Francis Poquet. His behaviour we hear both before and at his Execution was morose and sullen, seemingly ignorant of and unconcerned about his unhappy Condition. He refused the Assistance of a Protestant Divine, and when the Sheriff told him about one o'Clock that it was Time to move, he declared he would not stir until he had

---

[65] "Weebear" is undoubtedly an attempt by an English colonist to spell the French name "Oubert" as the second news report suggests.

eat his Dinner, which was brought him. When he ate and drank heartily, he then went off without the least seeming Trouble or Terror on his Mind. *The Pennsylvania Gazette*, October 30, 1760

During one several day period in 1738, there was a rash of suicides by hanging. Were they all related, the product of the power of suggestion, the effects of a fall moon or were the three of them merely a coincidence?

We have from Burlington a most melancholy Account of the Death of a Boy of 5 Years old, last Week, who hanged himself on the stake of a Fence with a Rope he had been playing with in the Yard. He was first discovered by means of the crying of a younger Child, "Brother wont speak to me". 'Tis thought that the abundance of Discourse he had heard of the late Execution of Negroes for Poisoning had fill'd his Mind and put him on imitating what he had heard was done, not knowing the Danger. It is said that he dreamt much of that Execution the Night before, and telling his dream in the Morning, added "And I shall die to Day" which was not then regarded. *The Pennsylvania Gazette*, June 8, 1738

Woodbridge in New Jersey, March 28. On the 26th Instant, one Jonathan Walker, a good liver amongst us, being sick, and only one Woman in the house to look after him, in the Height of his Fever, he attempted to go out of the House, which the Woman endeavouring to hinder, he threw her down, then run out and cast himself into a deep Well and there perished. He has left eight children behind him, their Mother being dead 3 Months before. *The New England Weekly Journal*, April 17, 1727

Philadelphia, June 1. Yesterday in the Forenoon a Man pretty well advanced in years, well dressed, came to the House of Joseph Gregory of Glouster in West-Jersey and wanted a Passage to Philadelphia, and seemed impatient at the Ferry Boat's stay, and asked for some Water to drink, which was brought to him, then he took a walk in the Orchard, leaving his Saddle-Bags and Hat in the House. About an hour after, he was found hanging by his Garters from a Limb of an Apple-Tree astride over the Fence. We have not yet learnt his Name.

We also hear from Chester, that last Saturday a Boy hang'd himself in the Work-House. *The New York Gazette*, June 12, 1738

The hundreds of advertisements for runaways, escapees and deserters, which describe in detail any abnormalities about the person sought, are sources for learning the maladies and deformities of the colonists. As mentioned, small pox scarred many, as well as causing permanent hair loss. Scars of all other sorts were commonplace as were other evidences of accident and misadventure. Several runaways had their ears bitten off by horses; were crippled from ill setting broken bones; had missing fingers, limbs and eyes; or suffered permanent damage from gunshot wounds. Others were described as having one leg, arm, thumb or even ankle larger than the other.

Other disabilities were due to birth defects ("splaw footed"; "bowlegged" ; "bandy legged"; "knees bending somewhat inward"; "turns out his feet much as he walks and his knees are inclined to strike one another"; "walks with his leg turned outward"; "his right foot twisting and the toe of the same inclining to turn outward as he walks and his right knee bending inwards towards the left"; "turns out his feet pretty much as he walks"; "hunched back"; "round shouldered, slow in speech, a little hard of hearing, stoops and rocks much in his walk".

Speech defects of lisping, stammering, stuttering or "speak[ing] by clusters, hard to understand" were widely reported. Others squinted, had an eye permanently shut or eyes sunk deeply into their heads or were hard of hearing. Still others stooped as they walked, were round shouldered or were missing their teeth.

Dermatologists would have had no end of business in those days as the following symptoms were among those described: "great ringworms on her breast and arms"; "ring worm on his face"; "all around his neck and above his shirt collar and all over his body his skin is greyish like a fish scale"; "face somewhat bumped".

Other ailments are not so easy to diagnose, at least to a layman, but sound either serious or potentially so: "is a little swelled with the dropsy"; "much afflicted with a dry cough"; "yellow complexion"; " has a great lump on his throat"; "troubled with a phthisick"; "hoarse in his speech as if he had a cold"; "he goes crooked and often groans in his sleep"; or "he halts as he walks seemingly rocking".

It has been suggested that the American colonists were not as well educated as their parents had been in Europe, which, upon reflection, makes perfect sense. Carving homes out of the frontier was a dawn to dusk task, to which education, as well as other preferred accompaniments to civilization, were necessarily secondary. But education was present and increasingly becoming a part of the Colony's life.

Education was almost exclusively for males. In fact among hundreds of notices and accounts in colonial newspapers relating to education, only one was directed to young women:

As Thomas Powell, of Burlington, Schoolmaster, has been applied to sundry times to take Girls to Board and hath hitherto declined it because he thought it inconvenient to board a Number of each Sex in the Same House, William Fentham, Latin and French Master, in the same School, begs leave to inform the Public that Girls may be conveniently boarded and taught Needle-Work by his Wife, who has opened a School for that Purpose, and may have the benefit of being instructed in English, Writing, Arithmetic and French by

Thomas Powell and William Fentham

N.B. The Boarders will have an Opportunity of speaking the French Tongue in the House. *The Pennsylvania Gazette*, April 21, 1763

For the few boys in the position to be educated, there were, like today, college prep courses and business courses of several varieties.

Mr. Campbell in Burlington, by the first of September next, proposes to teach young Men the classick Authors. If any Gentlemen are inclined to send their Sons to him, they may depend upon diligent Attendance.

N.B. The said Cambell will board two or three Boys at his House. *The Pennsylvania Gazette*, July 5, 1744

Writing, arithmetick vulgar and decimal, merchants accompts by the Italian method double entry, sundry branches of the mathematics, as navigation survey &c. and algebra, all carefully taught in Burlington, near the Court-House by

Thomas Craven

The Pennsylvania Gazette, February 7, 1749

The Languages, as Latin, Greek, Hebrew &c. also the Arts and Sciences, Philosophy and Theology &c. are to be taught faithfully by John Henry Goetschius, A.M., and Dutch Minister at Hackensack and Schralenburg, where may be had proper Lodging and other Necessaries. *The New York Gazette Revived in the Weekly Post Boy*, November 20, 1749

Bartholomew Rowley (at his School in Burlington) professes to teach the Latin and English Grammar, Albany's Syntax and Prodia, School Authors, Rhetorick, Gordon's Geographical Grammar, Arithmetic, &c. N.B. That universal Comprehension of Natural and Civil Story, i.e. Cosmography, may be read in said school. *The Pennsylvania Gazette*, September 19, 1751

The schools were small and most required the students to board on site or in the neighboring town. There was keen competition for students as reflected in the Notices printed in the popular press of the 1700s seeking students and explaining all the positive attractions of their schools and curricula.

This is to inform the Public that the Subscriber hath opened a Boarding-School Elizabeth-Town, in East-New-Jersey, for the accommodation and instruction of Youth in Writing, Arithmetic both vulgar and Decimal Extraction of the Roots, Geometry and Trignometry, with their Application in Surveying, Guaging, Menturation, Navigation &c., Merchants Accompts in the most approved method; as also, Boys to be instructed in the Beauty and Propriety of the English Tongue, which shall be taught as a Language; the best English Authors shall be read & explained; the Art Rhetoric or Oratory, shall be taught with great Care and Exactness; Specimens of the Boys proficiency therein shall be given every Quarter. Those Gentlemen who are pleased to encourage said School may depend upon the greatest Care being taken over the Morals of their Children that a just veneration may be early risen in their tender Mind for Virtue, as well as Learning. The School-House is very pleasantly Situated in an open and wholesome Air; its hoped the undertaking will meet with due Encouragement, especially from those who know the importance of a proper British Education and the great Advantages Boys must necessarily have from their being always under the Inspection of a Master. Boys will be admitted into said School who can read tolerably well on very reasonable terms by

Robert Cather

The Pennsylvania Journal, April 1, 1762

Ephraim Avery
Takes this Method to inform the Public that he open'd
A School

At Second- River in East-New-Jersey, opposite to Col. John Schuyler's, where he teaches writing and reading English, the Latin and Greek languages, arithmetick, both vulgar and decimal; likewise, Algebra, trigonometry, surveying, guaging, plane, traverse, and mercator's sailing, by several different methods, according to Atkinson's and Wilson's epitomes; Any gentleman of the City of New York, or in the Country, that will favour him with their children may depend upon their being instructed in any of the above mentioned branches, with the utmost care and expedition.

N.B. It would not be improper to acquaint you that the place is agreeably situated on a navigable river, the inhabitants very kind and civil; boats, almost daily pass and repass from hence to New York. Gentlemen need not give themselves any trouble to provide lodgings or wood for the School, both of which said Master engages to procure on very reasonable terms. *The New York Mercury*, November 29, 1762

Burlington, July 5, 1763. The Subscriber having for Strong Reasons left T. Powell and procured a commodius Room, proposes to open School the 11th of July, in which the following Branches of literature will be taught viz. Latin, French, English, Writing, and Arithmetic and the strictest Attendance given. Having also provided Conveniences for Boarders, those who are inclined to put Children under his Tuition, will have in all probability in a reasonable time the Satisfaction of finding them capable of conversing in the French Tongue, as he proposes to give frequent lectures and to render it familiar by the Constant Practice and Use of it in the Family. The Encouragement of the Public in this Useful Undertaking shall be gratefully acknowledged in the closest Application to the Benefit of the Scholars, from their friend William Wyatt Fentham, late Latin Master in Thomas Powell's School. *The Pennsylvania Gazette*, July 14, 1763

This will inform the Public that it is the Design of the Subscriber to open up a Grammar School, on the 20th Day of April, at Hackensack, under the Inspection and Direction of the Rev. Mr. Goetschius. All Gentlemen who are disposed to having their Sons instructed in the learned Languages as being very necessary and useful to a farther Progress in the liberal Arts and Sciences, may depend upon a constant Attendance, a strict and accurate Instruction by their humble Servant,
Stephanus Voorhees, A. M.

N.B. The Terms of Admission will be as moderate as in any Latin School perhaps to be found viz. Twenty Shillings entrance, and Twenty Shillings per Quarter. It is supposed by Gentlemen who are well acquainted in the Place that Board and Tuition will not exceed Twenty Pounds per Annum. The agreeable Situation of the Place, together with many other Conveniences, I hope will be of a considerable Motive to engage the Attention of such Gentlemen as are disposed to have their Sons educated. *The New York Gazette or Weekly Post Boy*, April 3, 1766

Hackensack, at the New-Bridge. We the subscribers, being encouraged by the favorable notice, and approbation of many gentlemen of character, both in city and country, to pursue our present business, do hereby, from an expectation of further encouragement, inform the public, that it is our honest design in conjunction with each other, in order to extend our usefulness to mankind in general, to continue to teach the learned languages. A necessary and beautiful accomplishment for young gentlemen who desire to make any considerable figure in life, as they are the proper foundation of all other advances in speculative knowledge, in the approved method; with the same accuracy and care as formerly, and hope our good intentions, together with our diligence, and assiduous labour, will always be such, as to merit the assistance and approbation of all gentlemen of letters.

Strangers may have satisfaction, as to the character of the school, by applying to a number of competent judges, in New York, whose sons are now under tuition; and as another inducement the situation of the place is almost sufficient of itself to recommend it.

It is healthy, pleasant, and inviting; it abounds with innocent and necessary pleasure and amusement: But, at the same time, youth are very little exposed to vice, or dangerous examples to corrupt their morals.

The neighbourhood is exceedingly well calculated for boarding children, and is heartily disposed to encourage so public a utility. Board may be procured in the best families, at the usual price. All possible care is, and will be taken, for good accommodations. There is sufficient room for boarding twice the number of scholars that are at present in the school, without exposing them to any inconvenient distance.

There is also a third person to teach English, writing and arithmetic, who instructs the latin scholars in those branches of education, such a portion of time every day, as not to interfere with their stated studies, for a small additional consideration per quarter.

We are the publick's much obliged,
Most obedient humble servants,
Stephanus Voorhees
Francis Barber

N.B. We will esteem greatly to our honour, whenever any gentleman shall think it fit to come and inspect our school, and be informed as to our manner of instruction, and shall be glad to receive instruction ourselves, as to the method, or anything else that tend to promote the public good. *The New York Journal or General Advertiser*, January 14, 1768

There is lately opened a Grammar School in Lower Freehold, Monmouth County, East New-Jersey, known by the name of Mattisonia Grammar School, where the learned languages are taught and Youth qualified to enter any of the American Colleges, or fitted for any Public Business, as the Arts and Sciences, and especially the several Branches of the Mathematics, will also be taught with Accuracy and Care. The School to be under the Patronage and Inspection of Rev. Messrs. William Tennent[66] and Charles M'Knight[67] and Dr. Nathaniel Scudder[68], who

---

[66] William Tennent, a Presbyterian minister from a family of famous preachers, was the subject of an interesting event in his twenties. In frail health, he one day collapsed and appeared to be dead. Prepared for his funeral with the mourners assembling, Tennent's friend and doctor appeared, having been away at the time of death. For unknown reasons, but described as a refusal to accept his friend's death, the doctor had the funeral postponed and remained with the body for three days, praying and watching. Finally, the family would allow him no longer and, as funeral preparations were renewed, the Rev. Tennent popped up from his death bed for a moment, only to return to unconsciousness. It was enough however to maintain the vigil and Rev. Tennent began to slowly emerge from what must have been a coma caused by a stroke. It took him six weeks to be able to leave his bed, longer to regain his speech and, as he had lost his memory entirely, he had to relearn everything back to the alphabet.

One thing that the Reverend did remember, however, was what is now known as an out of body experience during which the dying man saw what lay beyond. Franklin Ellis in his 1885 Edition of the History of Monmouth County describes Rev. Tennent's recitation of the experience as follows: "He felt as if caught up by some invisible power and carried up; away in the distance he beheld a sight of inexpressible glory, indescribable and beautiful. His first thought was "Blessed be God, I am saved at last." His agony and disappointment were great when his heavenly conductor informed him that he must return to earth. Then he gave a groan, and as he opened his eyes, saw his brother Gilbert and the Doctor and heard them disputing about his funeral."

Rev. Tennent was also a great supporter of the Revolutionary cause and, on his

will be careful that it is always furnished with an able Teacher and engage frequently to visit and Examine the Members as to their literary Improvement.

All Gentlemen who will favour the Undertaking, may depend upon having Justice done to their Children.

The House for the School, finished in a genteel Manner, is situated in a very healthy place and good Neighbourhood, where the Morals of Youth will be in no Danger of being corrupted and the whole expense of Boarding and Tuition will not exceed Twenty Pounds.

N.B. The above School is in Mr. Tennent's Parish. *The New York Journal or General Advertiser*, December 24, 1766

Elizabeth-Town, New Jersey, July 11. Mr. Reeve, master of the grammar school established here . . .hath lately signalled his intention. . . of resigning. . . We have chosen Mr. Joseph Periam, who proposed to resign his Office as a Tutor in the College of New Jersey. . . Mr. Periam, having long taught the mathematics in the college, with distinguished approbation and success, proposes, besides what has been heretofore taught in the school, to instruct, if requested, in this important branch of knowledge, not only young gentlemen who have studied the Latin and Greek languages, but others who do not intend a college education.

---

death bed, reportedly asked God, if possible, to let him live "to see a happy issue to the severe and arduous controversy my country is engaged in."

[67] We do not know which Charles M'Knight this was. There was Rev. Charles M'Knight who also was a well known Presbyterian preacher throughout Monmouth County. Also an avid supporter of the Revolution, his parsonage in Middletown was burned by the British and he was taken prisoner to New York and placed in festering prison ships anchored in the harbor. Eventually, released he was so weakened by the captivity that he soon died. Or the reference could be to Rev. Charles M'Knight's son, a medical doctor of the same name, who was a captain in the Colonial Army.

[68] Dr. Scudder was perhaps the greatest patriot of the three founders of this School. A medical doctor from Freehold, he was a delegate to the Continental Congress and a member of the Committee on Correspondence, part of the network throughout the colonies that served to encourage and support independence. He was also a colonel in the Monmouth militia. In October, 1781, he would be shot at Black Point, in Rumson. New Jersey, by a quasi military band of British sympathizers/bandits, stationed on Sandy Hook and known as the Refugees.

As this gentleman is skilled in penmanship, a particular attention will be paid, if desired by the parents, to the handwriting of the pupils. These will be required to spend some time every day in improving themselves in this useful and ornamental part of education. There employment herein will differ, according to their different capacities. Some in writing the usual copies; others in transcribing fairly, from approved authors, either letters to acquire a taste for the epistolary stile; or to select pieces to be committed to memory, which they will be taught to pronounce with grace and propriety. Those of riper judgments will be required to write their own thoughts in the forms of letters, descriptions &c. These transcripts and compositions will be carefully reviewed and errors pointed out in such manner as will be most likely to make them accurate in writing and spelling.

We need not mention that care will be taken to instruct them in geography, so far as is necessary to understand the use of the Globes, [in] the classical authors, [and] in Oratory, as these have heretofore been taught when desired in this school.

As it is important that Youth, even before they leave the grammar-school, should be instructed in the principles of christianity, Mr. Periam will engage to teach them such of our protestant Catechisms as may be most agreeable to their parents or governors. *The New York Gazette and Weekly Mercury*, July 24, 1769

This Joseph Periam who had taken over at the Grammar School in Elizabeth must have memorable school master as one of his earlier flings at education suggests:

Proposals for teaching the Latin Language, so that the student may save three-Fourths of his time and above half of his money.

The Subscriber, lately a tutor of the college of New Jersey, proposes to teach a very few boys the Latin language . . . .The number of students will not exceed six . . . The mode of teaching will be somewhat new, and, perhaps, has never been practiced, in America at least. But tho' I make no secret of the mode, yet, the public are not so much concerned in knowing that as my terms.

If I teach the Latin language in one year, so that at the years end (sickness and unforeseen accidents excepted) the student appears, upon examination, to be well acquainted with it, not only as well as most in any college on the continent are at their commencing Bachelors of arts, but be able with propriety and facility to translate Latin into English and English into Latin and understand the grammatical construction, then, I shall expect 40 Pounds Proc. but, if I fail in the attempt, then I shall expect no compensation.

To be taught thus would be by the far cheapest for the student, which may appear from the following considerations.

'Tis well known, that, at the rate Youth are generally taught, one of an indifferent or middling genius, would require at least 4 years to obtain a competent knowledge of the Latin language, such a knowledge I mean as has just been mentioned.

In each of these four years, suppose the student to expend for tuition 4 Pounds, for board 26 Pounds, for Apparel and other expenses, 30 Pounds, in all 60 pounds per Annum, which in 4 years amounts to 240 Pounds. This then is the whole expense to the student while learning the Latin language, after the usual rate of teaching.

Again supposing a student learns the Latin language in one year, according to the proposal above mentioned, in this one year, suppose the student to expend for tuition 40 Pounds, for board, 26 Pounds, for apparel and other expenses 30 Pounds, in all 96 Pounds. This then is the whole expense of the student, while learning the Latin language after the rate proposed.

Thus we see that above 140 Pounds is saved, besides three years of precious time.

If, besides saving his time and money, he should learn the language, not only without the wearisome groping which disgusts almost every youth and, in many ways, fixes a lasting aversion to study, but should even contract every day a greater fondness and relish for study, which fondness 'tis highly probable he will retain all of his life after, I refer to all who have ever thought about the preciousness of time, of the pain-ful fatigue which grammar-school boys generally undergo, and of a valuableness of a relish for study, whether it would not be a good and cheap bargain, for a youth to pay not only 40 Pounds, but even a 100 pounds to Be thus taught.. . .

No abatement or allowance will be made for such as have spent any time at the Latin. The subscriber would prefer such as never had. . . .

Joseph Periam
The Pennsylvania Journal, October 16, 1766

"Study at Home" courses, or, at least, an ancestor of them, were also available in Colonial America to those who did not have the opportunity to have a more formal education.

Just Published by Thomas Powell, Master of the Boarding School at Burlington,

The Writing Master's Assistant

containing a concise and practical System (in Copper Plate) for teaching to Write; designed for both the Use of Schools and private Families; insomuch that Masters may teach a much greater Number of Scholars by the Use of it, than by the common Methods of Schools and the Parents may by the proper Application of it (if far distant from a School) instruct their own Children to Write in a short time. A Person may improve an indifferent Hand or One, who has never learnt before, may learn, if of a proper Age, without the Help of a Master.

N.B. Directions how to hold the Pen, how to sit and how to use the Plates severally, are prefixed to the Work. Sold by David Hall at Philadelphia and by the Author at Burlington, Price Five Shillings. *The Pennsylvania Gazette*, August 2, 1764

The University, of course, was the highest form of education in Britain and the Continent. It would take almost a century before the Colony could mature so much as to have an institution like that of its own. The College of New Jersey's (today Princeton) birth was announced in the newspapers of the day:

Whereas a Charter with full and ample Privileges, has been granted by his Majesty under seal of Province of New Jersey bearing date 22d October, 1746 for erecting a College within the said Province, to Jonathan Dickinson, John Pierson, Ebenezer Pemberton and Aaron Burr, Ministers of the Gospel, and some other Gentlemen as Trustees, by which Charter equal Liberties and Privileges are secured to every denomination of Christians, any different religious Sentiments notwithstanding.

The said Trustees have therefore thought proper to inform the Public that the design to open the said College the next Spring and to notify to any Person or Persons who are qualified by preparatory Learning for Admission that some time in May next at latest, they may be there admitted to an Academic Education. *The New York Gazette Revived in the Weekly Post Boy*, January 12, 1747

Also acknowledged was the College's first graduation exercises:

We have Advice that on Wednesday the 9th of Last Month, was held at Newark, the first Commencement of the College of New-Jersey, when the Rev. Mr. Aaron Burr was unaminously chosen President of said College by the Trustees and Six young Scholars were admitted to the Degree of Bachelor of Arts. After which, his Excellency Jonathan Belcher, Esq, Governour and Commander in Chief of that Province, having declared his Desire to accept from that College the Degree of Master of Arts, the other Trustees in a just Sense of the Honour done the College by his Excellency's Condescension, most heartily granted his Request and the President, rising uncover'd, address'd himself to his Excellency, and according to the Authority committed to him by the Royal Charter, admitted him to the Degree of Master of Arts. *The Boston Weekly News Letter*, December 1, 1748

Discussed in the press as an exchange of letters from readers (a primitive form of the editorial/letter to the editor section of today's papers) was the purpose of the College and from what ranks its students should come. In it is plainly obvious the growing dislike in America for a privileged class, a sentiment that will later fuel a revolution.

The College of New Jersey, upon which we all have had our eyes fixed, for furnishing our Churches with a gracious, holy, humble and learned Ministry, have wisely judged that gentlemens sons are the only likely persons to answer our expectations; and accordingly have passed an Act that none shall be admitted to the College, but those that are able to continue for four years; and they have provided a Professor of Divinity, who, if well attended for a year or two more, will fit these gracious, holy, humble (and I may add rich) youths for the Ministry; and the experience at a moderate computation will not exceed 300 pounds, which is but a trifling sum for a gentleman, in that important business. You will imagine, perhaps, that the pious Poor are to be shut out. No; a gentleman of that faculty told me "if a young man of exemplary piety, promising abilities, and sufficiently forward

-216-

in learning to enter the junior class, would, upon a certificate that he and his parents were so poor, that they were not able to support him more than two years, make application for admission, he might be taken in as a poor scholar."

B.O.

The Pennsylvania Chronicle, June 27, 1768

It has been an old saying, "cast dirt plentifully and some of it will stick." Fully of this sentiment it seems was the Author of that letter, signed B.O. . . . . But he has something to say respecting the College of New-Jersey, as well as the Synod. In his historical narration, he evidently designs to represent the board of trustees in an injurious light. I shall leave that Respectable Body to speak for themselves, although it is probable that they will judge such ill-natured sneers unworthy of their notice, whether their act of admitting none to the College save the first class, be in fact a prudent regulation or not may be dubious; doubtless they thought it to be proper at the time of passing it, although I know some not inconsiderable friends of that institution that think otherwise. Some future period will better discover the truth in that point. *Supplement to the Pennsylvania Journal*, July 21, 1768

Being wealthy was not enough to gain entrance to the College. A knowledge and, indeed, fluency in subject matters today's students rarely ever even takes was a requirement for admission, as the following Notice from the College's Trustees stipulates.

The Trustees of the College of New Jersey give notice that, at the earnest solicitation of many particular persons and societies friendly to the institution, they have entirely repealed the law that was to have taken place in September next, absolutely requiring four years residence and resolved to admit upon the same footing as before. They think it however necessary to notify that every scholar who pretends to enter any of the superior classes, must come fully prepared and expect a strict and impartial examination. And, that no school master or others concerned in the scholars may have reason to complain of advantages being taken against them, it is thought proper now to publish the original law of admission and to give full information as to how the trial is to proceed. The law for admission into the Freshman class, enacted in the year 1748, and which has still been the law for the examination is in the following words: " None may expect to be admitted but such as being examined by the president and tutors, shall be found able to render Vergil and Tully's orations into English and to turn English into true and grammatical latin, and be so well acquainted with the greek so as to render any part of the four Evangelists in that language, into latin or English and to give the grammatical construction of the words." By another law, enacted in the year 1760, it is ordered "that all who are admitted to the freshman class shall be acquainted with vulgar arithmetic, which shall be considered a necessary term of their admission."

These laws will be strictly observed and it is expected that the scholars should not only explain the authors therein specified but be well acquainted with the grounds of the languages and such parts of education as by their nature must be supposed to go before the above classical performances viz. Reading English with propriety, spelling the English language and writing it without grammatical errors.

As to the superior classes, whoever desires to enter the Sophomore, must either come and sit down with the freshman of the preceding year, before commencement, and be judged at the same time, or if it comes later than their public examination, three must be balloted from the class which he desires to enter, and by fair comparison with them, he will be admitted or degraded. The same rule will be observed as to those desiring admission to the junior class.

It is expected and desired that Masters of large schools who send a number of students to college, should come with them themselves and be present and assist at their examination. By this means, they will have the opportunity to see justice done to them and all suspicion of unfairness and partiality will be effectually prevented. *The New York Gazette and Weekly Mercury*, May 1, 1769

Indeed, the entrance requirements were so difficult that the College had to create a "prep" school in Princeton to prepare applicants for admission.

Prince-Town, October 25. The Publick is hereby notified that as soon as a competent Number of Scholars offer themselves, an English School will be opened, under the Inspection of the President of the New-Jersey College and as an Appendage to the same, in which it is proposed to be taught the English language grammatically and that the Boys, when found capable, be exercised in Compositions, as well as in pronouncing Orations publickly; also Writing, Arithmetick and the popular branches of Arithmetick by a proper Master or Masters; and, in the mean time, until this scheme is ripe for Execution, such as desire, may be well accommodated at the English common school at the Town, now taught by Mr. Simon Williams, a graduate of this College, who writes a good hand and has had long experience in Teaching. Gentlemen's Sons can be conveniently boarded at several Places in Town and one Gentlewoman in particular has taken a large commodius House for that very purpose. It may be depended on that all possible Care and Pains will be taken both with respect to the Morals and Instruction of the Youth. *The Pennsylvania Journal*, November 10, 1763

Throughout the world, students seem to lead the protests that eventually change society. As the American Revolution approached, the Princeton students of 1770 were no different. The object of their wrath were those New York merchants who were breaking the agreements reached among the citizens in towns throughout all the colonies to no longer import from Britain until certain rights and liberties were granted them:

This afternoon the Students at Nassau Hall, fired with a just indignation on reading the infamous letter from the Merchants in New York to the Committee of Merchants of Philadelphia informing them of their Resolution to send Home Orders for Goods contrary to their Non-Importation Agreements, at the tolling of the College Bell, went in Procession to a Place fronting the College, and burnt the Letter by the Hands of a Hangman, hired for the Purpose, with hearty Wishes that the Names of all Promoters of such a daring Breach of Faith, may be blasted in the Eyes of every Lover of Liberty and their Names handed down to Posterity as Betrayers of their Country. *The New York Gazette or Weekly Post Boy*, July 16, 1770

We are credibly informed from Princeton that the senior Class at Nassau Hall have unanimously agreed to appear at their ensuing Commencement dressed in American Manufactures. How happy ought we to esteem ourselves, when we see some of our youth, who will probably fill some of the highest Stations in their Country, when their Fathers have fallen asleep, so early declaring their Love for their Country; and we hope this will meet with that esteem which is their due and that many at this critical Juncture will follow the laudable Example in encouraging our own Manufactures. *The New York Gazette or Weekly Post Boy*, July 30, 1770.

One might judge the differences between the substance of the education of two and a half centuries ago with that of today by the following press reports of The College of New Jersey's graduation exercises, which appeared designed to demonstrate that the graduates had indeed been educated and learned how to think during their undergraduate days, rather than merely to amass information and learn job skills as most today seem to think is the purpose of education:

On Wednesday last, was held at New Brunswick, the Anniversary Commencement of the College of New-Jersey, at which, after the usual publick Disputations, the following young Gentlemen were admitted to the degrees of Bachelors of Arts viz

John Brown	John Moffat
William Burnet	John Todd
John Hoge	and
Thomas Kennedy	Eleazer Whittlesey

After which, a handsome Latin Oration was pronounced by Mr. Burnet, one of the Graduates, and the Ceremony concluded to the Universal Satisfaction of a numerous Audience, the whole Affair being conducted with great Propriety and Decorum. *The New York Gazette Revived in the Weekly Post Boy*, October 2, 1749

Princetown, September 30. Yesterday the Trustees of the College of New-Jersey, with his Excellency the Governor, attended the Commencement. After the usual Procession, and a solemn invocation of the of the Divine Blessing, on the Business of the day, and the Candidates for the Honours of the College, the Exercises were introduced by an elegant salutatory Oration in Latin, pronounced by Mr. James Manning, one of the Candidates for Bachelor's Degree. The Young Gentlemen gave an agreeable Specimen of their skill is Disputation, which was carried on alternately in the Syllogistic and Forenic Way. The Subject of the First which was syllogistic, was the following Thesis, *Conservatio non est continua Creatio*[69], which was well defended and opposed. This, agreeable to the order aforementioned was succeeded by a forsenic Dispute on this Question, "Whether a Prince, endowed with the Virtues of Civil Government, but not with Military, is to be preferred to one of the most shining, military Genius, if he is destitute of the Virtues necessary for the governing in Peace?" Which was decided in the affirmative after being debated on both Sides with much Spirit and Eloquence. To relax the Attention of the Audience, an English oration on Politeness was pronounced by Mr. Joseph Periam, which gave universal Satisfaction from the Justness of the Sentiments, the Elegance of the Composition, and Propriety with which it was deliver'd. The Thesis next debated was *Anima humana dum in Corpus infunditur, a Deo immediate creatur*[70], which afforded Pleasure to the learned Part of the Auditory. The Exercises of the Forenoon were concluded by a forsenic Dispute on this

---

[69] Although my Latin is rusty, this translates roughly into "Preservation of the status quo is not progress".

[70] Man's soul is breathed into him at his creation.

Subject: "Whether Moral as well as Mathematical Truths are capable of Demonstration?" which was judiciously maintain'd and determined in the affirmative to general Satisfaction.

The Entertainments of the Afternoon were begun with a Dispute, which was very ingeniously managed by the Respondent, on this Thesis *Sensus Moralis, qua simplex Perceptio, atque Moralis Obligationis Fundamentum non datur*[71]. The last question being debated by the Bachelors being "Whether Noah's Flood was Universal?" gave agreeable Amusement to the Auditory, by the popular and pertinent Manner in which it was canvassed. A valedictory Address in English, pronounced by Isaac Allan, with a graceful Ease and Propriety, closed the Exercises of the Candidates for the Honour of Bachelor's Degree.

The following Thesis was also learnedly defended and opposed by the Candidates for Master's Degree *Deus Hominum sine Virtute morali, non priaris creavit, neque creare potuit.*[72]

. . . . [a]nd the whole concluded with a poetical Entertainment, given by the Candidates for Bachelor's Degrees, interspersed with Choruses of Music, which with the whole performance of the Day, afforded universal Satisfaction to a polite and crowded Auditory. *The New York Mercury*, October 11, 1762

Princeton, September 26, 1763. Yesterday his Excellency our Governor, with the other Trustees, attended the Anniversary Commencement of the College of New-Jersey.

The Exercises of the Day were introduced by a Short, Elegant, Latin Oration, pronounced by the President, to which succeeded a well composed Salutory Oration, delivered by one of the Young Gentlemen of the Senior Class and then the following Theses were Maintained and Opposed by the Candidates for the Bachelor's Degree, viz. The Preacher of the Gospel has the best opportunity of exercising the art of Rhetoric, in its whole Extent; that Ceremonious Behaviour, usually called polite Manners, is not Vain and Senseless Parade but useful and necessary; Brute Creatures Think but have not Human Reason; *Ars typographica plus utilitatis, quam detrimenti, veritati et bonis moribus attulit; Necessitas moralis, lubentiae*

---

[71] Whether a sense of morality and man's obligations can be learned by natural thought alone?

[72] God neither creates, nor is capable of creating man without moral victory.

rationali nequaquam repugnat[73]. The four former in the Forensic, the latter in the Syllogistic Way. The several Disputants acquitted themselves to general Satisfaction. The Entertainment was agreeably Diversified by two Elegant, English Orations, one on Peace, the other on Reputation, which were well pronounced.

A Beautiful Harangue on the Advantages of Health, introduced the Exercises of the Candidates for the Masters Degree. This was succeeded by a Latin Disputation on this Thesis *Nulla simplex imperii civilis forma est quam optima,*[74] which was Maintained and Opposed with great Judgment. A spirited Valedictory Address concluded these Exercises. *The Pennsylvania Journal*, October 14, 1763.

One thing has not changed in education and that is the lack of sufficient funding to do all that has to be done. Public lotteries, for example, helped finance the College of New Jersey, but still there was a shortfall:

We are informed that at a Meeting of the Trustees of the College of New-Jersey, lately held at Nassau College, the Revd. Mr. Blair, Professor of Divinity in said College, requested liberty to resign said office, as he considered the present revenue of that college insufficient for the support of a professorship and that the instruction of pupils in that branch may at present devolve upon the President of the College. The Trustees gave him the thanks of the board for his service to that institution, and considering the application as an act of generosity and disinterestedness in him, added the highest testimonials of their approbation of his character and conduct. *The Pennsylvania Journal*, May 11, 1769

---

[73] Whether the art of printing is more beneficiial or detrimental to virtue and good morality.

[74] The Natural form of human order is superior to all others.

From the earliest days, the enactment of laws and their subsequent administration and enforcement were essential to colonial America. That meant able judges, a speedy and convenient resolution of conflicts and, most importantly an honest system that put the litigants on equal footing. Witness the thanks and praise that the citizenry of Middlesex and Somerset Counties showered on the Governor in 1712 and ask yourself whether the same could be said today:

To his Excellency Robert Hunter Esqr, Captain General and Governour in Chief of the Provinces of New-Jersey, New York, Vice Admiral of the Same &c.

The Humble Address of the Grand-Jury for the Counties of Middlesex and Somerset at the Sessions held at Perth Amboy in the Province of New-Jersey, the fourth Tuesday in May, 1712,
Sheweth

That the sense of our duty Excites our Thankfulness to Providence and sincere acknowledgments to Her Majesty for the Felicity we enjoy under your Excellency's Administration. Amongst the numerous Instances that could be given, we beg leave to point out a few, without which the Province would have continued unhappy.

1. Your Excellency's early Care after your Accession to the Government in settling the Courts upon the surest Basis, by appointing Persons as well qualifyed as Judges, as the Infant Circumstances of the Country would allow; they are men of known Probity, whose Reputation have remain'd unsullied with the Stains of Corruption.

2. Your Excellency Appointing Surrogates in remote parts of the Province which gives a general ease to the Country by preventing that great trouble and excessive charge to which many were formerly exposed in Travelling from the most Distant Places of the Province to Burlington for Probate of Wills, Letters of Administration and Licenses of Marriage.

3. The Celerity of Justice which is equally to be valued with doing whereof we were so happy to have almost as many actions Tryed of late in a little Time as had been at the Supreme Court, since the Province happily fell under her Majesties's immediate Government.

4. The discouragement of harassing Her Majesties Subjects after that violent way of procedure by Information, which rendered that ancient

and happy constitution of Presentments by Grand Inquest useless.[75] It is with the greatest joy that we express our Felicity that by Your Excellencies goodness we now see Justice flow in its proper channel and firmly hope that neither crafty Artifices nor subtil insinuations will be able to divert it out of its right current.

We pray Your Excellency to believe that we shall not be wanting in our Duty to lay hold of all opportunities to demonstrate our Loyalty to Her Majesty and gratitude to Your Excellency in rendering Your Administration easy over.
Her Majesties Dutiful Subjects and Your
Excellencies Obedient Servants.
The Boston News-Letter, June 9, 1712

As settlements increased, more and more laws were created, which necessarily added to the administration of the judicial system which had to interpret the new laws and adjudicate disputes regarding them. The following laws were passed in a single legislative term, a formidable achievement considering the frontier and part time nature of the legislative process:

May 16, 1768. We hear from Perth Amboy, that on Tuesday last his Excellency the Governor of New Jersey, gave his Assent to the following 23 Acts of the General Assembly of the Province, viz.

An Act for the Support of Government

An Act for the Relief of Insolvent Debtors

An Act to erect and establish Courts in the several Counties, for the trial of small causes

An Act to appoint Commissioners to furnish the Barracks.

---

[75] Today, the Grand Jury system by which a group of citizens meet in secret to determine whether there is sufficient evidence to bring criminal felony charges against an individual, is often criticized as being obsolete, a tool of the prosecutor and lacking in its secrecy the elementary fairness required by the Constitution. Ironically, as history often is, the Grand Jury system was a major step forward in the protection of individual rights when it wrested from the Crown in England. Before that it was the Crown, the Kings and his minions, who determined whom should be charged with what crimes and when they would be tried -- obviously a powerful weapon in a dictator's hands. They would present the charges by way of an "information". When the power to accuse went to the Grand Jury, usually comprised of twenty four or more citizens, the rules of secrecy prevented the King from finding out how the jurors voted, thus strengthening their resolve to vote freely whether or not to indict a person.

An Act for better regulating Constables, Vendues, and Taverns.

An Act to continue an Act for granting a bounty on Hemp, Flax, etc.

An Act for the Trial of Slaves for Murder and other Crimes etc.

An Act for the Septennial Election of Representatives to serve in General Assembly, in the Colony of New-Jersey.

An Act for chusing Representatives in the Counties of Morris, Cumberland, and Sussex.

An Act to regulate the Fishery in the Eastern Division from the mouth of Rariton, Northward.

An Act to impower the Inhabitants of Bridgewater and Bedminster in the County of Somerset to repair their Highways by Hire.

An Act to impower the Inhabitants of Pequanock in Morris County, to repair their Highways by Hire, etc

An Act to repair Public roads in South Amboy by Hire etc.

An Act to repair and amend the roads and streets in the North Ward of Perth Amboy etc.

An Act to build a Bridge over South-River etc.

A Supplementary Act to an Act to regulate the method of taking Fish in Delaware River etc.

An Act to enable Creditors more easily to recover debts from joint partners.

An Act appointing Commissioners to sell a Quantity of gun powder and lead etc belonging to the Colony.

An Act to oblige the Assessors to deliver Duplicates of their Assessments.

An Act to oblige Town-Officers to hand over the Laws to their Successors.

An Act to enable the Owners and Possessors of the Lower Meadows on Woodbury Creek, to dam out the Tide.

And to two Naturalization Bills, after which his Excellency was pleased to prologue the General assembly to the 31st Instant. *The New York Gazette or Weekly Post Boy*, May 16, 1768.

New York, December 18. The 6th Instant a Session of the General Assembly of the Province of New Jersey, ended at Burlington, during which session Twenty-six Acts passed . . . Among those Acts passed were An Act for the Trial of Causes under Ten Pounds; an Act for the Relief of Insolvent Debtors; An Act against Horse-Stealing; an Act to Regulate the Ferries; an Act for the Preservation of Oysters; an Act for the Preservation of Deer; and An Act to lay a duty on Negroes imported. *The New York Gazette and Weekly Mercury*, December 18, 1769.

In the earlier days, while there were judges, there were few lawyers. A party to a lawsuit either often represented himself or allowed a more objective and educated friend or neighbor be his advocate in the adversary system that remains unique to English Common law. But soon, lawyers began to become part of the fabric of the legal system, from the Chief Judge down to the lawyer just starting out in his practice:

Lewis Gordon, Attorney at Law

Hereby gives Notice that he has removed from Easton to Bordentown, where he may be spoke with by those who shall be pleased to favour him with their Business. He also draws Deeds and all other Instruments of Writing, examines Titles and rectifies or supplies their Defects with the greatest Care and Accuracy. *The Pennsylvania Gazette*, April 1, 1756.

London, July 7. Yesterday Nathaniel Jones of the Middle Temple, Esq., Barrister at Law, kissed His Majesty's Hand on his being appointed Chief Justice of New Jersey in America. *The New York Mercury*, August 27, 1759

There were, of course, the usual digs taken at lawyers. Some were subtle, others explicit:

London, September 16. Divers Gentlemen have lately gone over to New York and other Provinces of North America to claim lands given their predecessors almost a century ago. On the estate of one gentleman, 'tis said,

Elizabeth-Town is now built, which will now turn out to be of great value to him. It is probable this will give the American lawyers some business. *The Pennsylvania Journal,* November 6, 1766

To the Freeholders and Inhabitants of the Province of New Jersey
Gentlemen,

I Congratulate you on the prospect we have of the Legislature of this Province, meeting on the 10th of this Month, as I am in Hopes that you will lay before that Body all those Grievances which you apprehend this Province has groaned under some Years past, thro' the Oppression of some Lawyers, who, though rioting in Luxury, have acquired Estates from the Toil and Labour of the Necessitous, whose Cries, I trust, have reached the Ruler of Heaven and Earth.

Now is the Time Gentlemen to Petition, now before the whole Province in sunk in the insatiable Gulf of their Oppression and Vice. Now, while some little Property remains as yet out of their Reach and when there is some reason to think that many Members of the Legislature are convinced of the Necessity to restrain them in their Bills of Cost. . .

It has been said that, in the Opinion of some of you, it will be in vain to petition for these Purposes. . . . Let me beseech you, Gentlemen, not to be discouraged altho' several of the Honourable Council are Lawyers by Profession, who, no doubt, have great weight there; they are Gentlemen of known Honour and Integrity and eminent in their Profession, scorning low Arts of common Practioners. . . Have they not Families and Children who can not all be Lawyers? Surely, they will look forward to the Interests of their own as well as our Descendants. . . .

A Plantation Man
The New York Journal or General Advertiser, October 5, 1769.

In 1770, there was an uproar against attorneys that had many causes. Some accused lawyers of selling out those who claimed they had title to the their property through valid Indian Deeds. Others repeated the usual charges of overcharging and underworking to which all lawyers grow hardened. But, in some instances, the dislike for lawyers went deeper than a particular event or perceived character trait. It reflected an underlying economic problem. All over the colonies, property owners were losing their farms and other properties to foreclosure and, even then, for only a portion of their values. Lawyers and the Courts took the brunt of it as this pair of news reports from Monmouth County indicate:

From Freehold in Monmouth County in New Jersey, we learn that the inhabitants of that County are so irritated at the lawyers there, that on

Tuesday the 23rd of January, being the Time appointed for the holding Courts of Pleas and General Sessions of the Peace there, a great number of them assembled there in a tumultuous and riotous Manner and absolutely refused to permit one lawyer to come; the Magistrates were so intimidated that no Courts were opened or held there that time. *The Pennsylvania Journal*, February 12, 1770

New York, March 5. We hear from Freehold in Monmouth County that on Tuesday last, a Special Court of Oyer and Terminer was held there; that in the Forepart of the Day, a great Number of People met in the Courthouse in order to prevent the Courts being held or, rather, to prevent any Lawyers from coming there; but on some Gentlemen's cooly reasoning with them and representing the evil Consequences that must attend such illegal Measures, they all dispersed and suffered Business to go on as usual.*New York Gazette or Weekly Post Boy*, March 5, 1770

By the following reports from colonial news papers on specific litigations, the system seems, despite the catcalls, to have worked pretty well:

New-York, December 19. We hear from Newark that last week came on a Trial there in the Circuit Court between James Arnet, Plaintiff, and one Graham, late Quarter-Master in the 16th Regiment, Defendant. The Charge was for firing a Gun wilfully into a Barn in Elizabeth-Town, some Time ago, which set it on Fire and burnt it up, together two valuable Horses that were in it. The Evidence being pretty clear, Verdict was given for the Plaintiff, with full Costs of Suit. *The New York Gazette or Weekly Post Boy*, December 19, 1768

The King v. John Searson

The Prisoner, being set at the Bar, and charged with the Indictment, pleads not guilty; and for trial puts himself on God and his Country.
On Motion of Mr. Attorney General, ordered, That the Sheriff do return his Pannel, and that the Trial come on. The Sheriff returned the Pannel and twelve of the jurors were sworn.

The Jury, without going from the Bar, say that the Defendant is not guilty and so say they all. Whereupon, he was ordered to be discharged. And Francis Kay, the Prosecutor [the accuser], having frequently contradicted himself in his Testimony and it appearing to the Court that the Prosecution was malicious, the Sheriff was commanded to take the said Francis Kay into his Custody. *The Pennsylvania Gazette*, December 14, 1769

At the Supreme Court held at Perth-Amboy, on Thursday the 7th instant, came on the famous Trial of Traverse of an Indictment found by a

Grand Jury in September Term, 1766, against the Justices and Freeholders of the County of Middlesex, charging them with the Crime of raising divers Sums of Money on the Inhabitants of the County, and that great part thereof so raised, they had illegally applied to discharge and pay their own Expenses; against the Form of an Act of the Governor, Council and General Assembly etc.

Upon this Trial it must be confessed, the Defendants laboured under certain great Disadvantages, besides the dexterity and sanguine Efforts of the Attorney General were displayed and pushed to the utmost in this Matter. But from a just Exertion of the Abilities of the Attornies, who spoke on the Part of the Defendants, as well as from the Verdict of a virtuous Jury, who did Honour to their Country, and who themselves must have been injured if the Charge had been just, the said Justices and Freeholders were honourably acquitted; and it may be said to the Satisfaction of the rest of the Inhabitants, equally concerned in interest, if any, or the least part of the Charge had been true: Upon the Whole there appeared great Malignity in this Prosecution. *The Pennsylvania Gazette*, November 13, 1766

A letter from a visitor from abroad, who was obviously impressed by the criminal justice system in operation, was proudly published by the Press.

The expectation I had of meeting with people I had business with made it necessary for me to attend here [Sussex County, New Jersey] from the 18th to the 21st Instant and gave me an opportunity of gratifying my curiosity in observing the course of criminal proceedings in this new country. On the 18th Mr. Justice Read came to the Court-House, attended by the proper officers and published his Majesty's commission of Oyer and Terminer for that county. The Grand Jury was qualified and charged, and Mr. Attorney General, having prepared several bills of indictment, he preferred them to the Grand Jury, who came into Court at about four o'clock in the afternoon, and delivered two bills, one against one Robert Seamor, for the Murder of an Indian Man and another against one David Ray for manslaughter. The prisoners were set to the Barr and arraigned and pleaded not guilty. The Court enquired of them if they had any witnesses in their favour and offered them the aid of the Court to oblige them to attend the next day, at which time they were informed, their trials would be brought on. A guard of two Constables and twelve men were ordered to secure the gaol and to be relieved from time to time by a like number.

On the 19th, about ten o'clock in the morning, the Court met, and the prisoners were set to the barr, when Ray retracted his plea and was burnt in the hand. Then the Court proceeded on to the Trial of Seamor which lasted three hours. The prisoner behaved with great boldness and challenged several of the jurors who were set aside. The evidence against the prisoner was as follows; from his behaviour to the Indian before their going from the house together; Seamor's being possessed of the Indian's Guns and Goods; proof of his breaking the back and the legs of the dead body and burying of him were presumptions very violent; and some witnesses were also produced that Seamor had confessed to them the murder and declared that he would destroy any Indian that came his way. The evidence was produced by the Attorney General very judiciously and the Court took much pains to explain to the Jury, with great clearness, the nature of this kind of evidence and to shew the absolute certainty, arising from these facts, which were proved with undeniable evidence; and the prisoner acknowledged at the barr that he had the plunder, but said he had bought them of a sailor, who went to Philadelphia. The Jury agreed on their Verdict and brought Seamor in guilty.

The Court-House was exceedingly crowded and the prisoner remanded to prison. He behaved with great insolence and denied the fact; this night twenty-five militia took post at the Goal. On Saturday morning, the court met and passed sentence on the prisoner and ordered his execution between three and four o'clock in the afternoon. The Judge in his address to the prisoner seemed to calculate his discourse pretty much to the audience by painting the heinousness of the crime; the terrible effect it might have had on the frontiers, if the Indians had been possessed by the same spirit of revenge with the prisoner; the ingratitude of it, as it was known that the Oneida Nation. to which the murdered Indian belonged, had during the whole course of the last war, cooperated with his Majesty's Troops. The prisoner persisted in denying the fact and seemed to expect a rescue, but I did not observe a murmur among the people and the most sensible were fully convinced of the justice of his sentence. An Indian of note, I suspect, as he were of a good aspect, and wore a plume of feathers upon his head, attended the trial and the execution, and the Court seemed solicitous for his protection from insult, nor did anything of the kind happen. I understood that great pains had been taken to procure him to attend.

At the time appointed, the Sheriff brought the prisoner out, and, then, for the first time, he seemed dismayed, for he was encircled by a strong detachment from the adjacent companies of militia. At the Gallows, he made a short prayer and declared that he had lived a dissolute and wicked life, and was guilty of the fact for which he was about to suffer and then he was executed.

The people behaved very orderly and I heard the Indian, who had attended the trial and the execution, say, that he should pass through several of the Indian towns in his way to Sir William Johnson and would report the justice of his brethren, the English, on this occasion. The Indian was delivered to a guard, who set off with him immediately, and engaged to see him safe from the frontiers. Through the whole I saw great good order and regularity. *The Pennsylvania Journal*, January 1, 1767

The Philosophers' and Poets' Corner

*Perhaps more so than today, the newspaper of the colonial period
served as a forum for the making of speeches and pleas of an intellectual and
moral nature. Consider the following rhetoric on virtue of patriotism that
true "sons" have for their "fatherland":*

Non Nobis nati sed patrae

No Man is greater in my Esteem than he that is truly actuated by
a national Spirit to preserve the Interest of his Country; what Man is so
brutal and groveling upon Earth that, upon reading the lives of ancient
Patriots, will not be stirred up to a generous Emulation of their noble virtues
and Rouze his soul into a deep Contemplation of the immortal Honours that
flow from a resolute contempt of Death. Was not Cato a greater Example
than Ulysses or Atlas, who, without the concurrent help of any, supported
the sinking commonwealth, till at last as inseparable Companions they were
crushed together? The brave Man dreads nothing more than being affected
with the weakness of effeminacy; his mind is not inflamed by the imaginary
appearance of things; he courageously erects a Bulwark between him and
selfish fondness; he is not enslaved by the menaces or glories of Fortune; he
considers himself under the Relation of being his Country's Guardian, and
in opposition to all Accidents, he maintains his Places reckoning it a Duty
incumbent to sacrifice his private Interest to the advantage of the Repulick.
The desire of Security is a caution of base and inglorious Minds. Let us
therefore learn of Phaeton, who was not dismayed at his Father's telling him
the dangerous consequence that might attend his undertaking, but rather grew
importunate to stand in the station which Phoebus trembled in; when the
Case of our Nation calls us for assistance we ought to consider Life as a
particle of flying Time, and act boldly in defence of her injured Rights
despising the dissolution of our earthly frame to become an inimitable
example to future ages - - - I cannot help reflecting upon the Debauches of
these times, who being neither willing to Serve, nor fit to Command, choose
rather to be smothered with perfumes than honorably fall a victim to the
mercy of their Enemies; some of them place their felicity in wealth; some
in Disengagement from public Affairs; some in Sensuality and in learning
the Art of voluptuousness; some in popular applause within the Walls of an
invincible Garrison; others in Colours and metals; but what do these falls
and fading Enjoyments contribute to surviving Fame? When Pluto's infernal
Minister summons them to appear before the lawful tribunal of inexorable
Rhadamanthus, they are judicially sentenced into the vile and contemptible
Cavern, which has this Inscription, *nos numeros fuimus fruges consumere
noti*: Soon are they buried in the silent Grave of oblivion and their existence
no longer remains recorded than that of the quick decaying Mushroom. This
is the reward that is due inglorious Softhings, whose Lifes and Estates the
noble and courageous bear Arms and lye in trenches to defend, dreading the

Chyrugeon, more than the Enemy; they fear not their own end, being fully persuaded that an end they must have, and that all created beings are subject to Temporary Limitation; nay, even if the Earth shined upon her Womb and Disclose all the Secrets of the Subterranean Regions, they look down with undaunted Courage; they expose themselves to the fury of Earthquakes, Thunder, the threat of God's Demons, fire, Lighting, Seas, the Glowing of the Scythian sands, in short the total Dissolution of the Universe and at length they are stigmatized by the Incorrigible base and disingenuous Policy of the effeminate Part of Mankind with the odious and the ungenerous epithet of foolhardy, rash and Inconsiderate.

What a sumptuous apology do these reptiles make for the Gallantry of their contempt? What deep characters must these titles imprint on the noble Mind of the brave Man who is ready to deposit his life for the publick safety. Let us defy Death, press and persevere, until we are crowned with consultatory Honours and the Spoils of publick Enemies; then shall the Annals of time receive our Fame and register it among the heroes of the golden Age, who were defenders and establishers of their Country. . . . If one could but see the Mind of a courageous Man, as it is illustrated with the true principles of Generosity, would he not be charmed at such an object and decline to set his Heart upon things trivial and contemptible. Did not Socrates leave us an example how easy a thing it is to gain the ascendent over the two great terrors of Mankind, Death and a Goal. In fine we ought always to reflect upon the Law of Man as the Law of Nature and that merely to live is common with irrational Creatures. *The New York Weekly Journal,* October 13, 1740

"Liberty", another British concept, that was being honed on the frontier, was likewise a subject fit for philosophical reflection. Note that the editor to whom the following piece was "sent" was John Peter Zenger, who had earlier been defendant in a libel action that established for the first time anywhere the essential right of freedom of the press.

Mr. Zenger,

The inserting the following Lines of Liberty will oblige,
Your very humble Servant
S.

By Liberty, I mean a latitude of Practice within the Compass of Law and Religion. 'Tis standing clear of inferior Dependances and private Jurisdiction; he who is Master of his Time and can chuse his Business and diversions, he who can avoid disagreeable Company and he alone when his Humour or Occasions require it, is as free as he ought to wish himself. Tis true, as the World stands, general Liberty is impractical. If one had nothing but a Soul to keep, he need not go to Service to maintain it. But a Body at present is a very indigent sort of a Thing. It can't subsist upon its growth, but stands in want of continual Supplies; this circumstance of eating and drinking is a cruel Check upon many a Man's Dignities and makes him hold his Life by a servile Tenure. However, he that lies under this Incumbrance should make his best of it and not quarrel with the Order of Providence. At the worst Death would knock off his Chain shortly; in the mean Time, his business is to play with it. But where the Necessaries of Life may be had at a cheaper rate, 'tis folly to purchase them this Way; he that will sacrifice his Liberty to his Palate and convey over his Person superfluities is a Slave of his own making and deserves to be used accordingly.

Dependance goes somewhat against the Grain of a generous Mind, and 'tis no wonder why it should be so, considering the unreasonable advantage which is so often taken of the inequality of Fortune, the Pride of Superiors and the wanton Exercises of Power, make Servitude much more troublesome than Nature intended. Some People think that the Life of Authority consists in Noise and Imperiousness, in Menacing and Executions; to let their Servants live easy is in some Measure to make them their equals; therefore, they love to brandish their Advantage, to part with nothing without a stroke of Discipline and to qualify their Favours with Penance and Mortification; but to be enfranchised from Arbitrariness and ill Humour, is not the only convenience of Liberty. This State affords great Opportunities for the Improvement of Reason, it gives Leisure for Reading and Contemplation, for an acquaintance with Men and Things and for looking into History of Time and Nature. He that has the Business of Life at his own disposal and has no Body to account to for his Minutes but God and himself may if he pleases be happy without Drudging for it; he needs not flatter the vain, nor be tired with the Impertinent, nor stand to the courtesy of Knavery and Folly, he needs not dance after the Caprice of a Humorist, nor bear a Part in the extravagance of another; he is under no anxieties for fear of displeasing, nor has any difficulties of Temper to struggle with, his Fate does not hang upon any Man's Face; A Smile will not transport him, nor a Frown ruin him. For his Fortune is better fixed than to float upon the nice and changeable. This Independence gives easiness to the Mind and vigour for Enterprize and Imagination, a Man has nothing to strike a Damp upon his Genius, to overawe his Thoughts, and Check the Range of his Fancy. But he that is embarass'd in his Liberty is apt to be unassur'd in his Actions, palled and dispirited in his Humour and conceptions so that one may almost read his Condition in his Conversation. 'Tis true, a peculiar Greatness of Nature, or the Expectations of Religion may relieve him, but then not every one is furnished with these Advantages. The Reason why Parmenie could not rise up to Alexander's height of thinking, was possibly because he was under his Command.--- Longinus observes that there were no considerable Orators in Greece, after their Government was altered by the Macedonians and Romans; according to him their Elocutions and their

Freedom seemed to languish and expire together; when they were once enslaved, the Muses would keep Company no longer, the Vein Rhetorick was seared up, the force of Demosthenes spent and no sublime to be had for Love nor Money.

Now tho' Freedom within a rule is very desireable, yet there is scarcely any one Thing has done more mischief than this word misunderstood; absolute Liberty is a jest; 'tis a visionary and Romantick Privilege and utterly inconsistent with the present State of the World; the generality of Mankind must have more understanding, and more Honesty, too, than they are likely to have as long as they live, before they are fit to be at their own Disposal; to tell People they are free is the common artifice of the Factious and Seditious. The State Gipsies pick the Pockets of the ignorant with this specious Cant, and with informing them what mighty Fortunes they are all born to; and what is this fine freedom after all, that these Sparks can help to; why are they free to be out of their Wits and to be undone if they take their Advice, to lose their Conscience, their Credit and their Money and to be ten Times more press'd than they were before.

There is still a more extravacent Notion of Liberty behind; some People are for repealing the Laws of Morality, for throwing open the inclosure of Religion and leaving all in common to licentiousness and violence; they are for making their Inclinations the Rule and their Power the Boundary of Actions. They hate to let an Opportunity slip, or any Capacity lay idle, but are for grasping at all Possibilities of Pleasure and playing their Appetite to whatever comes their Way; to tie Men up from enjoyment and cramp them with Prohibitions is an encroachment upon the Rights of Nature. These ungenerous Impositions are it seems the Dotages of Age, the Results of Spleen and Impotence; or at best the Pretences of designing Power, which lays an Embargo upon some Branches of Trade to engross the Advantage to itself. I wonder why these Men don't improve their Principle farther. Why they don't dance upon the Battlements of Houses, jump into a Furnice for Diversion? To forbear these Things are not great Restraints upon the Liberties of Motion and make many of the Faculties of Nature insignificant; they ought to step into the Rescue of Fevers and Phrensy and not let their Acquaintance lie under such an ignominious Confinement, especially when their spirits are up and they are so well disposed for Satisfaction; why do they not draw up a Remonstrance against Jails, Pillories, and Executions? What have they no Sense of the Grievances of their Fellow Subjects? Can they see their own generous Principles suffer, their very Charter violated and do nothing towards a relief? They asking your Pardon to embark in such Expectations might endanger their Interest and come home to them at last; and to speak truth, they are for having this Arbitrary Privilege in no Hands but their own; for touch them in their Honour or Property you will find them with a Zeal for Justice and Restitution. Then the Laws are defective and give too little Damages and therefore though they venture their necks for it, they must have a Supplemental Satisfaction, their own Case, one would think, might show them the unreasonableness of their Scheme and that a Liberty against Virtue and Laws is only a Privilege to be unhappy and a Licence for a Man to Murder himself. *The New York Weekly Journal*, July 7, 1740

The subject matter was not always as ponderous as patriotism and liberty. Sometimes, it was more humorous, although the underlying animus one suspects was serious.

Mr. Zenger,

The inserting the following in your next Journal without deferring it to another opportunity will oblige

Your very humble Servant,
Peaceable

The most dangerous and mischievous Creature call'd a Spunger or Hanger-on, with which most of the great families are pestered; they have little to recommend them, unless it be an out-dress, a few drunken Jests or Scraps of Poetry, or perhaps some broken Characters of Men and Things with a little of the intrigues and humors of the Times; and by virtue of these Qualifications, they fancy themselves Companions fit [for] the greatest Man in the Province. And will be sure that upon the smallest Invitation to crowd themselves upon him, if they meet with any Encouragement;

and it's ten to one by degrees grow familiar and after that impudent and at last intolerable.

In one Point indeed they are Philosophers, as carrying all they have along with them and truly that is little enough too; their Furniture in general is so wretched and scandalous that you may soon learn them by their garb, an old laced Hat, a Cockade, or a Velvet Jocky Cap, a Touper, a short black Bob, a laundry Waistcoat, a bawdy Song or two, a few drunken Healths and about a dozen or to puns and quibbles set them up; and with these they'll will be perpetually grating and dinning your Ears, till they have worn them as threadbare as their Coats; and after all, must be forc'd to be laugh'd or kick'd out of 'em, before they will quit them too.

As for Money they never have any, nor never pretend to any unless it be now and then a five or ten shilling note borrowed or the Fragments of a Tavern Reckoning, to Heel piece a Pair of Shoes or recruit the Snuff Box. In short, these are drones in the strictest Sense of the Definition. And if you once suffer 'em to crawl in your Hive (to keep up to the Nature of the insect) they'll be sure and disturb your Cell, devour your Honey, and in all respects as bothersome and pernicious to Servants and Trades People as well as to the Families that they can fasten themselves upon as drones and Wasps are to Bees.

The Town swarms with this kind of gentry and a Man of Fortune cannot set his Foot in it from his Voyage or Travels, but that there are several of them come instantly humming and buzzing about him; I tell you that Idleness and all its direful Consequences being seen in every Corner of N. Jersey, that's is so scandalous and reproachful that neither Heaven, Earth, or Hell itself will own or patronize it.

How unreasonable then is it, I think I may say, how infamous and unaccountable for Men of Fortune and Reputation to pick up such loose and profitless Creatures and take 'em into their Bosoms, introduce them into all Conversations, and make them their inseparable Companions and give them absolute Power to Rule and sway their Families. I am astonished when I see the Fort, on a Birth Day, and an Assembly half filled with these Leaches, who thrust themselves into all Company and Business along with their Patrons, sucking and spunging upon them, and in the literal Sense, eating them up alive.

I would not be misunderstood; I am dissuading the fortunate and great against relieving and supporting distressed Gentlemen in their Necessities. No, I would not have them defy the example of that Liberality, by whose Effects themselves live. But then, I would not have them abuse the Divine Recedent by fostering a sort of Sluggish Creatures that have brought about their own Wretchedness by Whoring and Gaming. *The New York Weekly Journal*, May 11, 1741

Poetry was a frequent vehicle for delivering a message, a medium long since abandoned in today's world, unless a remnant of it persists in the advertising jingles of Madison Avenue and in greeting cards. Often it was written in celebration of a friend's nuptials, as was the following:

To a Young Lady on her Marriage
by a young Lady

Dear Polly on your Bridal Day,
Accept my Muse's first Essay;
The Theme inspires me while I send
The warmest wishes of a Friend.
Kind Heaven to reward your Truth,
Now smiles and sends the faithful Youth,
Whose Heart and Constancy you'll prove,
And find them perfect as his Love.
In him, is every virtue join'd,
In you, each charm of Face and Mind;
Sure Cupid has obtained his sight,
Else how could he have aimed so right?
No More kind Fortune dost thou prove,

"An unrelenting Foe to Love,"
For here too mutual Hands we find,
Where Youth and Gentleness are joined.
Your Bliss, your Friends and Parents share,
And joyful, hail the happy Pair
May ev'ry Day like this be crown'd,
And Love and Friendship still abound.
And as each circling Year goes past,
Still finds you happy as the last.
New York Journal or General Advertiser, September 20, 1770

Poetry also delivered political messages, here a roundtable, as it were, of opinions, which forty five years later result in revolution:

The following lines were put over the Door of the General Court, viz.

Our Fathers crost the wide Atlantick Sea
And blest themselves when in the Desart Free
And shall their Sons, thro' Treachery or Fear
Give up thar Freedom which has cost so dear!
What-e'er Pretence our Enemies may frame,
The Man is alter'd, but the Cause the same
From Caesar's Court should Cato fawning come
Be sure that Cato is no Friend to Rome.

A stranger passing by, and seeing several Persons read the above Lines, caused him to stop, and having perused the same, he took a piece of Chalk and writ underneath the Lines the following, viz.

Their Fathers crost the wide Atlantick Sea
To be in Deserts from their Deserts Free
And shall their Sons with glaring Insolence
Support a Cause so void of common Sense?
What-ev'er Pretence this stubborn People frame
The Case is alter'd, but the Men the same
From Caesar's Court should a new Ruler come
Be sure they'll starve him, as they've others done.
New York Gazette, November 2, 1730[76]

To Mr. William Bradford
Sir:

I am a Boston Man by Birth and meeting with your Last Weeks Gazette, I found a Satyr on the New-England Verses, written by a

---

[76] Bradford was not nearly as pro independence as his student Zenger had been.

Gentleman passing thro' Perth Amboy. Reading them, I called for Pen, Ink and Paper and wrote the following Answer to it, and seeing it is Poetry, I write this in his own stile, viz.

> Presumptuous Traytor, we can make't appear
> It was not Treasons made our Fathers Fear
> Nor Hal- - - res made them fly for Safety here
> But it was cruel Paptists, cursed Parts
> That made them Venture into wild Desarts
> To avoid their Malice and Blood thirsty Hearts
> And having crost the wide Atlantick Sea
> And purchas'd dear a perfect Liberty
> We'll keep it still and what is that to thee?
> Know this, vile Traytor, we have cause to sing,
> Our Dear-bought Liberty's a Precious Thing
> Under the Influence of a Gracious King.
> Great George is Merciful and well doth us use,
> Tho' some of us his Mercy hath abused,
> Which we that's Loyal, beg, will be excus'd.
> Now should a Salary be fixed outright
> On him that's appointed to guide us Right[77],
> Then all our Dear-bought Freedom takes its Flight.
> Of Liberty, the Jews of Old did sing,
> When either under High Priest or a King,
> Then shall we give up such a Precious Thing?
> Oh no, we're strong, and we'll stand our Defence,
> Altho you're pleas'd to call it Insolence;
> This for our Freedom is a good Pretence.
> *New York Gazette*, December 5, 1730

Or, it might more be in the nature of a ridicule, a cousin for the political cartoon today.

On the Virginia Assembly offering up their prayers for wisdom for Lord B----t.

> The Assembly in devoutest strain
> Ask for my Lord the gift of Brain
> Wisdom alone will hardly do
> Next beg a little patience too
>   New Jersey
> *The Pennsylvania Chronicle*, June 5, 1769

---

[77] This referred to a dispute that was occurring in several Provinces at the time where the Royal Governor insisted that his salary be appropriated five years in advance, a step that diminished the Province's and its General Assembly's Power of the purse string over him.

From the first Americans, the paleo-indians who crossed over to America from Asia at least 12,000 years ago (and, as likely, double or triple that) to the most recent arrival, America has always been a land of immigrants.

Throughout the 1700s, there was a constant flow of settlers from western Europe and slaves from Africa. Seventy five per cent of the white immigrants to the colonies south of New England came as indentured servants --- an individual, who in exchange for his passage and other payments (sometimes the satisfaction of a debt back home) agreed to come to America and work for his sponsor for a fixed period of years, often ten. The Notices of Runaway indentured servants indicate that the majority of them were from the British Isles, England, Scotland and Ireland, both north and south. A small percentage were from France Germany, Sweden and Holland.

News reports from colonial America put flesh on the statistics relating to these early immigrants. They came to America as servants and slaves, soldiers and convicts, seekers of religious freedom and deserters:

New-Castle, August 14. There has come in this last Week about 2000 Irish People and abundance more are daily expected. In one Ship about 100 of them dyed in their passage hither. It is computed that there is about 6000 come into this River since April last. *New England Weekly Journal*, August 25, 1729

Philadelphia, October 19. Last Sunday arrived here Capt. Tymberten, in 17 Weeks, from Rotterdam, with 220 Palatines, 44 died in the Passage. About 3 Weeks ago, the Passengers dissatisfied with the length of the Voyage were so imprudent as to make a Mutiny and, being the stronger Party, have ever since the Government of the Vessel, giving orders among themselves to the Captain and Sailors, who were threatened with Death in the case of Disobedience. Thus, having sight of Land, they carried the Vessel twice backwards between our Capes and Virginia, looking for a Place to go ashore, they knew not where. At length they compelled the Sailors to cast Anchor near Cape May and eight of them took the Boat by force and went ashore, from whence they have been five Days coming up by Land to this Place where they found the Ship arriv'd. Those concerned in taking the Boat are committed to Prison. *The Boston Weekly News-Letter*, October 27, 1732

We just now hear that the Snow Irene, Capt. Garrison is arrived at Sandy Hook from London with upwards of One Hundred Passengers on board of the Moravian Brethren.[78] *The New York Gazette Revived in the Weekly Post Boy,* May 1, 1749

Just imported from the River Gambia, in the Schooner Sally, Barnard Badger, Master and to be sold at the Upper Ferry (called Benjamin Cooper's Ferry), opposite to this City, a Parcel of Likely Men and Women

SLAVES

with some Boys and Girls of different Ages. Attendance will be given from the hours of nine to twelve o'Clock in the Morning and from three to six in the afternoon, by

W. Coxe, S. Oldman & Company

N.B. It is generally allowed that the Gambia Slaves are much more robust and tractable than any other Slaves from the Coast of Guinea and more capable of undergoing the Severity of the Winter Seasons in the North American Colonies, which occasions their being vastly more esteemed and coveted in this Province and those to the northward than any other Slave whatsoever. *The Pennsylvania Journal,* May 27, 1762

Just arrived here from Jersey, and to be seen (in the Ship Lark, Joshua Pickman Master, lying at the Long Wharff, Boston) very likely Boys and Girls time of Service for Years, to be disposed of by the said Master, or Jonathan Belcher, Esq., at his Warehouse in Merchant's Row. *The Boston News-Letter,* October 22, 1722

Last Week came to this City, two French Soldiers, who say that 19 more, with an Old Indian, deserted the French Forces at Mississippi and have been 8 Months on their Journey hither over land; They inform us that they, with many others, were sent from Old France, about 18 Months ago, to settle at New Orleans, but not liking the Country, they chose to come this Way; the rest of their Company, they say, are in the Jerseys. *The Pennsylvania Gazette,* November 23, 1752

New York, July 27. The 17th and 46th regiments are now embarked upon the transport destined for England and the 28th she embarks at Amboy. They have been more than 10 years in America and the 17th carries home no more than 90 men, out of 750, that came to America in it. *The Pennsylvania Journal,* July 30, 1767

---

[78] Moravians, German speaking religious pacifists from Bohemia and Moravia, settled in such large numbers that the Moravian community had a ship built which ferried the new American across the Atlantic. It was also the Moravian community of Gnaden-hutton in Sussex County that was so savagely attacked by the Indians in 1755.

The Ellen, Capt. Clark, arrived here Thursday last, in 58 days from Bristol. He has brought about 50 Artificers in the Iron Way, which we hear are all to be employed at Mr. Hasencliver's different Works. *The New York Journal or General Advertiser*, October 8, 1767

Based on the number of passengers who did not survive the crossing, the trip over was obviously dangerous.

New York, September 10. Last Week arrived at Sandy-Hook and is since gone up to Amboy, the Brig Charming Sally, Capt. Heyshaw, of this Port, from Hamburgh, having had a passage of 16 Weeks from Land to Land in which they were reduced to the short Allowance of a Bisket a Day per Man, for a great while, and in all probability some of them would have perished, had they not met with a Boston Vessel a few Weeks ago, who helped them to a small Supply. The last Piece of Meat they had was dressed the Day they got into the Hook. *The New York Gazette or the Weekly Post Boy*, September 10, 1753

Not all of these new Americans came voluntarily as the following account of an immigrant's end reflects.

New York, February 12. On Saturday last Richard Roche, born in Ireland and about 26 Years of Age was executed here persuant to his Sentence. He acknowledged that he was whipped in Dublin for keeping Company with an Idle Woman, who had stolen some Goods there and that they had some Time after come in a Transport Vessel to America, that he broke opened and robbed a house at Salem N.J., for which he was whipped there also. *The Pennsylvania Gazette*, February 27, 1753

British soldiers enlisted for lengthy terms, as much as ten years at a time, and usually for an upfront cash bonus. Thus, it was not unusual for the poor of the British Isles to enlist, be sent to America and thereafter to desert and become colonists themselves, usually on the frontiers. Consider the following Public Notice regarding a trio of deserters named Murphy. Probably brothers based on the surname and common physical characteristics--- maybe from Ireland[79], but perhaps American born --- they undoubtedly are ancestor, assuming they were not apprehended and executed as traitors, to thousands of Americans today.

---

[79] Murphy is the most common surname in Ireland and there were many in the Ulster area of Northern Ireland, from whence came many colonists, most as indentured servants, during the 1700s.

Eight Pistoles Reward

Broke out of Gaol of the County of Burlington, on Saturday the 9th of this Instant, the following deserters from the New Jersey Regiment, viz.

John Murphy; Aged about Thirty years; Five feet Seven inches high; red hr and of a sandy Complexion marked with the Small Pox, very apt to get into Liquor, then very Talkative.

William Murphy; by trade a blacksmith; Aged about Twenty six years, Five foot Nine Inches high; grey eyes and of a sandy complexion;

James Murphy; Aged about Twenty two Years, Five feet eight inches high; has red hair and grey eyes and of a sandy complexion, by trade a Shoemaker

Whoever takes up the said Deserters and delivers them to the County of Burlington shall have the above Reward or two Pistoles for each of them, paid by
Joseph Imlay
The Pennsylvania Journal, September 14, 1758

Enough Germans came in the first half of the 1700s as to require a newspaper of their own:

Henry Miller

Printer in Second-Street between Race and Vine Streets Begs leave to acquaint the public that every Monday he publishes a German Newspaper, which circulates not only through all of Pennsylvania, but likewise goes to Georgia, South and North Carolina, Virginia, Maryland, The Jerseys, New York, Albany, up to the Mohawk River, Nova Scotia and the West Indies. Such Gentlemen and others in town and country, who will be pleased to favor him with the insertion of their advertisements, may depend upon having them truly and idiomatically translated gratis.

He also takes this public opportunity gratefully to acknowledge the encouragement given to his paper both by the town and the country, from the first publication thereof two years ago, and humbly begs the further continuance of his kind customers favours, assuring them that their orders shall at times be punctually obeyed by
their obliged and humble servant,
Henry Miller

N.B. He likewise performs all sorts of printing work in any language correct and neatly. *The Pennsylvania Journal*, January 12, 1764

Yet, while thousands were coming to America, thousands were leaving her -- or at least her civilized coasts. The frontier was an irresistible urge to some of the colonists, tempted by advertisements like the following:.

Whereas a Proposal is now on Foot, for settling a very extensive Colony upon the finest Part of Ohio and Application been also made, previous to the Peace, for that Purpose, it is necessary to acquaint the Public with the Proposals, as they are the most advantageous of the Kind ever known and I may venture to say that ever will be. The Situation, Fertility of the Soil, and innumerable other Advantages that attend this Colony, over and above any that can be mentioned in the American Empire, are Inducements enough for any sensible Man to settle there, without the least Hesitation, but as Mankind are fond of being secure in the real Enjoyment of something independent, it is proposed that every Family who becomes Proprietors and Settles, in this Colony, are to have 300 Acres of Land, to be granted by Patent, to them and their Heirs forever. It is also proposed that 400,000 Acres are to be sold to Gentlemen Proprietors, which will be granted in patents, from One Thousand to Ten Thousand Acres each, these are proposed to be sold at the Rate of 50 Pounds per One Thousand Acres, which will raise the sum of 20,000 Pounds which is to be employed in Purchasing the Colony, Provisions, Cattle and Farming Utensils &c. . . . . The Name of the Colony is to be New Wales, in Honour of his Royal Highness, the Prince of Wales, who is to be the sole Proprietor of the Colony. . . . The Number of Families proposed to form the first Settlement are 4000. *The Pennsylvania Gazette*, April 21, 1763

Whereas, a certain tract of land hath been lately obtained in the Province of Nova Scotia, lying on the north side of the Bason of Menis, called Philadelphia Township, whereon some good families are now settled and many more engaged to go. This is to give notice, that any person inclining to become settlers on the said land, will meet with very good encouragement, the particulars of which, will be made known by applying to James James, at Pile's Grove, Daniel Lethgow at, at Salem Bridge, James Thomson, at Hancock's Bridge, Benjamin Davids, at Crosswicks, John Jones, in Germantown, or to Nathan Sheperd, William Ball, John Lukens, James Haldane and Benjamin Armitage, in Philadelphia. And as a proper vessel will be provided to carry families and goods to the aforesaid lands, early next spring, those who propose to become adventurers, are desired to be speedy in their application, and enter into articles with some of the above mentioned persons. *The Pennsylvania Chronicle*, February 1, 1768

Make no mistake about it. The frontier was dangerous as the following confirms:

New York, June 15. We have an account from Goshen that on the 18th of the last Month, four of the Inhabitants of that Place, viz. Robert

Thompson, Anthony Car, Silas Houlse and Abraham Finch, set our from thence with the Design to view the Land called the Great Patent at the Head of the Delaware River; and five Days later, in the long dark wet weather we had at that Time, they all got lost in the Woods. They continued wandering about twelve days, almost starved and, in their Rambling, met with an old Indian Hut where they found a piece of raw deerskin, which they roasted and ate as a delicious morsel, having nothing else to eat for above six Days, but a few wild Herbs they had picked up. At length, growing faint, they killed one of their Horses to eat. In this Extremity, they at least perceived a high Hill, to the top of which they travelled and from thence happily discovered a House at the Minisinks. *The Pennsylvania Gazette*, June 18, 1752

The virgin lands to the west belonging to France were tempting to many Americans:

By a private letter from Trenton-Ferry, we are assured that upwards of twenty Frenchmen have passed over there within a few weeks past, who all said they were Deserters from Mississippi and represent that Country to be in a deplorable condition for want of Supplies from France and that at this time a Conquest of the whole Dominion could be made with far less than 500 Men. *The Pennsylvania Gazette*, April 26, 1753

Those that set out for the frontier did do with a sense of adventure:

A Correspondent writes us that a Body of upwards of 500 stout active industrious Men, completely armed and accoutred, are arrived at or near the Minisinks, from New England, (with Carts, Oxen and Horses and various Instruments of Mechanism and Husbandry) on their way to possess and settle the Lands they claim on the Susquehannah, from whence a small party were lately forced by a superior number of Proprietary Agents and Partisans from this Province. They are continually joined by People from different Parts of New Jersey, in which Province they met with the greatest Hospitality. They are in high Spirits, on their near Approach to what they call the American Canaan or Land of Promise. *The Pennsylvania Chronicle*, May 8, 1769

The newspapers of the Colonial period did not have sports pages as we know them, principally because only one of the sports popular today had been invented. That was "the Sport of Kings" -- horse racing -- and it was a preoccupation of many.

Notice is hereby given that there is to be given Gratis, at Mount-Holly in the County of Burlington, on Wednesday the 19th of September Twenty Pistoles to be run for by as many Horses, Mares or Geldings as any Person or Persons shall think fit to put in. They are to put in Twenty Shillings for every Horse, Mare or Gelding and enter them four Days before the Day of the Running. They are to run three Heats, one Mile at a Heat, on a straight Course, and to carry weight for Inches. A Horse, Mare or Gelding to carry 140 weight at 14 Hands high and for the first inch Higher to carry fourteen Pound, and for every inch above that seven Pound; and all Horses that are under sized to be equivalent to the same. Any one Horse, Mare or Gelding that should win two Heats and save the Distance the third, shall win the Prize. And the next Day the Betts to be run for: everyone that saves his Distance the first Day is entitled to Run, the Horse that wins the Prize excepted. The Horses are to be entered at John Budd's or Caleb Shinn's. *The Pennsylvania Journal*, August 30, 1750

Articles for a Twenty and a Ten Pound Purse, or Plate, to be run for on the Course of Elizabeth-Town, in the Field of Isaac Hatfield, about a Mile from the Bridge, on the 5th and 6th Days of October, 1762, viz.

On Tuesday, the 5th Day of October next, A Plate or Purse Value Twenty Pounds, to be run for by any Horse, Mare or Gelding (the Winning Horse of the last Hundred Pound run for at New-York only excepted) each Horse, Mare, or Gelding, to carry Ten Stone, Saddle and Bridle included, to run the best of three Heats, and three Rounds of the Course to each Heat; to leave all the Posts on the left Hand, and no Crossing or Jostling, but for the last half mile of each Heat and that only by the two foremost Horses.

On Wednesday, the 6th Day of October next, A Plate or Purse Value Ten Pounds, to be run for by any Horse, Mare or Gelding, the winning Horse of the above mentioned York Plate and the winning and distanced Horse of the above Twenty Pound Plate also excepted, to run the best of three Heats, three Rounds as above, to each Heat; to carry eight Stone, Saddle and Bridle included, no Crossing or Jostling, but as allowed for the above Twenty Pound Plate.

On Thursday, the seventh Day of October, the Entrance Money to be run for by the Beaten Horses, who run for the above Plates and saved their Distance.

Each Horse that runs for any of the above mentioned Plates, to be entered six Days before each of the respective Days of Running, with Jecamiah Smith (there will be appointed proper Judges and Managers) and to pay Entrance for the Twenty Pound Plate or Purse, Twenty Shillings, and for the Ten Pounds, Ten Shillings, or pay double for each if they enter at the Post. *The New York Mercury*, September 13, 1762

The Elizabeth-Town
Free Masons Plate
Of Twenty Pounds Value

To be Run for in the Field of John Vander Belt, on the South Side of Staten-Island, on Tuesday the Fourth Day of October next, (being the first Day of the Elizabeth-Town Fair) by any Horse, Mare or Gelding (those blooded only excepted) to carry Nine Stone, the best of three Heats, Three Miles each Heat, Three Pounds for Each. The Owner of each Horse, Mare or Gelding must enter them the Day before and pay unto Mr. Thomas Dongan or Jacob Vander Belt, the Sum of Twenty Shillings for each. The Entrance Money to be Run for the Next Day, by all but the Winning Horse of the preceding Day and those distanced. Those that Neglect to Enter till the Day of Running must pay Double Entrance at the Stake. Not less than Three will be permitted to start for the above Plate. All Disputes that may arise will be determined by three Master Masons, who are appointed for that Purpose. *The New York Gazette*, August 15, 1763

To be run for at the City of New Brunswick, on Monday, the 3d of November next, free for any horse, mare or gelding not being of the whole blood (Smoaker excepted) a purse of 20 Pistoles, the best in three heats, at 2 miles each heat; the horses to be entered with Mr. Henry Birker, at 4 dollars each horse. Any entered on the day of starting to pay double entrance. Proper judges will be appointed to determine any disputes that may arise, and each horse is to carry 9 stone; and so in proportion. The entrance money will be run for on the next day by any except the winning horse. *The Pennsylvania Gazette*, September 18, 1766

A Purse of Fifty Dollars

To be run for on Monday the second day of May next, at Perth-Amboy, free for any horse, mare or gelding, not more than halfblood, (Mr.

Morris's mare excepted) carrying weight for age, to run the two mile heats; (any horse winning two heats to be entitled to the purse) not less than four reputed running horses will be allowed to start; the entrance money to be run for the day following; the winning and distanced horses excepted, to be entered on or before the thirteenth day of April, with Richard Carnes, jun. or Isaac Bonnell, paying three dollars, entrance or double at the post. For further sport, the same day, a complete saddle, bridle, and whip will be run for by common horses. *The New York Journal or General Advertiser*, April 7, 1768

To add to the excitement of the race was the rivalry developing between the British bred horses and those of the American countryside.

Since English Horses have been imported into New York, it is the opinion of some People that they can out run The True Britton. This is to satisfy the Publick that I will Run him with any Horse that can be produced in America; to run on Long Island the Four-Mile Heats, or One Heat, carrying Eleven Stone, for Three Hundred Pounds or more, any time between this and the Tenth of April, only giving me one Month's Notice. If no Person thinks proper to accept of this Proposal, I desire that they will never mention running with him again, as I purpose keeping him for Covering.

A. W. Waters
The New York Gazette, January 17, 1763

An Advertisement, subscribed by A.W. Waters, having appeared in the last New York Gazette, in which the whole Continent of America is challenged, in the most illiterate, unsportsman-like Terms, to start a Horse for the Sum of Three Hundred Pounds against one in his Possession, called the True Briton. And as the Breed of English Horses are squinted at, with great Contempt, I take the liberty to acquaint the Public that I will start a Horse lately purchased by me of Mr. Holmes, of Carlisle, in Old England, to run for One Hundred Pounds over Haerlem Course, the best of three Four Mile Heats, against his boasted Favorite, each carrying Nine Stone on the Tenth of April next. And I will bet One Hundred Pounds that mine is better bred and a Third Hundred Pounds that he is much better qualified for a Stallion, being far superior to his Horse, in Shape, Strength and Action. It may be proper to observe to this redoubted Advertiser that all Five Year Old Horses carry no more than Nine Stone; and he is cautioned not to look upon such a Shaped animal as the Briton is to be invincible, until he has beat a Good Horse which he once most unsuccessfully attempted. Remember Pacolet, Master Abraham. One Word more and I shall be done with the Jersey Hero. I will engage to run the Produce of a Mare that shall be covered by my Horse against the Produce of one covered by the Briton, in April, when they are rising Four Years Old, at Eight Stone seven pounds each, for Three Hundred Pounds, pay or play. And this challenge I am indebted to give, that the Publick may be informed, I rely as much upon the goodness of my Horse as a Stallion, as I do upon his Racing Performance. If therefore the Briton is not approved in Shape, Strength and Racing Form, and if the Owner declines to consent to what I have offered, desire he will not presume to rank him with any others than the common Mongrels of the Country from whence he was derived and that he will be forever silent upon the Subject of Matching and Racing.

J. Leary
The New York Gazette, January 24, 1763

Will be Lett

To cover Mares for the ensuing Season, at Connecticut Farms, in the Borough of Elizabeth, New-Jersey, within four Miles of the Town, by Jeremiah Smith

The Hero

Bred by Mr. John Holmes, of Carlisle, in Old England. The Hero was got by Young Sterling, his Dam by Slipby, which was own Brother to Saup's; his Grandam by Partner, his Great Grandam by Greyhound, her Dam by Wastrel Turk, her Grandam by Old Haut-Boy, her great Grandam by Place's White Turk, her dam by Dodsworth and out of a Lyton Barb Mare. Young Sterling was got by Old Sterling, out of Matchieu's Dam; Matchieu won the Whip at New-Market; his Pedigree is certified by the Breeder. Terms of Covering as follows: Five Pounds Proc. at the first Covering, the Mare to have the Benefit of the Season, for which purpose I have provided Pasture for the Mares at a Distance and will take proper care of those that are sent to be covered, for Three Shillings Proc. per Week. Hero is Fifteen Hands and a Half High, well shaped, and by Good Judges, allowed to be the most compleat Horse they ever saw in America.

Jecamiah Smith

N.B. The Challenge lately given by the Owner of the True-Briton, should have been accepted by the Master of Hero, had not the Horse so lately arrived from England; but, in the fall, in all probability, the Publick may have the Satisfaction of seeing the so-much-dreaded True-Briton, beat by the Hero on his own Terms. *The New York Gazette*, March 14, 1763

Some races never got off the starting mark:

Beaver-Pond, May 28, 1768. Last Monday, a Thousand People were drawn to this Place, by an Advertisement for a Twenty Pound Plate. Three Horses etc. were to start, or No Race; only Capt. Rutgen's Queen Kate, got by Ariel, and Mr. Hird's Lady Leggs, got by Briton, appeared. The Owners, to divert a very respectable Company, as there was not a sufficient Number to run for a Plate, agreed upon a Sweepstakes, but the Jersey Sportsman refused to gratify the Spectators with a Contest, pretending that the sum was too trifling to hazard a Heat upon, so that after paying Forfeit, he left the Field and the Superiority of the Two Racers left undecided. Should he be valiant enough to face this Blood of Ariel, a Plate in the Fall, whether in Pennsylvania , or at Home, may assure him that a Briton filly is a s superable in our Northern Colonies as the Plains of Upper Marlborough. *New York Gazette and Weekly Mercury*, June 6, 1768

With others, there was dramatic entertainment in addition to a neck and neck race:

New York, October 12. On Tuesday last at Powlas Hook Races, four Horses started for a 50 Pound Purse (the best two out of three Heats of 3 Miles each) which was won by Mr. Anthony Rutger's (junr) Horse Luggs. Mr. Morris Hazard's Horse Partner had the Misfortune in the last Heat to run over a Dog, which occasioned him to fall and throw over his Rider (who was much hurt), otherwise it was doubtful which of the Two would have won, Partner having won the second Heat. *Extraordinary Supplement to the New York Journal or General Advertiser*, October 12, 1769.

The only other activity which could arguably be called "sport" was wagering, principally in card games but also in the many lottery games advertised in the press. Today, we think that "Lotto" and similar games were invented only in the past few decades as more and more States needed to add to revenues without further increasing taxes. It was not really different in colonial times. In fact, lotteries pre-date our Nation by many years, having developed before in England and even earlier as methods of distributing lands among citizens. Typically, lotteries were licensed, fundraisers for charitable and public works, with celebrities or other public figures endorsing specific lotteries. For example:

Notice is hereby given that the New Brunswick Lottery for building a Parsonage House not being quite full, there are some tickets still to be disposed of by the Managers and B. Franklin; And that, notwithstanding the Limitation of three months in the tickets for the Fortunate to receive their Money, they may at any time, after the Drawing thereof, come and demand their Prizes.

A Fortnight's Notice will be given in this Paper before the Time and Place of Drawing. *The Pennsylvania Gazette*, November 17, 1748

The Tickets in the New-Brunswick Lottery for Building a Church, being not all disposed of, has occasioned the Drawing to be postponed a little; mean time, the Managers continue selling Tickets as usual. *The New York Gazette Revived in the Weekly Post Boy*, October 3, 1748

Scheme
Of A
Lottery
For the Use of
The College of New Jersey

The Legislature of the Colony of New Jersey, having been pleased to Countenance this Rising Seat of Learning, so far as to Pass an Act, enabling the Trustees to erect and draw a Lottery, for raising any Sum not to exceed Three Thousand Pounds, Proclamation Money, it is hoped that the generous design in making this Law will be carried out into Execution, by all those who wish well to the Institution or who are desirous of promoting Useful Knowledge in these Infant Countries, and to prepare our own Youth to sustain the Publick Offices in Church and State. The following Scheme is calculated for raising the Sum of Two Thousand Nine Hundred and Ninety-Nine Pounds Eighteen Shillings and Six Pence, Proclamation Money. There are to be 13,333 Tickets at Thirty Shillings Each, whereof 4, 488 will be Fortunate, subj. to a 15 per Cent. Deduction, viz.

Number of prizes		Value of each
1	of	1000 pds
1	of	750 pds
1	of	500 pds
4	of	200 pds
10	of	100 pds
20	of	50 pds
50	of	20 pds
100	of	10 pds
4299	of	3 pds
1	first drawn	20 pds
1	last drawn	32.10 pds

4488 Prizes
8845 Blanks

13333 Tickets at Thirty Shillings each is 19,999.10 pounds

So that it is evident there are not two Blanks to a Prize. The Drawing is to begin the fourth Day of April next, at Nassau Hall, in Princetown, or as soon before as the Lottery is filled under the Inspection of Three of the Trustees of the College. Robert Ogden and William Peartree Smith, Esqrs., of Elizabeth-Town; Jonathan Sergeant Esq. of Maidenhead and Mr. Ezekiel Forman, Merchant, of Princetown are appointed Managers and will be under Oath for the Faithful Execution of their Trust. *The New York Mercury*, January 9, 1764

We whose names are hereunto subscribed, sons of some of the principal families in and about Trenton, being in some measure sensible of the advantages of Learning, and desirous that those who are deprived of it thro' the poverty of their parents might taste the sweetness of it with ourselves, can think of no better or other Method for that purpose other than the following

Scheme
of a Delaware Island Lottery

for raising 225 Pieces of Eight toward building a House to accommodate an English and Grammar-school and paying a Master to teach such children whose parents are unable to pay for their schooling. It is proposed that the House be 30 Feet long, 20 Feet wide and one story high and built on the Southeast corner of the Meeting House yard in Trenton. . . .*The Pennsylvania Gazette*, April 26, 1754

Scheme of a Lottery

By Virtue of an Act of the Colony of New York made and passed the 19th day of May, 1761, for raising the sum of 3000 Pounds to be employed for and towards purchasing so much of Sandy Hook as shall be necessary and thereon to erect a proper LightHouse. The said lottery to consist of 10,000 tickets, at Forty shillings each, whereof 1684 are to be Fortunate, from which 15 per cent is to be deducted. *The Pennsylvania Journal*, July 9, 1761.

Soon, lotteries became more like raffles and began to be used as a method of relieving the debt of an individual, of selling property and even raising cash.

The method of disposing of landed estates by way of Lottery, having been in practice in most Countries time out of mind and, as no lotteries have been more common in America, in particular, it is presumed the following scheme for disposing of 46 Acres of Excellent Meadow Ground, situated on the Southwest end of Petty's Island, nearly opposite the City of Philadelphia, being the present property of Alexander Alexander, will be equally acceptable to the Publick with any Lottery yet set foot on the Continent. And it is well known that no tract can be more pleasant or better situated for a Country Seat than Petty's Island, from every part of which there is a most delightful Prospect up and down the river Delaware, of all outward and inward bound shipping, of the Jersey and Pennsylvania Shores and a full View of the City of Philadelphia. *The Pennsylvania Journal*, June 11, 1761

And they began to be more and more criticized:

Fallit vituem specie Vertutis et Umbra[80]

My dear Countrymen:

Upon perusal of my opponents last performance in support of lotteries, I at first determined not to be led out of my way but to proceed in my principal design of discovering to the public, the partiality of the design and the unlimited power confer'd by the [lottery operators] . . . In support of these assertions I give the solemn declaration of the British Parliament, by which it appeared that all lotteries were in their opinion unjust, fraudulent and common nuisances, the same were the sentiments of the legislature of New Jersey and this province. . . .

Pennsylvanicus
The Pennsylvania Journal, March 1, 1759

Indeed, lotteries became illegal in New Jersey, as in some other provinces, forcing the operators to go "off shore" and operate from islands in the Delaware River:

The Drawing of Biles Island Lottery for finishing the Lutherian Church in Bedminister Town, and County of Somerset, East-New Jersey, will punctually begin drawing on Tuesday, the first day of May next, on Biles Island, in Delaware River, near Trentown, without any further delay. *The Pennsylvania Journal*, April 12, 1759

---

[80] translated:" Vice imposes on the Public under the pretext and mask of Virtue."

Unlike the television news bulletin, which strikes in blitzkrieg fashion and, in fifteen seconds, departs back to the newsroom, the newspaper is intended to be a Reader's Companion for the day, a week or until a fresh paper replaces it. Thus, the publication usually contains some forms of reader amusement, most often a cross word puzzle, but sometimes a quiz, a brain teaser, a word game or other test of the reader's memory, powers of observation or knowledge. The following challenges to the colonial readership may well mark the evolution of this section of the paper:

Burlington County, November 30. On the 15th Instant at Night, one John Antrum, was watching for Venison in his Corn-Field and a Horse happening to come into the Field, he took him for a Deer and shot him dead. It is said he must pay for the same. Query: whether he ought to pay for the same, since it was by Mistake and the Horse a Trespasser. *The Pennsylvania Gazette*, December 4, 1729

Mr. Bradford,

A Neighbor of mine having dream'd a dream, not only Once, but Twice, and with some Concern has told it Publickly, I therefore send it to you to Print it, which will oblige one of your constant Readers,
S.D.

That I was at the City of New York, walking upon the south side of the Town, and as I stood upon the Dock I saw a Cart drawn by two Oxen and two Horses and a White Man to drive it. Many Spectators saw it, as well as I, and wondered to see it drive so furiously. I asked Whose Team it was? Answer was made that it was Col. M----'s. I asked, Where they were going that they drove so furiously? Answer was made. It was going to M----l. By this time, I saw the Team run furiously into the River, in sight of all the Beholders, where it perished. But so soon as the Team was sunk, I saw a great Mastiff Dog go into the River and fetch the Driver out and did shake him. And the Driver turned instantly into a Beast with a pair of Horns upon his head. *The New York Gazette*, April 3, 1738

Mathematical Question

Suppose in an oblique angled triangle, whose Base and one side is unknown, the Length of the other side 25, the angle included by the known side and Base 41 Degrees and the Area 275; thence to find all the unknown parts without reducing it to two right angled Triangles. *The New York Gazette or Weekly Post Boy*, February 13, 1766

(solution)

We have received Solutions of the Mathematical Question in our 2 last Papers, from 4 different Persons, but, as we have no Algebraical Figures and the angled Figures could not be had without considerable Expense, we hope such Matters will not be expected to appear in our Paper, unless the Persons who send them will procure the Mathematical Figures and send Money to pay for their Insertion, as the Gentlemen did who proposed the Question. We shall however for this once, insert, gratis, One of the Answers, which is more easily expressed than the rest viz.

Elizabeth-Town, Feb 24,1766

To the Printer.

The Mathematical Question proposed in your last two Papers is to be performed as follows.

1. As the Radius is to the given Side, so is the side of the given Angle to the Perpendicular.

2. Divide the area by half of the Perpendicular, gives the Base. The Question will then be reduced to the 4th and 5th Cases of oblique Triangles in Trigonometry, having two sides and the included angle given, from which the others are easily found.

A.C.

This Gentleman (and some of the rest in their Town) propose Questions in Mathematicks, which, if they please, shall be inserted. *The New York Gazette or Weekly Post Boy*, February 27, 1766

As they still do today, colonial news papers broadcast the sad news as to who have passed on. Markedly unlike today, however, little attention was given in those Death Notices to the material accomplishments of the deceased. Rather, his or her virtues and positive character traits were recognized and lauded, as much as an example to the living as in eulogy to the dead. This applied even to Royalty:

Perth Amboy, New Jersey, June 6. A Message from his Excellency J. Belcher, Esq., Governor and Commander in Chief of the Province of New Jersey.

Gentlemen of the Council and General Assembly:

The 28 of the last Month I had the Honor to receive a Letter from his Grace, the Duke of Bedford, one of his Majesty's principal Secretaries of State, of the 21st of March last, and which is couched in the following terms:

Whitehall, March 21, 1751

Sir:

It is with great Concern that I am now to acquaint you with the Death of His Royal Highness the Prince of Wales, who expired of a violent Pleuritick Fever about 10 o'Clock last Night. The grief upon this melancholy Occasion is great and general. It is however a great Comfort to His Majesty's faithful servants to find that his Health is entirely re-established and that Her Royal Highness, the Princess of Wales, and the rest of the Royal Family are as well as can be expected in the present Circumstances. I most heartlily condole with you upon this unfortunate Occasion and am
Your most obedient humble Servant
Governor Belcher, New Jersey

The Death of this Prince, who next under His Majesty, was the Darling and Delight of the British Nation, has drawn a gloomy Scene for the Prospect of all of His Majesty's Dominions, and I think it is my Duty to say, I shall be glad to join with you, as speedily as may be, in an Address of Condolence, to our most Gracious Sovereign, upon this very melancholy Occasion, and, at the same Time, to Congratulate His Majesty upon the entire re-establishment of his Health (after his late Indisposition) the value of whose precious Life is doubly enhanced to all his good and faithful Subjects, by the Death of the late Heir Apparent to his Crown and his Kingdom.

J. Belcher

Pennsylvania Journal, June 13, 1751

There was little doubt in the mind of the Colonist as to what was right and what was wrong. Morals were not the object of discussion and speculation as if their substance could change by the direction from which one held them out and studied them. God and Government pronounced the rules with clarity and good creatures and citizens complied as was their happy duty. Without any doubt, these virtues are part of the genetic code of our Nation, as is the expectation that they will continue to be esteemed and follow.

Note in the following the emphasis that is placed upon how a person performed his or her task on earth, the type of neighbors they were, their generosity and their devotion to "virtue", as the backbone of a good man's existence:

On Monday the 20 Currant, Dyed here in the Afternoon the Reverend John Harrinan, Pastor of the Church in this Place, aged about 60 Years, Who the same day at a Church Meeting told his people that his time of Departure drew near and exhorted them to Peace and Unity one with another and to stand fast in the Covenant that they had engaged themselves to. *The Boston News Letter*, September 3, 1705

On Thursday at Amboy dyed the Rt. Hon. my Lady Hay, much lamented by all that knew her, being a Lady of rare Endowments and Vertues, one of the best of Wives, and a most excellent Mother and has left His Excellency Brigadier Hunter our Governour the most afflicted Man alive. She was Interr'd here in the Chappel in Fort George. *The Boston News-Letter*, August 13th, 1716

Philadelphia, April 29. Last Week died at Amboy, John Barclay, Esq. in an advanced Age, a pious Man, an excellent neighbour and of very great Service to the Publick, but much more particularly where he lived and is very much lamented by all that knew him. He was Brother to Robert Barclay, Laird of Ure in the Kingdom of Scotland, the famous Quaker, who wrote *Barclay's Apology*. *The Boston Weekly News-Letter*, May 6, 1731

New-Brunswick. On Wednesday last departed this Life in the 70 Year of her Age, Mrs. Anne Depepyster, Widow of the late Coll. John Depeyster deceased. She was possessed of every Virtue that adorns the Sex; her Indisposition was short, for on Saturday last she was taken Speechless, with an Appoplectic Fit, and on Friday interred, her loss is much lamanted by all who had the Happiness to Converse with her. *The New York Weekly Journal*, January 28, 1740

Last Thursday Se'nnight, died at Perth Amboy, in an advanced Age, the Hon. Andrew Johnson, Esq. one of his Majesty's Council for the Colony of New-Jersey and Treasurer of the Eastern Division of that Province. A Gentleman of so fair and worthy a Character, that truly to attempt to draw it, would be throwing away Words. He was really equal to what Pope means, when he says " An honest Man is the noblest Work of God." *The New York Mercury*, July 5th, 1762

New York, April 5. To the unspeakable loss of his Family and Public, on Friday Evening last, died the Honourable James Alexander, Esq. in the Sixty fifth Year of his Age.

A Gentleman in his Disposition, generous, courteous and humane, delicate in his sense of Honour, steadfast in Friendship, of strict Probity, temperate in his Diet and in Business indefatigable. The Relations of Husband, Father and Master he sustained with the highest Reputation. In these Parts of the World few Men surpassed him either in the natural Sagacity and Strength of his Intellectual Powers or in his Literary Acquirements. . . . He was also eminent in his Profession of the Law. . . . Always true to the Interest of his Country, well knowing that the Rights of the Crown are the Bulwark of the Liberties of the People, that the Liberties of the People are the Safety and Honour of the Crown and that a just Temperament of both in the Administration of the Government constitutes the Health of the Political Body. . . . *The New York Mercury*, April 5, 1756

One of our Correspondents from the Country writes us as follows, viz.

Amwell, in Hunterdon County, New-Jersey

Messieurs Hall and Sellers,

Altho' I am one of your constant Readers, yet I have been a little surprized, that I found no Mention made in any of the public Papers of the Death or Character of John Reading Esq., late of this Place, especially as his

Station and Character was eminent. That God who has said, "The Righteous shall be had in everlasting Remembrance," no Doubt expects that we should actively concur in accomplishing that sacred Declaration. And, besides, as Example teaches more powerfully than Precept, so, illustrious Examples of Virtue being set before us, excite us to a noble Emulation. These Considerations have induced me to give you the following Strictures of his Character - - - The God of Nature endowed Mr. Reading with good, natural Powers - - - a Genius above the Common Level. His Judgment was clear and manly; his Thoughts under good Command; his Expressions ready and pertinent. He justly supported the Character of being a strictly honest Man; one of unshaken Integrity and Uprightness. He was under the Advantage of an early liberal education; and had his mind enriched with a useful store of Knowledge - - - all which Things conspired to qualify him to act with Dignity in the several important Stations in which he was placed in Life;· and he had the deserved Honour of being entrusted with some of the most important Offices in the Government. He was early appointed a Member of His Majesty's Council in this Province, and was twice the President-Governor of it, which important Offices he executed with a becoming Dignity, Judgment, and Fidelity. And though distinguished with honourable Trusts, he did not appear at all elevated by them, but behaved with that Meekness and Gentleness, that Evenness and Agreeableness, that happily marked his whole Character; and with Condescension and Respect to the meanest and poorest, as well as to the greatest. He was remarkably inoffensive and cautious in his Conduct, and steady, solid and grave in his Deportment; yet he was not remorse or sullen, gloomy or impolite. It might be said, without flattering Panegyric, that he never undertook any trust, to which he was not eminently faithful, nor sustained any relation, whether of a Husband, Parent, Friend, Counsellor, or ruler, but he was conscientious in the Discharge of it. And he had the rare art of doing worthily without appearing conscious of it. He was temperate in his Enjoyment, and charitable to the Poor; was far from being vain or showy in his Appearance; on the contrary, it was plain and unaffected; when he spake, it was with a natural Guard and Prudence; seldom did an unguarded Word drop from his Lips - - - He did not love to deal in Calumny or Detraction, or engage in Party Quarrels, but was a quiet and peaceful Member of Society; was scarcely known to speak to the Disadvantage of any, even though their conduct was disagreeable; but prudently concealed his sentiments in his own Breast, and suffered their own Actions to be the severest Libel on their Fame. He manifested an high regard to Religion, and was a constant Attendant at public Worship; was Catholic in his Sentiments, and loved good Men of every Denomination of Christians - - - He had a strict Regard to Truth, and was punctual to his Word - - - Was universally beloved, and died lamented on the Fifth Day of November last. *The Pennsylvania Gazette*, January 28, 1768

Extract from letter from Amwell, New Jersey, Oct 17, 1768. On Wednesday the 5th inst. a melancholy Accident happened here. On the afternoon of said Day, Captain Daniel Reading . . . and two other Gentlemen, each with his Fowl-ing Piece, charged with small Shot, went out . . . in the Pursuit of Game in the neighbouring Woods. . . [T]he Gun of [one of] the Gentleman . . . accidentally went off and Captain Reading . . . unhappily received the Charge. . . Skilful Surgeons were immediately called . . . , but notwithstanding many flattering Symptoms of a favourable Issue, yet, on the Morning of the 15th instant, he unexpectedly and suddenly expired. . .

Captain Reading's placid, easy, open, benevolent, engaging Disposition and Conduct, had rendered his the Object of universal Esteem and Affection wherever he was known. Hence, his Death is justly and very greatly regretted! It is not only an unspeakable Loss to a deeply afflicted Widow and a large Family of small Children, but to the particular Society to which he belonged, of which he was a very useful Member, and to all his Acquaintance. He was one of the most loving and affectionate Husbands, the tenderest of Fathers and a steady Friend; and his immature and unexpected Death, in the Prime of his Days, and in the midst of Usefulness, shews the Vanity of Man in his best Estate and the great Necessity of attending to our Lord's Admonition "Be ye also ready, for in such an Hour as ye think not, the Son of Man cometh."

It is said that the Gun, which was instrumental in the above unhappy Affair, had sundry times before gone off in the same unexpected and surprizing Manner. *The Pennsylvania Gazette*, October 27, 1768

New-Jersey, June 4. On Thursday last the Wife of Capt. Thomas Lawrence of Hackinsack was buried, aged Ninety four; Her Husband follow'd her to the Grave, at the Age of Ninety Seven, is a hearty Man and walks as upright as a Youth. *The Boston Weekly News-Letter*, June 9, 1737

On the sixth Instant, departed this Life Edward Tonkin, Esq. of Burlington County, in New-Jersey, a Gentleman, who will be long remembered with Esteem and Regret, by as many as who had the Pleasure to know him. We hear that he left a handsome Legacy to St. Mary's Church in Burlington. *The Pennsylvania Chronicle*, April 17, 1768

Stoney-Brook, in New-Jersey, On the 8th Instant departed this Life, in the 68th Year of his Age, John Clark, a Man of an amiable Character, ... of whom it may be truly said, that he was a loving Husband, a tender Parent, an indulgent Master, and an obliging Neighbour; which makes his

Death greatly lamented. His remains were decently interred in the Quaker's Burying-Ground (of which Society he was a Member) at this Place, on the Tuesday following, attended by a large Concourse of People. *The New York Gazette or Weekly Post Boy*, May 23, 1768

Elizabeth-Town, August 12, 1768. On Wednesday Morning last, departed this Life, after a short Illness, the Hon. Samuel Woodruff, Esq., one of his Majesty's Council for this Province. A gentleman universally known for his undaunted Resolution, unshaken Fidelity, and Just Decisions, in the Character of a Magistrate, and for his Benevolence, Hospitality, public Spirit and Liberality, few, if any, exceeded him. In his private Life were most eminently joined, the affectionate Husband, the tender Parent, kind Master, faithful Friend, and to crown all, the cheerful and devout Christian. By his sudden Fall, several public and important Places of Trust are become vacant, all of which he filled with distinguished Integrity. His remains were decently interred Yesterday Afternoon in the First Presbyterian Church, attended by a numerous Concourse of People, from this and the neighbouring Towns, when a very pertinent and judiciously applied Sermon was preached by the Rev. James Caldwell, from Isaiah vii,1,2: " The righteous perished, and no Man lath it to heart, and Merciful Men are taken away, none considering, that thee Righteous is taken away from the Evil to come. He shall enter into Peace, they shall rest in their Beds, each one walking in his Uprightness." *The New York Gazette and Weekly Mercury*, August 15, 1768

Perth-Amboy, September 19. On the 6th Instant died here in the 71st Year of his Age, Doctor John Johnston, very much lamanted by all who knew him and to the unexpressible loss to the Poor, who were always his particular care. *The American Weekly Mercury*, September 14, 1732

Burlington, October 16. Yesterday about eleven in the Forenoon, at the Point House, died of a Fever after nine Days Illness, James Smith Esq., one of his Majesty's Council and Secretary for the Province of New-Jersey, much lamanted in general as justly deserving the fair Character he bore; being a Man of great Benevolence, Moderation and Justice in the Offices he fill'd and regretted by his Acquaintance as a chearful sincere Friend. *The Pennsylvania Gazette*, October 19, 1732.

Elizabeth-Town in East-Jersey, April 1, 1734. On Saturday 29th of March was here inter'd the Body of Peter Sonmans, Esq. Chief Proprietor of East New-Jersey. He was Son to Arents Sonmans, late of one of the States of Holland, which Government, after having finished his Study in

Lyden, he quitted and came to England where he had the Honor of some considerable Offices under his Late Majesty King William, coming 1705. Coming a second Time into this Country where he had so considerable an interest, he was appointed one of her Late Majesty's Hon. Council Agent to the Proprietors Survey-General, General Receiver of the Quit-Rents and Ranger of the Forests, as well a s Sea-Coast, he was in two succeeding Elections Chose Representative for the County of Bergen, in which Station he Manifested himself a true Patriarch to his Country.

He was justly esteemed for his Charity, and Clemency, his sincerety in Friendship, Patience in Oppressions and undaunted Spirit in Dangers, manifested his just Merit of the Motto of his Arms *"Patientia Fido - - - In Augustis intrepidus"*[81]; much more could be said but for Brevity's Sake is omitted. *The American Weekly Mercury*, March 28, 1734

Burlington, July 19. On Saturday last died here the Hon. Col. Peter Bard, after a very short Indisposition. He had during his residing among us acquir'd the Characters of a Worthy Magjstrate, a sincere Friend, and a Father to the Poor. His Death is greatly lamented by all who had the Honor of his Acquaintance. *The American Weekly Mercury*, July 18, 1734

Last Monday died, in the Eightieth Year of her Age, and on Thursday was decently interred, in the Family Vault at Morrisania, Isabel Morris, Widow and Relict of his Excellency Lewis Morris Esq., late Governor of the Province of New Jersey: A Lady endowed with every Qualification requisite to render the Sex agreeable and enetertaining, through all the various Scenes of Life. She was a Pattern of conjugal Affection, a tender Parent, a sincere Friend and an excellent Oeconomist.

She was Liberal, without Prodigality; in Person, Amiable,
Frugal, without Parsimony; in Conversation, Affable
Chearful, without Levity; In Friendship, Faithful
Exalted without Pride; of Envy, void.
She pass'd through Life, endow'd with every Grace,
Her Virtues, black Detraction cannot deface
Or cruel Envy e're eclipse her Fame
Nor, mouldering Time, obliterate her Name.

In Honour to her Memory, this is offer'd by an Admirer of her transcendant Virtues. *The New York Gazette revived in the Weekly Post Boy*, April 6, 1752

---

[81] Enduring loyalty and ancient bravery

To the Printers

Tho' I believe the Character of Elizabeth Morris, inserted in the last Gazette to be just, yet I think the following Particulars (perhaps unknown to the Essayist of that Account) are worth preserving.

She was born in Elizabeth-Town in New-Jersey, married to Anthony Morris in 1700, lived with him above Twenty Years and survived him above Forty-six Years and her Conduct, in every Station of Life, was truly honourable. Her Husband was a noted Preacher among Friends, one of the first Settlers, and held considerable Offices in the Government of this City and Province and some of his Descendants (by preceding Wives) of the Fifth Generation, followed the Corpse of his Widow to the Place of Interment. *The Pennsylvania Gazette*, February 19, 1767

New-York, January 9. On Wednesday December 28th 1768 at his Seat in Morris County, departed this life, Captain Robert Troup, age at 60. With all the Fortitude of a Hero, he joined the Meekness, Benevolence and Compassion of the Christain. Warmed with true British Ardour in the late Wars, he signaliz'd himself in the course of his Country and achieved Victories worthy of the Cognizance of Fame. A tender and loving Husband, a kind Parent, a sincere Friend and an Example of steady Veracity and diffusive Charity. He finished his Course lamanted by all around him.

"His humble Stone, what few vain Marbles can,
May justly say, Here lies an honest Man."
Pope
The New York Gazette and Weekly Mercury, January 9, 1769

New York, February 6. Saturday the 28th ult. died at his house at New Barbados Neck in Bergen County, aged 89 Years, Warner Richards Esq. He was born on the Island of Barbados and was the last Survivor of a Number of Gentlemen who came from that Island and purchased the Neck upwards of 60 Years ago. He was remarkable for a very vigorous and strong Constitution. *The New York Gazette or Weekly Post Boy*, February 6, 1769.

As is sadly the case today, while some lives were full, others ended all too soon:

New-York, April 1st. We have the Melencholy News from the Borough of Elizabeth, in New-Jersey, that Mr. Nathaniel Bunnel, Son of

Joseph Bunnel, Esq., one of his Majesty's Judges of the Supreme Court of that Province, died some Time last Week, whose Death was occasion'd by an unhappy Blow on the back part of his Head, which he received from a Rail, that lay in the Cart-rut which the Wheel of the Cart flung up when he went over it; t'is said he lived a week after this sad Accident happen'd but never came to perfect Senses, nor spoke but a few Words. He was a very Hopeful Gentleman, useful to the Church he belonged to, helpful in Publick Affairs, charitable to the Poor, a dutiful Son, a kind and loving Husband, and a tender Father; and he lived in good Repute among his Neighbours, was respected by his Acquaintance and Friends, was beloved and is much lamented by his Parents and Family; he has left a wife and six Children, the youngest but a Fortnight old. *The New-York Evening Post*, April 1, 1745

Bordentown N. Jersey, January 23, 1768. Departed this Life, greatly and deservedly regretted (being the day on which he entered his twentieth year) Mr. Peter Imlay, son of John Imlay, Esq. of this Place, after a long and painful Illness, which he underwent with the Fortitude of a Christian --- He was remarkable for his early Piety, and steady Course of Life, frequently expressing a grateful Sense of the Divine Goodness towards him. When Death approached, he calmly resigned his Breath to him who gave it, and with the utmost Composure of Mind waited the Period that was to relieve him from all the Embarrassments of human Nature. *The Pennsylvania Chronicle*, February 1, 1768

After a short illness, on Saturday the Fifth of July, Miss Polly Rickets, Daughter of Colonel William Rickets, of Elizabeth-Town, departed this Life in the Sixteenth Year of her Age, removed from the Guilt and Misery of a Sinful World, without partaking of either; the Joy, Pride and Comfort of her Parents, admired by all her Relations and Friends, the Delight of all who knew her; religious; humble, modest, charitable and dutiful: Virtues by Heaven inspired are an Offering fit for Heaven and this, on such melancholy Occasions, should lead us to dry up our Tears, yield a perfect Resignation to the Divine Will and rather congratulate the Deceased on such timely Departure. *The New York Mercury*, July 14, 1760

In some instances, as in this 1768 obituary of a Middletown hard cider maker, one can see, like a fossil trapped in amber, the political dilemma the ordinary citizen was under as the Revolution to begin centuries of revolutions approached --- i.e., allegiance to the Crown, dislike of Parliament and a yearning for independence that could not be put back in the bottle.

On the 30th ult. died at Middletown, in New Jersey in the 28th year of his age, Mr. William Wiley, an eminent distilller .... a gentleman of acknowledged uprightedness and integrity, whose benvolent mind, and rectitude for life, added to his agreeable converse, and engaging manner, rendered him universally beloved and respected. He was a strenuous asserter of the liberties of his country - - - a zealous advocate for the welfare of Britain and America, whose interests, from the solidity of his judgment he was led to consider as inseparably connected; but an enemy to every measure that wore the least glimmering of oppression; He bore a lingering and painful disorder, with that fortitude and resignation which so eminently characterizes the christian and the man; fully convinced of this great truth "Death is victory; It binds in chains the raging ills of life."

He met his dissolution with that cheerfulness and serenity which are ever the emanations of a conscious virtuous mind, and which none but the truly pious can form a proper idea of, in full assurance, that a life devoted to the cause of virtue would be rewarded with an inheritance among the blessed. *The Pennsylvania Chronicle*, July 4, 1768

The weather is a time proven topic of interest, a fact not lost on the early newspapers. Unusual meteorological events were and are newsworthy. Blessed with a collection of reports on aberrant weather, taken over a course of 65 years, it is possible to identify weather patterns in New Jersey and their most extreme variances.

Cold, very cold weather seemed to predominate in the first fifteen years of news reporting in America but, as time passed, the stretches of arctic chill seemed to shorten, with two or three year cycles of extremely cold being reported every twenty years or so afterwards. These reports seem to reflect the breakup in America of the Little Ice Age, an abnormally cold period reported in Europe during the middle centuries of the closing millenium.

New York. Christmas day was the Coldest that was ever felt here; Hudsons River was froze over and continued fast several days, the severe cold lasted three days. *The Boston News-Letter* January 14, 1706

Burlington, January 22. We have had here a very severe Winter; Delaware River so froze that Loaden Slaes go from thence upon it to Philadelphia. *The Boston News-Letter*, February 2, 1708

Lathrop from Boston is put into a Creek of Delaware River below, but the River is fast at Burlington where they pass over on the Ice. *The Boston News-Letter*, January 3, 1715

Philadelphia, March 5. Our river has been full of Ice again and we have as Winter like Weather as any we have had and a great snow upon. *The Boston News-Letter*, April 1, 1717

New York, January 19. On the 9th, 10th, 11th and 12th Instant great numbers went over Hudsons River upon the Ice from New-York to New-Jersey, since which the weather has grown very warm, like the Spring, and all the Ice gone. *The Boston News-Letter*, January 25, 1720

Boston. Last Week and the beginning of this we had an extream cold Season, and on Friday last a Rope-Maker's Jersey Boy being at Work was so overcome with the Cold that he fell down Speechless and being carried home he died soon after. *The New England Weekly Journal*, January 11, 1737

New-York. Last week Capt. Barnes from S. Carolina left his Sloop at Shrewsbury where she is froze up. *The New York Weekly Journal*, February 9, 1741

By the Philadelphia Papers of last Thursday, we learn, that the Navigation of their River was then stopt by the Ice; the extreme Cold about that time hindered the Posts from performing their Stages; the Rivers of Hackinsack and Newark, were both shut up, but not so hard as to permit Horses to cross and even a Footman, in going over the Hackinsack River, broke through and narrowly missed being lost. *The New York Gazette or Weekly Post Boy*, January 9, 1767

New York, April 24. A Letter from the back Part of Elizabeth-Town, greatly laments the cold Weather all last Week and particularly Monday Night last was said to be the coldest that was ever known at this Season. The Ice in many Places was a full Inch thick and the great Peach Orchard belonging to Mr. Miller of that Borough, consisting of upwards of 11,000 fine Trees, being then in full Bloom, was entirely blasted for this Year and about 100 Pounds damage for its Owner. Indeed, it is thought that the Peaches are universally gone in this Manner, as well as certain other Fruits in Bloom, tho' it is hoped that the Apples may not have suffered so much, they being not yet open. We are assured also that the Wheat in all the Clay Soils, in the Jerseys, is prodigiously thrown out and perished, during the Winter, so that the Crops in all such Land will certainly fall very short. "When God's Judgments are on the Earth, the Inhabitants thereof should learn Righteousness." *The New York Gazette or Weekly Post Boy*, April 24, 1769

Winter storms can be paralyzing and destructive. Reports of unusually high tides and winter floods, as in the 1992 "Northeaster of the Century", can be found in the colonial press:

New York, January 23. Last Monday Night and Tuesday Morning, we had here a very violent Gale of wind at South East-East, which has done considerable damage to several vessels and craft being at our Wharfs, and had not the Wind suddenly chop'd about to the West as it did a few hours before High Water and checked the Tides, to all appearance all the Wharfs would have been quite overflowed.

We hear that in the same Storm, a Rhode Island Sloop, from St. Kitts, was cast away near Sandy Hook; the Men saved and only eight or ten Casks of Rum of the Cargo; but have not yet heard the Name of Vessel or Master. *Pennsylvania Journal*, February 5, 1751

New York, February 12. By the Philadelphia Post, we learn that the late high Tide has done considerable Damage at New Brunswick, most of the

Houses, nigh the River, flowing with Water; that at Elizabeth-Point, the Wharffs are much hurt; that the Bridge on Staten-Island is almost rendered impassable for Man and Horse; and that a Negro Boy, of about 15 Years of Age, was drove upon Staten Island Beech, supposed to be drowned with the Tide, on Thursday Night last, and that the Coroner's Inquest was holding upon him as he came along. *The Pennsylvania Journal*, February 27, 1753

New York, January 25. The Storm on Sunday the 10th inst. has made prodigious Devastations in several parts of the Government of New Jersey; five or six Mill-Dams upon one small stream in the West Part of Woodbridge; a fine new Bridge built last Summer and but just finished in the Fall, which cost above 300 Pounds, across the Raritan River at a Place called Bound-Brook, was swept away and some Pieces of it found 30 Miles below. At New-Brunswick and the Landing, the Water was all over their lowest Streets and many Stores and other Houses with Goods therein damaged. As there had been snow on the Ground and a Thaw of three or four Days before the Storm came on, the Sea-Water rising so high prevented the Freshes going off so speedily as it otherwise would, and the great Rains falling at the same time gives Room to think that more Damage is done throughout the Country than we yet have an Account of. *The New York Mercury*, January 25, 1762

March 28, 1768. We hear from Salem County, New Jersey, that on Saturday Evening the 19th Inst. there was the highest Tide there, that has been known by the oldest Man now living, which occasioned the Loss of several Hundred Sheep and Lambs, besides many horned Cattle, Hogs, etc and had done great damage to the Tide Banks. *Supplement to the New York Journal or General Advertiser*, April 2, 1768.

When the cold weather ended and the thaw began, New Jersey, especially her interiors, were threatened anew by Nature in the form of flooded ice filled rivers:

New York, February 5. We hear from New Brunswick that in the great and sudden Thaw we had on Monday and Tuesday last, the fine Bridge, lately built across the Rariton River, near Bound Brook, was carried away by the ice falling against it, with the Rapidity of the Current. *The Pennsylvania Journal*, February 12, 1770

Philadelphia. We hear from Brunswick upon Rariton River that at the breaking up of the Ice a vast deal of Damage was done at the Ferry there, the Fresh occasioning, such as Inundation that whole Barns and Warehouses were born down and carried away and much Wheat, Flower, Beef and Pork lost. The Water was many Feet high in the Dwelling Houses at the Landing, but we hear of nobody drowned. *The Pennsylvania Gazette*, February 22, 1733

Philadelphia, February 27. We have these further Accounts of the Damages done by the Freshes & Ice, at New-Brunswick, the Water was all over the City and has damaged abundance of Wheat, carried away a Barn, the Ice turn'd a House quite round, undermined the House of Wm. Cox, carry'd away Mr. Antil's Barn, Stable and Hay, together with several Hogs, Turkies & Fowls, likewise carried away a large quantity of Wheat & Salt. We likewise hear that the Freshes have done great Damage at Trenton, that it carried away the Dam of the Iron-Works & the Dam of the Grist Mill, Bridge & Dying House, with a large Copper was carried down the Stream & abundance of other Damage. There was a Horse drowned lately with a Cloth Side-Saddle and we hear that the Woman is since taken up at Glouster, but can't learn as yet who she is.

New York, Last Week there was a great Flood in Rariton River in New Jersey, which did a great deal of Damage. It carried away three Barns with Corn & Cattle in them. At New-Brunswick, it broke several Store-houses & Wharffs and quite destroyed Mr. Hude's Store-house with near 3000 Bushels of Wheat in it & other Damage. *The New England Weekly Journal*, March 19, 1733

We hear from different parts of the Country that great Damages have been done by the late Freshes in the Rivers and Creeks by carrying off Stacks of Hay, breaking Bridges, ruining Mill-Damns and the like.

At Brunswick vast Damages were done on the breaking up of the River Rariton, which carried away several Storehouses and destroyed large quantities of grain. The Damages done in that Town only is said to amount to upwards of 2000 pounds.

The Ice in the River Delaware remains yet and People continue to pass over it but 'tis now becomes so rotten that several Men and Horses have broke through and narrowly escap'd drowning. *The American Weekly Mercury*, February 3, 1737

Spring and early summers are the times for violent tornado like storms, sometimes accompanied by hail.[82] *Notice the dates of the following storms:*

We hear from Newark in East-New Jersey that some time last week they had there a most violent Hurricane, the extent of which was about 40 Rod and tore up every Thing in it's way, particularly a Barn and some Timber near it which it carry'd to a very great height and distance. *The American Weekly Mercury*, May 6, 1742

---

[82] Surprisingly, New Jersey is listed among the areas of the United States where tornados are regularly reported.

New York, March 23. Last Tuesday we had here a considerable Shower of Rain. About a Week before that we had a pretty smart Snow Storm, attended with a great deal of thunder, to the Surprise of Most since it is no common Thing here to have Snow and Thunder both at once. And we hear that the Snow was so violent at that Time near Woodbridge that a Boy in the Field was struck down and stunned, but happily without further damage. *The New York Gazette revived in the Weekly Post Boy*, March 23, 1752

Being at Burlington yesterday, I was a spectator of one of the most extraordinary storms of hail and rain as perhaps has been seen in America; at least, some very old men said they had never seen one like it. It had begun to gather in the North about one o'Clock and continued brewing, as I remember, until about two, now and then threaten[ed] with a rumbling thunder. . . . After several heavy rumbling thunders, a north and by east wind took place and drove with fury. At first, there came a little rain that was soon after followed by some large stones of hail, which, with the rain, increased for the space of 8 or 10 minutes. [T]hen appeared to me a most amazing prospect. It seemed as if the whole body of the clouds were falling, half rain, half hail. The street appeared as another Delaware, full of floating ice. . . . The thickest of it continued for 15 or 20 minutes more and then abated gradually. After it was over, there looked as if there had fell a snow and in some places the hail had drifted 6 inches thick, some of which remained on the ground until night, notwithstanding it continued warm after the storm. The wind was for the most part N. by E. and the rain and hail went in a vein of about one and a half miles in breadth.

As soon as the gust was over, I took a walk to see how the fields &c. had fared and found a scene of desolation. The rye, flax and oats were cut to pieces. The peas, beans and garden truck, where the storm fell thickest, intirely ruined. The trees appeared as if the caterpillars had been stripping them of their verdure. Cherries, apples, peaches and leaves, almost covered the ground in places. . . .*The Pennsylvania Gazette*, June 1, 1758

Last Sunday s'ennight, at Night, a shower of Hail (attended with terrible Thunder and Lightning) fell at Sandy Hook, some of which was, 'twas said, as big as Pidgeon's Eggs. One of our Pilot Boats, then lying in the Cove, was struck with the Lightning, which shattered her Topmasts all to Pieces and did her considerable other Damage. What is very remarkable, a Boy that lay asleep in the Fore-Castle close to the Bulkheads, received no hurt, whilst they were split in a surprizing Manner. *The Pennsylvania Journal*, April 10, 1753

New York, May 20. We hear from Flushing and several other places on Long Island that last Tuesday se'nnight a very hard Shower of Hail fell in these parts. . . Most of the Hail Stones being as big as Pigeon

Eggs. 'Tis said the Hail was large and plentiful also at many places up the North River[83], as well as in the Jerseys. *The New York Gazette and Weekly Post Boy*, May 20, 1754

Philadelphia. On Tuesday last, in the afternoon, we had a Shower of exceeding large Hail here, which however lasted but a short Time, and soon after, the wind blowing very high, continually shifting and attended with Thunder, a Water-Spout appear'd on Delaware opposite to Kensington, which carried up Coopers Creek and supposed to break on the Shore, where, it is said, considerable damage is done, tho' we have no particular Account thereof. We hear that a School House was beat down, the Roof of a Dwelling House blown off, a great deal of Garden Ground destroyed, that a new Wherry was lifted up by it and broke to Pieces by the Fall and that a great many Trees were torn up by the Roots. *The Pennsylvania Gazette*, June 6, 1754

New York, June 10. On Tuesday afternoon last we had here a very Sudden Gust of Wind and Rain, attended with Thunder and Lightning, from the W.N.W.

A Brunswick Boat in coming across our Bay at the Time the Squall happened, was overset thereby, and five out of eighteen Passengers in her drowned in the Cabin. . . The other thirteen were taken off her deck by one of the Staten Island Passage Boats, who being near, bore away to their relief. We are told she had on board between a Thousand and Twelve Hundred Pounds worth of Linnen, manufactured in the Jersies, and brought hither for sale. . . . *The New York Gazette or the Weekly Post Boy*, June 10, 1754

Tuesday afternoon we had a violent gust of wind and Rain with very hard Thunder, which had done considerable damage by blowing down chimneys, tearing off Roofs of Houses, overturning small wooden Buildings, Barns &c. and has tore up a prodigious number of Trees. At the same Time, a small Boat, coming down from Burlington, was overset, with five men in her, two of which were drowned. . . A young man was also killed near Glouster Point by the fall of a Barn. *The Pennsylvania Journal*, June 24, 1756

New York, July 5. The Gust of wind that was felt in Philadelphia the 22 ult. . . . was felt in a very severe manner at Newark Mountains in New Jersey where the Orchards, Fences, Corn Fields and Wood Land, for about a Mile and a Half in Length are entirely ruined, many large Trees being broke down and carried to an incredible distance from the Place where they stood. Houses and Barns to the amount of 25 are quite blown away. .

---

[83] The Hudson River was sometimes called the North River.

. A new House, belonging to one Dodd, almost finished, was entirely blown away and a Barrel of Wool that happened to be in one of the Chambers, was carried a quarter of a Mile off and three days later was found in a Swamp. *The New York Mercury*, July 12, 1756

During the summers, there were reports of too much rain or not enough:

By letters from Philadelphia June 29th, we are informed that of late up in the Country to the Westward, they have had violent Rains that caused a fresh, whereby the Water rose 20 feet perpendicular in a few hours; it flooded all the Meadows near Sculkill River and drowned many Cattle. The Current was so impetuous that it carried away several Mills and Bridges and broke Damms and spoiled the Flower and Corn. The like fresh has not been known these Twenty years past. The Damms and Bridges in New Jersey are either wholly destroyed or much damaged by the Freshes. *The Boston News-Letter*, July 10, 1721

New York, July 1. From Woodbridge and Piscataway in New Jersey, we hear, that last Saturday se'ennight, the greatest Quantity of Rain fell, for the Time it lasted, as ever was known in the Parts, which has broke away several Mill-Dams and done much damage to many Fields of Corn, Flax &c. *The New York Gazette or the Weekly Post Boy*, July 1, 1754

Since our last we have had very great Falls of Rain, by which we hear, great quantities of Hay are destroyed; and that all the Bridges and Mill dams on the Amboy Road and all the Mill Dams on Reckless's Stream, and many others in different Parts, are carried away but we have not heard much Damage done to the Grain. *The Pennsylvania Gazette*, July 10, 1766.

New York July 10. We hear from New Jersey that Abundance of Damage has been done there by the great Rains which fell on Thursday Night, Friday and Saturday last. It is said that the Cloud from whence the heavy Rain fell did not extend further to the N. than Bound Brook. But in other parts, about Spotswood, Second River &c. the Floods there have been very great and swept away all before them, not a Bridge or a Mill for many miles was left standing. We have already heard of the Loss of between 20 and 30 mills. *The New York Gazette or Weekly Post Boy*, July 10, 1766

We have had the greatest Rains and the most constant for ten or twelve Days past, that has ever been known in my Memory and which still continues. I am informed that fourteen Mill-Dams in this [Cumberland] and Salem County are carried away by the Freshes. The Wetness of the Season gives us a Melancholy Prospect with respect to the Harvest, already begun, which before was very promising. *The Pennsylvania Gazette*, July 17, 1766.

Extract of a Letter from Cohansy in Cumberland County, New Jersey, August 19, 1769

"We have had the most excessive dry season here almost ever known. Our Corn, in some Places, quite cut off and our Pasture Fields burnt up, so that scarce any green appeared until last Wednesday Morning we had such a violent Gust, that we were almost flooded. Wherever the Waters found a Descent, they ran with such Rapidity, that Bridges, Mill-dams, Fences &c. were carried away but happily it did not last long. *The Pennsylvania Gazette*, August 31, 1769

New York, July 9. We have Advice from several Parts of East New Jersey that the late hot Weather has much blasted many Fields of Wheat to the great Disappointment of the poor Farmer's Hopes. *The Pennsylvania Gazette*, July 16, 1761

Summertime also had its own type of storms, often accompanied by hail, lightning or more tornados. Witness the following accounts of those summer explosions:

We hear from West New Jersey that on Tuesday last there was a prodigious Quantity of Hail fell, about seven Miles from Hattenfield, which covered the Ground, some of which was Measured about two Inches Round but has not done much Damage as we hear of. *The American Weekly Mercury*, June 14, 1739.

From News-Brunswick we hear that on Tuesday last they had a strong Gust of Wind, accompanied with some Rain and Hail of an amazing Bigness. We are informed that in one House it struck 28 Holes through the Roof; the Damage to the Grain is so great, that some who have already brought their last Crop to the Market countermand the same, lest they should want Bread. At Amwell a Boy was kill'd by the Hail and a Man and his Wife were much hurt thereby. *The Boston Weekly Post-Boy*, August 14, 1749

From Pamerpoch in West Jersey, we hear that on Saturday last in the Afternoon, they had a heavy Thunder Gust, attended with a prodigious fall of Hail, which has done much damage by beating down the Cabages, Tobacco &c. It is said for Truth that the Hail that fell that Afternoon lay in most Parts of the Village nearly four Inches deep, the largest of some of the Hail Stones were of an Uncommon Size. *The Boston Weekly News-Letter*, June 17, 1742

Burlington, August 11. Friday last we had a violent gust which killed two Mares within a few miles of this City. *The Pennsylvania Gazette*, August 7, 1736.

There has been this summer little Hail, but on Wednesday the 26th of July, a small cloud arose, to my thinking, not unlike what we have often met in the Latitude of Cape Hatteras; it began about a mile to the North Eastward (for distance from Monmouth Court-House) and in less than half a Mile to the South Eastward it took the Corn and Buckwheat that was standing as clean as it could have been mowed; it lay to Thursday about 11 o'Clock. I myself had the opportunity of seeing some of the Stones; I can't say more than this, there was Rhombus and Rhomboides and I think in Geometrical Figures, its beyond me to describe; one I weighed which was two Ounces and a half Troy. *The Boston Weekly Post-Boy*, August 14, 1749

We have an Account from Ash-Swamp, near Elizabeth-Town, that about 10 Days ago, a Shower of Hail, incredibly large, fell in a Vein of some Miles in those parts, which laid waste and entirely consumed every Field of Wheat and Corn that was within its Compass; Limbs of Trees broke to Pieces and Birds and Fowles, scarce one with its reach, escap'd. 'Tis said some of the Hail-Stones were as big as Hen's Eggs. *The Boston Gazette or Weekly Journal*, July 24, 1750

We hear from Penn's Neck, in Salem County, New-Jersey, that the Hail Storm, mentioned in our last two Papers, did considerable damage to several Plantations there, in three or four of which, it is said, the Grain is entirely destroyed. *The Pennsylvania Gazette*, July 7, 1768

Lightning killed with such regularity that it is a tribute's to Benjamin Franklin's courage and curiosity that he, a newspaper editor with knowledge of the danger, so risked his life in that experiment of flying a kite in an electrical storm.

From Hackensack we hear that the House of Adolph Brower was struck with Lightning, himself and a Negro Man were struck, who died immediately; with much ado his Corps and some of the Household Goods were saved from the Flames but the Negro was consumed. *The Boston Evening-Post*, July 19, 1742

From Great Egg Harbour we have an Account that on Friday Night last the House of Elisha Smith was struck with Lightning in a very surprizing Manner, without hurting any of the People in it, viz. Both Ends of the House were intirely broke in, and the Roof laid open, and the End of an old House adjoining it was likewise beat in and the Roof of it damaged. There were eleven Persons in both Houses, but none of them received any Hurt. *The Pennsylvania Gazette*, April 12, 1750

New York, August 26. We hear from Shrewsbury that, last Tuesday in the Afternoon, the House of Joseph Price in that Town, was struck with Lightning, accompanied by a violent Clap of Thunder, which went thro' and shattered the House pretty much, knocked down three of his People and kill'd two Horses that stood in the Door. *The New York Gazette revived in the Weekly Post Boy*, August 26, 1751

On Tuesday evening, the 20th Instant, the House of James Dilkes, Farmer, of Mantua Creek, Glouster County, was struck by Lightning, when his Wife was instantaneously killed and three of his Children badly hurt; a Dog which was lying at the Children's feet was burnt to Death. The Lightning came down the Chimney, the Top of which it shattered to Pieces and tore the end of the House asunder. *The Pennsylvania Gazette*, May 29, 1766

Philadelphia, May 25. On Tuesday last they heard several hard Claps of Thunder in the Jerseys which has done some damage. It killed a Lamb and two Ewes near Burlington. At the same time a very hard Clap split a Tree near to a Woman who sat at her Door but did no damage. A Dog was at the same time hurled a considerable distance away by the same but not killed. *The New England Weekly Journal*, June 5, 1732

On Wednesday last about 12 o'Clock, a sudden clap of thunder struck upon the House of Ebenezer Prout near this Place (Trentown); he was sitting at the Front Door and one William Pearson at his right hand; his only son a Boy about 9 Years old, who stood within 3 Foot of them with his back toward the Door, was struck down dead, the hair of his head burned off closely, his Jacket, Shirt and Breeches were torn all to Pieces, but no part of his body touched. The Posts of the House were split, the Rafters shattered as small as you can imagine. The Woman of the House being in the new Room (where the Thunder did the greatest Execution) was so much hurt that we despair of her Life, her youngest Daughter is in the same condition; William Pearson is much hurt but like to recover. The Man of the House is not hurt. The Boy was buried yesterday. *The American Weekly Mercury*, August 12, 1732

New York, July 13. We have advice from New Brunswick, that on Thursday Evening last, they had a hard Gust with Thunder, Lightning and Rain, wherein the Presbyterian Meeting-House in that Town was struck with the Lightning and shattered pretty much. Mr. Schuyler's Still-house was also struck and the Mast of a Boat shiver'd to Pieces, and, across the River, a Brew House of Mr. Antil's was also shatter'd.

And the Friday before that, there was a violent Storm of Hail and Thunder at Trenton, which damaged many trees, as well as grain, many of the Hailstones being bigger than Pidgeon's Eggs. *The Pennsylvania Gazette*, July 17, 1752

We hear from Hattonfield, over the River, that on Sunday last, during the Violent Gust (which we had also here) one Clemens being in his Barn making up a Mow of Corn, was struck down by the Lightning; and, on recovering, he perceived the Corn and the Barn to be in Flames, out of which he made his Escape, but the Barn was burnt down to the ground with every thing in it, notwithstanding the great Fall of Rain, to the Damage of 100 pounds. *The Pennsylvania Gazette*, July 14, 1737

Piscattaway, May 26. On the 19th Instant we had very hard Showers of Rain (which was very much wanted) attended with Thunder and Lightning. At New-Market in this Province, as a Country-man with a Team and six Oxen was driving along, the two foremost and hindmost Oxen were instantly struck dead, and the middle yoke not hurt, nor the Person that drove them. *The New York Gazette*, June 12, 1738

Philadelphia, May 28. We hear from Salem that the House of William Tufts was burnt by Lightning last Week; also a Barn in Glouster County. *The New York Gazette or the Weekly Post Boy*, June 4, 1753

Last Friday, the House of John Archer in Glouster County, New Jersey, was struck with Lightning and set on fire, whereby the House with most of the Furniture was consum'd, but no Person hurt. *The Pennsylvania Journal*, July 26, 1753

New York, August 6. The same Night a hard Clap of Thunder struck a green tree at Freehold, set it a Fire and kill'd a Horse under it, which belonged to one Sarah Pearant. *The New York Gazette or the Weekly Post Boy*, August 6, 1753

We hear that on Friday last, the Pilot boat belonging to Jacob Hart, being off our Capes was struck with lightning, which split her main-mast to pieces, went into the hold, thro' the cabin, where it almost suffocated two persons and then passed out of the cabin door into the air. *The Pennsylvania Journal*, August 17, 1769

From Fairfield in Cumberland County in New Jersey, we learn that Thursday last Se'nnight, as a Lad was plowing in a Field, a Thunder Gust came on, when a sharp Flash of Lightning killed five Oxen out of six that were in the Plow; the Lad was likewise struck down at the same time, but happily recovered again son afterwards. *The Pennsylvania Gazette*, June 4, 1767

We hear from Crosswicks, in New Jersey, that on Tuesday Evening, the 30th ult. two Horses belonging to Mr. Abel Middleton of that Place were struck down by a Flash of Lightning, as they were standing under a Tree in his Pasture. *The Pennsylvania Chronicle*, July 6, 1767

Philadelphia, July 9. By a Gentleman from Trenton we learn that on Tuesday the ult. in the Evening Mr. William Justis of that Place was struck dead by a Flash of Lightning. Mr. Yard of the same Place who was standing very near him was struck backwards at the same time, but happily recovered soon afterwards; The Lightning made four Spots on his Breast, of a green and yellowish Colour, but without the least Pain. *The Pennsylvania Gazette,* July 9, 1767

Gradually, as knowledge grew from experiments such as Franklin's, protections from lightning were developed. As suggested by the following, it was a tentative process at first:

Mr. Holt,
Sir,

Having lately seen in one of the public Papers (but forgot which) an Account of the Light House[84] being struck by Lightning, I was induced to inquire after the particular Circumstances of that Affair, especially, as I knew it to have a Metalline Conductor, and that, if it really were so, there would not be wanting those, who from the Prejudice of Education and their Non-Knowledge of the Efficacy of conducting Wires, would be ready to infer and propagate the Inutility of them, for the preservation of Edifices &c. You will oblige the Public and one of your constant Readers, by assuring them, that the Light House at Sandy Hook, has not been struck, so as to exhibit any appearance or Signs thereof whatsoever, and that the veracity of the Informant is indisputable, as well as his knowledge of the Premises, which he derives from his Proximity thereto. *The Pennsylvania Journal,* September 18, 1766

Late summer, early autumn is when hurricanes attack the Atlantic coast, as undoubtedly occurred on September 8, 1769:

New York, September 21. The Storm of Wind and Rain which came on, on Friday Morning the 8th Instant, and continued to 8 or 9 o'Clock at Night, has had very terrible and melancholy Effects in all Places from which we have yet had Opportunity to hear. From some of the People belonging to the Vessels that were lost at Barnagat in the late Storm, we have the following Accounts: The Sloop Sally, Cap't Pike, with 4 other Hands, having on board 30 Barrels of Mackrel and 4,000 Cod Fish, left Newport the 3rd Instant; on Friday the 8th, Wind very high at E.N.E. being near Barnagat Beach, attempted to beat off, but were soon driven into the Surf and left to the Mercy of the Winds and Waves. About a Quarter of a

---

[84] The lighthouse referred to here is the one that still stands on Sandy Hook, warning incoming vessels to New York to beware the barrier beach. Part of Gateway National Park, it is open to the Public as are the beautiful ocean beaches of the Park.

Mile South of the Inlet, the Sloop was driven on Shore on the Beach, where two or three Planks starting, she soon filled with Water and Sand and a Bank of Sand was driven up against her, which covered the Deck above two Feet before the People left her. By the Help of their Boat, they all got on Shore on the Beach, where the Boat was dashed to Pieces and one poor Man had most of his Ribs on one Side broken. They lay on the Beach all night and next Morning were taken off and carried ashore, where the wounded Man, the Capt. and Mate were lodged in the House of one Mr. Chamberlayne and intended to save all they could from the Vessel. The People lost every Thing but the Clothes on their Backs.

The Sloop Porgie, Christopher Johnson, Master, who left Edenton, in North Carolina, the 22d of August, loaded with Pitch and Turpentine, bound for New-York, about the same Time unfortunately arrived at the High-Lands of the Nevisinks, as also a fine large black Sloop extremely well found, having a square Topsail and supposed to be from the West Indies. Both of these Sloops finding it impossible to avoid driving on Shore, brought too, within the Breakers at Barnagat and threw out their Anchors. The large Sloop having a new Cable, made fast around the Mast at full length, seemed likely to ride out the Gale, but the Cable of the Porgie immediately parting, in wareing she was driven foul of the other Sloop and thereby lost her Bowsprit. As she was driving past, a Person on board the large Sloop was heard to say "Lord, Help Him. Poor Man. He is gone." The Porgie presently was driven on the Beach and dashed to Pieces, but the People providentially escaped and saved much of the Cargo. Soon after they were on Shore, about 6 in the Evening, the Wind suddenly shifted to N.N.W. and blew a more violent storm than before, with heavy Rain and Hail. Next Morning there was nothing to be seen of the large Sloop, which it is supposed was driven on the Breakers without her. A short, thick made Negro Man, with a Broad Face, pitted with Small-Pox, was seen on board of her and, after the Storm, the Body of such a Negro and those of 6 white Men, drowned, were taken up on the Shore and buried. The white men all wore their own hair, except one, supposed to be the Captain or the Mate, whose Head was shaven. During the Storm, a Brig was seen to the Eastward, standing S.S.E. A small Sloop was driven on Shore, within the Inlet, another with Rails, from Brunswick, and another at Egg-Harbour, all likely to be lost. Two other Sloops and 2 Schooners it is thought will be got off.. . .

Captain Ferns, from the Grenades . . . spoke with Captain Allen of Nantucket, who informed him, the Fleet of Whalers had suffered great Damage in the same Gale. *The New York Journal or General Advertiser,* September 21, 1769

The colonial press even reported an earthquake in New Jersey, severe enough to wake people in the night:

New-York, March 1. We are credibly informed, that a smart Shock of an Earthquake, was felt about 4 o'Clock in the Morning of the 21st ultimo, at Middletown, (New Jersey) and other Parts adjacent. *The New York Mercury*, March 1, 1762

If northeasters, tornados, hurricanes and even earthquakes could not destroy colonial America, there was an extraterrestrial threat to it. Or so was the dire prediction of a comet's tail slapping the earth, as reported in the press:

Mr. Holt,

I Observed the Comet this morning at 2 0'Clock and find its Progress toward the Sun. I believe at the Rate of about three Degrees in 24 Hours. It is now to the Southward of the Sun, but is falling as fast to the North that I think it will pass on that Side. By a Calculation I made this Morning, I find the Sun at half after 7 0'Clock, 2,793,104 Miles North at the Place where the Comet was at Two. In less than 30 Days I expect it will be parallel with the Sun. Should it become between us and the Sun the Tail will probably extend to the Earth. And, therefore, it becomes all to be prepared for the Consequences so alarming as to those which must then follow.

If somebody who has instruments, has not sent you some exact Calculations, you may publish these, but, if better are come to Hand, these are needless. The Publication of those sent you last Week are now, I suppose, unnecessary for the same Reason. *The Pennsylvania Gazette*, September 7, 1769

When you are looking for a home or a job, the classified section of your daily or Sunday paper is the place to begin. They are collections of terse, often abbreviated, pay by the word or line, no nonsense descriptions of what is available in the marketplace and for how much. Samples from today's paper include:

BY   Owner,4BR,3bth,EIK,LR,DR,fin bsmt,poss Mthr/Dtr,cent air;conv.pub trans NYC, asking 235K

or

Drivers Wanted ---
CDL lic. req'd, 5 Boros & LI,.NJ,CT

The ancestors of these advertisements are apparent (no pun intended) in the very first edition of the first of the colonial papers. In fact, a principal purpose, and financial necessity, of the newspaper was to engage in such advertising. However, back then, the "Notices to the Publick" were not so abrupt and concise as they are today. While colonial papers too charged by the word or line, their advertisements, usually composed by the subscriber himself, were more descriptive and, at times, even chatty. Always, they were polite and respectful to their customer/reader. Yet despite those differences, the resemblance between today's classified advertisements and those of the past is unmistakable and unbroken.

Real Estate for Sale

Newly marrieds, serious buyers, and the merely curious, all scan the real estate for sale section of their newspapers, imagining and searching for the ideal home. The colonial papers offered for sale properties of all descriptions, a sampling of which suggests much about life in those times. For example, how the houses of the period were laid out can be seen in the following.

A Very good Dwelling House in the County of Bergen, about Forty Eight Foot in length and Twenty Four Foot broad, with a large Cellar-

Kitchen, A Dairy and Stone Cellar all joyn'd together; the said Dwelling House has two large Rooms and an Entry, with a large flush Garrit and Bolting House near the same and an old Store House, Stable and Negroes Kitchen adjoining to each other, and a well built Smoak-House, with a Fowl-House thereunto adjoining, with a very good Garden to the same, the Land thereunto belong contains one Acre or something more. *The New York Evening Post*, February 3, 1746

One could look for a home in the wooded countryside:

To be Sold on Reasonable Terms

A Farm lying in the Township of Barnard's or Baskin-ridge in Somerset County, about a mile from Jacob Vanderveer's mill, near the Low Dutch Meeting house, near a good market for all sorts of produce, also within a mile and a half of the English Church; containing about 322 acres, having a good dwelling house thereon, and a large dutch Barn covered with cedar shingles, with good out houses for Negroes or other uses and good barracks; about 220 acres cleared and in fence; a fine piece of meadow and much more can be made; there is on said farm an exceeding fine orchard of about 300 apple trees, noted for yielding the best of cyder, several large fine pear trees and about 50 peach trees and a number of cherry trees, black walnuts and a thriving young nursery, all in good order; most of said farm in good fence, well watered having fine constant springs in every field and a spring of water by the dwelling house that waters a large piece of meadow; its well timbered to support the clear land, fine white oaks and many fine poplar trees fit for building or sawing, being near to a saw-mill; the title is indisputable, both from Elizabeth-Town and Proprietors. For further particulars, inquire of Capt. William Graham, living on said premises. *The New York Mercury*, December 13, 1762

A very good Tract of Land, containing 3314 Acres in the old Purchases, on the Head of the Rariton River, about six miles from a Saw Mill and Grist Mill upon Black River and near a Pond of Water called by the Indians Kant-Kan-i-auning in the County of Hunterdon. It is well timbered and Watered and sundry Places upon it convenient to erect Mills. For Title and Conditions of Sale, enquire of said Francis Many, Sale-Maker, in Water Street, near the Arch Wharf, Philadelphia. *The America Weekly Mercury*, February 19, 1740

TO BE SOLD

A Plantation in Middletown, adjoining on Shrewsbury River, and on the Mill Creek, so that the Farm, or more properly Neck of Land, is two-thirds or more fenced with Water, where there is very good fowling and a great Plenty of Fish, Clams and the very best of Oysters, all within 6 or 8 Rods of the Door. The said Farm, lying about 4 Miles from Sandy-Hook, containing 240 Acres of good Land for Grass or Grain of any sort, 150 Acres of which is cleared and all in good Fence, joining East and West on Two Brooks and North-East and N. West by the above said River and Creek, so that every field is well watered with 15 or 20 acres of good Salt Meadow belonging to the same. On it is a large Dwelling-House, Kitchen and Out-Houses, with a large Stone Cellar under the House, with two good Apple Orchards, a good Dutch Barn. Any Person inclined to purchase the same, let them apply to John Teunisson, now living on the Premises, who will agree on reasonable Terms and will give an indisputable Title for the same. *The New York Gazette*, January 17, 1763

To be Sold by Thomas Kearny [a] tract of land at a Place commonly called Waycake, in the Township of Middletown and County of Monmouth New Jersey . . . containing 450 Acres, well timber'd, partly joining Navisinks Bay and partly by a Navigable Creek, about 30 Acres of clear Land and a small Orchard, the greatest part arable and choice Pasturage, several Acres of which may be made good Meadow; it is very commodious for Domestic or Foreign Trade, being a noted Landing; likewise fit for Fowling, Fishing, Hunting, Oystering, Clamming. . . . *The New York Gazette revived in the Weekly Post Boy*, September 25, 1752

TO BE SOLD

A Neck of land, lying in Shrewbury, in Monmouth County and in the Province of East New Jersey, containing about one thousand Acres; about Three Hundred of which is Salt Meadow; it is bounded between Mosquito Creek and Kettle Creek, a Fence of about three-quarters of a Mile, will fence in the whole; there may be kept on the Neck at least Three Hundred Head of Cattle, Winter or Summer; and at least five Hundred or six Hundred Sheep, with little or no Fodder and as many Hogs. *The New York Journal or General Advertiser*, August 6, 1767.

There were also available homes, with possible commercial uses, in the larger towns of the Province:

A Lot of ground situate in Bordentown, fronting the two main streets, containing one acre, on which is erected a commodious two story brick house, well built and completely finished, with a good dry cellar under same, a two story brick kitchen, with apartments for servants, a good well at the door with a pump in the same.

A good garden, a stable, chair and hay house. The dwelling house is pleasantly situated and commands an agreeable prospect of the River Delaware and is in every way calculated for a gentleman's country seat. *The Pennsylvania Chronicle*, August 1, 1768

A Very good Two Story Brick House and a Wooden Dwelling House and a good Stable and other out houses, Situate in Trenton being by the Road leading to York and near the Grist Mill is very convenient for any Business whatsoever, with one Acre of Ground belonging to the same, which fronts on two very publick streets in said Town and has a good Spring before the Door. *The American Weekly Mercury*, July 17, 1740

A House and Homestead, near the Center of the Town of Newark containing about 3 Acres or more, all in good fence, with two Buildings upon it, a Stable and Garden, not inferiour to any in this Town or the next adjacent. *The New York Weekly Journal*, November 2, 1741

A Convenient House for a Merchant or Storekeeper in the City of New Brunswick, Province of East New Jersey, of two Stories under Roof, on each Floor six Rooms and in each a Fire Hearth, together with a good Store House newly repaired. *The New York Weekly Journal*, January 11, 1742.

A House and Lot in Princeton, a pleasant and agreeable Situation opposite the College, being 46 foot front, and 36 feet deep, with 10 Rooms, 8 with Fireplaces, a large new Stable 40 foot long and 20 broad with a good Well and a large Garden with a Variety of Fruit Trees, a large Bed of the best Asparagus &c., all enclosed with a good boarded Fence, fit for a Merchant or a Tavern. Whoever inclines to purchase may apply to Elias Boudient, Attorney at Law at Elizabeth Town[85] *The Pennsylvania Gazette*, November 5, 1761

---

[85] Mr. Boudinot, as his name is correctly spelled, was destined to have a long and interesting life, culminating in his being named President of the Continental Congress in 1783.

There were magnificent estates back then also. Witness the empire which Charles Hoff, Jr. had collected in his (and,perhaps, his father's) lifetime and which he now was breaking up and selling off:

To be sold by the Subscriber, living in the Township of Kingwood, in the County of Hunterdon, and Province of New Jersey, the following Premises: One over-shot Stone Grist Mill, with about 100 Acres of Land; a Stone dwelling house with a frame House adjoining and Buildings convenient for keeping Store, so as to front between 60 and 70 Feet, at which Place a Store hath been kept upwards of 20 Years past; two bearing orchards, the one grafted fruit; about 10 Acres of Meadows, a Frame Barn, Stables &c., this Mill chiefly employed in grinding Grists, having a very great run of Country Custom. Also one Breast Grist-Mill, chiefly kept for Merchant's Work, at which a considerable Quantity of Flour is made yearly; a Saw-mill for accommodating the Works with Boards, Stuff &c. with about 100 Acres of Land; A Stone Dwelling House and Two Log Houses; 15 Acres of Meadow and a Quantity of Swamp for making more Meadow; with a well frequented Stone Tavern and Stone

Kitchen, the House affording five Rooms and a Cellar; the said Tavern is in the Cross-roads, leading from Trenton and New Brunswick to the Forks of the Delaware &c.; a Well of good Water at the Door and a very good Spring not 60 Paces distant. The Tavern, with some Meadows and about 30 Acres of Land (15 whereof Woodland) may be sold separate. Likewise to be sold a Fulling mill and Stone Dwelling House, with about 30 acres of Land, about 4 Acres thereof Meadow . . . The Subscriber also has for sale, a Forge with two Fires, for refining Pig Metal into Bar Iron, with 70 or 100 Acres of Land, together with a Coal House and other Houses for accommodating Workmen, being capable of making about 50 Tons of Bar Iron yearly. The said Forge lies very convenient to a Tract of Land called the Great Swamp, from whence it has been supplied with a considerable quantity of Coal Wood gratis and more is offered on the same terms. . . The Reason of it being divided into Parcels is to accommodate Purchaser, as it was thought it might be a heavy Purchase for one Person; but if any such Purchaser present, it may all be sold together. The whole pleasantly situated in a little Country Village, convenient to Places of Worship of three different Denominations viz. Church, Presbyterians and Quakers, the farthest not exceeding three Miles. The Terms of Sale will be the Purchaser or Purchasers to pay Half down at entering on the Premises and the Remainder in reasonable Payments. A sufficient Warrant and Deed will be made, on paying the one Half of the Purchase Money, and giving Security for the Remainder by me.

Charles Hoff, jun.

The Pennsylvania Gazette, August 12, 1762.

The prize property on the market may have been what today, one suspects, must be part of the City of Hoboken but which, before the Revolution, was an island farm on the western shore of the Hudson River.

The Island called Hoobock, in New Jersey, directly opposite the City of New York, lying on Hudson's River, containing between seven and eight hundred Acres, two thirds of which is Upland and one third is Salt Meadow. It is in the best order, has on it a Garden of about five Acres, filled with a choice selection of English Fruits, such as Peaches, Pears, Plums, Cherries, Necterns and Apricots. There is upon it a very large House. . . and another very good one adjoining, both under one Roof. . . and under the whole are very large convenient cellars, together with an extraordinary Kitchen. A few Feet distance from the Dwelling is a large new Kitchen, which has three Rooms on each side, therefore more fitting for a Family, likewise the most commodious Dairy for at least thirty Cows.
There are other Out Houses, as, a new Smoke House, Fowl House, a large Stable with Stalls for ten Horses on one side and a fine roomy Place on the other to work in when dirty Weather, over which is a Granery with Appartments for all Kind of Grain and at the contrary end a Hay Loft, which will contain a great Quantity of Hay ; besides all which there is a very large roomy Barn for Cows on the one side and another for Horses on the other. There are likewise on the Farm a good Cyder Mill and a House over it, the Loft of which will hold about 20 Loads of Hay.

There will be let with the Premises, a good Waggon, Cart, Ploughs, Harrows and Farm Utensils of every Sort, as also a 100 good Sheep, among which are English Rams; also thirty good Milch Cows and thirty Head of Cattle, from one to four Years old.

Besides an old orchard which in good years will produce 70 or 80 Barrels of Cyder, there are also sat out near a 1000 Apple Trees, all grafted with the best of Fruits, some of which bore last year.

This farm has a Right in Bergen Commons, to turn out what Cattle you please and be supplied with Timber for Fencing and firing; is finely supplied with Fish and Oysters in great Abundance, all around it, and scarce any Thing in America can equal its convenience for Marketing, as, in good weather, you may cross [the Hudson River to New York City] in Half and Hour; and in the different Seasons of the Year abound with Plenty of Wild Fowl; and the Farm itself all in good Clover; of the Salt Hay [it] may be mowed at least 500 Loads per Year and of Fresh at present Sixty but more may be brought.

In short, a Farm equal to this, for all Convenience is not to be met with, and in Point of Situation nothing can exceed it and is remarkably healthy. *The New York Mercury*, December 1, 1760

Much of the labor force that worked on the farms and along the shore of colonial New Jersey was comprised, aside from the owner and his family, of indentured servants and slaves. But as multi year contracts of indenture expired and the sons of freemen grew up, independent workers of varying specialties emerged and, with little exception, seemed constantly in demand during the 1700s. For example:

Philadelphia, November 6, 1746. Josiah White of Mount Holy, near Burlington, in the Jerseys, wants a jouneyman shearman[86], and if a good hand, will give him good encouragement. Said White grinds clothiers shears. *The Pennsylvania Gazette*, November 6, 1746

On George's Road, in New Jersey, near Brunswick, a good Blacksmith, that understands shoeing of Horses and Country Work. Whoever wants employment shall have a good House and some Land with Iron, Steel, &c. and all Sorts of Tools necessary for carrying on Business. For further Particulars, enquire of the Printer hereof or of Mr. Thompson, at the Sign of the Ship, in Brunswick. *The New York Mercury*, July 5, 1762

A Person is wanted who is well qualified to settle Merchant's Books and Accompts, such a one that can be any Ways Recommended, may be sure of Employment for some Months and be reasonably rewarded, by applying to

John Johnson
John Barbarie
Stephen Skinner
The New York Mercury, September 6, 1762

This is to give notice to all able bodied freemen, not inhabitants of the County of Sussex, who are willing to enter into the Service of the Province of New Jersey, in defending the frontier parts of said Province, that in their application to me the subscriber, at Fort John's or elsewhere in the County of Sussex, they shall immediately be enlisted and be upon the Province pay at Two Shilling, Proclamation Money, per day.

Jacob Dehart
The New York Mercury, July 19, 1756

---

[86] A "shearman" is some who "cuts". It can sheep, wheat or, as here, cloth.

Ready Money may be had for clearing and putting into Grass about 25 Acres of Marsh, on Oldman's Creek in Glouster County, which is already banked in. Any Person willing to undertake the above may hear of Terms, by applying to the Subscriber, in Market Street, Philadelphia. He also wants a sober honest Lad, who can write a tolerable Hand and understands something of Arithmetic, as an Apprentice. *The Pennsylvania Gazette*, September 10, 1767

A Fuller[87] that can be well recommended for a good Work-Man, in Lower Freehold, in East-New-Jersey, near Monmouth Court-House by applying to the Subscriber, living in that Place.

Charles Gordon

The Pennsylvania Gazette, September 29, 1763

Wanted. A Person that understands the tanning and currying business well. A proper Person for that business and who can be well recommended may hear of good encouragement by applying to Francis Quick, at Kingwood, in West New Jersey. *The Pennsylvania Gazette*, June 1, 1758

County of Burlington, in New Jersey, 1764. The following Tradesmen are wanted, viz. a Shoemaker, a Taylor and Wheelwright[88], who, if they come well recommended for Sobriety, Honesty, and Industry may find good Encouragement by applying to the Subscriber, where convenient Dwelling-Houses and Shops may be had at a moderate Rent of

William Foster

The Pennsylvania Gazette, February 23, 1764

Wanted

A Man that has been brought up a Butcher and hath judgment in buying cattle &c. Any such Person, well recommended for sobriety, honesty and industry, may meet with good encouragement by applying to Stacy Potts at Trenton. *The Pennsylvania Gazette*, May 20, 1767

---

[87] A "fuller" works with cloth, cleaning and processing it.

[88] A "wheelwright" makes or repairs wheels and wheeled vehicles.

Wanted immediately, a Good Cooper[89], for packing Pork and Beef. A Person of a good Character may meet with Encouragement, by applying to the Subscriber, living in Burlington County, who has good Staves and a fine Conveniency to work in; and, for the future, the Person may, if he chuses, provide Staves for himself.

William Foster
The Pennsylvania Gazette, November 3, 1757.

Wanted at Etna Furnace, Burlington, a good Keeper or person accomplished in Castings. . . . *The Pennsylvania Gazette*, November 24, 1768

Wanted at Aetna Furnace, Burlington, . . . a middle aged woman not subject to liquors, fit to be entrusted with the Care of a large Family, but not to Cook. *The Pennsylvania Gazette*, November 24, 1768

At Etna Furnace, Burlington County, which will begin to be in Blast the Middle of April, are wanted a good Keeper, two Master Colliers[90], Moulders and Stock-takers. Those who apply in Season and come well recommended, will be encouraged. The Wood should be running in February or beginning of March. *The New York Gazette or Weekly Post Boy*, January 23, 1769

Good Encouragement given by Hawxhurst and Noble, at Sterling Iron Works for Wood cutters, Colliers, Refiners of Pig and Drawers of Bar Iron; also a Person well recommended for Driving a four horse Stage between said Works and the Landing.

N.B. Pig and Bar Iron and sundry English Goods to be sold by William Hawxhurst in New York. *The New York Mercury*, December 24, 1759

---

[89] a barrelmaker

[90] Colliers burned forest lumber to the right texture of charred wood to be used in the manufacture of iron. The production of iron was an essential of colonial survival and New Jersey became the leading producer of it until the Revolution.   This was bog-iron, a hydrous peroxide of iron containing 40% metallic iron, formed by a complex process that transferred, by means of percolating ground waters, the iron from the greensands and other cretaceous formations of a hundred million years ago into the decayed vegetation that lay in woodland swamps and pools. Once extracted, had to be purified in the furnaces and forges of an "iron works". Some of these iron works became major employers. The first of them in New Jersey, located at the Falls at Shrewsbury --now Tinton Falls -- had a workforce of seventy men which included: "foundersd, smiths, anchor smiths, miners, carpenters, colliers, wood cutters, carters and common laborers".

A Person that understands the nailing business in its different branches or who has been employed in that manufactory. Such a person bringing proper recommendations, will meet with good encouragement, by applying to Joseph Riggs, Esq. or Joseph Hadden, in Newark, New-Jersey, who are entering largely in that business. *The New York Gazette and Weekly Mercury*, February 29, 1768

At Etna Furnace, in the County of Burlington, good colliers, two good carpenters, a good Smith that understands the making flatt or padd iron handles, a stone Cutter, a person used to grind flatt irons and waggon boxes, will meet with encouragement. *The Pennsylvania Journal*, March 3, 1768

Vesuvius Furnace, at Newark, in New Jersey. A Single Man, well recommended, who understands moulding and casting of Iron Hollow Ware, in all its branches, may hear of good Encouragement, by applying to Mr. James Abeel, Merchant, in New-York, or to Moses Ogden, at said Furnace. *The New York Gazette and Weekly Mercury*, March 28, 1768

Wanted by the subscriber, living in the township of Upper Freeehold, in the County of Monmouth, East New Jersey

A Person who understands the business of Fulling and Dying Cloth, that can be well recommended, to be employed by the Month, Year or on Shares, which may be agreed on by the Parties when met; The Fulling-Mill and all Implements suitable to carry on the Business, is now in good repair and has a constant Stream of Water. For further particulars, enquire of Robert Brown, on the Premises, or John West, at the Old Ferry, Philadelphia. *The Pennsylvania Gazette*, January 8, 1767

Wanted Immediately

A Fuller, who understands fulling, dying, shearing and pressing Cloth, in all its Branches, and one who can be well recommended for Care and Trust; such a Person will meet with extraordinary Encouragement, by applying to Samuel Kitchen, in Amwell Township Hunterdon County, West-Jersey. The Fuller to work on Shares or by the Year. Apply to said Kitchen at his Mills. *The Pennsylvania Gazette*, June 8, 1769

Even the Government was hiring and it sounded like a great deal!

For the New Jersey Regiment under the Command of Colonel Peter Schuyler

To every abled body Volunteer will be given Twelve Pounds Proclamation Money and Clothes, a Blanket and other Necessaries, to the Value of Eight Pounds more; and they are to be enlisted only to the first day of November next; so that the Bounty Money, Clothes and Pay will amount in the whole to Five Pounds a Month; that is three shillings and four pence a day, besides Subsistence. All Persons who are willing to serve their King and Country upon this Occasion, are to repair to some of the Officers, who have Warrants to recruit for this Service at Salem, Glouster, Burlington, Bordentown, Trenton &c. *The Pennsylvania Gazette*, April 12, 1759

One position that was always in demand was that of the school teacher, as witnessed by the following which are only a few among scores and scores of such pleas.

Philadelphia, September 11, 1746. Notice is hereby given that there is in the Town of Bethlehem, and County of Hunterdon, in West-Jersey, two or three Vacancies for Schools where 18 or 20 pounds a Year hath been given with Accommodations. Any Schoolmaster well qualified with Reading, Writing and Arithmetick and wants Imployment, may repair to John Emley, living in the aforesaid Place and undoubtedly find Imployment. *The Pennsylvania Gazette*, September 11, 1746

Notice is hereby given, that a good School Master is very much wanted at the Landing, near New-Brunswick, where a full School may be had as soon as a Master will settle there, as there is not one in all that Place. *The New York Gazette Revived in the Weekly Post Boy*, March 16, 1747

Any schoolmaster, or mistress, that shall come well recommended to be of a sober behaviour and can spell well and write in a good common hand, may find encouragement for keeping of a school, by applying to William Foster, near Mountholly, in West-Jersey. *The Pennsylvania Gazette*, November 2, 1749

A single Person is wanted that is qualified for a School Master, Such a One will meet with Encouragement by applying to Martin Beekman or Abraham Dumont, near Rariton River, about seven Miles above the Landing. *The New York Gazette Revived in the Weekly Post Boy*, April 9, 1750

Wanted at the Boarding School at Burlington

A Sober single Man, qualified to teach the Latin Language, if he understands French, he will suit the better; Such a Person by applying to Thomas Powell, Master of the said School, will meet with good Encouragement. *The Pennsylvania Gazette*, January 6, 1763.

Moore's Town, Burlington County. Wanted, a Schoolmaster to teach the English Language grammatically, write a genteel Hand, Arithmetic, and the useful Branches of the Mathematics, and, if he could teach some Latin, it would be more agreeable to some of his Employers. Good encouragement will be given to one that comes well recommended. Enquire of John Cox or Joshua Bispham, living near the said place. *The Pennsylvania Gazette*, August 2, 1764

The colonists looked to advertisements and notices in the newspapers to learn about goods, newly arrived from Europe, which were offered for sale. For example:

Just imported from London and to be Sold by John Gifford of Perth Amboy, by Wholesale or Retail very reasonable for ready Money a Choice parcel of cutlary, Haberdasher hard ware as Knives and Forks, Scissors, Penknives, Silver and Steel strings for Watches, Ivory Combs, Mettle Buttons, fine French large and small Seed Necklaces, Garnets etc, Brass Box Dials, Nice Bath Thimbles, choice Spectacles of several Sorts, fine Snuff Boxes, smelling Bottles fine Lancets, Ivory Nutmeg Grators, four and six leafed Pocket Books, Buckles of sundry Sorts, and other sundry Goods. *The New York Weekly Journal*, June 30, 1740

Lot and Low in New York [have] imported in the last vessels from Europe, a fresh assortment of goods to be sold on the most reasonable terms at their Store, in Smith Street, among which are Women's white cotton stokings, men's white silk [stockings], white and brown tread stockings, silk breeches pattern, silk caps, women's white and black silk mits; black worsted mits; Irish camblets, tammies, calimancos, poplins, missinets, silverets, bombazeens, cambricks, linnens, silk handkerchiefs, pewter quart and pint and 1-2 tea pots, basons, dishes, plates, checks, hollands &c. *The New York Mercury*, May 4, 1761

Edward Arnold, near the Bridge in Elizabeth Town, has imported a general Assortment of Goods fit for the Season. Also a great Variety of Pictures, Paper Hangings, Looking Glasses and Tea Boards, all of which he will sell wholesale and retail, as cheap as they are to be had in New York. *The New York Mercury*, December 8, 1760

Just Imported and to be Sold by
Garret and George Meade
At their Store in Walnut-street

A Few hogsheads of old Barbados spirit fit for immediate use, rum, Muscovado Sugar in barrells, cotton and a few hogsheads of the best Teneriffe wine. *The Pennsylvania Journal*, September 1, 1763.

To be sold by
Stephen Skinner
In Perth Amboy

Madeira wine by the pipe and quarter cask, West India rum by the hogshead, molasses, rice and sundry other merchandize. *The New York Mercury*, February 6, 1764

Specialized services and products were also advertised:

A Parcel of seasoned Deck Plank of 30 feet long, very hearty and a Quantity of choice seasoned Ceader and Pine Board to be sold. Inquire of Frets Wright in Burlington. *The Pennsylvania Journal*, October 19, 1752

Salem County, May 26. Notice is hereby given to all Masters of Vessels and others that want Live Stock, such as sheep, hogs, ducks and geese, and all sorts of poultry. Any person favouring us with his Custom, may depend upon our doing our best endeavours to oblige them. *Pennsylvania Gazette*, June 7, 1770

Jonathan Hanson, Mast-maker

Takes this opportunity to acquaint the public in general and his friends in particular that he carries on the business of mast-making at the South side of Mr. James Penrose's wharf and has collected together a large variety of good Jersey, Delaware and New-England spars, and from his long experience and known abilities in the said business, he hopes his former customers and others will continue their custom, which will be gratefully acknowledged by their humble servant
                    Jonathan Hanson
The Pennsylvania Journal, May 25, 1769

A Fire Engine with a Suction Pipe, made by Nuttal of London, that will discharge 170 Gallons in a Minute, the Distance of Fifty Yards and may be worked either by the Suction Pipe when near a River or a Pond, or by the Cistern in the usual Way; lately imported, and to be sold, on no other account, that it being too large for the Use of Burlington, but would suit Philadelphia or any other populous Place. For Terms apply to Daniel Ellis, Esquire, Richard Well or William Dillwyn in Burlington.

N. B. They would take a smaller one in Exchange, if nearly new and in good Order. Proposals, either to purchase or to exchange, will be duly answered. *The Pennsylvania Chronicle*, March 16, 1767

To be Sold
by Nicholas Gouverneur

Ringwood refined and stamped Bar Iron and Share Moulds. The Quality of which Iron being tough and hard is very fir for ship building and County Work and is esteemed equal to the best of Sweedish Iron. *The Pennsylvania Journal*, May 24, 1759

The Chalybeate Waters

Near Glouster, having acquired great esteem, and having been much frequented, many persons, who gave them a regular trial, have found very singular and salutary effects from them; it is expected, as the excellent virtues of these springs become more known, many will be desirous to be convenient, where they can have frequent and easy access to them, every morning and evening, which will be necessary, as the waters drank at the spring are found to be much more efficacious. And, as many were prevented from attending them regularly the last season, from the difficulty of getting good and convenient lodging, the Subscriber takes this method to inform the ladies and gentlemen, that he has taken a large and convenient house in Glouster, very pleasantly situate, with six good lodging rooms on the first floor and will entertain those who are pleased to favour him, on very low and reasonable terms. *The Pennsylvania Gazette*, May 7, 1767

Philadelphia, November 19. We hear from Burligton that the new constructed light travelling Waggon, contrived by Richard Wells, Esq., on a full Trial last Week, was found to answer its Design to great Exactness. Among other Improvements, his Invention to discharge the Horses, in case of their running away, is particulary worth attention. This is done, at the expense of about a Pistole, by the Riders (in the inside of the Carriage) only pulling a String, when the Horses go off and leave the Carriage standing. An Invention that bids fair to be of great Use and Safety to those who ride in the close Carriages. *The Pennsylvania Gazette*, November 19, 1767

Mary Ogden (widow of Moses Ogden)

Acquaints the Public that the business of Shoe-making is carried on as usual and Orders for any Article in that way, shall be complied with in the best and expeditious Manner. *The New York Gazette and Weekly Mercury*, January 2, 1769

Books and other printed materials appeared to be items in demand. They varied in content and audience. Tomes on morality on the frontier were matched with the practical and entertaining Franklin almanacs:

Just published at New-York, and to be sold by the Printer hereof, a Companion for the Young People of North America, particularly recommended to those within the Provinces of New-York, New-Jersey, and Pennsylvania, calculated for the Promotion and Furtherance of Christian Decorum among Families, to excite a laudable and Christian Emulation among Young People, to pursue the Paths that lead to real Religion: By Attempting to discover the Beauties of a Virtuous life and to remove all objections against being religious. By Ahimaaz Harker, a Candidate for the Ministry. *The Pennsylvania Chronicle*, April 4, 1768

This Day is published and sold by Andrew Steuart, at the Bible-in-Heart, in Second Street, Philadelphia, a Narrative of the unhappy Life and miserable End of Samuel Stoddard, late of Egg-Harbour, in the County of Burlington, Province of West-New-Jersey, who was tried at the Supreme Court, held at Burlington aforesaid, on Saturday, the 6th of November, 1762, for the barbarous, cruel and inhuman Murder of Jacob Gale, late of Egg-Harbour aforesaid, of which Crime he was found guilty and, according to Sentence, was executed at the City of Burlington, on Tuesday the 23rd of the same Month. This Narrative, which is written in his own Hand, lays before you a series of unheard of Villainies and most atrocious Crimes . . . . It appears from his own Confessions that he was a crafty subtle Person and carried on his sinful Practices of Art and Dissimulation, especially with the Women.

Together with a most surprising Dream or Vision, which he had about 18 Months before his Death and his last Speech and dying Words, which he spoke to the People and delivered to the Sheriff in his last Moments. To the whole is added an Account of his Trial before the Hon. Robert H. Morris, Chief Justice of the said Province. *The Pennsylvania Gazette*, December 16, 1762

Just Published

The New-Jersey Almanack for the Year 1742 By William Ball, Philomath. Printed and Sold by B. Franklin. *The Pennsylvania Gazette*, October 22, 1741

Speedily will be published and sold by the Printers hereof, *Poor Richard's Almanack* for 1756, containing, besides the usual astronomical Calculations, a Variety of usual and entertaining Observations, viz. How Pennsylvania may have Three Millions, Two Hundred and Eighty Pounds in seven years, of which every Farmer may, if he pleases, have his share; the Praises of Astonomy; ditto of Religion, Conversations, Rules to be agreeable in it; how New Jersey may clear One Hundred Thousand Pounds in the year 1756; the advantage of Temperance in promoting a Man to High Station etc, etc. *The Pennsylvania Gazette*, October 23, 1755

Just Published, the Vade Mecum[91] for America: or, a Companion, for Traders and Travellers; Containing I. An exact and useful Table showing the Value of any Quantity of any Commodity, ready cast up from one Yard to One Pound to Ten Thousand; II A Table of Simple and Compound Interest; III The Names of the Towns and Counties in the several Provinces and Counties of New England, New-York and the Jersies; as also the several Counties in Pennsylvania, Maryland and Virginia, together with the Time and Setting of their Courts. . .*The Boston Weekly News-Letter*, April 20, 1732.

The Map of Pennsylvania, New Jersey and New-York Provinces by Mr. Evans we hear is now printing of and will soon be published. *The New York Gazette Revived in the Weekly Post Boy*, June 12, 1749

This Day is published (Price Six Pence) and to be sold
by the Printer hereof,

Liberty, a Poem

Lately found in a Bundle of Papers, said to be written by a
Hermit in New-Jersey
The Pennsylvania Chronicle, January 23, 1769

---

[91] Latin for "go with me".

To be sold by the Printer hereof, Hutchinson's History of the Massachusetts Bay --- Grove on the Last Supper --- Lady Montagu's Letters --- An Essay on Economy --- Considerations on the Propriety of imposing taxes on the British Colonies for the Purpose of raising a Revenue by Act of Parliament --- The Worship and Principles of the Church of England, being a Sermon preached by Thomas Davies, A.M. a Missionary from the Society --- Liberty, a Poem, lately found in a Bundle of Papers, said to be written by a Hermit in New-Jersey --- Answer to Pilate's Question -- What is Truth? --- The main Point, Faith distinguished from Counterfeits --- Directions for making Calcined or Pearl Ashes. *The Pennsylvania Chronicle*, May 22, 1769

Just Published and to be sold by the Printer hereof, Price 2s. 3d by the Dozen or 2s. 6d. single

A Complete Introduction to the Latin Tongue, wherein is contained all that is necessary to be learn'd of the Several Parts of Grammar, in a plain, easy, traditional Method, Comprehending the Substance of what has been taught by some of the best Grammarians, viz. Liily, Ruddiman, Phillipps, Holmes, Bp. Wettenhall, Cheever, Clark, Read &c. Published principally for the Use of the Grammar School at Newark and recommended to all who design to send their Children to New-Jersy College. *The New York Gazette revived in the Weekly Post Boy*, April 27, 1752

Now on Sale at the News-Printing Office in Beaver Street
Poor Roger's American Country
Almanack
Also to be sold at the same Place
The New-Jersey Almanack,
Copernicus Weather Guesser,
And Dutch Almanacks for 1769
The New York Journal or General Advertiser, December 1, 1768

Now in the Press and will shortly be published, the Hermit of New Jersey, a Collection of Poetical Essays, consisting of several short Fugitive Pieces. an Ode to Liberty and a Dialogue, between Lorenzo and the Hermit, on Human Happiness. *The Pennsylvania Chronicle*, December 5, 1768.

The Printer of this Paper proposes to offer to the Publick the whole contents of a Book, some time since published in England, said to be designed for use in the Colonies called "Memoirs of the Culture of Silk". . . . The Legislature of New Jersey, about 18 Months ago, had such a good

Opinion of it, that they passed a Law for the Encouragement of the Planting of Mulberry Trees, for it is a known Maxim, that where ever Mulberry Trees will thrive, there silk may be raised. . .*The New York Gazette or Weekly Post Boy*, January 9, 1767

Most of the items advertised for sale, however, related to everyday needs:

To Be Sold By James Abeel, Near the Albany-Pier Hollow-Ware of all kinds, made at Vesuvius Furnace, at Newark, in New-Jersey, and allowed by the best Judges to be far preferable to any made in America. *The New York Journal or General Advertiser*, June 23, 1768

To be sold by William Morris, jun., at his store in Trenton, opposite John Jenkins, good rum by the hogshead and salt by the hundred bushels, or less quantity, at the Philadelphia Price and freight up from thence. *The Pennsylvania Gazette*, April 10, 1746

Lately set up at Trenton in New-Jersey, a Planing and Blade Mill, by Isaac Harrow, an English Smith, who makes the undernamed Goods, viz.

Dripping Pans	Garden Spades	Garden Sheers
Frying Pans	Common Shovels	Glover Sheers
Chafing Dishes	Peel Shovels	Sheep Sheers
Broad Axes	Cooper Axes	Scythes
Falling Axes	smoothing Irons	Mill Saws
Carpenter Tools	Cow Bells	Cross cut Saws
Coopers Tools	Bark Shaves	Hand Saws
Tanners Knives	Pot Ladles	Coffee Roasters
Curriers Knives	Melting Ladles	Hay Knives
Skinners Knives	Fireshovel Pans	Fodder Knives
Ditching shovels	Cloathiers Sheers	Tobacco Knives

As also sundry other Sorts of Goods not herein mentioned; likewise all sorts of Iron Plates for Bell-making or any other Use. All Persons that have occasion for any of the above mentioned Goods, may be supplied by George Howell, Last-Maker in Chesnut-Street Philadelphia or by the Maker at Trenton aforesaid, at as Reasonable Rates as any that come from England. *The American Weekly Mercury*, September 5, 1734

Ogdens, Laight & Company
At Vesuvius Furnace
In Newark, East New Jersey

Makes all kinds of hollow ware and other castings usually made at air furnaces, such as forge hammers and anvils, pots, kettles, griddles, pyepans of various sizes, potash kettles and sugar boilers, calcining plates, plain and ornamental chimney backs, jaumb and herth plates neatly fitting each other, Bath stoves for burning coal, iron stoves for work shops and ship cabbins, Dutch and perpetual ovens, boiling plates, boxes for carriages of all kinds and sizes, half hundred and small weights. As their metal is of the best quality and the construction of their furnace manner of working and moulding the most improved; their ware is equal, if not superior, to any made in America or imported; particularly the metal for hammers and anvils for forges is excellently well tempered and found on repeated trials to be in general superior to English Hammers &tc.

N.B. Bar iron will be taken in payment for hammers and anvils at market price. *The New York Gazette and Weekly Mercury*, October 30, 1769

Choice Deer Skins of all Sorts to be sold by David Ball and Martha Swain, at Springfield in the Borough of Elizabeth, New Jersey, for Cash only. *The New York Mercury*, December 24, 1759

Benjamin Randolf . . . has for sale at the Sign of the Golden Eagle, in Chestnut street, a quantity of wooden Buttons of various and intends, if encouraged, to keep a general assortment of them.

The people of New Jersey (in general) wear no other kind of buttons and say they are the best and cheapest as can be bought both for strength and beauty and he doubts not but that they will soon recommend themselves to the public in general. *The Pennsylvania Gazette*, January 18, 1770

To be Sold
By John Mecom

Opposite the White Hart Tavern, in Albany-street, New Brunswick, the following articles which he will sell cheap for Cash: 3d, 4d, 5d, and 6d trunk nails, hob [nails] ditto, tacks and brads of all sorts, 4d, 6d, 8d, 10d, 12d, 20d and 24d nails; paving, socket, long and short firmer chisels, gouges of all sorts, plane irons, coopers drawing knives, carpenters hammers, broad axes and wood ditto, shoemakers knives and hammers, awls and awl hafts, shoe tacks, an assortment of horne, split bone and sham buck knives and forks, Barlow's and common pen-knives, buck, ditto, burnt bone ditto, pistol capt and cutteau knives of all sorts, brass, iron, japanned and steel snuffers, brass chafin dishes, round and square iron ditto, shovels and tongs with or without brass heads, an assortment of door, chest, cubboard and pad locks, hinges of all sorts, carpenters two feet and nine inch solid joint rules, iron squares, chalk lines, horn and ivory combs, steel and white metal shoe and knee buckles, mourning ditto, White's steel plate hand and pannel, tennent, sash and dovetail and compass saws, files and rasps, taylors and sheep shears, women scissors of all sorts, iron shovels and spades, long and short scythes, Scotch snuff in bladders, writing paper and a general assortment of sadlery and many other articles in the ironmongery and cutleryway, too tedious to mention. Said Mecom makes and sells all kinds of jewelellers and goldsmiths ware. Those therefore that will favor him with their Custom may depend upon being served on the utmost reasonable terms. *The New York Mercury*, June 18, 1764

Boston and Philadelphia Rum,
Bohea Tea
by the Chest; and
Carolina Leatheer
to be sold by
Reed and Pettit

The Pennsylvania Journal, January 12, 1764

To be disposed of very reasonably, a New, light and very genteel Post Chariot, esteemed by good Judges who have viewed it, equal to any imported from England. Enquire of M. Williamson, at Elizabeth-Town, in New Jersey. *The New York Mercury*, April 23, 1764

Aaron Miller, Clock-Maker in Elizabeth Town, New Jersey makes and sells all sorts of Clocks, after the Best Manner, with expedition; He likewise makes Compasses and Chains for Surveyors, as also Church Bells of any size, he having a Foundry for that Purpose and has cast several which have been approved to be good . . . *The New York Gazette revived in the Weekly Post Boy*, November 16, 1747

Best Flour in pound and half pound bottles; a quantity of good flax; muscovado and loaf sugar; rice, coffee, chocolate and tea; raisins in keggs; pepper, nutmeg and allspice; allom; copperas; brimstone; redwood and logwood; iron pots, kettles, skillets, bake irons, tea kettles, and said irons, knives and forks; best double worm grimlets; crumb creek scythe stones; a few barrels of Burlington Pork and sundry other things, to be sold by Benedict Dorsey, in Third-Street, nearly opposite the Work House. *The Pennsylvania Gazette*, September 10, 1767

To be sold at public Vendue, on Tuesday the 14th of August next, at the House of William Rea, in Kingwood, an Assortment of Shop Goods, consisting of Broadcloths, Kerseys, Naps, Serges, Saggathies, Damasks, London Shaloon, Durants, Tammies, Calimancoes of various colors, Thicksets, Fustians, Jeans, Cotton and striped Holland, narrow and wide Cottons and Linen Checks, Irish Linens, Cambricks, Lawns, Muslin, Camblets, Cambletees, Silk Handkerchiefs, sewing Silk, Ribbons, Tapes, Bindings, Earthen-ware, Delf-ware, Tea Cups and Saucers, Tea-pots, Scythes, Frying-pans, Window Glass, Wine Glasses, Felt Hats, Fine ditto, Pewter Dishes and Spoons, Tea Kettles, Knives and Forks, Scissors, Razors &c., Feather Bed and Bedding, black walnut desk, Tables, Chairs, Hand Irons, and sundry other household Goods and Farming Utensils. *The Pennsylvania Gazette*, June 21, 1764

To be sold at Newark, East New-Jersey, on Mr. Samuel Governieur's Wharf, a Vessel in Frame of the following Dimensions, That is to say, 41 Feet Keel, 18 Feet Beam, and 8 1/2 Feet Hold. Said Vessel measures about sixty four Tons, Carpenter's Tonnage; the Timber is well seasoned and very good. Any person inclining to purchase said Vessel, may apply to me, the Subscriber, living in Newark as aforesaid, who will sell said Vessel cheap.

Joshua Attwood
The New York Gazette and Weekly Mercury, April 11, 1768

Any Gentlemen of New York may be supplied with hogshead Hoops and Staves, by Marius Glanvil, Merchant at Bound-Brook, giving timely Notice, to Mr. Joshua Mullock, in Pearl Street,who has to sell a quantity of Oats by the Bushell and Irish Butter by the Firkin.

Marius Glanvil
The New York Mercury, January 3, 1763

The Sturgeon Manufactory is now carried on by Elijah Bond, near Trenton, under the care and inspection of Mrs. Broadfield, whose knowledge and experience in that branch of business is well known, where any person may be supplied, either for shipping or home consumption, at Fifteen Shillings for a single three-gallon keg, or Twelve Shillings and Six Pence by

the quantity, and in proportion for larger kegs: -- warranted good
N.B. They are also sold at Coxe and Furman's store, in Water Street, at the
same rates. *The Pennsylvania Chronicle*, May 30, 1768

Services, of course, of all varieties were also available.

Mount Holly, 7th Month 27,1768. The subscriber thinks it
necessary to inform the public in general, and his friends in particular, that
he is now carrying on his business of clock and watch making, mending, and
cleaning, at his house in Mountholly, where those who are pleased to favour
him with their custom, may depend upon its being done with the greatest
care and dispatch.

He also finds himself under the necessity to desire all those indebted
to him, to consider his late misfortune, and discharge their respective
balances immediately, in order to enable him to carry on his business in the
best manner his present low circumstances may admit, for the maintenance
of himself and family.
Richard Dickinson
New York Gazette and Weekly Post Boy, August 8, 1768

Wines and other alcohol products always sold well:

To Be Sold
by Robert Ritchie

A large parcel of Madeira and St. Michael's Wine, by the Pipe,
Hogshead or quarter cask, the most part of the latter is above three years old
and of a fine quality, Jamaica Spirit, muscavado sugar and an assortment of
dry goods, very cheap for cash or on short credit. *The Pennsylvania Journal*,
November 10, 1763

TO BE SOLD By
Robert Lettis Hooper, Junr;

At his Store in Water-Street, three Doors above Chesnut Street,
Three-penny, Ten-penny, Twelve-penny and Twenty-penny

Nails by the Barrel, Madeira Wine by the Pipe or Quarter Cask, Loaf Sugar,
and a Cargo of good Lisbon Salt, which he will retail at 2/10 per Bushel.
Robert L Hooper, Junr.
The Pennsylvania Journal, December 23, 1762

Choice rack'd Newark Cyder in barrels, to be sold by Francis Thurman, living in Wall Street, opposite Mr. Christopher Bancker'. *The New York Mercury*, May 12, 1755

Like our garage sales of today, the 1700s saw similar sales of assorted goods at the same time. There were also, then as now, estate sales. Imagine rummaging through the possessions of the late Governor himself!

Tomorrow being the twelfth day of this Instant, at two o'clock in the forenoon, at the Fort will be exposed to sale by Publick Vendue the following Goods, belonging to the Estate of the late deceased Excellency Governour Montgomery viz.

A fine new yellow Camblet Bed, lined with Silk and lac'd, which came from London with Captain Downing, with the bedding; one fine Field Bedstead and Curtains; some blew Cloth lately come from London, for Liveries; and some white Drop Cloth, with proper Trimming; some Broad Gold Lace; a very fine Medicine Chest with great variety of valuable Medicines; a parcel of Sweet-Meat & Jelly Glasses; a Case with 12 Knives and twelve Forks, with Silver Handles guilded; some good Barbados Rum; a considerable Quantity of Cytorn Water; a Flask with fine Jesseme Oyl; a fine Jack with Chain and Pullies; a large fixt Copper Boyling Pot; a large Iron Fire-Place; Iron Bars and Doors for a Copper; a large lined Fire Skreen and several other Things. All to be seen at the Fort.

And also at the same Time and Place there will be sold One Gold watch of Mr. Tomkins make and one Silver Watch; two Demi-Peak Saddles, one with blew Cloth Laced with Gold and the other Plain Furniture; two Hunting Saddles; one Pair of fine Pistols; a fine Fuzee mounted with Silver and one long Fowling Piece.
New York Gazette, October 11, 1731

Normally, however, the pickings were not so exotic:

"oxen, cows, horses, and young cattle, a pair of timber wheels, and waggon, a desk and bookcase, a case of walnut drawers, sundry feather beds, and other articles of household furniture, too tedious to mention. *The Pennsylvania Journal*, April 7, 1768

At the same time and place will also be sold, negroes, horses, cattle, sheep, hogs, waggons, ploughs, harrows, farmers utensils, household furniture, green wheat, and some shop goods. *The New York Gazette and Weekly Mercury*, April 11, 1768

Sadly, among the merchandise noticed for sale, were human lives. The colonists, only generations from being slaves themselves as serfs in feudal Europe, appeared to have little repulsion in enslaving others. A major portion of immigrants to the America in the 1700s came either as slaves from Africa or as indentured servants (whose captivity was for a dozen years or so rather than a lifetime) from Western Europe, principally England and Northern Ireland.

Just arrived here from Jersey, and to be seen (in the Ship Lark, Joshua Pickman Master, lying at the Long Wharff, Boston) very likely Boys and Girls time of Service for Years, to be disposed of by the said Master, or Jonathan Belcher, Esq., at his Warehouse in Merchant's Row. *The Boston News-Letter*, October 22, 1722

If any Person has a Jersey, English or Irish Boy's Time to dispose of that can Shave or Cook, may hear of a Purchaser by Enquiring of the Printer hereof. *The New England Weekly Journal*, July 15, 1740

A Jersey Girls time (aged about 16 who can handle her needle well) to be disposed of five years, Enquire of the Printer hereof and know further. *The New England Weekly Journal*, March 29, 1731

To Be Sold

A Very Likely Jersey Lads Time of Service for four Years, who was at the Carpenter's Trade several Years; and a likely Jersey Girls Time for Six Years and a half. Inquire of Capt. Peter DeJersey, in Winter Street, where the said servants may be seen. *The Boston Weekly News Letter*, May 25, 1738

To Be Sold

Two likely Negro Men, one of them a Ship-Carpenter by Trade and the other understands a Team or Plantation Work; Also a Negro Wench with two small children; the Wench understands House Work. Any Person inclining to purchase may apply to Susannah Marsh, Widow, at Perth-Amboy, who will dispose of them on reasonable Terms. *The New York Weekly Post Boy*, March 9, 1747

Just imported from the River Gambia, in the Schooner Sally, Barnard Badger, Master and to be sold at the Upper Ferry (called Benjamin Cooper's Ferry)[92], opposite to this City, a Parcel of Likely Men and Women

SLAVES

with some Boys and Girls of different Ages. Attendance will be given from the hours of nine to twelve o'Clock in the Morning and from three to six in the afternoon, by

W. Coxe, S. Oldman & Company

N.B. It is generally allowed that the Gambia Slaves are much more robust and tractable than any other Slaves from the Coast of Guinea and more capable of undergoing the Severity of the Winter Seasons in the North American Colonies, which occasions their being vastly more esteemed and coveted in this Province and those to the northward than any other Slave whatsoever. *The Pennsylvania Journal*, May 27, 1762

He has to dispose of (to be delivered when he embarks, probably the beginning of May) Two healthy, likely Negro Wenches, one about 29 Years of Age unmarried. The other about 24 Years old, married, has a very likely Child (a Girl) about 4 Years old and has no Children since. The Wenches have both had the Small-Pox and can be recommended from seven years Experience as sober, honest, good Servants. *The New York Journal or General Advertiser*, February 4, 1768

Said Thomas has two young negro wenches for sale, the one with or without two children. the other about fourteen years of age. *The New York Gazette and Weekly Mercury*, February 15, 1768

---

[92] Camden

On the Road: Transportation, Lodging and the Mail

A stage coach was the usual method of land transportation for those who did not want to walk or ride their own horse and competition was brisk. One enterprising line even had a futuristic ring to its marketing, calling its coach "The Flying Machine".

As today, colonial New Jersey's transportation had three "markets". The first, like the commuters of the 20th century, were those coming the shortest distances, from farms and villages, fifty miles or fewer away, to the larger towns like Elizabeth, Newark and New York City:

Good News for the Publick

The long wished for Ferry is now established and kept across the North [Hudson] River, from the Place called Powles's Hook to the City of New York; and Boats, properly constructed as well as for the Conveniency of the Passengers as for the Carrying over of Horses and Carriages, do now constantly ply from one Shore to the other. The Landing on the New York Side is fixed at the Dock commonly called Mesier's Dock, the Distance between the two Places being about three Quarters of a Mile, and as the Boats may pass and re-pass at all times of the Tide with almost equal Dispatch, it is thought by far the most convenient Place for a ferry of any yet established, or that can be established, from the Province of New-Jersey to the City of New-York. And what will give it the Preference by far of all the other Ferries, in the Winter season, is rarely a day happens but that the Boats may pass at this Ferry without being obstructed or endangered by Ice. Constant Attendance is given at Powles's Hook[93], by Michael Cornelisse, where the best of Stabling and Pasture is provided for Horses.

Also, that a Ferry is established and kept across the Kill Van Kull and the Boats constantly attend for that Purpose, at the Place formerly belonging to John Beak, and commonly called Moodases, situate near the Dutch Church, on Staten-Island, from whence Passengers are transported directly to the said Powles's Hook, so that a short, safe, easy and convenient Way is fixed by Means of the two Ferries for all Travellers passing to the City of New-York from any of the Southern Governments. *The New York Mercury*, July 16, 1764

A new erected Stage for Passengers kept by Thomas Davis of Newark, will set out from thence every Wednesday and Thursday, about 8

---

[93] Powles Hook is referred to often in the colonial press, principally because of its location across the Hudson from New York, in what today is Jersey City, originally a Dutch settlement. For some reason, the spelling "Paulus" later replaced "Powles", the location now known as Paulus Hook.

o'clock in the Morning, and proceed to the Ferry at Powles Hook, opposite the City of New-York; and from thence set out again for Newark, between 2 and 3 o'Clock in the Afternoons of the same Days. Fare for each Passenger, One Shilling. *The New York Gazette and Weekly Mercury*, April 11, 1768

The following is a new plan for a Stage Waggon, from Powlas-Hook, proposed by the Subscribers, viz. A Waggon to set off in the week (Sundays excepted) one from Powlas-Hook, and another from Mr. James Bank's, at Newark, at precisely half an hour past 7 o'clock in the morning, and at a half an hour past 4 in the evening; meet at Capt. Brown's Ferry and exchange passengers; and every Monday, Wednesday and Saturday, Ward's Waggon returns immediately from the said Ferry through Newark, to Elizabeth-Town; stays there until 3 o'clock in the afternoon, and then returns back again through Newark to Powlas-Hook. Passengers from Bank's will always be on a sure footing on the Elizabeth-Town days, as well as for other times, for if the waggon should be full from Elizabeth-Town, for New York, Ward will have other waggons ready at Bank's, for the passengers who wait there at the appointed times.

All persons who are pleased to encourage this undertaking, are desir'd to be punctual to the times above mentioned, as the waggons must be very exact in meeting at Capt. Brown's Ferry; and they may depend (God willing) on constant attendance and good usage,
By their humble Servants
Mathias Ward and John Thompson

Fare for passengers from Powlas-Hook, to Newark, is 1 shilling 6 pence, to Elizabeth-Town 1 shilling. To begin (if God permit) on Friday the 15th inst. *The New York Gazette and Weekly Mercury*, July 11, 1768

The Publick are desired to take Notice that the Stage from the New-Bridge, for Powles-Hook, will ride but once a week, after the Holy Days, till the Severity of the Season is over. Attendance will be give on every Tuesday, at the usual Hours, by the Publick's most obliged and
Very humble Servant,
Andrew Van Buskirk
The New York Gazette and Weekly Mercury, December 19, 1768

There was also a great deal of other travel within the Provinces of East and West New Jersey, but involving greater distances. This second market included, for example, the route between Trenton and New Brunswick which was a popular one, as the following indicate:

To Accomodate the Public

There will be a Stage Waggon set out from Trenton to Brunswick, Twice a Week, and back again, during next Summer. It will be fitted up with Benches and Cover'd over, so that the Passengers may sit Easy and Dry and Care will be taken to deliver Goods and Messages safe.

Note, the Waggon will set out, for the first Time, from Wm. Atlee's and Tho. Hooton's in Trenton.

On Monday the 27th of March next and continue going every Monday and Thursday from Trenton and return from Brunswick every Tuesday and Friday.

Every Passenger to pay two Shillings and Six Pence and Goods and Parcels at the cheapest Rates. *The American Weekly Mercury*, January 31, 1738

Whereas there was a Stage-Waggon that went twice a Week from Trenton to Brunswick and back again, in the Summer Season 1738, the Conveniency of which from its Certainty and Cheapness, and the inconveniences People labour'd under from being detained and paying extravagant Rates, has induced several People to apply to the Owners, promising their Assistance and Encouragement; This is to give Notice that the Stage-Waggon will be continued and go twice a Week certain, from Trenton Ferry every Monday and Thursday, and from Brunswick back again every Tuesday and Friday, during this Summer. The Waggon will be covered over so the Passengers may sit easy and dry, and care will be taken to deliver Goods and Messages safe. To encourage People to travel and Send Goods by the said Waggon, the following low Prices are fixed: Every Passenger 2 shilling, 6 pence Proc., Merchant Goods 2 shilling per C., Household Goods, Boxes etc at the cheapest Rates, perform'd by William Atlee and Joseph Yeates.

Note. The waggon will set out on Monday the 21st of this Instant April, from the Ferry at Trenton. *The Pennsylvania Gazette*, April 10, 1740

Notice is hereby given that William Wilson at Brunswick has purchased the Stage Waggon that belonged to William Atley of Trenton, which Waggon now goes constantly twice a Week, on the following Days, from Brunswick every Monday and Thursday and from Trenton every Tuesday and Friday, in which Waggon Passengers and Goods may be carried safe & dry. All Persons sending Goods from Philadelphia are desired to direct them to the care of Thomas Hutton in Trenton and those from New York to William Wilson in New Brunswick, where care shall be taken to forward them speedily and in good Order. *The Pennsylvania Journal*, June 7, 1744

Perth Amboy, being on the Coast and the capitol of the Eastern Division of the Province of New Jersey, was another popular stage destination:

This is to give Notice that on the first Day of May next, will be ready and well fixed, a Stage Wagon, to carry Passengers and Goods between Perth Amboy and Bordens-Town, which will attend at Amboy Ferry on every Tuesday, and at Bordens-Town every Thursday, on which Days all Persons intending to transport themselves or Goods, may be carried from either of said Places to the other for Four Shillings a Passenger and all Goods at reasonable Rates.

Security is given by the Wagoner for the safe conveying all Goods delivered into his Charge.

All Persons having Goods to transport as aforesaid may send them to Joseph Borden at Bordens-Town or Pontius Stelle at Amboy, who will take proper Care they shall be sent according to Order. *The American Weekly Mercury*, April 24, 1740

These are to inform all Persons that there is a Ferry settled from Amboy over to Statten-Island which is duly attended, for the convenience of those who have the occasion to pass and Repass that way. The Ferriage is Fourteen Pence Jersey Currency, for Man and Horse and Five Pence for a single Passenger. *The New York Gazette*, July 4, 1737

There was even a market for transportation and lodging for summertime getaways to the "Jersey Shore", an attraction that continues to this day:

Shrewsbury Stage from Burlington

This is to acquaint the Publick, that there is a convenient Stage Waggon erected and kept by Joseph Haight at the Sign of General Wolfe, in Burlington, to go from Burlington to Shrewsbury or elsewhere during the Summer Season, which Stage will go once a Week, if Occasion requires, from the date hereof and to carry six Persons. John Ferguson's Stage Boat will attend at Crooked Billet Wharff, in Philadelphia, every Wednesday in each Week and the Waggon will set off Thursday Morning. The Price of the Waggon to Shrewsbury will be Forty-five Shillings, if Four Persons or under, if above and not exceeding six, Fifty Shillings. All Gentlemen and Ladies that will please to favour us with their Custom may depend that there will be good Attendance given and the People civilly used by their humble servants,

Joseph Haight, John Ferguson
The Pennsylvania Gazette, June 14, 1764

This is to acquaint the Public that I have moved from Bordentown to Black Point, about 6 Miles from Shrewsbury Town, where all Gentlemen and Ladies, who intend going there for the Benefit of the Salts, may depend upon good Accommodation and best Usage from their humble Servant

John Brown

The Pennsylvania Gazette, June 14, 1764

But the third transportation market, then as now, was not within New Jersey but through it. The New York to Philadelphia run, with some brief stops in between, was the prime market, the object of much competition among both carriers and routes:

This is to give Notice that there is a Stage-Wagon now ready, which will attend at Perth Amboy Ferry every Tuesday and at Burlington every Thursday, they being the two most convenient Places for a speedy Transportation of any yet practiced from New-York to Philadelphia. Said Wagon will go the old Post Road from Amboy as far as the Crosswicks Bridge and if Ladings presents, will go with it to Burlington; or it may be carried at a small Expense from Bordenstown to Burlington or Philadelphia by Water, in a few hours Time. Passengers will be carried from either the first mentioned places to the other for Four Shillings Procl per P, and all Goods at reasonable Rates. Security is given by the Wagoner for the safe conveying all Goods delivered into his Charge.

All Persons having Goods to be sent per said Wagon may order them to be left with Pontius Stelle at Amboy or Joseph Borden at Bordens-Town, who will take proper Care they shall be sent according to Order. *The New York Weekly Journal*, May, 19, 1740

This is to give Notice to all Gentlemen and Ladies that have Occasion to transport either themselves, Goods, Wares, or Merchandizes from New-York to Philadelphia, that by the Subscriber, there is now a Stage-Boat well fitted for that Purpose, kept, and if Wind and Weather permit, shall attend at the late Col. Moore's Wharf in New-York every Wednesday in every week (and at other times if Occasion) and to proceed to the Ferry at Amboy on Thursday, where on Friday morning, a Stage Waggon well fitted, shall be ready to receive them and immediately proceed to Borden's Town where there is another Stage-Boat ready to receive them and proceed directly to Philadelphia. All People may depend upon the best Usage and all Passengers and Merchandize shall be transported at the same Rates as are customary from New-Brunswick to Trenton. And as the Passages by Water are much shorter and easier performed than the Brunswick-Way, and the Roads generally drier, it is hoped this Way will be found the most deserving of Encouragement.

Daniel O'Brien

N.B. The said O'Brien puts up at Mr. John Thompsons at the Thistle & Crown, known by the Name of Scotch Johnneys. *The New York Gazette Revived in the Weekly Post Boy*, November 26, 1750

Notice is hereby given to all Persons whatsoever that may have occasion to transport themselves, Goods or Merchandise from New-York to Philadelphia, that, by the Subscriber, there is a Stage Boat, well fitted for the purpose, kept, and, if the weather permits, shall attend at the late Colonel Moore's Wharf in New-York, every Wednesday in every Week (and on Saturday also if Freight offers) and to proceed to Mr. John Cluck's, near Amboy Ferry on Thursday, where there is a wharf storehouse and good Entertainment, and on Friday Morning, a Stage Waggon, well fitted, shall be ready to receive them and to proceed directly to Bordentown, where there is another Stage Boat ready to receive them and to take them to Philadelphia. And whatever Goods or Passengers shall come in the Stage Waggon to Mr. Cluck's shall be immediately taken off by the Boat on Friday morning and brought to New-York. All Persons may depend on the best Usage and all Passengers and Merchandise carried at the most Reasonable Rate. The said Waggon will attend at Mr. Cluck's on Tuesday Morning also, providing a Freight offers of not less Fifteen Shillings Value. And as Passages this way are generally performed in 48 hours less than they can be by way of New Brunswick, it is hoped that the Undertaking will meet with the encouragement it deserves.

Daniel O Brien

N.B. The said O Brien will touch at Amboy every Friday Morning, at Captain Steven's Wharf, and will do business for any Gentlemen or others at reasonable Rates. He likewise will do business for any Persons, living on the Stage Waggon Road, with the utmost Care, at a reasonable Rate, they sending their Orders in Writing with the Money. *The New York Gazette revived in the Weekly Post Boy*, March 25, 1751

This is to give notice to all persons that shall have occasion of transporting themselves, goods, wares, or merchandize from Philadelphia to New York or from the latter to the former, that by Joseph Borden, Jr. there is a stage boat, well fitted and kept for that purpose, and if wind and weather permit, will attend at the Crooked Billet Wharff in Philadelphia every Tuesday in every week and proceed up to Bordentown on Wednesday and on Thursday morning a stage-waggon, with a good awning, kept ny Joseph Richards, will be ready to receive them and proceed directly to John Cluck's opposite the City of Perth Amboy, who keeps a House of good entertainment and on Friday morning a stage-boat, well fitted and kept by Daniel Obryant will be ready to receive them and proceed directly to New York and give her attendance at the White Hall slip near the Half-moon battery.

If people be ready at the stage days and places, 'tis believed they may pass the quickest 30 or 40 hours, the cheapest and safest way that has yet been made use of, if due attendance be given by us, the subscribers, which we shall endeavour to do as near as possible. Also people living on or near the road may have their business done by letters or otherwise. Due care shall be taken in the delivery of letters, verbal messages &c. by us

Joseph Borden, Jun., Joseph Richards and Daniel Obryant

N.B. All passengers and goods that shall come to Bordentown on Sunday or Monday, in every or any week, by any Trenton shallops, White Hill shallop or Bordentown shallops or boats or in other whatsoever, whose wagon hire shall amount to Sixteen Shillings or upwards shall, upon first notice, have a waggon and be transported to the above Cluck's, opposite Amboy, where, if the stage-boat is not ready to receive them (but 'tis intended she shall), it must be allowed they have the greatest chance for dispatch of any other place whatsoever, for all the Brunswick, the place above Brunswick called the Landing and all the river boats must pass that place in whom people may have passage. *Pennsylvania Gazette*, April 4, 1751

The Public is hereby informed that there is a Ferry erected at and opposite Bordentown, from which there is an exceeding good Road, well cleared and safe for Carriages that leads in to the Post Road, about five miles above Bristol, which makes it the nearest and by far the pleasantest Road from Philadelphia to Bordentown, Allentown, Amboy, Middletown, Shrewsbury, Freehold &c. and is several Miles nearer to New York than the Post Road. There are good Boats and good Houses of Entertainment at both the aforesaid Ferries and also at convenient Stages, on the Roads leading to the several Places above mentioned.

J. Borden, jun. J. Kirkbride

N.B. Any Number of Gentlemen or Ladies, not exceeding five, may have a ganteel covered light Waggon to convey them from Bordentown to Shrewsbury, upon any Monday, from the date hereof, for Thirty-five Shillings, the Run down, by me.

B. Cook

The Pennsylvania Gazette, August 12, 1762

This is to give Notice to the Public that the Stage Waggon kept by James Barnhill in Elm Street, near Vine Street, in Philadelphia and John Masherew, at the Blazing Star, near New-York, intend to perform the Journey from Philadelphia to New-York in two days, and from there to Philadelphia in two Days also, commencing the 14th of April next and to continue seven months, viz. to the 14th of November; and the remaining five months of the year in three days (the waggon seats to be set on springs). They purpose to set off from New-York to Philadelphia on Mondays and

Thursdays as they now do, punctually at sun-rise, and change their Passengers at Prince Town and return to Philadelphia and New York the following Days. The price each Passenger ten shillings to Prince Town, ten shillings to Powle's Hook, opposite New-York, Ferriage free, and three pence each mile any distance between. Gentlemen and Ladies who are pleased to favor us with their custom, may depend upon due attendance and civil usage,

By their Humble Servants
John Barnhill and John Mesherew
The Pennsylvania Journal, February 13, 1766

That the Stage-Waggons, kept by John Barnhill, in Elm Street, in Philadelphia, and John Mercereau, at the New Blazing Star, near New York, continues their stages in two Days, from Powles-Hook Ferry. opposite New York, to Philadelphia; returns from Philadelphia to Powles Hook in two Days also; they will endeavour to oblige the Publick by keeping the best of Waggons and sober Drivers, and sets out from Powles-Hook and Philadelphia, on Mondays and Thursdays, punctually at Sunrise and meets at Prince Town the same Nights, to exchange Passengers, and to return the day after; Those who are kind enough to encourage the Undertaking, are desired to cross Powles-Hook Ferry the Evening before, as they must set off early; The Price for each Passenger is Ten Shillings to Prince Town, and from thence to Philadelphia, Ten Shillings more, Ferriage free. There will also be but two Waggons, but four sets of fresh Horses, so it will be very safe for any Person to send Goods, as there are but two Drivers, they may exchange their Goods without any Mistake. Persons may now go from New York to Philadelphia and back again in five Days, and remain in Philadelphia two Nights and one Day to do their Business in. The Public may be assured that this Road is much the shortest, than any other to Philadelphia, and regular stages will be kept by the Publick's obliged humble Servants.

John Mercereau and John Barnhill
The New York Gazette or Weekly Post Boy, May 9, 1768

Since almost any trip away from home in the 1700s included at least one night's lodgings elsewhere, inns were important to the traveller. Innkeepers, like merchants anywhere, had to vie for the business:

Capt. Terret Lester is Removed to the House where Thomas Inglis lived on the Dock in Amboy, where there is good entertainment for Man and Horse. He also keeps a Passage-Boat to ply between New York and Amboy, by which Passengers may be accommodated and Goods carefully conveyed and also stored in his Ware-House when there is occasion. *The New York Gazette*, April 3, 1738

Margaret Johnson (formerly the Widow Cheetwood) Who, for many

Years, kept the Nag's Head Tavern, near the Bridge, in Elizabeth-Town, begs leave to inform her old Customers and Friends, that she now keeps a Public House, near the Bridge, in Elizabeth-Town, in the large and commodious House lately belonging to the Estate of Colonel Peter Schuyler, deceased, commonly called the White House, at the sign of the Nag's Head, where good Entertainment may be had, both for Man and Horse. *The New York Gazette*, September 19, 1763

The Subscriber, at the Royal Oak Inn, in Trenton, after returning thanks to the Public in general, and his friends in particular, begs leave to acquaint them, that he is removed from the house he lately lived in, to the brick corner house, opposite Samuel Tucker's Esq; formerly kept by Robert Rutherford, where he hopes for the continuance of their favours, to their very humble servant,
Renselaer Williams
The Pennsylvania Chronicle, May 23, 1768

The Subscriber, who lately kept the King's Arms Tavern, in Princeton, begs Leave to acquaint his Friends in particular, and the Public in general, that he has removed to the commodious Inn, in Princeton, long known by the name Hudibras; where having furnished the House with the best of Liquors, and proposing from time to time to supply it with the best Provisions he can procure in the Situation; he flatters himself that he should be able to entertain Travellers and others in the best Manner, and he is determined to apply himself to give general Satisfaction. He hopes for the Continuation of the Custom of his Friends, and that of any other Gentlemen, who will please to favour him with their Custom, shall be gratefully acknowledged; by the Public's
Obliged humble Servant
Jacob Hyer

N.B. As the Stage-Waggons from New-York to Philadelphia, and back, put up at his house, any Person inclining to send Goods or Parcels by that Conveyance, may depend on their being carefully forwarded.
He continues to follow the Hatter's Business in all its Branches, as usual.
The New York Gazette or Weekly Post Boy, June 20, 1768

The Subscriber takes this method to acquaint the Public, that she has opened her house opposite the college, in Princeton, New-Jersey, to accommodate all persons who travel in the stage-waggons, or otherways, with private lodging.
Parnel Davenport

N.B. The said Parnel Davenport, widow, continues boarding as usual. *The Pennsylvania Chronicle*, July 4, 1768

Mrs. Johnson Notifies the Public that she has removed to the large and commodius House, commonly called the White House, at the Sign of the Duke of Rutland, in Elizabeth-Town, where she proposes to keep public House of Entertainment, and hopes for the Favour of her old Customers. *The Pennsylvania Gazette*, June 30, 1768

Publick Notice is hereby given that John Graham, who formerly kept the Sign of the Duke of York, at White-Hall, in New York, now keeps the Sign of the Marquis of Granby, in Elizabeth-Town, in the most Publick part of the Town and the most noted Tavern for these many Years past, formerly kept by Mrs. Chetwood, but lately by Mr. John Joline. All Gentlemen Travellers or others, who will be so kind as to favour him with their Custom, may depend upon being used well; he is well provided with Pasture and Stabling.

John Graham

New York Mercury, May 14, 1764

The Publick is hereby informed that the Subscriber, who lately kept a Publick-House at the Sign of the Black Horse, in Mansfield, is removed to Trenton, where he keeps a Publick-House at the Sign of the King of Prussia, in King Street and is well accommodated with Houseroom, Stabling and Pasture. All Travellers, Gentlemen and Ladies and others that will favour him with their Custom may depend upon good Entertainment, both for themselves and their Horses and civil treatment from their humble Servant,

Richard Cox

The Pennsylvania Gazette, June 7, 1764

The Public are hereby informed that the Subscriber has just opened, a genteel house of entertainment in the City of New-Brunswick, at the Sign of the Tree of Liberty, where travellers and others may be well accommodated with every Thing necessary for their comfort and subsistence. He hopes for his Endeavours to merit the Esteem of the Public; he may be gratified with a reasonable share of their Custom.

Henry Bicker

N.B. He still carries on the Business of a Hatter, where Persons may always be supplied with Hats of every Sort and Quality, such as the best Beavers and Castors. *The New York Journal or General Advertiser*, October 16, 1766

Verdine Elsworth

Begs leave to acquaint the Public in general that he has lately removed from New York, to Powles-Hook Ferry and has improved and fitted up the House belonging to the Ferry in the best Manner, for the

Entertainment of Travellers and also such of his Friends as chuse to favour him with their Custom, who may depend upon being entertained in the genteelest Manner. And that he has also a very neat cover'd waggon and Pair of Horses which they may at any Time be accommodated with, upon timely Notice, as also with Horses and Chairs and likewise Saddle Horses. By their very Humble Servant,

Verdine Elsworth

The New York Gazette and Weekly Mercury, July 3, 1769

Necessarily associated with transportation and inns was the colonial postal service, which followed the same routes and used the taverns as collection boxes. The following announcement of an expansion in service shows the extent of the colonial postal system as of 1732:

General Post Office in Virginia, July 8. The Post Office that was first begun in America 38 years ago has never yet been established Southward of Philadelphia, but since the Hon. Alexander Spotswood, Esq. has been appointed Post-Master-General of all his Majesty's Dominions in America and the West-Indies, he has been taking measures to carry the Post toward the South Coasts, and by his Care and Application, has extended it about 350 Miles further than the City of Philadelphia to the City of Williamsburg in Virginia. *The New York Gazette*, July 31, 1732

New Jersey residents would be surprised to learn that the General Post Office was located in Woodbridge, New Jersey with New York City and Philadelphia being merely local post offices which received their concessions from Woodbridge. But, as the next account indicates, Woodbridge lost its favored position to better and quicker serve the postal patron in light of the traffic between the two cities.

For the Benefit of Trade and Commerce
General Post Office, Woodbridge, January 2, 1764

This Day at 1 o'Clock, a Post Rider with the Mail for Philadelphia sets out from New York Post Office, for the First Time, in order that the Stage between those two Cities, may be performed three times a Week, if Weather permits, by which means letters will pass from one to the other in less than 24 hours. The Mail is to reach Philadelphia on Tuesday and to return to New York before Wednesday Noon, to be discharged again from New York Office at 1 o'Clock on Wednesday to be in Philadelphia on Thursday; It is to be at New York again on Friday and at Philadelphia on Saturday; and so to continue Weekly till further Orders. *The New York Mercury*, January 2, 1764

The less popular routes were privately serviced:

Joseph Burwell, Post Rider

Takes this method to inform the Public that he has engaged to ride from the Union Iron works, in New Jersey to Philadelphia, for one year commencing the first day of December, 1768; that during the three Winter months, viz. December, January and February, he performs the said Stage once in two weeks and the other nine months, he proposes to ride weekly. He sets out from his house in Quaker Town, on Wednesday, arrives at the Indian King, in Market-street, Philadelphia, on Thursday morning and sets out again in the afternoon, on his return back. Such Persons who have any Business to transact, that he can serve them in, are desired to be ready at the times appointed, when he will receive their commands and execute the same, with the greatest Care and Fidelity, with grateful Acknowledgments to those who are pleased to employ him. *The Pennsylvania Gazette*, December 22, 1768

The U.S. Postal Service's tradition that the mail must go through, despite adversities, is proven by the following account on one colonial postman's perseverance:

New York, May 29. On Thursday Night last the Post Boy, that rides between New Brunswick and this City, had his horse stole out of the Stable at Brunswick Ferry, and another not being readily to be got, he came off with the Mail on his Back and travelled Ten Miles on Foot, by which means we have no Philadelphia News Papers this Week, he not being able to bring them along on his Back from Brunswick. However, they came to Hand last Night, but we don't find any Thing very material in them. *The New York Gazette or Weekly Post Boy*, May 29, 1769

Notice was given to the "Publick" of businesses of all varieties that were for sale. For example:

A very good Fulling Mill at Fishing Creek, in the County of Cape May, with all the Materials, as with Press, Shears, Trenters, and Copper, with One Hundred Acres of Land. *The Pennsylvania Gazette*, October 16, 1735

Philadelphia, September 15, 1748. This is to give publick notice that in West New Jersey and the County of Burlington, in the Township of Chesterfield, that there is to be sold a good malt-house made of brick work, and a brew- house, joining together, with copper tubs, coolers, malt-mill, spouts and pumps, all convenient for the brewing of good beer, situate at Borden-town, on a large wharff, upon the River Delaware, which is so convenient, that you may lower your beer into the boats or shallops, which are passing almost every day either to Philadelphia, Burlington or Trenton, and also at the other end of the brew-house, on the said River, there is also a large waggon-road to the several store houses on the said River, where the waggons are passing almost every day, and by this conveniency, you may send your beer to any of the towns round about. Any person inclining to purchase the above, may apply to
Nathaniel Farnsworth
The Pennsylvania Gazette, September 15, 1748

To be sold or lett for a term of years by Benjamin Biles, at Trenton, a tanyard, well accustomed, with a lot of ground of two acres and a third of an acre, a good bark-house, mill-house, bark-mill, beam-house, a good stone currying shop and leather-house, vatts enough to tan 800 hides, besides calf-skins, per year. . . *Pennsylvania Gazette*, January 1, 1751

A Large and commodius well built grist-mill with two pairs of stones, two water wheels, within the house, turned by a constant stream of water, three boulting chests, with conveniences for screening the wheat, boulting and hoisting the meal by water, with other utensils necessary for the same. . . *Pennsylvania Gazette*, January 1, 1751

To be sold at publick Vendue, on Wednesday the first Day of June next, on the Premises or at a Private Sale Before, situated in the County of Hunterdon, on Lamenton River, in New Jersey, a good New Forge or Finery, with three Pairs of Bellows and three Fire Places and all the Utensils belonging to it, with a good Coal-house and Out-houses for Forge-Men to live in. *The Pennsylvania Gazette*, April 28, 1763

A Commodious Brew-House 70 Feet long and 48 Feet wide, with all the Appurtenances thereunto belonging, being in very good order; it has in it a Malt Cellar of 70 Feet long and 14 Feet wide, being an earthen Floor, with a good Brick Arch overhead; the Copper containing 23 Barrels; in said Brew-House is a very good Malt Mill which goes with a Horse; . . . with a very good Beer Cellar with a Brick Floor;. . . with a stream of very good Water running through the same which was never known to fail in providing a sufficient Supply of Water for said Brew-House . . . Any Person inclining to purchase same may be supplied with two Negroes who understand something considerable of the Brewing business. . . .*The New York Gazette*, September 19, 1763

A Saw-mill, together with the lands thereunto belonging, lying on one of the South Branches of the Little Egg Harbour River, within 4 Miles of a Landing, where the Produce may be transported either to New York or Philadelphia. . . Any Person inclining to Purchase may know the Terms by applying to John West, at the Old Ferry, Philadelphia. *The Pennsylvania Gazette*, October 18, 1763

The Ferry over Delaware, commonly called Dunk's Ferry, near the mouth of Neshamminy, in Buck's County, Pennsylvania, about 16 miles from Philadelphia, on the great road to Burlington. It is a very good situation for a tavern, there being a great number of travellers passing that way, both by land and water. There is a good house for the purpose and 100 acres of good Land, with proper ferry-boats in good order. To be entered on in May next. For further particulars, enquire of John Kidd, near the premises. *The Pennsylvania Gazette*, January 21, 1768

The Subscriber, having for many years, made it her business to cure Sturgeon in North America, which has been esteemed preferable to any manufactured by other persons and Obtained the first premium of Fifty Pounds sterling from the society of arts and commerce in London; takes this method of acquainting the public, that she intends, as soon as possible, to leave this part of the world, but is desirous and willing to instruct a sober industrious person or family in the whole art, secret and mystery of manufacturing sturgeon in the several branches, consisting of making isinglass, pickling, cavear, glue, and oil; the subscriber has lately fallen upon a method of doing the isinglass equal to any whatever. Whoever has a mind to treat with the subscriber, may apply to her at Mr. Elijah Bond's fishery near Trenton, where is every thing convenient for carrying on the business, and plenty of fish throughout the whole year furnished by Mr. Bond's fish pond.

Margaret Broadfield

N.B. The sturgeon manufactory is now carried on by Elijah Bond, near Trenton, under the care and inspection of Mrs. Broadfield, whose knowledge and experience in that branch of business is well known, where any person may be supplied, either for shipping or home consumption, at Fifteen Shillings for a single three-gallon kegg, or Twelve Shillings and Six Pence by the quantity, and in proportion for larger keggs: -- warranted good

N.B. They are also sold at Coxe and Furman's store, in Water Street, at the same rates. *The Pennsylvania Gazette*, August 11, 1768

A Forge, on Mononlopan river, commonly called South river, not above four miles from the landing on said river, where boats go to New-York and it is the nearest but one to a landing, of any forge in the Provinces of New-York or New-Jersey so that all the land carriage is but four miles; the forge has three fires and is capable to make 120 tons of barr-iron per annum, with as ag good a stream as most any in the country . . . The only reason for disposing of the works is that the Owners live at some distance and cannot easily overlook the works. Pigs may be had at New York at the market-price and will not cost above 6s. or 7s. per ton for transportation, till within four miles of the works; or, if the purchasers should be inclined to turn the works into a blomary, ore of a good quality is at hand in great quantities and to be had on very reasonable terms. There is a sufficient quantity of coals on hand to make 40 or 50 tons of barr-iron and 1000 cords of wood ready cut to carry on the coaling business in the spring . . . Teams of oxen, carriages and other utensils will be sold at first cost. *The Pennsylvania Journal*, February 19, 1767

New York, May 4. We hear from Newark that Ezekiel Ball, an ingenious Mechanic, has invented a new Machine for leveling the Roads with great Expedition; it is made in the form of a Triangle, with a small expense, and is drawn by Horses, cutting off the Ridges and filling in the Ruts to Admiration and deserves to be highly recommended to the public; if any Gentleman is desirous of knowing in what Manner it is made, the Model may be now seen at his house. *The New York Journal or General Advertiser*, May 4, 1769

A Fulling-mill and dye-house, with all the tools and utensils on the business of a fuller and dyer at Trenton, now in the possession of the subscriber, living in Trenton, on reasonable terms. *The Pennsylvania Gazette*, June 28, 1753

The Iron works in Mount Holly was the subject of a number of advertisements in the early 1760s. Apparently, it was a troubled business :

The Iron Works, known by the name of Mountholly Ironworks, viz. one Forge or Finery with three Fireplaces, three Pair of Bellows, and all the Utensils thereunto belonging. Also one forge or Chasery, with One Fire Place and One Pair of Bellows, with all the Utensils belonging to it, built for the Conveniency of the Hammer- Man, where he meets with no interruption from the Finers, both built upon the main Branch of the Rancocus-Creek,

Water carriage from the Forges to Philadelphia, a large compleat Coal-House, four good framed Dwelling-Houses, three of which are made for two Tenements each, for the workman. . . with about 500 Tons of Bog iron on the Bank. . . Any Person inclining to Purchase may be informed of the Price and the Incumbrances upon it by applying to

Peter Bard

The Pennsylvania Gazette, October 27, 1763

To be sold by way of Public Vendue, on Tuesday, the First day of May next, at the House of Zachariah Rozell, Innholder, at Mounyholly, the Iron-works, commonly called and known by the Name of Mountholly Ironworks, consisting of one Finerey, with three Fire-places, and three Pair of Bellows and all the other Apparatus for carrying on the Works; also a Chasery, with one Fire-place and one pair of Bellows, for the Conveniency of the Hammer-man, where he meets with no interruption from the Finers; a commodius Coal-house, with about 500 tons of bog ore on the Bank, several commodius houses to accomodate the Workmen; also 360 acres of land, six acres of which are cleared and drained Meadow and fifteen acres more may be made; a genteel Dwelling-house with a handsome Garden and other Conveniences, pleasantly situated for the Owner or Overseer. . . There is plenty of Wood contiguous to the Works. *The Pennsylvania Gazette*, April 19, 1764

Philadelphia, April 23, 1764. Whereas public Notice was given in the Gazette of last Week that the Mount-holly Iron-Works would be exposed to Sale by public Vendue, on the first Day of May next, We, the subscribers, being Assignees in Trust to the Estate of James Child, do think it our Duty to inform the Public that we are possessed of a mortgage on the said Estate, by which we claim 470 pounds, and in Consequence of this Right, did some time since order a Writ of Ejectment against the Tenant in Possession, which Writ, we are informed, has been since issued and served, so that the Cause is now In Court.

Samuel Neave, Jeremiah Ward, Francis Richardson
The Pennsylvania Gazette, April 26, 1764

Mount-Holly, May 2, 1764. Whereas an Advertisement was published in the last Pennsylvania Gazette, by the Assignees of James Child, in Opposition to the sale of Mount-Holly Iron-Works, this is to give Public

Notice that the Tenant in Possession, conceiving that James Child has no Equitable Right to the Monies said to be Due on the Mortgage and, of Consequence, none on the Land, he is determined to contend the Matter. In the mean time to satisfy the Scruples of the Purchaser, the Subscriber will consent that the whole Monies pretended to be due upon the Mortgage, shall be retained by the Purchaser, and if the final Decision of the Suit shall be in Favour of the Mortgagee, then the Purchaser shall be discharged by Receipt upon the Payment of the Money in his hands to the Mortgagee or his Assignees; otherwise the money reserved, to be paid to the Subscriber. Good Security shall be given for the Performance of the above Articles to indemnify the Purchaser.

To be sold by Public Venue, on Saturday, the 19th of the instant May, the above said Mount-Holly Iron-works with all the Apparatus thereunto belonging, Houses, Land &c., as mentioned in a former Advertisement, and which was adjourned in order to obviate the Difficulty raised by said Advertisement. *The Pennsylvania Gazette*, May 10, 1764

Lost and Found

Public Notices inserted in the newspapers also sought the return of loss or stolen items:

Stolen away from Benjamin Smith in Trentown, on the 22nd Day of October, two Horses, one a large Dapell grey about Seven Years old, he Paces pretty fast, has no Brand, one of his fore Legs is crooked, his knees bends in pretty much. The other a Middlesize, of a dark Brown, about Nine Years Old, he will go a small travelling pace, has two Slits in his off Ear and one hind Foot white. Whoever secures the said Horses, with the Person that took them away, and gives Notice to the Owner, shall have Five Pound as a Reward, and all reasonable Charges, paid by
Benjamin Smith
The American Weekly Mercury, October 26, 1732

On the 3d Instant was taken away from the Plantation of Mr. Samuel Bayard at Hobook in New-Jersey, a large new Perriagua, of about 31 Foot in length, in breadth 5 Foot, the Side under the Wales painted white, between the Rails blue, the inside dark red, made of three pieces of White-wood, with a small Keel, painted on the Quarters with a Kind of a Snake, on each side of the Stern-post is a Star painted yellow; the Head of the Stern is gouged out to lay the Boltsprit in and on her Forecastle is a Cleet to fix the Boltsprit in. Whoever takes up the said Perriagua and gives Notice so that she may be had again, shall have Twenty Shillings Reward, paid by
Samuel Bayard
The New-York Gazette, April 16, 1733

Whereas a large Brass Wash Kettle and a Parrot Cage were some time ago lost out of a Brunswick Boat or carried to a wrong Place by Mistake, whoever can give an Account thereof to the Printer of this Paper so that the Owner may have them again shall have Five Shillings Reward with Thanks. *The New York Weekly Journal*, June 15, 1741

Stolen or turn'd adrift on Tuesday Night, the 28th Day of December, 1742, from the Town Wharff in the City of Burlington, a small Ferry-Boat about 14 feet Keel and about 5 feet and a half wide, with a plain upper streak and a Bead on the lower Edge, one Side something crusht, and a new piece put in, and Benches from the after-Thwart to the Main-Thwart on each Side, about 4 Years old, with Rudder-Irons, and a small Chain, the Locker-Board abaft is lost.

Whoever takes up the said Boat and brings her to the City of Burlington, or gives Notice thereof to Thomas Hunloke, of the said City of Burlington, shall be rewarded for their Care and Trouble.

Thomas Hunloke

The Pennsylvania Gazette, January 13, 1743

Lost a few Days ago, a double Letter-Case or Pocket-Book with 4 Tickets of the Elizabeth Town Raway Lottery in it; all belong to --- Bruster, one of which is a prize of 1 pound 8 shilling, which is marked on it in Figures; also another Ticket in the same Lottery which is a prize of 1 pound 8 shilling, with John Steelman's name on it; Likewise a New York Lottery Ticket belonging to Henry Davis; and several Papers of Consequence, which are of no Service to any Body but the rightful Owner. Whoever has found the same, and will bring it to Obadiah Wells or the Printer hereof, shall have Ten Shillings Reward and no Questions ask'd. *The New York Gazette revived in the Weekly Post-Boy*, December 5, 1748

Went adrift from the Ship Samuel and Judith, at Sandy-Hook, the 27th of last Month, a ship's Yawl, 20 Foot long and about 6 foot Broad, with five Oars, suppose to be drove ashore under the High Land of Navesink; Whoever finds the said Yawl and brings her to the said Ship shall have 40 Shillings Reward, paid by John Griffiths. *The New York Gazette Revived in the Weekly Post Boy*, November 13, 1749

Lost, last Fall, in Morris-Town, in East Jersey, a Dog, of the Pointer kind, all white, his Tail dockt and has had his off thigh broke; answers to the name Cato. Whoever brings the said Dog to Mr. Waters at Elizabeth Town Point shall have Five Shillings Reward. *The New York Gazette revived in the Weekly Post Boy*, March 25, 1751

Was put upon a Trenton Shallop, a considerable time ago, at Philadelphia and brought up to Trenton, by Asher Carter, a quantity of new Pewter. Any Person, proving their Property and paying Charges, may have it again by applying to Nathaniel Parker, at Trenton Ferry. *The Pennsylvania Gazette*, April 19, 1764

A Mistake

On Friday the 6th instant, two pieces of dowlas, and one piece of brown Shallon, tied together, and directed to William Graham, Taylor, at Elizabeth-Town, were put on board of a Boat at White-Hall Wharf, which was then supposed to be the Boat commanded by Capt. Dobbs, belonging to Elizabeth-Town; but as said Graham has not received the said Goods, and as Capt. Dobbs denies that they were put on board his Boat, and carried elsewhere by mistake, the Person therefore who has them will please to deliver them to the Printer hereof, or to said Graham of Elizabeth-Town, and he will thankfully be rewarded for same. *The New York Mercury*, January 11, 1768

Some time since, a Sack of Furs, that came in the Stage from Philadelphia, was sent to John Dennis of Elizabeth Town, thro' a mistake, for one that he expected from thence, they resembling each other. Any person that will return said John Dennis his furs, shall have theirs, proving their property and paying the charges of this advertisement. *The New York Mercury*, June 21, 1756

Lost, last Fall, in Morris-Town, in East Jersey, a Dog, of the Pointer kind, all white, his Tail dockt and has had his off thigh broke; answers to the name Cato. Whoever brings the said Dog to Mr. Waters at Elizabeth Town Point shall have Five Shillings Reward. *The New York Gazette revived in the Weekly Post Boy*, March 25, 1751

Glouster, August 16. Stolen from the subscriber, on Monday night the 14th of this instant, 4 wheels of a large waggon, well tiered with black gum hubs, one of the boxes of the little wheels loose and cannot be fastened without new bushing; also a new skiff, 18 feet keel, 4 feet beam, Moses bottom, a chain ten feet long and the upper streaks painted a lead colour. If any person or persons will give information, so that the thieves may be brought to justice, shall Three Pounds reward, or Thirty Shillings for the Wheels and Skiff paid by

William Hugg

The Pennsylvania Gazette, August 24, 1769

The Notices also sought the owners of many types of property that had been found and searched for the owner.

Taken up a Drift, in Salem Creek, on the 20th of January, about 200 Feet of 2 Inch Oak Plank, a Quantity of Oak Scantling, some Inch Cedar Boards, in a Raft, with a Battoe. The Owner of such Raft and Battoe, by applying to Ranier Vanhist, Esq., living on Salem Creek, and proving his Property and paying the Charges, may have them again. *The Pennsylvania Journal*, February 25, 1762

Found, a Silver Watch, on the Great Road leading from Haddonfield to Glouster, the 21st of January last. The Owner, proving his Property, and paying Charges, may have it again, by applying to Benjamin Sykes, living in Chesterfield, Burlington County. *The Pennsylvania Gazette*, February 9, 1764

Taken up, a seven inch cable almost new, also an anchor of about 200 weight. Any Person claiming the same may have it again by sending or applying at the House of Isaac Stathem in Greenwich, Cumberland County. *The Pennsylvania Journal*, November 26, 1767

Trenton, December 30, 1765. There is now in our Possession four Kegs, without any Direction, that were delivered on board one of our Boats at Philadelphia, about nine Months ago; any Person that proves their Property to said Kegs and pays the charges may have them back again.
Furman and Hunt
The Pennsylvania Gazette, January 9, 1766

February 13, 1768. Taken up, adrift, about the eighth of January last, at the Mouth of Cohansey Creek, a Moses built Boat, about the size of a Ship's Yawl. whoever has lost the same, by applying to Benjamin Reeve, living in Greenwich Town, Cumberland County, West New-Jersey, proving their Property, and paying Charges, may have it again. *The Pennsylvania Chronicle*, February 15, 1768

Was left at Powles-Hook Ferry House, in New York, some of them a considerable time ago, 2 Surtouts and a close bodied coat. Whoever has left them, by applying to William Sloe at the Fery House, proving their property, and paying the Charges, may have them again. *The Pennsylvania Chronicle*, May 23, 1768

January 9, 1769. Took up something more than two Months since, a small yawl or Moses Boat. The Owner, describing her and paying Charges, may have her again, by applying to John Hartshorne, at Black Point, in Shrewsbury. *The New York Gazette and Weekly Mercury*, January 9, 1769

Taken up at the Mouth of Alloway's Creek, two Scows; one thought to be a Mud-Scow, the other a Ferry one. The Owner of them or either of them by proving his property and paying charges may have them again by applying to William Willis at the Head of the above Creek. *The Pennsylvania Gazette*, September 8, 1763

However, before we begin to think that colonial days were not unlike our own, we catch glimpses of some of the differences between now and then, differences repugnant to a free and humane civilization:

We hear from Cape May that about the beginning of this Instant a Whale came ashore about 15 Miles to the Eastward of the Cape, she had about 4 foot and a half Bone, had a hole in her supposedly made by an iron and was therefore concluded to have been killed by Whale-Men. And about the middle of this Instant another Whale came ashore at Absecun Beech, about 40 Miles to the Eastward of Cape May; she had about 7 Foot-Bone and had in her 2 or 3 Irons. The said Whales are saved and it was thought proper to give this Notice that they who struck them may know where to apply for their right in them. *The American Weekly Mercury*, April 22, 1742

On the 5th of this instant March, a Whale came ashore dead about 20 Mile to the Eastward of Cape May. She is a Cow, about 50 Foot long and appears to have been killed by Whalemen but who they are is yet unknown. Those who think they have a Property in her are advised to make their Claim in Time. *The Pennsylvania Gazette*,

The Beginning of April came ashore about 15 Miles Eastward of Cape May, a dead Whale, about four and a half foot Bone with a Hole in her suppose'd to be made by an Iron. And about the Middle of the Month another 40 Miles Eastward of the Cape, with 2 or 3 Irons in her, a valuable Fish being of near 7 foot Bone. *The Boston Weekly News-Letter*, May 13, 1742

Run away, the 13 of August last, from Benjamin Vining, near Salem in Salem County, a Servant Man named John Clark, an Irish lusty stout fellow, aged about 50 Years, grizle Hair'd and grey Beard, by Trade a Gardner and a good Workman at that or any kind of Country Work; had on Ozenbrigs Shirt and Trowsers, a good Felt Hat, Kersey Jacket and Shoes and Stockings.

He is apt to Drink hard and then has the Brogue on his Tongue; he has about three years to serve; Whoever takes him up and gives Notice to the Printer hereof or to me the Subscriber, so that I may have him in possession to sell him wherever he may be, shall have Twenty Shillings as a Reward and all reasonable Charges paid by

Benja. Vining

The American Weekly Mercury, August 30, 1733

Run away Cato, a Mulatto slave, mid sized, American born; 20 Years of Age; has very wide mouth, bushy hair, walks with his knees bending forward; He is an extream handy fellow at any common work, especially with horses and carriages of almost any sort, having been bred to it from a little boy and to the loading and unloading of Boats; a good deal used to a farm; can do all sorts of house work and very fit to wait upon a Gentleman; speaks very good English and Low Dutch, also pretty good High Dutch; is noted for his sense and particularly for his activity at any thing he takes in hand. . . . *The Pennsylvania Gazette*, January 13, 1743

Taken up by John Deare, a New-Negro Man, about 30 Years old; has had the Small Pox very thick; he had nothing on but a Crocus shirt; he can speak no English. Whoever owns him may apply to the said John Deare and have him again, paying Charges. *The American Weekly Mercury*, August 2, 1733

Notice is hereby given that there has come to the House of John Leonards at South River Bridge, near Amboy, in the Eastern Division of the Province of New Jersey, a Negroe Man, who was forced to the said House for want of Sustenance; he is a middle sized Man; talks no English or feigns that he cannot; he calls himself "Popaw"; his Teeth seems to be Fil'd or Whet sharp; he will not tell his Master's Name. Whoever ownes the said Negro may have him from the said Leonard on coming or sending for, paying according to Reward (if any be) or, if not, according to the Laws of this Province and also reasonably for his Diet 'till fetched. *The American Weekly Mercury*, July 14, 1726

Newspapers of the colonial period also served to publish official notices required by the Government. They ranged from Proclamations of the Royal Governor on important subjects to routine notices such as when and where the courts would sit. There were notice regarding runaway indentured servants or slaves, deserters, suspected thieves and escapees from gaol.

Other notices were required under particular statues. Typical would be the notice given creditors of a debtor advising them to appear and explain why the debtor should not be released from his obligations[94]:

Pursuant to an Act of the General Assembly of the Province of New Jersey, lately published, entitled "An Act for the Relief of Insolvent Debtors", we the Subscribers, being now confined in the Gaol of the County of Essex, and having petitioned to the Judges of the Inferior Court of Common Pleas, for the Benefit of said Act, filed a Schedule of Effects, do give notice to all our Creditors to appear on the 30th Day of June next, at two o'clock in the Afternoon of the same Day, before the Judges of the said Court at the Court House of the County of Essex, in Elizabeth Town and shew cause, if any they have, why we should not be discharged agreeable to the Directions of said Act.

James Baley and Samuel Yeomans
The New York Gazette or Weekly Post Boy, May 30, 1768

Public Notices also served to allow an individual, who believed he had been cheated, to publicly dishonor his prior obligation to another, just as you would "stop payment" on a check today.:

---

[94] England had debtor prisons where the ower of the unpaid obligation would be confined until somehow his debt was paid. Colonial America, although designed according to British laws, never embraced the concept of imprisoning persons who could not pay their obligations. Perhaps, it was because so many of the colonists themselves had been indentured servants or had come to America to escape economic servitude. In fact, quite early, some of the Provinces periodically provided legislation that allowed a debtor to be released from his obligations so as to start life anew. They were opposed by the Crown but this did not deter the colonial legislatures who continued to pass these opportunities at a fresh start. Of course, the Constitution provided Bankruptcy Courts, along the same line --and using almost identical language -- as the colonial legislation. On the other side of the Atlantic, Charles Dickens, seventy five years after the American Revolution, was written about the horrors of the British debtor prisons.

Burlington, January 22, 1761. Whereas, Isaac Connerro of New York, on or about the 30th Day of December last, obtained a Note of Hand of George Eyre in a fraudulent manner and by Force for the Sum of Ten Pounds, these are therefore to forbid any Person from taking any Assignment of the aforesaid note for we are determined not to pay the same or any Part thereof, as the said Isaac Connero is greatly indebted to the Estate of George Eyre, deceased, per order of George Eyre during his lifetime.

Jehu Eyre, Executor

The Pennsylvania Gazette, January 29, 1761

Or to tell creditors that a person has died and that they should seek repayment from the man's estate.

The Creditors of Doctor John Budd, late of Salem, are requested to send their Accounts to the Auditors, appointed by the Court for the settlement of his Affairs, that they may receive their Dividends of the Estate. *The Pennsylvania Chronicle*, April 25, 1768

Cape May, April 28. Patrick Steward, a Scotchman, Practioner of Physick and Surgery, late of Somerset, who left there four Sons and three Daughters, on the 27th of March last died intestate[95] at my House in Cape May, New Jersey, leaving in my Hands some few Assets to be administered. Those having legal Right to the administration thereon are desired to take the same upon them in three Months after Date and discharge my Bill of Funeral Expenses &c. or I shall otherwise be obliged to administer, to reimburse myself according to Law. *The Pennsylvania Gazette*, June 1, 1758

---

[95] that is, he died without a will directing how his property should be divided.

The newspapers and their Publick Notices also provided the opportunity for those separated by years or distance to attempt to find each other, as with the "Personals" ads of our own papers:

Whereas Thomas Burridge of the City of Glouster, who came over to New York in one Capt Totterdel of Bristol in the year 1713, who I hear is married and lives in some Part of New Countries, either in Pennsylvania or the Jerseys, if he will come or send to Obadiah Hunt, he may be informed of an Estate fallen to him, likewise a Legacy to a Sister of his, who came over some time after him. *The American Weekly Mercury*, May 10, 1722

This is to inform Mr. Richard Wright of the Kingdom of Ireland, who lately kept a School at Perth Amboy, that his brother Joseph Wright is arrived in these Parts and having made diligent inquiry after him cannot learn whither he has removed. If the said Richard Wright would send an Account thereof to the Printer of this Paper, his Brother may hear of him and they may have a Meeting. *The Pennsylvania Gazette*, September 30, 1731

Philadelphia, April 29, 1767. If Edward Duffle be living (who has been absent from Philadelphia between 12 and 13 years) by applying to Elizabeth Duffle, Burlington, may hear of something greatly to his advantage. *The Pennsylvania Gazette*, May 7, 1767

If George Scients, who came to Philadelphia from Frankfort in Germany, about 14 years ago, is living and will apply to Richard Moore, in Allowy's Creek in Salem County, he may hear of his brother Henry Scients, who will be very glad of the opportunity of seeing him. *The Pennsylvania Gazette*, March 30, 1769

Whereas a certain Joseph Pledger, a Shop Joiner by Trade, left the Town of Salem, West New Jersey in the Year 1765; if the said Joseph Pledger be living, he is desired to return to the said Town of Salem where he may be informed of something greatly to his advantage. But should he be dead, it will be taken very kind if any person will inform me of it.
Robert Johnson
The New York Gazette and Weekly Mercury, April 24, 1769

Whereas about 6 or 7 Weeks ago one Samuel Smith of the Borough of Elizabeth in New-Jersey came to this City and bought sundry Goods, but in his way home was lost near Elizabeth-Town Point. The Persons who sold him the said Goods are desired to inform the Printer hereof that his Friends may know their Contents and which of them remained unpaid for. *The New York Gazette revived in the Weekly Post-Boy*, January 2, 1749

If Joseph Wall and Jacob Wall and their kinsman John Wall, who are supposed to be born at Worcester in Old England and to be lately arrived in America, applies to Ebenezer Large in Burlington, they may be informed of something very much to their advantage. *The Pennsylvania Gazette*, February 14, 1749

If all or either of the following persons, be living, by applying to Jonathan Thomas, postmaster in Burlington, they may hear of something considerable to their advantage, viz.

Daniel Philips, who came from Kingsbridge in England and is supposed to reside in New Jersey. Mark Casey, a sailor or shoemaker, who came from Cork about seven years ago to Pennsylvania. Michael Casey, his brother, a shoemaker, who also came from Cork to Pennsylvania about seven years ago. Or any persons of the name Place, who had an uncle in England called Aaron Place. *The Pennsylvania Gazette*, April 12, 1750

Conrad Frech living in Old Springfield Township, Burlington County, New Jersey, wants to know where his Wife's Sister Christina Specht resides. She was born at Gumbererthosen, in the Elector Palatine Dominions and came with her Brother and Sister to this Country 14 Years ago and was a bound Servant for 9 Years in New Jersey. Whoever knows anything about her is desired to give Intelligence to the aforesaid Conrad Frech, or if this should come to her Knowledge, she is invited to come to her said Brother-in-Law and Sister, or to let them know where she lives. *The Pennsylvania Gazette*, October 28, 1762.

John Jacob Bernaht, a Native of Dehingen, near Schaffhausen, in Switzerland, takes this method of informing himself whether his brother John Ulrich Bernaht be yet alive, and if he is, where he resides. They both arrived in Philadelphia from their native Country about 13 Years ago, but were soon separated, since which Time, the first mentioned has heard nothing of the latter. If this should come to his Knowledge, he is kindly invited to come to his Brother John Jacob, at Mountholly, in New Jersey or send him at least intelligence of the Place of his Residence. And any other

Person that knows any thing about him is requested to do the same, the Favours shall be acknowledged by

John Jacob Bern

The Pennsylvania Gazette, March 22, 1764

Frederick Shlemb, born at Longen Condto, in Germany, and who came to this country last fall, wants to know where his brother Peter Shlemb is; he has been in the country 13 years; if alive, he may hear of his brother, by enquiring of Deterick Taub, shoemaker, in Second-street, Philadelphia.

N.B. Said Peter Shlemb, lives somewhere in New Jersey. *The Pennsylvania Gazette*, January 14, 1768.

Some of the notices suggest inheritances:

These are to inform John, Robert and Moses Molegan, who came from Ireland, that they have a Legacy left them by one Thomas M'Keterick, and by applying to Hugh M'Collom, executor, living at Freehold, in Monmouth County, East New Jersey, they may be further informed. *The Pennsylvania Gazette*, February 10, 1757

Walter Fyson, who lived formerly at Snailwell near Barnwell, or New Market, that was a farmer and afterwards followed the trade of woolcomber; if he be living and will send a letter to Samuel Berry Bristol, he may hear of an estate that has fallen to him of the value of 27,000 Pounds Sterling. Any person who can give Notice of the Place of his Residence to Samuel Berry, shall receive a Reward of 100 Pounds Sterling. Or any person that proves him to have been alive within five years or his death will receive 200 Pounds Sterling of

Samuel Berry

The New York Mercury, October 17, 1757

Often missing children were the ones sought in the notices:

Whereas John, the Son of Peter Aris Hodgkinson, a Boy about the age of 13 Years, was taken by a Spanish Privateer, in his Passage from Dublin to Philadelphia, in a Brigt. commanded by Zacharia Whitepaine, and as his Father can have no satisfactory Account of him at present, if any Person will take care of said Boy, if on the Continent among the English Inhabitants and send word to his Father in Burlington or conduct him or cause him to be conducted thither, they shall receive Five Pounds for said Boy, or reasonable Satisfaction for their Information, by

Peter Aris Hodgkinson

The Pennsylvania Gazette, December 14, 1744

Whereas as a little Boy, named James Newell, about 12 Years of Age, came into this country on a Vessel caled the Rose, from Belfast, and was bred a Sailor; if any Person can give said Hugh Newell any Account of him, he shall be well rewarded for his Trouble; he may be wrote to, by directing it to the Care of Joseph Borden, in Bordentown. *The Pennsylvania Gazette*, January 15, 1767

Whereas Philip George Steigleman, a Dutch lad about twelve years old, son of John Steigleman, was bound to some Person in the Jerseys about Two Years ago, which his Father cannot find out, this is therefore to request the Master of said lad to send word to his father, who lives with George Swope, about five miles this side of Lancaster. *The Pennsylvania Journal*, April 30, 1767

We can all recognize the "mother" in the following Personal notice from 1761:

Notice is hereby given to Alexander Martin, Merchant in Salisbury, North Carolina, that his Father Hugh Martin of Hunterdon County, New Jersey, died the 9th of March last and left him and his Brother James Executors. Wherefore, said Alexander Martin, if not inconvenient to his Business, is desired to return home to settle his late Father's Affairs, but if his coming should be attended with any Disadvantage to him, he is requested not to come by his Mother. *The Pennsylvania Gazette*, December 10, 1761

Some of these Public Notices have a story behind them, which, unfortunately, we will never know:

Perth Amboy, July 2, 1723--- Publick Notice is hereby given that one John Wilson Marriner being on board the Sloop William, William Fraser Master, belonging to Amboy, who was taken by the Pyrates, the said Wilson was forced on board the Pyrate Sloop against his will and when the Man of War took the Pyrate's Sloop he was carried along with the rest of the Pyrates and put in Prison in Rhode Island. *The American Weekly Mercury*, June 27, 1723

A

Abbit, John, 79
Abeel, James, 288, 297
Ackerman, Abraham, 61
Absecom Beach(Abequon Beach)(Abescomb Beach), 57, 81, 82, 83, 84, 327
Adair (Odear), James, 48, 49
Adamson Anthony, 40
Aetna Furnace, 287; see also *Etna Furnace*
Ageman,Thomas, 24
Alamo, 125
Ageman, William, 24
Albany, 46, 47, 115, 242
Albany County, 112
Albany Dock, 35, 297
Albany Street, New Brunswick, 298
Albany, Captain Richard, 98
Albertis, Benjamin, 55
Albertis, Severns, 55
Aldsworth (first name unknown), 65, 66
Alexander, Alexander, 252
Alexander, James Esq., 257
Alfe, Jurri, 71
Allan, Isaac, 221
Alleghany, 107
Allen, Nathan, 149
Allen, Captain (first name unknown), 277
Allens-Town, 149, 311
Allemingle Township, 116
Allen, William Esq., 49
Allen, (first name unknown), 152
Alloway's Creek, 327, 331, Amboy, 22, 25, 26, 69, 70, 73, 76, 81, 82, 93, 96, 116, 120, 140, 164, 166, 168, 169, 181, 189, 240, 241, 256, 308, 309, 310, 311, 312, 328, 334; *see also* Perth Amboy
Amboy Ferry, 309, 310
Amboy Road, 271

American Philosophical Society, 140
Ammile, Jaquez, 98
Amwell, 109, 176, 200, 257, 272, 288
Anguilla, 75
Annapolis, Maryland, 174
Anderson Furnace, 20
Anderson, Justice (first name unknown), 107
Andover Iron Works, 19
Andres, Joseph, 43
Andrews, Lewis, 120
Anen (Annin), James, 102, 103
Antigua, 75, 76, 77, 88, 91
Antil, (first name unknown), 268, 274
Antill, Honorable Edward Esq., 68, 153, 159
Antill, Mrs. (first name unknown), 89
Antrum, John, 253
Appalachia, 125
Applegate, Ebenezer, 70
Archer, John, 275
Arkansas, 125
Armitage, Benjamin, 243
Arnet, James, 228
Arnold, Edward, 291
arson, 29, 72
Ashcraft, Captain (first name unknown), 77
Ash Swamp, 41, 273
Ashford, Mary, 185
Ashford, Thomas, 185
Ashton, Benjamin, 175
Ashton, Elizabeth, 175
Atlee, William, 307
Attwood, Joshua, 300
Auble, Matthias Andrew, 15, 16
Augusta County, Virginia, 24
Augustine, 93
Avery, Ephraim, 209
Ayscough, Dr. Richard, 196

B

Badger, Captain Barnard, 240
Baker, Captain (first name unknown), 191
Bain (first name unknown), 35
Baines, Robert, 151
Baldwin, Nehemiah, 126
Baley, James, 329
Ball, David, 298
Ball, Ezekiel, 319
Ball, Samuel, 52
Ball, William, 243, 295
Bancker, Christopher, 302
Bank, James, 306
Barbarie, John, 285
Barber, Francis, 211
Barbados, 46, 76, 91, 98, 191, 262, 291
Barclay's Apology, 256
Barclay, John Esq., 256
Barclay, Robert, 256
Bard, Col. Peter, 261
Barker, Joshua, 200
Barley, Daniel, 184
Barnard Townshp, 280
Barnegat, 72, 76, 77, 84, 95, 276
Barnegat Beach, 276
Barnegat Inlet, 77
Barnes, Captain (first name unknown), 266
Barney's Gut, 77
Barnhill, James, 311, 312
Barnwell, 333
Barre, Colonel (first name unknown), 146
Baskinridge, 62, 280
Bason of Menis, 243
Bates, Thomas, 198
Bayard, Samuel, 323
Bay of Honduras, 11, 75, 95
Bayonne Prison (France), 97, 98
Bayton, Peter Esq. 52
Beach, Reverend (first name unknown), 173
Beak, John, 305

Beard, William, 58
Beaver Pond, 249
Bedford, Duke of, 255
Bedloe's Island, 52
Bedminister, 225, 252
Beekman, Martin, 289
Belcher, Jonathan Esq., 216, 240, 255, 256
Belfast, Ireland, 334
Bell, Tom, 46-47, 48, 50
Bellus, Philip, 31
Benezel, Stephen, 141
Benson, John, 59
Bergen County, 45, 58, 123, 124, 164, 201, 261, 262, 279, 284, 326
Bermudas, 75, 91, 92
Bern, John Jacob, 333
Bernaht, John Jacob, 332
Bernaht, John Ulrich, 332
Bernard, Governor, 114
Berrien, John, 142, 143
Berry, Peter, 60
Berry, Samuel, 333
Besha's Land, 110
Beson, Captain (first name unknown), 92
Bethlehem, 107, 289
Bible-in-Heart, 294
Bicker, Henry, 314
Biddle, Owen, 140
Biles, Benjamin, 317
Biles Island, 252
Bill, Captain (first name unknown), 75
Birker, Henry, 246
Bispham, Joshua, 290
Blair, Alexander, 34
Blair, Rev. (first name unknown), 222
Black Point, Rumson, 150, 212n, 309, 326
Black River, 109, 280
Blazing Star, 8, 9, 311; *see also* New Blazing Star
Blewfields, 11
Block Island, 91

Bloomfield, Dr. Moses, 198
Blue-Point, 78
Bohemia, 240n
Bombay Hook, 17, 96
Bond, Elijah, 300, 319
Bond, (first name unknown), 73
Bond, Captain (first name unknown), 90
Bonnell, Isaac, 247
Boone, Daniel, 125
Bordeaux, 88
Borden, Joseph, 308, 309, 311, 334
Borden, Joseph Jr., 310
Bordentown, 226, 263, 282, 289, 308, 309, 310, 311, 317, 334
Boston, 66, 75, 76, 89, 91, 93, 153, 240, 241, 265
Boston locations
Long Wharf, 240
Merchant's Row, 240
Winter Street, 303
Boston News-Letter, 1
Boudient, Elias, 282; *see also* Boudinot
Boudinot, Elias, 282n
Bound Brook, 176, 183, 184, 267, 300
Bourn, Merica, 184n
Bourns, (first name unknown), 43
Bowen, Captain (first name unknown), 75
Bowers, Captain (first name unknown), 117
Bowers, Lemuel, 118
Bowery, New York, 66
Bowman, Mary, 22
Bowne, Safety, 31
Bows, Thomas, 24
Bradford, William, 237, 237n, 253
branding, 33, 34, 43, 45, 229
Brant (first name unknown), 87
Bridgewater, 225

Brig Charming Sally, 241
Brig Nancy, 84
Brig Orange, 92
Brig Pelling, 75
Brig Rachael and Betty, 18
Briggs, John, 57
Brink, Esther, 116
Brink, Garret, 116
Brink, Stephen, 116
Bristol, 17, 48, 76, 84, 85, 241, 311, 331, 333
Bristol, Ennion Esq, 49
Broadfield, Edward, 165, 165n
Broadfield, Margaret, 165n, 300, 319
Brooks, (first name unknown), 53
Brower, Adolf, 65, 273
Brown, John, 85, 220, 309
Brown, Robert, 288
Brown, Captain (first name unknown), 306
Brown, Reverend Mr.(first name unknown), 139
Brunnel (first name unknown), 58
Brunswick, 15, 34, 53, 68, 70, 72, 267, 268, 270, 277, 285, 307, 311, 316, 323; *see also* New Brunswick
Brunswick Ferry, 316
Brunswick Gaol, 184
Bruster,(first name unknown), 324
Buck, Aaron, 29
Buck's County, Pennsylvania, 318
Budd, Doctor John, 330
Budd, John, 32, 245
Bunnel, Nathaniel, 262
Bunnel, Joseph Esq., 263
Burcham, Timothy, 32
Burlington, 6, 24, 25, 27, 33, 34, 51, 52, 53, 54, 55, 57, 65, 74, 94, 102, 103, 120, 121, 124, 137, 143, 146, 155, 166,

Hutton, Thomas, 307
Hyer, Jacob, 313
Hylton, Captain Ralph, 185
Hyndshaw's Fort, 111

I

Imlay, John, 263
Imlay, Joseph, 242
Imlay, Peter, 263
Inglis, Thomas, 312
Indian tribes
  Alleghany, 107
  Cayugas, 114
  Conestagoe Indians, 119
  Conoys, 114
  Delawares, 107, 114,
    120
  Iroquois, 6, 105
  Leni Lenape, 6, 100,
    104, 105, 105n
  Minisinks, 114
  Mohawks, 107, 114
  Mohegans, 114
  Nanticokes, 114
  Munsee, 6
  Oneidas, 101, 114, 230
  Onondaga, 114
  Opings, 114
  Oswego, 112, 115
  Senecas, 114, 115, 120
  Shamokin, 107
  Shawanese, 107
  Tuscaroras, 107, 114
  Tuteloes, 114
  Unami, 6, 114
The Indian King Tavern, 151
The Indian Queen, Philadelphia,
34
Ireland, 60, 125, 203, 241,
241n, 331
Iroquois, 6

J

Jackson, Thomas, 138
Jackson, William, 24
Jackson's River, Virginia, 24
Jackques Bay (Jakeses Bay), 53,
78
jail break, 30
Jamaica, 11, 76, 84, 89, 93, 95,
122, 190, 191, 301
Jamaica, Long Island, 43, 189
James, James, 243
Jamestown, Virginia, 5
Jenango, 110
Jenkins, John, 297
Jennings, Solomon, 99
Jersey City, 8n, 305
Johnson-Hall, 120
Johnson, Hon. Andrew Esq.,
257
Johnson, Captain Christopher,
277
Johnson, Isaac, 138
Johnston, Doctor John, 170, 260
Johnson, John, 13, 14, 73, 285
Johnson, Doctor Lewis, 154
Johnson, Margaret, 312
Johnson, Nicholaus, 42, 43
Johnson, Robert, 331
Johnston, Captain Thomas, 116
Johnson, Sir William, 120, 230
Johnson, Mrs.(first name
unknown), 314
Johnston, Captain (first name
unknown), 115
Johnson, Dr. (first name
unknown), 204
Joline, John, 314
Jones, Captain Francis, 91
Jones, Dr. John, 197
Jones, John, 50, 243
Jones, Captain John, 84, 85
Jones, Nathaniel, 226
Juanita, Pennsylvania, 111
Justis, William, 27

K

Kant-Kan-i-auning, 280
Kay, Francis, 228
Kearny, Thomas, 281
Keen, Mounce, 145
Kelly (first name unknown)
Kennedy, Captain Archibald
Esq., 173
Kennedy, Thomas, 220
Kensington, 270
Kentucky, 125
Keppel, Commodore (first name unknown), 95
Kerr, Captain Walter, 84, 85
Kettle Creek, 281
Kidd, Captain, 78n
Kidd, Captain William
Kidd, John, 8, 9, 319
Killigrove, Henry, 30
Kill Van Kull, 305
King, Constant, 70
King, Gilbert, 147
King Road, 84
King's Arms Tavern, 313
Kingsbridge, England, 332
King's Evil, 195, 195n
Kingston, 184
Kingsland, Gastavus, 36
King Street, Trenton, 314
Kingwood, 283, 286, 300
Kip, Captain (first name unknown), 75
Kilsaye, Dennis, 27
Kirk, Thomas, 30
Kirkbride, J., 311
Kitchen, Samuel, 288
Knoulton Township, 31
Kolb, Colonel (first name unknown), 8, 9

L

Lacawse, 119
Laghowexin Settlement, 116
Lahay, John, 79

Lambert (first name unknown), 124
Lamenton River, 318
Lancaster County, 119, 334
Large, Ebenezer, 332
Lashley, Andrew, 16
Lathrop, Captain (first name unknown), 91
Lathrop, (first name unknown), 265
Lawrence, John, 196
Lawrence, Robert, 23, 163
Lawrence, Captain Thomas, 259
Lawrence, Captain (first name unknown), 52
Lawrance (first name unknown), 15
Leaming, Jeremiah, 154
Leary, J, 248
Leary, (first name unknown), 152
Lebanan, 74
Leacy, Cadry, 28
Leddel, Louisa, 181
Leddel, William, 181
Lee, Captain John, 76
Leeds, Titan, 27
Leek, John, 204
Lemon, Richard, 28
Leni Lenape, 6, 99, 104, 105, 105n
Leonard, Captain John, 11, 100
Leonard, John, 328
Leslie, Charles Scham M.D., 193
Lester, Captain Terret, 312
Lesyear, (first name unknown), 186
Lethgow, Daniel, 243
Levy, Nathan, 176
Lewis-Town, Delaware, 141
Liberty, a Poem, 295
Liberty and Cluster Pilot Boats, 30
Liberty Island, 52n
Lippincott (first name unknown), 29

Middleton, Abel, 275

Middlesex County, 60, 70, 136, 145, 146, 223, 229

Middletown, 30, 52, 54, 61, 150, 154, 174, 199, 212n, 263, 264, 278, 281, 311

Mill Creek, 281

Miller, Aaron, 299

Miller, Henry, 242

Miller, John, 200

Miller, (first name unknown), 266

Millstone, 142

Minck, Captain Henry, 78

Minisink, 67, 107, 108, 110, 116, 119, 244

Minisink Indians, 114

Mississippi, 240, 244

Moffat, John, 220

Mohawks, 107, 114, 118

Mohawk River, 242

Mohegans, 114

Molegan, John, 333

Molegan, Moses, 333

Molegan, Robert, 333

Mompesson, Roger Esq, 43

Monmouth County, 22, 25, 26, 41, 47, 88, 149, 151, 162, 163, 174, 177, 184, 187, 211, 211n, 212n, 227, 228, 281, 288, 333

Monmouth Court-House, 153, 273, 286

Monmouth Gaol, 22, 23

Mononlopan River, 319

Montesor, Captain (first name unknown), 116

Montgomery, Governor, 302

Montreal, 112

Montour, Captain (first name unknown), 120

Moodases, 305

Moore, Deliverance, 179

Moore, Henry Esq. 199

Moore, James, 179

Moore, Richard, 331

Moore, Susanna, 172

Moore, Thomas (aka Wilkies Tom), 30

Moore, Colonel (first name unknown), 172

Mooretown (Moore's Town), 102, 103, 290

Moor, Mary, 53

Moravians, 106, 107, 240, 240n

Morehead's Meeting House, 141

Morgan, Barnabas, 35

Morgan, (first name unknown), 11

Morough, Thomas, 39

Morris, Anthony, 262

Morris, Elizabeth, 262

Morris, Isabel, 261

Morris, John, 34

Morris, Lewis, 127, 261

Morris, Hon. Robert H., 294

Morris, William jun., 297

Morris, (first name unknown), 49, 247

Morrisania, 261

Morris County, 15, 22, 34, 58, 62, 64, 70, 132, 225, 262

Morris Town, 60, 162, 324, 325

Morris Town Gaol, 65

Mosquito Creek, 281

Mott, (first name unknown), 85

Mount Holly, 9, 61, 73, 151, 162, 245, 285, 289, 301, 332

Mountholly Ironworks, 320, 321, 322

Mount Vesuvius, 172

Mullen, Jane, 143

Mullen, John, 143

Mullock, Joshua, 300

Munsee, 6

Murder, 13-25

Murphy, 241, 241n

Murphy, James, 242

Murphy, John, 242

Murphy, William, 242

mutiny, 17

Muttony, David, 85

N

Nag's Head Tavern, 313
Nanticokes, 114
Nantucket, 277
Narrows, 89
Nassau Hall, 71, 219, 222, 251; see also College of New Jersey
Navesink Bay, 281
Navesink River, 149
Naversink (Neversinks), 80, 88, 90, 94, 138, 150, 277, 324
Neal, Captain Eliphalet, 80
Nealson, James Esq., 72, 72n, 73
Neave, Samuel, 321
Neshamminy River, 318
Neskopecka, 107
Nevill, Justice Samuel, 13, 132, 204
Nevis, 89, 91
Newark, 21, 22, 29, 33, 34, 51, 52, 58, 59, 72, 73, 126, 127, 131, 132, 139, 160, 175, 197, 204, 216, 228, 266, 268, 282, 288, 297, 298, 300, 302, 305, 306, 319
Newark Goal, 22, 44
Newark Mountains, 270
Newark, New Castle County, Del., 28
New Barbadoes Neck, 164, 262
New Blazing Star, 312; see also Blazing Star
New Bridge, 306
New Bridge, Hackensack, 210
New Brunswick, 18, 63, 68, 72, 74, 134, 139, 140, 142, 148, 153, 159, 166, 167, 173, 178, 189, 193, 196, 193, 203, 220, 246, 249, 250, 266, 267, 268, 272, 274, 282, 283, 289; 306, 307, 309, 314, 316; see also Brunswick
New Castle, 239
Newell, Hugh, 334
Newell, James, 334

Newfoundland, 95n
New France, 139
New-Jersey Almanack for the Year 1742, 295
New-Jersey Almanack for 1769, 296
New Jersey Medical Society, 197, 198
New London, 77, 199
New Market, 333
New Orleans, 240
Newport, Rhode Island, 77, 276
Newry, 8, 80, 81
New Stockbridge
Newtown Township, 202
New Windsor, 55
New York, 93, 96, 102, 105, 121, 122, 123, 138, 147, 150, 153, 160, 166, 168, 169, 172, 185, 190, 210, 212n, 219, 223, 226, 242, 251, 253, 265, 270, 284, 287, 288, 291, 292, 294, 295, 305, 306, 307, 309, 310, 311, 312, 313, 314, 315, 316, 318, 319, 320, 324, 326, 330, 331
New York City locations
  Albany Dock, 35, 297
  Beaver Street, 296
  Dye Street, 201
  Leary Street, 152
  Mesier's Dock, 305
  Col. Moore's Wharf, 309, 310
  New Street, 193
  Old-Slip, 35
  Pearl Street, 300
  Smith Street, 291
  Wall Street, 302
  White-Hall, 310, 314, 324
New York Evening Post, 130
New York Gazette, 132
New York Mercury, 198
New Wales, 243
Niagara, 111, 112, 115, 116
Niagara Falls, 115

Periam, Joseph, 212, 213, 214, 220
Perot, Richard, 47-51
Perkins, Elizabeth, 180
Perkins, Joseph, 180
Perkins, Captain (first name unknown), 88
Perkins, Lieutenant (first name unknown), 53, 54
Perth Amboy, 6, 25, 40, 69, 70, 92, 126, 131, 145, 150, 154, 169, 170, 172, 191, 199, 204, 223, 224, 225, 228, 238, 246, 257, 260, 291, 292, 303, 308, 309, 310 *see also* Amboy
Petty's Island, 252
Phalps, William, 112
Philadelphia, 8n, 15, 16, 20, 34, 37, 39, 45, 47, 48, 52, 54, 65, 66, 75, 76, 77, 80, 81, 83, 89, 91, 92, 103, 112, 119, 133, 134, 140, 146, 150, 151, 152, 155, 161, 189, 193, 194, 195, 203, 205, 215, 219, 239, 243, 252, 265, 266, 270, 271, 292, 297, 307, 308, 309, 310, 311, 312, 313, 315, 316, 317, 318, 321, 324, 325, 326, 331, 332, 333
Philadelphia locations
 Arch Street, 194
 Arch Wharf, 280
 Chesnut Street, 297, 298, 301
 Church Alley, 151
 Crooked Billet Wharf, 308, 310
 Elm Street, 311, 312
 Fourth Street, 154
 Jersey Market, 161
 John Latham's Wharf, 36
 Market Street, 151, 286, 316
 New Ferry House, 146
 Old Ferry, 288
 Penn Street, 20
 Race Street, 154, 242
 Second Street, 141, 294, 333
 Society Hill, 193
 State House Square, 140

Third Street, 300
Vine Street, 242, 311
Walnut Street, 291
Water Street, 280, 301, 319
Philadelphia Township, Nova Scotia, 243
Philipsburg, 176
Philips, Daniel, 332
Pickman, Captain Joshua, 240
Picquet, (first name unknown), 115
Pierson, John, 215
Pike, Captain (first name unknown), 276
Pilesgrove, 145, 178, 179, 243
Piscataway (Piscataqua), 15, 32, 40, 59, 73n, 136, 177, 184, 271, 275
Piscatawy [New Hampshire], 80
Pitt, William, 146
Pittsburgh, 102
Place, Aaron, 332
Pledger, Joseph, 331
Plumb Island, 78
Plymouth Bay Colony, 5
Point no Point, 17
Pompton, 58, 99
Poneo, Mary, 176
Poneo, Gabriel, 176
Poor Richard's Almanack for 1756, 295
Poor Roger's American Country Almanack, 296
Poquet, Francis (John), 204
Port Royal, 91
Porter, Israel, 199
Port St. Peiers, 98
Potowmack River, Md., 32
Potter, Captain (first name unknown), 89, 95
Potter's Town, 21
Potts, Stacy, 286
Powell, Margaret, 193
Powell, Thomas, 207, 209, 213, 290
Powell, (first name unknown), 49